D0778736

*Is There a Text
in This Class?*

801.95
F529

WITHDRAWI

Is There a Text in This Class?

The Authority of
Interpretive Communities

Stanley Fish

151781

HARVARD UNIVERSITY PRESS
Cambridge, Massachusetts
London, England   1980

LIBRARY ST. MARY'S COLLEGE

Copyright © 1980 by the President
and Fellows of Harvard College

All rights reserved

Printed in the United States of America

Library of Congress Cataloging in Publication Data

Fish, Stanley Eugene
 Is there a text in this class?

 Includes bibliographical references and index.
 1. Criticism   I. Title.
PN81.F56   801'.95   80-19438
ISBN 0-674-46725-6

To my parents,
Ida and Max Fish

Preface

THE ANSWER this book gives to its title question is "there is and there isn't." There isn't a text in this or any other class if one means by text what E. D. Hirsch and others mean by it, "an entity which always remains the same from one moment to the next" (*Validity in Interpretation*, p. 46); but there is a text in this and every class if one means by text the structure of meanings that is obvious and inescapable from the perspective of whatever interpretive assumptions happen to be in force. The point is finally a simple one, but it has taken me more than ten years to see it, and, in what follows, it will take me almost four hundred pages to elaborate it. Along the way I have had a great deal of help: from my students at the University of California at Berkeley, The Johns Hopkins University, and the University of Southern California; from the members of two NEH summer seminars (1974, 1976); from the faculty and students (themselves faculty) who made the 1977 session of the School of Criticism and Theory so intense an experience; and from a number of colleagues and friends, Leo Braudy, William Cain, Rob Cummins, Hubert Dreyfus, Frank Hubbard, Steven Mailloux, Ellen Mankoff, David Sachs, and John Searle. Lee Erickson performed the invaluable service of refusing to let me off the hook for an entire year. Lee Patterson and Christy-Jo Anderson gave me the gift of a chance conversation. Of two others I can only say what is a very conventional thing to say, that this book is as much theirs as mine; Kenneth Abraham and Walter Michaels worked it out with me in classrooms, in restaurants, at parties, on basketball courts, and, once, even on the radio. Jane Parry Tompkins has encouraged me and inspired me and given meaning to everything in my life.

Chapters 1–12 have been previously published in the following journals and collections: chapters 1 and 3 in *New Literary History* (1970, 1973); chapter 2 in *Approaches to Poetics,* edited by Seymour Chatman (1973); chapter 4 in *Milton Studies* (1975); chapters 5, 6, 7, 11, and 12 in *Critical Inquiry* (1975, 1976, 1978, 1979); chapters 8 and 9 in *Modern Language Notes* (1976, 1977); chapter 10 in *Boundary II* (1980). I am grateful for permission to reprint.

S.F.

Contents

*Is There a Text
in This Class?*

Introduction, or *How I Stopped Worrying and Learned To Love Interpretation*

WHAT INTERESTS ME about many of the essays collected here is the fact that I could not write them today. I could not write them today because both the form of their arguments and the form of the problems those arguments address are a function of assumptions I no longer hold. It is often assumed that literary theory presents a set of problems whose shape remains unchanging and in relation to which our critical procedures are found to be more or less adequate; that is, the field of inquiry stands always ready to be interrogated by questions it itself constrains. It seems to me, however, that the relationship is exactly the reverse: the field of inquiry is *constituted* by the questions we are able to ask because the entities that populate it come into being as the presuppositions—they are discourse-specific entities —of those questions. In 1970 I was asking the question "Is the reader or the text the source of meaning?" and the entities presupposed by the question *were* the text and the reader whose independence and stability were thus assumed. Without that assumption—the assumption that the text and the reader can be distinguished from one another and that they will hold still— the merits for their rival claims could not have been debated and an argument for one or the other could not have been made. The fact that I was making such an argument was a direct consequence of the fact that it had already been made, and the position I proceeded to take was dictated by the position that had already been taken. That position was best represented, perhaps, by William Wimsatt and Monroe Beardsley's essays on the affective and intentional fallacies (so called), essays that pled a successful case for the text by arguing, on the one hand, that the intentions of the author were unavailable and, on the other, that the responses of the reader were too variable. Only the text was both indisputably there and stable. To have recourse either to the causes of a poem or to its effects is to exchange objectivity for "impressionism and relativism." "The outcome of either Fallacy, the Intentional or the Affective, is that the poem itself, as an object of specifically critical judgment, tends to disappear."

To the degree that this argument was influential (and it was enormously so) it constrained in advance the form any counterargument might take. In order to dislodge the affective fallacy, for example, one would have to show first that the text was *not* the self-sufficient repository of meaning and, second, that something else was, at the very least, contributory. This was exactly my strategy in the first of the articles presented in this book. I challenged the self-sufficiency of the text by pointing out that its (apparently) spatial form belied the temporal dimension in which its meanings were actualized, and I argued that it was the developing shape of that actualization, rather than the static shape of the printed page, that should be the object of critical description. In short, I substituted the structure of the reader's experience for the formal structures of the text on the grounds that while the latter were the more visible, they acquired significance only in the context of the former. This general position had many consequences. First of all, the activities of the reader were given a prominence and importance they did not have before: if meaning is embedded in the text, the reader's responsibilities are limited to the job of getting it out; but if meaning develops, and if it develops in a dynamic relationship with the reader's expectations, projections, conclusions, judgments, and assumptions, these activities (the things the reader *does*) are not merely instrumental, or mechanical, but essential, and the act of description must both begin and end with them. In practice, this resulted in the replacing of one question—what does this mean?—by another—what does this do?—with "do" equivocating between a reference to the action of the text *on* a reader and the actions performed *by* a reader as he negotiates (and, in some sense, actualizes) the text. This equivocation allowed me to retain the text as a stable entity at the same time that I was dislodging it as the privileged container of meaning. The reader was now given joint responsibility for the production of a meaning that was itself redefined as an event rather than an entity. That is, one could not point to this meaning as one could if it were the property of the text; rather, one could observe or follow its gradual emergence in the interaction between the text, conceived of as a succession of words, and the developing response of the reader.

In this formulation, the reader's response is not *to* the meaning; it *is* the meaning, or at least the medium in which what I wanted to call the meaning comes into being, and therefore to ignore or discount it is, or so I claimed, to risk missing a great deal of what is going on. In order to support this claim I performed analyses designed to demonstrate both the richness of literary experience and the extent to which that experience was unavailable to (because it was flattened out by) a formalist reading. I did not make use of it at the time, but the following passage from *Paradise Lost* might well have been the basis of such a demonstration:

> Satan, now first inflam'd with rage came down,
> The Tempter ere th' Accuser of man-kind,
> To wreck on innocent frail man his loss
> Of that first Battle, and his flight to Hell.   (IV, 9–12)

My contention was that in formalist readings meaning is identified with what a reader understands at the *end of a unit of sense* (a line, a sentence, a paragraph, a poem) and that therefore any understandings preliminary to that one are to be disregarded as an unfortunate consequence of the fact that reading proceeds in time. The only making of sense that counts in a formalist reading is the last one, and I wanted to say that everything a reader does, even if he later undoes it, is a part of the "meaning experience" and should not be discarded. One of the things a reader does in the course of negotiating these lines is to assume that the referent of "his" in line 11 is "innocent frail man." Within this assumption the passage would seem to be assigning the responsibility for the Fall to Satan: Satan, inflamed with rage, comes down to inflict the loss of Eden on a couple unable to defend themselves because they are innocent and frail. This understanding, however, must be revised when the reader enters line 12 and discovers that the loss in question is Satan's loss of Heaven, sustained in "that first battle" with the loyal angels. It is that loss of which Adam and Eve are innocent, and the issue of the Fall is not being raised at all. But of course it has been raised, if only in the reader's mind, and in the kind of analysis I am performing, that would be just the point. The understanding that the reader must give up is one that is particularly attractive to him because it asserts the innocence of his first parents, which is, by extension, his innocence too. By first encouraging that understanding and then correcting it, Milton (so my argument would go) makes the reader aware of his tendency, inherited from those same parents, to reach for interpretations that are, in the basic theological sense, self-serving. This passage would then take its place in a general strategy by means of which the reader comes to know that his experience of the poem is a part of its subject; and the conclusion would be that this pattern, essential to the poem's operation, would go undetected by a formalist analysis.

That claim would be attached to the more general claim I was making, that I had escaped formalism by displacing attention from the text, in its spatial configurations, to the reader and his temporal experience. In order to maintain this claim it was necessary to remove the chief objection to talking about the experience of the reader, to wit, that there are (at least potentially) as many experiences as there are readers, and that therefore the decision to focus on the reader is tantamount to giving up the possibility of saying anything that would be of general interest. I met that objection by positing a level of experience which all readers share, independently of differences in education and culture. This level was conceived more or less syntactically, as an extension of the Chomskian notion of linguistic competence, a linguistic system that every native speaker shares. I reasoned that if the speakers of a language share a system of rules that each of them has somehow internalized, understanding will, in some sense, be uniform. The fact that the understandings of so many readers and critics were not uniform was accounted for by superimposing on this primary or basic level (identified more or less with perception itself) a secondary or after-the-fact level at which the differences between individuals make themselves manifest. At times I characterized this secondary level as an emotional reaction to the experience of the first (whether the reader likes or dislikes the experience of Faulkner's delays, he will, in common with every other reader, experience them); and at other times I spoke of it as an act of intellection, more or less equivalent with what we usually call interpretation. In either case the assertion was that this subsequent and distorting activity was the source of the apparent variation in the response of readers to literary texts: "It is only when readers become literary critics and the passing of judgment takes precedence over the reading experience that opinions begin to diverge. The act of interpretation is often so removed from the act of reading that the latter (in time the former) is hardly remembered."

The distinction then was between the actual reading experience and whatever one might feel or say about it in retrospect. It was also a distinction between something that was objective and shared (the basic data of the meaning experience) and something that was subjective and idiosyncratic. From this it followed that the proper practice of literary criticism demanded the suppressing of what is subjective and idiosyncratic in favor of the level of response that everyone shares. In terms of my own criticism this provided me with a strategy for dealing with my predecessors. I treated their accounts of literary works as disguised reports of the normative experience that all informed readers have. These reports are disguised, I reasoned, because a reader who is also a critic will feel compelled to translate his experience into the vocabulary of the critical principles he self-consciously holds. He will, that is, be reporting not on his immediate or basic response to a work but on his response (as dictated by his theoretical persuasion) to that response. In relation to such critics I performed the service of revealing to them what their actual experience of a work was before it was obscured by their after-the-fact (interpretive) reflections.

In short, I was practicing a brand of criticism whose most distinctive claim was not to be criticism at all but a means of undoing the damage that follows in criticism's wake. This is particularly true of the essay on Milton's *L'Allegro,* where the argument is that as a poem whose parts are arranged in such a way as to exert no interpretive pressures it is unavailable to criticism insofar as interpretation is its only mode. It follows then that since others who have written on the poem have to a man sought to interpret it, they are necessarily wrong. They are wrong, however, in ways that point inadvertently to my description of its experience; for it is in response to the curious discreteness that characterizes a reading of *L'Allegro* that the critics are moved to fault the poem for a lack of unity or to supply the unity by supplying connections more firm and delimiting than the connections available in the text. Thus, the very efforts of my predecessors testify to their involuntary recognition of the truth of what I am telling them; their reading experience is finally exactly like mine; it is just that their critical preconceptions lead them either to ignore or devalue it. Not only did this strategy enable me to turn opposing positions into versions of my own, but it also gave me a way of answering the question most often asked in the classroom and in public meetings: How is it that readers who are at least as informed as you are (in the sense of having "literary competence") do not experience literature as you say they should? I simply said that they do, even though they may not (consciously) know it, and that if they will only listen to me they will learn how to recognize the configurations of the experience they have always had. In this way I was able to account for the (apparent) differences in literary response without having to give up the claim of generality.

Like any other polemical success, however, this one had its price; for by thus preserving generality I left myself vulnerable to the most persistent objection to the method, that in essence it was no different from the formalism to which it was rhetorically opposed. In order to argue for a common reading experience, I felt obliged to posit an object in relation to which readers' activities could be declared uniform, and that object was the text (at least insofar as it was a temporal structure of ordered items); but this meant that the integrity of the text was as basic to my position as it was to the position of the New Critics. And, indeed, from the very first I was much more dependent on new critical principles than I was willing to admit. The argument in "Literature in the Reader" is mounted (or so it is announced) on behalf of the reader and against the self-sufficiency of the text, but in the course of it the text becomes more and more powerful, and rather than being liberated, the reader finds himself more constrained in his new prominence than he was before. Although his standard is raised in opposition to formalism, he is made into an extension of formalist principles, as his every operation is said to be strictly controlled by the features of the text. The last paragraph of the essay urges a method of classroom teaching in which students are trained first to recognize and then to "discount" whatever was unique and personal in their response so that there would be nothing between them and the exertion of the text's control.

What I didn't see was that I could not consistently make the two arguments at the same time. That is, I could not both declare my opposition to new critical principles and retain the most basic of those principles—the integrity of the text—in order to be able to claim universality and objectivity for my method. I kept this knowledge from myself by never putting the two arguments together but marshaling each of them only to rebut specific points. When someone would charge that an emphasis on the reader leads directly to solipsism and anarchy, I would reply by insisting on the constraints imposed on readers by the text; and when someone would characterize my position as nothing more than the most recent turn of the new-critical screw, I would reply by saying that in my model the reader was freed from the tyranny of the text and given the central role in the production of meaning.

In short, I was moving in two (incompatible) directions at once: in the one the hegemony of formalism was confirmed and even extended by making the text responsible for the activities of its readers; in the other those same activities were given a larger and larger role to the extent that at times the very existence of the text was called into question. The tension between these two directions is particularly obvious in the second of these essays, "What Is Stylistics and Why Are They Saying Such Terrible Things About It?" The argument of this piece is largely a negative one, directed at those practitioners of stylistics who wish to go directly from the description of formal features to a specification of their meaning. My thesis was that such a move, because it is unconstrained by any principle, produces interpretations that are always arbitrary. I did not, however, deny either the possibility or the relevance of cataloguing formal features; I merely insisted that the value of those features could only be determined by determining their function in the developing experience of the reader. Linguistic facts, I conceded, do have meaning, but the explanation for that meaning is not the capacity of syntax to express it but the ability of a reader to confer it.

Thus I retained the distinction between description and interpretation and by so doing affirmed the integrity and objectivity of the text. In the second part of the essay, however, the argument is much more adventurous and (potentially, at least) subversive. Objecting to the formalist assumption that the reader's job is to extract the meanings that formal patterns possess prior to, and independently of, his activities, I proceed to give an account of those activities that greatly expanded their scope:

> In my view, these same activities are constitutive to a structure of concerns which is necessarily prior to any examination of formal patterns because it is itself the occasion of their coming into being. The stylisticians proceed as if there were observable facts that could first be described and then interpreted. What I am suggesting is that an interpreting entity, endowed with purposes and concerns, is, by virtue of its very operation, determining what counts as the facts to be observed.

This clearly weakens, if it does not wholly blur, the distinction between description and interpretation, and it goes a long way toward suggesting that linguistic and textual facts, rather than being the objects of interpretation, are its products. Typically, however, there is a loophole, a space for equivocation which allows me to avoid the more unsettling implications of my argument. The phrase "determining what counts as the facts" is capable of two readings: in one reading it is a radical assertion of the unavailability of facts apart from interpretation; in the other it merely means that of all the specifiable linguistic facts, only some are relevant to the act of interpretation, and these can only be picked out in the context of the reader's activities. (This is more or less the position taken by Michael Riffaterre in his critique of the Jakobson–Levi-Strauss analysis of "Les Chats.") That is, in one reading the status of the text is put into radical question, while in the other it is a matter of selecting from the text, which is still assumed to be stable and objective, those components that will be regarded as significant. The equivocation finally rests on the key word "interpretation." In the first statement of the position (in "Literature in the Reader") interpretation is characterized as a second-level response that prevents us from recognizing the shape of our immediate experience; but in this essay interpretation is identified with that experience when I declare that the reader's activities *are* interpretive. Again, however, this is a statement that points in two directions: it can either mean that a reader's activities are constitutive of what can be formally described or that formal features are prior to those activities and act in relation to them as promptings or cues. The article trades on these meanings and ends without confronting the contradiction that exists at its center.

The source of this contradiction was my unthinking acceptance of another formalist assumption, the assumption that subjectivity is an ever present danger and that any critical procedure must include a mechanism for holding it in check. Indeed, it was the absence of such a mechanism in the procedures of the stylisticians that was the basis of my attack on their work. It is not, I complained, that what they do can't be done, but that it can be done all too easily and in any direction one likes. Behind the phrase "any direction one likes" is the Arnoldian fear that, in the absence of impersonal and universal constraints, interpreters will be free to impose their idiosyncratic meanings on texts. So long as I subscribed to this fear and even used it as a polemical weapon, it was unlikely that I would ever see my way to abandoning the chief stay against it, the stability and integrity of the text. As it turned out, the removal of that fear depended on my reconceiving of the reader in such a way as to eliminate the category of "the subjective" altogether, and although I didn't know it at the time, that process had already begun in "How Ordinary Is Ordinary Language?" written in 1972. In that essay I challenge the opposition between a basic or neutral language that is responsible to or reflects the world of objective fact and a language that reflects the uniqueness of individual or subjective perception. This distinction in turn is attached to another, between the language we ordinarily use in managing the business of everyday life and the language of literature, and as a result "ordinary language" is detached from the realm of perspective and values (now the province of subjectivity and literature) and turned into a purely formal structure that exists apart from any particular purpose or situation. My strategy in the essay is to rescue ordinary language from this impoverishing characterization by arguing that at its heart is precisely the realm of values, intentions, and purposes which is often assumed to be the exclusive property of literature.

This, of course, has the effect of blurring the distinction between ordinary language and literature, and leaves me with the problem of explaining how, in the absence of formal criteria, literary texts come to be identified. I solve this problem in a way that was to have great consequences for the position I was developing. Literature, I argue, is a conventional category. What will, at any time, be recognized as literature is a function of a communal decision as to what will count as literature. All texts have the potential of so counting, in that it is possible to regard any stretch of language in such a way that it will display those properties presently understood to be literary. In other words, it is not that literature exhibits certain formal properties that compel a certain kind of attention; rather, paying a certain kind of attention (as defined by what literature is understood to

be) results in the emergence into noticeability of the properties
we know in advance to be literary. The conclusion is that while
literature is still a category, it is an open category, not definable
by fictionality, or by a disregard of propositional truth, or by a
predominance of tropes and figures, but simply by what we decide to put into it. And the conclusion to that conclusion is that it
is the reader who "makes" literature. This sounds like the rank-
est subjectivism, but it is qualified almost immediately when the
reader is identified not as a free agent, making literature in any
old way, but as a member of a community whose assumptions
about literature determine the kind of attention he pays and thus
the kind of literature "he" "makes." (The quotation marks indicate that "he" and "makes" are *not* being understood as they
would be under a theory of autonomous individual agency).
Thus the act of recognizing literature is not constrained by something in the text, nor does it issue from an independent and arbitrary will; rather, it proceeds from a collective decision as to what
will count as literature, a decision that will be in force only
so long as a community of readers or believers continues to
abide by it.

This statement is not without its equivocations, and they are
familiar. The notion of a decision by which persons do or do
not abide implies that what one believes is a matter of choice.
On this reading, the free and autonomous subject is not eliminated but granted the considerable power of determining the
beliefs that determine his world. The stronger reading would
be one in which the subject's consciousness was wholly informed
by conventional notions, with the result that any "decision" to
affirm this or that belief would itself be enabled by beliefs that
he did not choose. But that reading has not quite surfaced and
the argument remains poised between two characterizations of
the self: in one the self is constituted, no less than the texts it
constitutes in turn, by conventional ways of thinking; in the
other the self stands in a place of its own from the vantage point
of which it surveys conventional ways of thinking and chooses
among them.

The same hesitation also informs the conception of the text.
When I say that literature is made by "a decision to regard with

a particular self-consciousness the resources language has always possessed," the integrity of the text is still preserved because the "decision" (to pay a certain kind of attention, to put in one's literary perceiving set) merely brings out, in the sense of highlighting, properties the text has always had. This stops quite a bit short of the stronger assertion that the properties of the text (whether they be literary or "ordinary" properties) are the product of certain ways of paying attention. The symmetry between my position on the text and my position on the self reflects my continuing commitment to the assumption (shared by the formalists) that the text and the reader are independent and competing entities whose spheres of influence and responsibility must be defined and controlled. The crucial step will be to see that the claims of neither the text nor the reader can be upheld, because neither has the independent status that would make its claim possible.

That step is taken in "Interpreting the *Variorum*," in which the text and the reader fall together. The text goes first in response to an objection that I myself raise: If the content of the reader's experience is the succession of acts he performs, and if he performs those acts at the bidding of the text, does not the text then contain everything and have I not compromised my antiformalist position? My answer to this question indicates that for the first time I was directly confronting my relation to formalism rather than simply reacting to the accusation that I was a closet formalist. This objection will have force, I declared, only if the formal patterns of the text are assumed to exist independently of the reader's experience. This, of course, was the enabling assumption of my reader-oriented analyses and the basis for my claim of generality. I now proceeded to give it up by demonstrating that in my own analyses the formal features with which I began are the *product* of the interpretive principles for which they are supposedly evidence:

I did what critics always do: I "saw" what my interpretive principles permitted or directed me to see and then I turned around and attributed what I had "seen" to a text and an intention. What my principles direct me to "see" are readers performing acts; the points at which I find (or to be more precise, declare) those acts to have been performed become (by a sleight of hand) demarcations *in* the text; those demarcations are then available for the designation "formal features," and as formal features they can be (illegitimately) assigned the responsibility for producing the interpretation which in fact produced them.

This would mean, for example, that the moment crucial to my analysis of *Paradise Lost*, IV, 9–12, the moment when the reader mistakenly thinks that it is the loss of Eden of which Adam and Eve are declared innocent, is not discovered by the analytical method but produced by it. The "units of sense" that mark the points at which my readers "do things" are only units within the assumption that reading is an activity of a particular kind, a succession of deliberative acts in the course of which sense is continually being made and then made again. That assumption cannot be "proved out" or proven wrong by the analysis since it will be responsible for the shape the analysis necessarily has (a description of a succession of deliberative acts, each of which revises or modifies a previous understanding).

The extent to which this is a decisive break from formalism is evident in my unqualified conclusion that formal units are always a function of the interpretive model one brings to bear (they are not "in the text"). Indeed, the text as an entity independent of interpretation and (ideally) responsible for its career drops out and is replaced by the texts that emerge as the consequence of our interpretive activities. There are still formal patterns, but they do not lie innocently in the world; rather, they are themselves constituted by an interpretive act. The facts one points to are still there (in a sense that would not be consoling to an objectivist) but only as a consequence of the interpretive (man-made) model that has called them into being. The relationship between interpretation and text is thus reversed: interpretive strategies are not put into execution after reading; they are the shape of reading, and because they are the shape of reading, they give texts their shape, making them rather than, as is usually assumed, arising from them.

At this point it looks as if the text is about to be dislodged as a center of authority in favor of the reader whose interpretive strategies make it; but I forestall this conclusion by arguing that the strategies in question are not his in the sense that would make him an independent agent. Rather, they proceed not from him but from the interpretive community of which he is a member; they are, in effect, community property, and insofar as they at once enable and limit the operations of his consciousness, he is too. The notion of "interpretive communities," which had surfaced occasionally in my discourse before, now becomes central to it. Indeed, it is interpretive communities, rather than either the text or the reader, that produce meanings and are responsible for the emergence of formal features. Interpretive communities are made up of those who share interpretive strategies not for reading but for writing texts, for constituting their properties. In other words these strategies exist prior to the act of reading and therefore determine the shape of what is read rather than, as is usually assumed, the other way around.

Even this formulation is not quite correct. The phrase "those who share interpretive strategies" suggests that individuals stand apart from the communities to which they now and then belong. In later essays I will make the point that since the thoughts an individual can think and the mental operations he can perform have their source in some or other interpretive community, he is as much a product of that community (acting as an extension of it) as the meanings it enables him to produce. At a stroke the dilemma that gave rise to the debate between the champions of the text and the champions of the reader (of whom I had certainly been one) is dissolved because the competing entities are no longer perceived as independent. To put it another way, the claims of objectivity and subjectivity can no longer be debated because the authorizing agency, the center of interpretive authority, is at once both and neither. An interpretive community is not objective because as a bundle of interests, of particular purposes and goals, its perspective is interested rather than neutral; but by the very same reasoning, the meanings and texts produced by an interpretive community are not subjective because they do not proceed from an isolated individual but from a public and conventional point of view.

Once the subject–object dichotomy was eliminated as the

only framework within which critical debate could occur, problems that had once seemed so troublesome did not seem to be problems at all. As an advocate of the rights of the reader, I could explain agreement only by positing an ideal (or informed) reader in relation to whom other readers were less informed or otherwise deficient. That is, agreement was secured by making disagreement aberrant (a position that was difficult to defend since the experience with which one had to agree was mine). But given the notion of interpretive communities, agreement more or less explained itself: members of the same community will necessarily agree because they will see (and by seeing, make) everything in relation to that community's assumed purposes and goals; and conversely, members of different communities will disagree because from each of their respective positions the other "simply" cannot see what is obviously and inescapably there: This, then, is the explanation for the stability of interpretation among different readers (they belong to the same community). It also explains why there are disagreements and why they can be debated in a principled way: not because of a stability in texts, but because of a stability in the makeup of interpretive communities and therefore in the opposing positions they make possible.

It followed then that what I had been doing in essays like "What It's Like To Read *L'Allegro* and *Il Penseroso*" was not revealing what readers had always done but trying to persuade them to a set of community assumptions so that when they read they would do what I did. As soon as I realized this, I realized that I was assenting to a characterization of my position that I had always resisted: you're not telling us how we've always read; you're trying to persuade us to a new way of reading. I resisted that characterization because I wanted to be able to claim generality. That is, I wanted to put my accounts of *the* reader's experience on as firm a ground as the ground claimed by the champions of the text by identifying the *real* reading experience in relation to which others were deviations or distortions. What I finally came to see was that the identification of what was real and normative occurred within interpretive communities and what was normative for the members of one community would be seen as strange (if it could be seen at all) by the members of another. In other words, there is no single way of reading that is correct or natural, only "ways of reading" that are extensions of community perspectives. Once I saw this, the judgment that I was trying to persuade people to a new way of reading was no longer heard as an accusation because what I was trying to persuade them *from* was not a fundamental or natural way but a way no less conventional than mine and one to which they had similarly been persuaded, if not by open polemics then by the pervasiveness of the assumptions within which they had learned how to read in the first place. This meant that the business of criticism was not (as I had previously thought) to determine a correct way of reading but to determine from which of a number of possible perspectives reading will proceed. This determination will not be made once and for all by a neutral mechanism of adjudication, but will be made and remade again whenever the interests and tacitly understood goals of one interpretive community replace or dislodge the interests and goals of another. The business of criticism, in other words, was not to decide between interpretations by subjecting them to the test of disinterested evidence but to establish by political and persuasive means (they are the same thing) the set of interpretive assumptions from the vantage of which the evidence (and the facts and the intentions and everything else) will hereafter be specifiable. In the end I both gave up generality and reclaimed it: I gave it up because I gave up the project of trying to identify the one true way of reading, but I reclaimed it because I claimed the right, along with everyone else, to argue for a way of reading, which, if it became accepted, would be, for a time at least, the true one. In short, I preserved generality by rhetoricizing it.

The distance I have traveled can be seen in the changed status of interpretation. Whereas I had once agreed with my predecessors on the need to control interpretation lest it overwhelm and obscure texts, facts, authors, and intentions, I now believe that interpretation is the source of texts, facts, authors, and intentions. Or to put it another way, the entities that were once seen as competing for the right to constrain interpretation (text, reader, author) are now all seen to be the *products* of interpretation. A polemic that was mounted in the name of the reader and against the text has ended by the subsuming of both the text and reader under the larger category of interpretation. What one finds waiting at the "end," however, is a whole new set of problems. Having redefined the activity of criticism so that it was no longer a matter of demonstration but a matter (endlessly negotiated) of persuasion, I am faced with the task of accounting, within the new model, for everything that had been recognized under the old model as being constitutive of the literary institution: texts, authors, periods, genres, canons, standards, agreements, disputes, values, changes, and so on. That task is begun in some of the essays that follow, and especially in those written after "Interpreting the *Variorum*," but if the rehearsing of this personal history has taught me anything, it is that the prosecution of that task will also be, in ways that I cannot now see, its transformation.

Part One

Literature in the Reader

1
Literature in the Reader: Affective Stylistics

[THIS ESSAY, an early manifesto, was written in the summer of 1970 in response to a letter from Ralph Cohen, editor of the recently founded *New Literary History*. "We hear," wrote Professor Cohen, "that you believe something and we would like you to tell us about it." I had become aware that I believed something in the course of writing *Surprised by Sin: The Reader in Paradise Lost* (1967); the thesis of that book is that *Paradise Lost* is a poem about how its readers came to be the way they are. It follows, I argue, that the difficulties one experiences in reading the poem are not to be lamented or discounted but are to be seen as manifestations of the legacy left to us by Adam when he fell. Milton's strategy in the poem is to make the reader self-conscious about his own performance, to force him to doubt the correctness of his responses, and to bring him to the realization that his inability to read the poem with any confidence in his own perception is its focus. In 1967 this was a daring argument (several reviewers called it "dangerous") because it seemed to commit the affective fallacy; but it was less daring than it might have been because it was a special argument, made only for a poem whose relationship to its readers was unique. In the years that followed, however, I was encouraged to extend the methodology of the book to other poems and to advance the general claim that all poems (and novels and plays) were, in some sense, about their readers, and that therefore the experience of the reader, rather than the "text itself," was the proper object of analysis. My interest in making such a claim coincided with a three-month residence in Paris, during the spring and early summer of 1970, when I participated in a seminar at the University of Vincennes, along with Seymour Chatman, Christina Brooke Rose, Albert Cook, Bruce Morisette, and others. Both Tzvetan Todorov's *The Fantastic* and Roland Barthes's *S/Z* had just been published, and everyone was reading and talking about them. I returned to find Cohen's letter waiting for me and I wrote "Literature in the Reader" while I was preparing to teach a course in literary theory for the first time. The article summed up everything I then believed, and I find its argument powerful and compelling even now, although it is long since that I began to see its flaws. Those flaws are discussed in detail in the introduction to this volume, but they all reduce to the substitution of one kind of reified entity for another. In place of the objective and self-contained text I put "the basic data of the meaning experience" and "what is objectively true about the *activity* of reading"; and in order to firm up this new "bottom line" I introduced the notions of the "informed reader"—designed to take account of, by stigmatizing, all those readers whose experiences were not as I described them—and "literary competence"—designed to stabilize the knowledge the informed reader is presumed to have. All of this was attached to the disclaimer that my method is oriented *away* from evaluation and toward description, a disclaimer that placed me in the value-independent position that I would later declare to be unavailable. Finally, although I would not now subscribe to the tenets put forward in this article, I would still make a claim for the pedagogical value of the method. More than any other way of teaching I know, it breaks down the barriers between students and the knowledge they must acquire, first by identifying that knowledge with something that they themselves are already doing, and then by asking them to become self-conscious about what they do in the hope that they can learn to do it better.]

IF AT THIS MOMENT someone were to ask, "What are you doing?" you might reply, "I am reading," and thereby acknowledge the fact that reading is an activity, something you do. No one would argue that the act of reading can take place in the absence of someone who reads—how can you tell the dance from the dancer?— but curiously enough when it comes time to make analytical statements about the end product of reading (meaning or understanding), the reader is usually forgotten or ignored. Indeed, in recent literary history he has been excluded by legislation. I refer, of course, to the *ex cathedra* pronouncements of Wimsatt and Beardsley in their enormously influential essay "The Affective Fallacy":

The Affective Fallacy is a confusion between the poem and its *results* (what it *is* and what it *does*) . . . It begins by trying to derive the standards of criticism from the psychological effects of the poem and ends in impressionism and relativism. The outcome . . . is that the poem itself, as an object of specifically critical judgment, tends to disappear.[1]

In time, I shall return to these arguments, not so much to refute them as to affirm and embrace them; but I would first like to demonstrate the explanatory power of a method of analysis which takes the reader, as an actively mediating presence, fully into account, and which therefore has as its focus the "psychological effects" of the utterance. And I would like to begin with a sentence that does not open itself up to the questions we usually ask.

That Judas perished by hanging himself, there is no certainty in Scripture: though in one place it seems to affirm it, and by a doubtful word hath given occasion to translate it; yet in another place, in a more punctual description, it maketh it improbable, and seems to overthrow it.

Ordinarily, one would begin by asking, "What does this sentence mean?" or "What is it about?" or "What is it saying?" —all of which preserve the objectivity of the utterance. For my purposes, however, this particular sentence has the advantage of not saying anything. That is, you can't get a fact out of it which could serve as an answer to any one of these questions. Of course, this difficulty is itself a fact—of response; and it suggests, to me at least, that what makes problematical sense as a statement makes perfect sense as a strategy, as an action made upon a reader rather than as a container from which a reader extracts a message. The strategy or action here is one of progressive decertainizing. Simply by taking in the first clause of the sentence, the reader commits himself to its assertion, "that Judas perished by hanging himself" (in constructions of this type "that" is understood to be shorthand for "the *fact* that"). This is not so much a conscious decision as it is an anticipatory adjustment to his projection of the sentence's future contours. He knows (without giving cognitive form to his knowledge) that this first clause is preliminary to some larger assertion (it is a "ground"), and he must be in control of it if he is to move easily and confidently through what follows; and in the context of this "knowledge," he is prepared, again less than consciously, for any one of several constructions:

> That Judas perished by hanging himself, *is* (an example for us all).
> That Judas perished by hanging himself, *shows* (how conscious he was of the enormity of his sin).
> That Judas perished by hanging himself, *should* (give us pause).

The range of these possibilities (and there are, of course, more than I have listed) narrows considerably as the next three words are read, "there is no." At this point, the reader is expecting, and even predicting, a single word, "doubt," but instead he finds "certainty"; and at that moment the status of the fact that had served as his point of reference becomes *uncertain*. (It is nicely ironic that the appearance of "certainty" should be the occasion for doubt, whereas the word "doubt" would have contributed to the reader's certainty.) As a result, the terms of the reader's relationship to the sentence undergo a profound change. He is suddenly involved in a different kind of activity. Rather than following an argument along a well lighted path (a light, after all, has gone *out*), he is now looking for one. The natural impulse in a situation like this, either in life or in literature, is to go forward in the hope that what has been obscured will again become clear; but in this case going forward only intensifies the reader's sense of disorientation. The prose is continually opening, but then closing, on the possibility of verification in one direction or another. There are two vocabularies in the sentence; one holds out the promise of a clarification— "place," "affirm," "place," "punctual," "overthrow"—while the other continually defaults on that promise—"Though," "doubtful," "yet," "improbable," "seems." And the reader is passed back and forth between them and between the alternatives— that Judas did or did not perish by hanging himself—which are still suspended (actually it is the reader who is suspended) when the sentence ends (trails off? gives up?). The indeterminateness of this experience is compounded by a superfluity of pronouns. It becomes increasingly difficult to tell what "it" refers to, and if the reader takes the trouble to retrace his steps, he is simply led back to "that Judas perished by hanging himself"; in short, he exchanges an indefinite pronoun for an even less definite (that is, certain) assertion.

Whatever is persuasive and illuminating about this analysis (and it is by no means exhaustive) is the result of my substituting for one question—what does this sentence mean?—another, more operational question—what does this sentence do? And what the sentence does is give the reader something and then take it away, drawing him on with the unredeemed promise of its return. An observation about the sentence as an utterance— its refusal to yield a declarative statement—has been transformed into an account of its experience (not being able to get a fact out of it). It is no longer an object, a thing-in-itself, but an *event,* something that *happens* to, and with the participation of, the reader. And it is this event, this happening—all of it and not anything that could be said about it or any information one might take away from it—that is, I would argue, the *meaning* of the sentence. (Of course, in this case there is no information to take away.)

This is a provocative thesis whose elaboration and defense will be the concern of the following pages, but before proceeding to it, I would like to examine another utterance which also (conveniently) says nothing:

> Nor did they not perceive the evil plight.

The first word of this line from *Paradise Lost* (I, 335) generates a rather precise (if abstract) expectation of what will follow: a negative assertion which will require for its completion a subject and a verb. There are then two "dummy" slots in the reader's mind waiting to be filled. This expectation is strengthened (if only because it is not challenged) by the auxiliary "did" and the pronoun "they." Presumably, the verb is not far behind. But in its place the reader is presented with a second negative, one that cannot be accommodated within his projection of the utterance's form. His progress through the line is halted and he is forced to come to terms with the intrusive (because unexpected) "not." In effect what the reader *does,* or is forced to do, at this point, is ask a question—did they or didn't they?—and in search of an answer he either rereads—in which case he simply repeats the sequence of mental operations—or goes forward—in which case he finds the anticipated verb, but in either case the syntactical uncertainty remains unresolved.

It could be objected that the solution to the difficulty is simply to invoke the rule of the double negative; one cancels the other and the "correct" reading is therefore "they did perceive the evil plight." But however satisfactory this may be in terms of the internal logic of grammatical utterances (and even in those terms there are problems),[2] it has nothing to do with the logic of the reading experience or, I would insist, with its meaning. That experience is a temporal one, and in the course of it the two negatives combine not to produce an affirmative, but to prevent the reader from making the simple (declarative) sense which would be the goal of a logical analysis. To clean the line up is to take from it its most prominent and important effect—the suspension of the reader between the alternatives its syntax momentarily offers. What is a problem if the line is considered as an object, a thing-in-itself, becomes a *fact* when it is regarded as an occurrence. The reader's inability to tell whether or not "they" do perceive and his involuntary question (or its psychological equivalent) are events in his encounter with the line, and as events they are part of the line's *meaning,* even though they take place in the mind, not on the page. Subsequently, we discover that the answer to the question "did they or didn't they," is, "they did and they didn't." Milton is exploiting (and calling our attention to) the two senses of "perceive": they (the fallen angels) do perceive the fire, the pain, the gloom— physically they see it—however, they are blind to the moral significance of their situation, and in that sense they do not perceive the evil plight in which they are. But that is another story.

Underlying these two analyses is a method, rather simple in concept, but complex (or at least complicated) in execution. The concept is simply the rigorous and distinterested asking of the question, what does this word, phrase, sentence, paragraph, chapter, novel, play, poem, *do*? And the execution involves an analysis of the developing responses of the reader in relation to the words as they succeed one another in time. Every word in this statement bears a special emphasis. The analysis must be of the developing responses to distinguish it from the atomism of much stylistic criticism. A reader's response to the fifth word in a line or sentence is to a large extent the product of his responses to words one, two, three, and four. And by response, I intend more than the range of feelings (what Wimsatt and Beardsley call "the purely affective reports"). The category of response includes any and all of the activities provoked by a string of words: the projection of syntactical and/or lexical probabilities; their subsequent occurrence or nonoccurrence; attitudes toward persons, or things, or ideas referred to; the reversal or questioning of those attitudes; and much more. Obviously, this imposes a great burden on the analyst, who in his observations on any one moment in the reading experience must take into account all that has happened (in the reader's mind) at previous moments, each of which was in its turn subject to the accumulating pressures of its predecessors. (He must take into account influences and pressures predating the actual reading experience—questions of genre, history, and so on—questions we shall consider later.) All of this is included in the phrase "in time." The basis of the method is a consideration of the *temporal* flow of the reading experience, and it is assumed that the reader responds in terms of that flow and not to the whole utterance. That is, in an utterance of any length, there is a point at which the reader has taken in only the first word, and then the second, and then the third, and so on, and the report of what happens to the reader is always a report of what has happened *to that point*. (The report includes the reader's set toward future experiences, but not those experiences.)

The importance of this principle is illustrated when we reverse the first two clauses of the Judas sentence: "There is no certainty that Judas perished by hanging himself." Here the status of the assertion is never in doubt because the reader knows from the beginning that it is doubtful; he is given a perspective

from which to view the statement and that perspective is confirmed rather than challenged by what follows; even the confusion of pronouns in the second part of the sentence will not
be disturbing to him, because it can easily be placed in the context of his initial response. There is no difference in these two
sentences in the information conveyed (or not conveyed), or
in the lexical and syntactical components,[3] only in the way these
are received. But that one difference makes *all* the difference—
between an uncomfortable, unsettling experience in which the
gradual dimming of a fact is attended by a failure in perception,
and a wholly self-satisfying one in which an uncertainty is comfortably certain, and the reader's confidence in his own powers
remains unshaken, because he is always in control. It is, I insist,
a difference in meaning.

The results (I will later call them advantages) of this method
are fairly, though not exhaustively, represented in my two examples. Essentially what the method does is *slow down* the reading experience so that "events" one does not notice in normal
time, but which do occur, are brought before our analytical at-
tentions. It is as if a slow motion camera with an automatic stop-
action effect were recording our linguistic experiences and presenting them to us for viewing. Of course the value of such a
procedure is predicated on the idea of *meaning as an event,*
something that is happening between the words and in the
reader's mind, something not visible to the naked eye but which
can be made visible (or at least palpable) by the regular introduction of a "searching" question (what does this do?). It is
more usual to assume that meaning is a function of the utterance, and to equate it with the information given (the message)
or the attitude expressed. That is, the components of an utterance are considered either in relation to each other or to a state
of affairs in the outside world, or to the state of mind of the
speaker-author. In any and all of these variations, meaning is
located (presumed to be imbedded) *in* the utterance, and the
apprehension of meaning is an act of extraction.[4] In short, there
is little sense of process and even less of the reader's actualizing
participation in that process.

This concentration on the verbal object as a thing in itself and as a repository of meaning has many consequences, theoretical and practical. First of all, it creates a whole class of utterances which, because of their alleged transparency, are declared to be uninteresting as objects of analysis. Sentences or fragments of sentences that immediately "make sense" (a deeply revealing phrase if one thinks about it) are examples of ordinary language; they are neutral and styleless statements, "simply" referring, or "simply" reporting. But the application to such utterances of the question "What does it do?" (which assumes that something is *always* happening) reveals that a great deal is going on in their production and comprehension (every linguistic experience is affecting and pressuring) although most of it is going on so close up, at such a basic, "preconscious" level of experience, that we tend to overlook it. Thus the utterance (written or spoken) "there is a chair" is at once understood as the report either of an existing state of affairs or of an act of perception (I see a chair). In either frame of reference, it makes immediate sense. To my mind, however, what is interesting about the utterance is the *sub rosa* message, it puts out *by virtue of* its easy comprehensibility. Because it gives information directly and simply, it asserts (silently, but effectively) the "givability," directly and simply, of information; and it is thus an extension of the ordering operation we perform on experience whenever it is filtered through our temporal-spatial consciousness. In short, it *makes* sense, in exactly the way we make (that is, manufacture) sense of whatever, if anything, exists outside us; and by making easy sense it tells us that sense can be easily made and that we are capable of easily making it. A whole document consisting of such utterances—a chemistry text or a telephone book—will be telling us that all the time; and that, rather than any reportable "content," will be its meaning. Such language can be called "ordinary" only because it confirms and reflects our ordinary understanding of the world and our position in it; but for precisely that reason it is *extra*-ordinary (unless we accept a naive epistemology which grants us unmediated access to reality), and to leave it unanalyzed is to risk missing much of what happens—to us and through us—when we read and (or so we think) understand.

The problem is simply that most methods of analysis operate at so high a level of abstraction that the basic data of the meaning experience is slighted and/or obscured. In the area of specifically literary studies, the effects of a naive theory of utterance meaning and of its attendant assumption of ordinary language can be seen in what is acknowledged to be the sorry state of the criticism of the novel and of prose in general. This is usually explained with reference to a distinction between prose and poetry, which is actually a distinction between ordinary language and poetic language. Poetry, it is asserted, is characterized by a high incidence of deviance from normal syntactical and lexical habits. It therefore offers the analyst-critic a great many points of departure. Prose, on the other hand (except for Baroque eccentrics like Thomas Browne and James Joyce) is, well, just prose, and just there. It is this helplessness before all but the most spectacular effects that I would remedy, although in one way the two examples with which this essay began were badly chosen, since they were analyses of utterances that are obviously and problematically deviant. This, of course, was a ploy to gain your attention. Assuming that I now have it, let me insist that the method shows to best advantage when it is applied to unpromising material. Consider for example this sentence (actually part of a sentence) from Walter Pater's "Conclusion" to *The Renaissance,* which, while it is hardly the stuff of everyday conversation, does not, at first sight, afford much scope for the critic's analytical skill:

That clear perpetual outline of face and limb is but an image of ours.

What can one say about a sentence like this? The analyst of style would, I fear, find it distressingly straightforward and non-deviant, a simple declarative of the form X is Y. And if he were by chance drawn to it, he would not be likely to pay very much attention to the first word—"That." It is simply there. But of course it is not simply there; it is *actively* there, doing something, and what that something is can be discovered by asking the question "what does it do?" The answer is obvious, right there in front of our noses, although we may not see it until we ask the question. "That" is a demonstrative, a word that points *out,* and as one takes it *in,* a sense of its referent (yet unidentified) is established. Whatever "that" is, it is outside, at a distance from the observer-reader; it is "pointable to" (pointing is what the word "that" does), something of substance and solidity. In terms of the reader's response, "that" generates an expectation that impels him forward, the expectation of finding out *what* "that" is. The word and its effect are the basic data of the meaning experience and they will direct our description of that experience because they direct the reader.

The adjective "clear" works in two ways; it promises the reader that when "that" appears, he will be able to see it easily, and, conversely, that it can be easily seen. "Perpetual" stabilizes the visibility of "that" even *before* it is seen and "outline" gives it potential form, while at the same time raising a question. That question—outline of what?—is obligingly answered by the phrase "of face and limb," which, in effect, fills the outline in. By the time the reader reaches the declarative verb "is"—which sets the seal on the objective reality of what has preceded it—he is fully and securely oriented in a world of perfectly discerned objects and perfectly discerning observers, of whom he is one. But then the sentence turns on the reader, and takes away the world it has itself created. With "but" the easy progress through the sentence is impeded (it is a split second before one realizes that "but" has the force of "only"); the declarative force of "is" is weakened and the status of the firmly drawn outline the reader has been pressured to accept is suddenly uncertain; "image" resolves that uncertainty, but in the direction of insubstantiality; and the now blurred form disappears altogether when the phrase "of ours" collapses the distinction between the reader and that which is (or was) "without" (Pater's own word). Now you see it (that), now you don't. Pater giveth and Pater taketh away. (Again this description of the reader's experience is an analysis of the sentence's meaning and if you were to ask, "but, what does it mean?" I would simply repeat the description.)

What is true of this sentence is true, I believe, of much of what we hold ourselves responsible for as critics and teachers of literature. There is more to it, that is, to its experience, than meets the casual eye. What is required, then, is a method, a machine if you will, which in its operation makes observable, or at least accessible, what goes on below the level of self-conscious response. Everyone would admit that something "funny" happens in the Judas sentence from Sir Thomas Browne's *Religio Medici* and that there is a difficulty built into the reading and understanding of the line from *Paradise Lost;* but there is a tendency to assume that the Pater sentence is a simple assertion (whatever that is). It is of course nothing of the kind. In fact, it is not an assertion at all, although the promise of an assertion is one of its components. It is an experience; it occurs; it does something; it makes us do something. Indeed, I would go so far as to say, in direct contradiction of Wimsatt and Beardsley, that what it does is what it means.

The Logic and Structure of Response

What I am suggesting is that there is no direct relationship between the meaning of a sentence (paragraph, novel, poem) and what its words mean. Or, to put the matter less provocatively, the information an utterance gives, its message, is a constituent of, but certainly not to be identified with, its meaning. It is the experience of an utterance—*all* of it and not anything that could be said about it, including anything I could say—that is its meaning.

It follows, then, that it is impossible to mean the same thing in two (or more) different ways, although we tend to think that it happens all the time. We do this by substituting for our immediate linguistic experience an interpretation or abstraction of it, in which "it" is inevitably compromised. We contrive to forget what has happened to us in our life with language, removing ourselves as far as possible from the linguistic event before making a statement about it. Thus we say, for example, that "the book of the father" and "the father's book" mean the same thing, forgetting that "father" and "book" occupy different positions of emphasis in our different experiences; and as we progress in this forgetting, we become capable of believing that sentences as different as these are equivalent in meaning:

This fact is concealed by the influence of language, moulded by science, which foists on us exact concepts as though they represented the immediate deliverances of experience.

A. N. Whitehead

And if we continue to dwell in thought on this world, not of objects in the solidity with which language invests them, but of impressions, unstable, flickering, inconsistent, which burn and are extinguished with our consciousness of them, it contracts still further.

Walter Pater

It is (literally) tempting to say that these sentences make the same point: that language which pretends to precision operates to obscure the flux and disorder of actual experience. And of course they do, if one considers them at a high enough level of generality. But as individual experiences through which a reader lives, they are not alike at all, and neither, therefore, are their meanings.

To take the Whitehead sentence first, it simply does not mean what it says; for as the reader moves through it, he experiences the stability of the world whose existence it supposedly denies. The word "fact" itself makes an exact concept out of the idea of inexactness; and by referring backward to find its referent —"the radically untidy ill-adjusted character of . . . experience" —the reader performs the characteristic action required of him by this sentence, the fixing of things in their place.

There is nothing untidy either in the sentence or in our experience of it. Each clause is logically related to its predecessors and prepares the way for what follows; and since our active attention is required only at the points of relation, the sentence is divided *by us* into a succession of discrete areas, each of which is dominated by the language of certainty. Even the phrase "as though they represented" falls into this category, since its stress falls on "they represented" which then thrusts us forward to the waiting "deliverances of experience." In short, the sentence, in its action upon us, declares the tidy well-ordered character of actual experience, and that is its meaning.

At first the Pater sentence is self-subverting in the same way. The least forceful word in its first two clauses is "not," which is literally overwhelmed by the words that surround it—"world," "objects," "solidity," "language"; and by the time the reader reaches the "but" in "but of impressions," he finds himself inhabiting (dwelling in) a "world" of fixed and "solid" objects. It is of course a world made up of words, constructed in large part by the reader himself as he performs grammatical actions which reinforce the stability of its phenomena. By referring backwards from "them" to "objects," the reader accords "objects" a place in the sentence (whatever can be referred back to must be somewhere) and in his mind. In the second half of the sentence, however, this same world is unbuilt. There is still a backward dependence to the reading experience, but the point of reference is the word "impressions"; and the series which follows it—"unstable," "flickering," "inconsistent"—serves only to accentuate its *in*stability. Like Whitehead, Pater perpetrates the very deception he is warning against; but this is only one part of his strategy. The other is to break down (extinguish) the coherence of the illusion he has created. Each successive stage of the sentence is less exact (in Whitehead's terms) than its predecessors, because at each successive stage the reader is given less and less to hold on to; and when the corporeality of "this world" has wasted away to an "it" ("it contracts still further"), he is left with nothing at all.

One could say, I suppose, that at the least these two sentences gesture toward the same insight; but even this minimal statement makes me uneasy, because "insight" is another word that implies "there it is, I've got it." And this is exactly the difference between the two sentences: Whitehead lets you get "it" (the neat, trim, tidy, exact world), while Pater gives you the experience of having "it" melt under your feet. It is only when one steps back from the sentences that they are in any way equivalent; and stepping back is what an analysis in terms of doing and happenings does not allow.

The analysis of the Pater sentence illustrates another feature of the method, its independence of linguistic logic. If a casual reader were asked to point out the most important word in the second clause—"not of objects in the solidity with which language invests them"—he would probably answer "not," because as a logical marker "not" controls everything that follows it. But as one component in an experience, it is hardly controlling at all; for as the clause unfolds, "not" has less and less a claim on our attention and memories; working against it, and finally overwhelming it, as we saw, is an unbroken succession of more forceful words. My point of course is that in an analysis of the sentence as a thing in itself, consisting of words arranged in syntactological relationships, "not" would figure prominently, while in an experiential analysis it is noted chiefly for its weakness.

The case is even clearer and perhaps more interesting in this sentence from one of Donne's sermons:

> And therefore, as the mysteries of our religions are not the objects of our reason, but by faith we rest on God's decree and purpose (it is so, O God, because it is thy will it should be so) So God's decrees are ever to be considered in the manifestation thereof.

Here the "not"—again logically controlling—is subverted by the very construction in which it is imbedded; for that construction, unobtrusively but nonetheless effectively, pressures the reader to perform exactly those mental operations whose propriety the statement of the sentence—what it is saying—is challenging. That is, a paraphrase of the material before the parenthesis might read—"Matters of faith and religion are not the objects of our reason"; but the simple act of taking in the words "And therefore" involves us unavoidably in reasoning about matters of faith and religion; in fact so strong is the pull of these words that our primary response to this part of the sentence is one of anticipation; we are waiting for a "so" clause to complete the logically based sequence begun by "And therefore as." But when that "so" appears, it is not at all what we had expected, for it is the "so" of divine fiat—it is so O God because it is thy will it should be so—of a causality more real than any that can be observed in nature or described in a natural (human) language. The speaker, however, completes his "explaining" and "organizing" statement as if its silent claim to be a window on reality were still unquestioned. As a result the reader is alerted to the inadequacy of the very process in which he is (through the syntax) involved, and at the same time he accepts the necessity, for limited human beings, of proceeding within the now discredited assumptions of that process.

Of course, a formalist analysis of this sentence would certainly have discovered the tension between the two "so's," one a synonym for therefore, the other shorthand for "so be it," and might even have gone on to suggest that the relationship between them is a mirror of the relationship between the mysteries of faith and the operations of reason. I doubt, however, that a formalist analysis would have brought us to the point where we could see the sentence, and the mode of discourse it represents, as a self-deflating joke ("thereof" mocks "therefore"), to which the reader responds and of which he is a victim. In short, and to repeat myself, to consider the utterances apart from the consciousness receiving it is to risk missing a great deal of what is going on. It is a risk which analysis in terms of "doings and happenings"[5] works to minimize.

Another advantage of the method is its ability to deal with sentences (and works) that don't mean anything, in the sense of not making sense. Literature, it is often remarked (either in praise or with contempt) is largely made up of such utterances. (It is an interesting comment both on Dylan Thomas and the proponents of a deviation theory of poetic language that their examples so often are taken from his work.) In an experiential analysis, the sharp distinction between sense and nonsense, with the attendant value judgments and the talk about truth content, is blurred, because the place where sense is made or not made is the reader's mind rather than the printed page or the space between the covers of a book. For an example, I turn once again, and for the last time, to Pater.

> This at least of flame-like, our life has, that it is but the concurrence, renewed from moment to moment, of forces parting sooner or later on their ways.

This sentence deliberately frustrates the reader's natural desire to organize the particulars it offers. One can see for instance how different its experience would be if "concurrences of forces" were substituted for "concurrence, renewed from moment to

moment, of forces." The one allows and encourages the formation of a physical image which has a spatial reality; the mind
imagines (pictures) separate and distinct forces converging, in an
orderly fashion, on a center where they form a new, but still
recognizable and managable (in a mental sense), force; the other
determinedly prevents that image from forming. Before the
reader can respond fully to "concurrence," "renewed" stops him
by making the temporal status of the motion unclear. Has the
concurrence already taken place? Is it taking place now? Although "from moment to moment" answers these questions, it
does so at the expense of the assumptions behind them; the
phrase leaves no time for anything so formal and chartable as
a "process." For "a moment," at "of forces," there is a coming
together, but in the next moment, the moment when the reader
takes in "parting," they separate. Or do they? The phrase "sooner
or later" upsets this new attempt to find pattern and direction
in "our life" and the reader is once more disoriented, spatially
and temporally. The final deterrent to order is the plural "ways,"
which prevents the mind's eye from traveling down a single
path and insists on the haphazardness and randomness of whatever it is that happens sooner or later.

Of course this reading of the sentence (that is, of its effects)
ignores its status as a logical utterance. "Concurrence, renewed
from moment to moment, of forces" is meaningless as a statement
corresponding to a state of affairs in the "real" world; but its
refusal to mean in that discursive way creates the experience
that is its meaning; and an analysis of that experience rather
than of logical content is able to make sense of one kind—experiential sense—out of nonsense.

A similar (and saving) operation can be performed on units
larger than the sentence. One of Plato's more problematical dia-
logues is the *Phaedrus*, in part because its final assertion—"no
work . . . has ever been written or recited that is worthy of serious
attention"—seems to be contradicted by its very existence. This
"embarrassment" has been the cause of a great many articles,
often entitled "The Unity of the *Phaedrus*," in which the offending section is somehow accounted for, usually by explaining it
away. What these studies attempt to discover is the *internal*

unity of the *Phaedrus,* its coherence as a self-contained artifact; but if we look for the coherence of the dialogue in the reader's experience of it rather than in its formal structure, the "inconsistency" is less a problem to be solved than something that happens, a fact of response; and as a fact of response it is the key to the way the work works. Rather than a single sustained argument, the *Phaedrus* is a series of discrete conversations or seminars, each with its own carefully posed question, ensuing discussion, and firmly drawn conclusion, but so arranged that to enter into the spirit and assumptions of any one of these self-enclosed units is implicitly to reject the spirit and assumptions of the unit immediately preceding. This is a pattern which can be clearly illustrated by the relationship between the speech of Lysias and the first speech delivered by Socrates. Lysias' speech is criticized for not conforming to the definition of a good discourse: "every discourse, like a living creature, should be so put together that it has its own body and lacks neither head nor feet, middle nor extremities, all composed in such a way that they suit both each other and the whole."[6] Socrates, in fact, is quite careful to rule out any other standard of judgment: it is the "arrangement" rather than the "invention" or "relevance" that concerns him as a critic. Subsequently, Socrates' own effort on the same theme is criticized for its impiety, an impiety, moreover, that is compounded by its effectiveness as a "piece of rhetoric." In other words, Lysias' speech is bad because it is not well put together and Socrates' speech is bad because it is well put together.

Although neither Socrates nor Phaedrus acknowledges the contradiction, the reader, who has fallen in (perhaps involuntarily) with the standards of judgment established by the philosopher himself, is certainly confronted with it, and asked implicitly to do something with it. What he does (or should do) is realize that in the condemnation of Socrates' speech a new standard (of impiety) has been introduced, one that invalidates the very basis on which the discussion (and his reading experience) had hitherto been proceeding. At that moment, this early section of the dialogue will have achieved its true purpose, which is, paradoxically, to bring the reader to the point where he is no longer interested in the issues it treats—no longer interested because he has come to see that the real issues exist at a higher level of generality. Thus, in a way peculiar to dialectical form and experience, this space of prose and argument will have been the vehicle of its own abandonment.

Nor is that by any means the end of the matter. This pattern, in which the reader is first encouraged to entertain assumptions he probably already holds and then is later forced to reexamine and discredit those same assumptions, is repeated again and again. In the middle section of the dialogue, the two friends agree to explore the subject of "good" and "bad" writing; and Socrates argues against the sophist position that an orator "may neglect what is really good . . . for it is from what seems to be true that persuasion comes, not from the real truth" (p. 46). It is essential, counters Socrates, for a "competent speaker" to know the truth about all things and subjects, for unless he does —and here the reader anticipates some kind of equation between good writing and a concern for the truth—he will be unable to *deceive* ("When a man sets out to deceive someone else without being taken in himself, he must accurately grasp the similarity and dissimilarity of the facts"). While art and truth have been joined in one context—the ruthlessly practical context of manipulative rhetoric—a wedge has been driven between them in another—the moral context assumed at the beginning of the discussion. To the earlier insight that a well-made speech is not necessarily a "true" speech (in the moral sense), the reader must now add the further (and extending) insight that "well-madeness" is likely to be a weapon in the arsenal of Truth's enemies. So that what was at first a standard of judgment to which Socrates, Phaedrus, *and* the reader repaired, is now seen to be positively deleterious to the higher standard now only gradually emerging from the dialogue.

The important word in my last sentence is "seen"; for it suggests that what is being processed by the *Phaedrus* is not an argument or a proposition, but a vision. As an argument, in fact, the dialogue makes no sense, since Socrates is continually reaching conclusions which he subsequently, and without comment, abandons. But as an attempt to refine its reader's vision it makes a great deal of sense; for then the contradictions, the moments of "blurring," become invitations to examine closely premises too easily acquiesced in. The reader who accepts this invitation will find, on retracing his steps, that statements and phrases which had seemed unexceptionable are now suspect and dubious, and that lines of reasoning which had seemed proper and to the point are now disastrously narrow. Of course they—phrases, statements, premises, and conclusions—haven't changed (as Socrates remarks later, "written words . . . go on telling you the same thing over and over"), the *reader* has, and with each change he is able to dispense with whatever section of the dialogue he has been reading, because he has passed beyond the level of perception it represents.

To read the *Phaedrus,* then, is to use it up; for the value of any point in it is that it gets *you* (not any sustained argument) to the next point, which is not so much a point (in logical-demonstrative terms) as a level of insight. It is thus a *self-consuming artifact,* a mimetic enactment in the reader's experience of the Platonic ladder in which each rung, as it is negotiated, is kicked away. The final rung, the intuition which stands (or, more properly, on which the reader stands), because it is the last, is of course the rejection of written artifacts, a rejection that, far from contradicting what has preceded, is an exact description of what the reader, in his repeated abandoning of successive stages in the argument, has been *doing.* What was problematical sense in the structure of a self-enclosed argument makes perfect sense in the structure of the reader's experience.

The *Phaedrus* is a radical criticism of the idea of internal coherence from a moral point of view; by identifying the appeal of well-put-together artifacts with the sense of order in the perceiving (that is, receiving) mind, it provides a strong argument for the banishing of the good poet who is potentially the good deceiver. We can put aside the moral issue and still profit from the dialogue; for if the laws of beginning, middle, and end are laws of psychology rather than form (or truth), a criticism which has as its focus the structural integrity of the artifact is obviously misdirected. (It is the experience of works, not works, that have beginnings, middles, and ends.) A new look at the question may result in the rehabilitation of works like *The Faerie Queene* which have been criticized because their poetic worlds lack "unity" and consistency.[7] And a new look at the question may result also in a more accurate account of works whose formal features are so prominent that the critic proceeds directly from them to a statement of meaning without bothering to ask whether their high visibility has any direct relationship to their operation in the reader's experience.

This analysis of the *Phaedrus* illustrates, not incidentally, the ability of the method to handle units larger than the sentence. Whatever the size of the unit, the focus of the method remains the reader's experience of it, and the mechanism of the method is the magic question, "What does this——— do?" Answering it of course is more difficult than it would be for a single sentence. More variables creep in, more responses and more different kinds of responses have to be kept track of; there are more contexts which regulate and modulate the temporal flow of the reading experience. Some of these problems will be considered below. For the present let me say that I have usually found that what might be called the basic experience of a work (do *not* read basic meaning) occurs at every level. As an example, we might consider, briefly, *The Pilgrim's Progress*.

At one point in Bunyan's prose epic, Christian asks a question and receives an answer:

> *Chr*. Is this the way to the Celestial City?
> *Shep*. You are just in your way.

The question is asked in the context of certain assumptions about the world, the stability of objects in it, the possibility of knowing, in terms of measurable distances and locatable places, where you are; but the answer, while it is perfectly satisfactory within that assumed context, also challenges it, or, to be more precise, forces the reader to challenge it by forcing him to respond to the pun on the word "just." The inescapability of the pun reflects backward on the question and the world view it supports; and it gestures toward another world view in which spatial configurations have moral inner meanings, and being in the way is independent of the way you happen to be in. That is, if Christian is to be truly in the way, the way must first be in him, and then he will be in it, no matter where—in what merely physical way—he is.

All of this is *meant,* that is experienced, in the reader's encounter with "just," which is a comment not only on Christian for asking the question but on the reader for taking it seriously, that is, simply. What has happened to the reader in this brief space is the basic experience of *The Pilgrim's Progress.* Again and again he settles into temporal-spatial forms of thought only to be brought up short when they prove unable to contain the insights of Christian faith. The many levels on which this basic experience occurs would be the substance of a full reading of *The Pilgrim's Progress,* something the world will soon have, whether it wants it or not.

The method, then, is applicable to larger units and its chief characteristics remain the same: (1) it refuses to answer or even ask the question, what is this work about; (2) it yields an analysis not of formal features but of the developing responses of the reader in relation to the words as they succeed one another in time; (3) the result will be a description of the structure of response which may have an oblique or even (as in the case of *The Pilgrim's Progress*) a contrasting relationship to the structure of the work as a thing in itself.

The Affective Fallacy Fallacy

In the preceding pages I have argued the case for a method of analysis which focuses on the reader rather than on the artifact, and in what remains of this essay I would like to consider some of the more obvious objections to that method. The chief objection, of course, is that affective criticism leads one away from the "thing itself" in all its solidity to the inchoate impressions of a variable and various reader. This argument has several dimensions to it and will require a multidirectional answer.

First, the charge of impressionism has been answered, I hope, by some of my sample analyses. If anything, the discriminations required and yielded by the method are too fine for even the most analytical of tastes. This is in large part because in the category of response I include not only "tears, prickles," and "other psychological symptoms"[8] but all the precise mental operations involved in reading, including the formulation of complete thoughts, the performing (and regretting) of acts of judgment, the following and making of logical sequences; and also because my insistence on the cumulative pressures of the reading experience puts restrictions on the possible responses to a word or a phrase.

The larger objection remains. Even if the reader's responses can be described with some precision, why bother with them, since the more palpable objectivity of the text is immediately available ("the poem itself, as an object of specifically critical judgment, tends to disappear"). My reply to this is simple. The objectivity of the text is an illusion and, moreover, a dangerous illusion, because it is so physically convincing. The illusion is one of self-sufficiency and completeness. A line of print or a page is so obviously *there*—it can be handled, photographed, or put away—that it seems to be the sole repository of whatever value and meaning we associate with it. (I wish the pronoun could be avoided, but in a way *it* makes my point.) This is of course the unspoken assumption behind the word "content." The line or page or book *contains*—everything.

The great merit (from this point of view) of kinetic art is that it forces you to be aware of "it" as a changing object—and therefore no "object" at all——and also to be aware of yourself as correspondingly changing. Kinetic art does not lend itself to a static interpretation because it refuses to stay still and does not let you stay still either. In its operation it makes inescapable the actualizing role of the observer. Literature is a kinetic art, but the physical form it assumes prevents us from seeing its essential nature, even though we so experience it. The availability of a book to the hand, its presence on a shelf, its listing in a library catalogue—all of these encourage us to think of it as a stationary object. Somehow when we put a book down, we forget that while we were reading, *it* was moving (pages turning, lines receding into the past) and forget too that *we* were moving with it.

A criticism that regards "the poem itself as an object of specifically critical judgment" extends this forgetting into a principle; it transforms a temporal experience into a spatial one; it steps back and in a single glance takes in a whole (sentence, page, work) which the reader knows (if at all) only bit by bit, moment by moment. It is a criticism that takes as its (self-restricted) area the physical dimensions of the artifact and within these dimensions it marks out beginnings, middles, and ends, discovers frequency distributions, traces out patterns of imagery, diagrams strata of complexity (vertical of course), all without ever taking into account the relationship (if any) between its data and their affective force. Its question is what goes into the work rather than what does the work go into. It is "objective" in exactly the wrong way, because it determinedly ignores what is objectively true about the *activity* of reading. Analysis in terms of doings and happenings is on the other hand truly objective because it recognizes the fluidity, "the movingness," of the meaning experience and because it directs us to where the action is—the active and activating consciousness of the reader.

But what reader? When I talk about the responses of "the reader," am I not really talking about myself, and making myself into a surrogate for all the millions of readers who are not me at all? Yes and no. Yes, in the sense that in no two of us are the responding mechanisms exactly alike. No, if one argues that because of the uniqueness of the individual, generalization about response is impossible. It is here that the method can accommodate the insights of modern linguistics, especially the idea of "linguistic competence," "the idea that it is possible to characterize a linguistic system that every speaker shares."[9] This characterization, if it were realized, would be a "competence model," corresponding more or less to the internal mechanisms which allow us to process (understand) and produce sentences that we have never before encountered. It would be a spatial model in the sense that it would reflect a system of rules pre-existing, and indeed making possible, any actual linguistic experience.

The interest of this for me is its bearing on the problem of specifying response. If the speakers of a language share a system of rules that each of them has somehow internalized, understanding will, in some sense, be uniform; that is, it will proceed in terms of the system of rules all speakers share. And insofar as these rules are constraints on production—establishing boundaries within which utterances are labeled "normal," "deviant," "impossible," and so on—they will also be constraints on the range, and even the direction, of response; they will make response, to some extent, predictable and normative. Thus the formula, so familiar in the literature of linguistics, "Every native speaker will . . ."

A further "regularizing" constraint on response is suggested by what Ronald Wardhaugh, following Katz and Fodor, calls "semantic competence," a matter less of an abstract set of rules than of a backlog of language experience which determines probability of choice and therefore of response. "A speaker's semantic knowledge," Wardhaugh contends,

> is no more random than his syntactic knowledge . . . therefore, it seems useful to consider the possibility of devising, for semantic knowledge, a set of rules similar in form to the set used to characterize syntactic knowledge. Exactly how such a set of rules should be formulated and exactly what it must explain are to a considerable extent uncertain. At the very least the rules must characterize some sort of norm, the kind of semantic knowledge than an ideal speaker of the language might be said to exhibit in an ideal set of circumstances—in short, his semantic competence. In this way the rules would characterize just that set of facts about English semantics that all speakers of English have internalized and can draw upon in interpreting words in novel combinations. When one hears or reads a new sentence, he makes sense out of that sentence by drawing on both his syntactic and his semantic knowledge. The semantic knowledge enables him to know what the individual words mean and how to put these meanings together so that they are compatible. (p. 90)

> The resulting description could then be said to be a representation of the kind of system that speakers of a language have somehow internalized and that they draw upon in interpreting sentences. (p. 92)

Wardhaugh concedes that the "resulting description" would resemble rather than be equivalent to the system actually internalized, but he insists that "what is really important is the basic principle involved in the total endeavor, the principle of trying to formalize in as explicit a way as possible the semantic knowledge that a mature listener or reader brings to his task of comprehension and that underlies his actual behavior in comprehension" (p. 92). (Interestingly enough, this is a good description of what William Empson tries to do, less systematically of course, in *The Structure of Complex Words*.) Obviously the intersection of the two systems of knowledge would make it possible to further restrict (that is, make predictable and normative) the range of response, so that one could presume (as I have) to describe a reading experience in terms that would hold for all speakers who were in possession of both competences. The difficulty is that at present we do not have these systems. The syntactic model is still under construction and the semantic model has hardly been proposed. (Indeed, we will need not a model but models, since "the semantic knowledge that a mature . . . reader brings to his task of comprehension" will vary with each century or period.)[10] Nevertheless, the incompleteness of our knowledge should not prevent us from hazarding analyses on the basis of what we presently know about what we know.

Earlier, I offered this description of my method: "an analysis of the developing responses of the reader to the words as they succeed one another on the page." It should now be clear that the developing of those responses takes place within the regulating and organizing mechanism, preexisting the actual verbal experience, of these (and other) competences. Following Noam Chomsky, most psychologists and psycholinguists insist that understanding is more than a linear processing of information.[11] This means, as Wardhaugh points out, that "sentences are not just simple left to right sequences of elements" and that "sentences are not understood as a result of adding the meaning of the second to that of the first, the third to the first two, and so on" (p. 54). In short, something other than itself, something existing outside its frame of reference, must be modulating the reader's experience of the sequence.[12] In my method of analysis, the temporal flow is monitored and structured by everything the reader brings with him, by his competences; and it is by taking these into account as they interact with the temporal left-to-right reception of the verbal string that I am able to chart and project *the* developing response.

It should be noted, however, that my category of response, and especially of meaningful response, includes more than the transformational grammarians, who believe that comprehension is a function of deep structure perception, would allow. There is a tendency, at least in the writings of some linguists, to downgrade surface structure—the form of actual sentences—to the status of a husk, or covering, or veil, a layer of excrescences that is to be peeled away or penetrated or discarded in favor of the kernel underlying it. This is an understandable consequence of Chomsky's characterization of surface structure as "misleading" and "uninformative"[13] and his insistence (somewhat modified recently) that deep structure alone determines meaning. Thus, for example, Wardhaugh writes that "every surface structure is interpretable only by reference to its deep structure" (p. 49) and that while "the surface structure of the sentence provides clues to its interpretation, the interpretation itself depends on a correct processing of these clues to reconstruct all the elements and relationships of the deep structure." Presumably the "correct processing," that is, the uncovering of the deep structure and the extraction of deep meaning, is the only goal, and whatever stands in the way of that uncovering is to be tolerated, but assigned no final value. Clues, after all, are sometimes misleading and give rise to "mistakes." "For example, we sometimes anticipate words in a conversation or text only to discover ourselves to be wrong, or we do not wait for sentences to be completed because we assume we know what their endings will be . . . Many of the mistakes students make in reading are made because the students have adopted inappropriate strategies in their processing" (pp. 137–138). In my account of reading, however, the temporary adoption of these inappropriate strategies is itself a response to the strategy of an author; and the resulting mistakes are part of the experience provided by that author's language and therefore part of its meaning. Deep structure theorists, of course, deny that differences in meaning can be located in surface forms. And this for me vitiates the work of Richard

Ohmann, who does pay attention to the temporal flow, but only so that he can uncover beneath it the deep structure, which, he assumes, is really doing the work.

The key word is, of course, experience. For Wardhaugh, reading (and comprehension in general) is a process of extraction: "The reader is required to get the meaning from the print in front of him" (p. 139). For me, reading (and comprehension in general) is an event, no part of which is to be discarded. In that event, which is the actualization of meaning, the deep structure plays an important role, but it is not everything; for we comprehend not in terms of the deep structure alone but in terms of a *relationship* between the unfolding, in time, of the surface structure and a continual checking of it against our projection (always in terms of surface structure) of what the deep structure will reveal itself to be; and when the final discovery has been made and *the* deep structure is perceived, all the "mistakes"—the positing, on the basis of incomplete evidence, of deep structures that failed to materialize— will not be canceled out. They have been experienced; they have existed in the mental life of the reader; they *mean*. (This is obviously the case in our experience of the line "Nor did they not perceive the evil plight.")

All of which returns us to the original question. Who is *the* reader? Obviously, my reader is a construct, an ideal or idealized reader, somewhat like Wardhaugh's "mature reader" or Milton's "fit" reader, or to use a term of my own, *the* reader is the *informed* reader. The informed reader is someone who (1) is a competent speaker of the language out of which the text is built up; (2) is in full possession of "the semantic knowledge that a mature . . . listener brings to his task of comprehension," including the knowledge (that is, the experience, both as a producer and comprehender) of lexical sets, collocation probabilities, idioms, professional and other dialects, and so on; and (3) has *literary* competence. That is, he is sufficiently experienced as a reader to have internalized the properties of literary discourses, including everything from the most local of devices (figures of speech, and so on) to whole genres. In this theory, then, the concerns of other schools of criticism—such as questions of genre, conventions, intellectual background—*become redefined in terms of potential and probable response,* the significance and value a reader can be expected to attach to the idea "epic" or to the use of archaic language or to anything.

The reader of whose responses I speak, then, is this informed reader, neither an abstraction nor an actual living reader, but a hybrid—a real reader (me) who does everything within his power to make himself informed. That is, I can with some justification project my responses into those of "the" reader because they have been modified by the constraints placed on me by the assumptions and operations of the method: (1) the conscious attempt to become the informed reader by making my mind the repository of the (potential) responses a given text might call out and (2) the attendant suppressing, in so far as that is possible, of what is personal and idiosyncratic and 1970ish in my response. In short, the informed reader is to some extent processed by the method that uses him as a control. Each of us, if we are sufficiently responsible and self-conscious, can, in the course of employing the method, become the informed reader and therefore be a more reliable reporter of his experience.

Of course, it would be easy for someone to point out that I have not answered the charge of solipsism but merely presented a rationale for a solipsistic procedure; but such an objection would have force only if a better mode of procedure were available. The one usually offered is to regard the work as a thing in itself, as an object; but as I have argued above, this is a false and dangerously self-validating objectivity. I suppose that what I am saying is that I would rather have an acknowledged and controlled subjectivity than an objectivity which is finally an illusion.

In its operation, my method will obviously be radically historical. The critic has the responsibility of becoming not one but a number of informed readers, each of whom will be identified by a matrix of political, cultural, and literary determinants. The informed reader of Milton will not be the informed reader of Whitman, although the latter will necessarily comprehend the former. This plurality of informed readers implies a plural-

ity of informed reader aesthetics, or no aesthetic at all. A method
of analysis that yields a (structured) description of response has
built into it an *operational* criterion. The question is not how
good is it, but how does it work; and both question and answer
are framed in terms of local conditions, which include local
notions of literary value.

This raises the problem of the consideration of local beliefs
as a possible basis of response. If a reader does not share the
central concerns of a work, will he be capable of fully responding to it? Wayne Booth has asked that question: "But is it really
true that the serious Catholic or atheist, however sensitive, tol-
erant, diligent, and well-informed about Milton's beliefs he
may be, enjoys *Paradise Lost* to the degree possible to one of
Milton's contemporaries and co-believers, of equal intelligence
and sensitivity?"[14] The answer, it seems to me, is no. There
are some beliefs that cannot be momentarily suspended or assumed. Does this mean then that *Paradise Lost* is a lesser work
because it requires a narrowly defined (that is, "fit") reader?
Only if we hold a universal aesthetic in the context of which
value is somehow correlated with the number of readers who
can experience it fully, irrespective of local affiliations. My
method allows for no such aesthetic and no such fixings of value.
In fact, it is oriented *away* from evaluation and toward description. It is difficult to say on the basis of its results that one work
is better than another or even that a single work is good or bad.
And more basically, it does not permit the evaluation of literature as literature, as apart from advertising or preaching or
propaganda or "entertainment." As a report of a (very complex) stimulus–response relationship, it provides no way to
distinguish between literary and other effects, except perhaps
for the components which go into one or the other; and no one,
I assume, will assent to a "recipe" theory of literary difference.
For some this will seem a fatal limitation of the method. I welcome it, since it seems to me that we have for too long, and
without notable results, been trying to determine what distinguishes literature from ordinary language. If we understood
"language," its constitutents and its operations, we would be
better able to understand its subcategories. The fact that this

method does not begin with the assumption of literary superiority or end with its affirmation is, I think, one of its strongest
recommendations.

This is not to say that I do not evaluate. The selection of
texts for analysis is itself an indication of a hierarchy in my own
tastes. In general I am drawn to works which do not allow a
reader the security of his normal patterns of thought and belief.
It would be possible, I suppose, to erect a standard of value on
the basis of this preference—a scale on which the most unsettling of literary experiences would be the best (perhaps literature is what disturbs our sense of self-sufficiency, personal and
linguistic)—but the result would probably be more a reflection
of a personal psychological need than of a universally true
aesthetic.

Three further objections to the method should be considered
if only because they are so often made in my classes. If one
treats utterances, literary or otherwise, as strategies, does this
not claim too much for the conscious control of their producer-
authors? I tend to answer this question by begging it, by deliberately choosing texts in which the evidence of control is
overwhelming. (I am aware that to a psychoanalytic critic, this
principle of selection would be meaningless, and indeed, impossible.) If pressed I would say that the method of analysis,
apart from my own handling of it, does not require the assumption either of control or of intention. One can analyze an effect
without worrying about whether it was produced accidentally
or on purpose. (However, I always find myself worrying in just
this way, especially when reading Defoe.) The exception would
be cases where the work includes a statement of intention ("to
justify the ways of God to man") which, because it establishes
an expectation on the part of a reader, becomes a part of his
experience. This of course does not mean that the stated intention is to be believed or used as the basis of an interpretation,
simply that it, like everything else in the text, draws a response,
and, like everything else, it must be taken into account.

The second objection also takes the form of a question. If
there is a measure of uniformity to the reading experience, why
have so many readers, and some equally informed, argued so

well and passionately for differing interpretations? This, it
seems to me, is a pseudo-problem. Most literary quarrels are not
disagreements about response, but about a response to a response. What happens to one informed reader of a work will
happen, within a range of nonessential variation, to another. It
is only when readers become literary critics and the passing of
judgment takes precedence over the reading experience that
opinions begin to diverge. The act of interpretation is often so
removed from the act of reading that the latter (in time the
former) is hardly remembered. The exception that proves the
rule, and my point, is C. S. Lewis, who explained his differences
with F. R. Leavis in this way: "It is not that he and I see different
things when we look at *Paradise Lost*. He sees and hates the
very same things that I see and love."

The third objection is a more practical one. In the analysis
of a reading experience, when does one come to the point? The
answer is never, or no sooner than the pressure to do so becomes unbearable (psychologically). Coming to the point is the
goal of a criticism that believes in content, in extractable meaning, in the utterance as a repository. Coming to the point fulfills a need that most literature deliberately frustrates (if we
open ourselves to it), the need to simplify and close. Coming to
the point should be resisted, and in its small way, this method
will help you to resist.

Other Versions, Other Readers

Some of what I have said in the preceding pages will be familiar
to students of literary criticism. There has been talk of readers
and responses before and I feel some obligation at this point
both to acknowledge my debts and to distinguish my method
from others more or less like it.[15]

One begins of course with I. A. Richards, whose principal
article of faith sounds very much like mine:

> The belief that there is such a quality or attribute, namely
> Beauty, which attaches to the things which we rightly call beauti-
> ful, is probably inevitable for all reflective persons at a certain
> stage of their mental development.
> Even among those who have escaped from this delusion and

are well aware that we continually talk as though things possess qualities, when what we ought to say is that they cause effects in us of one kind or another, the fallacy of "projecting" the effect and making it a quality of its cause tends to recur . . .

Whether we are discussing music, poetry, painting, sculpture or architecture, we are forced to speak as though certain physical objects . . . are what we are talking about. And yet the remarks we make as critics do not apply to such objects but to states of mind, to experiences.[16]

This is obviously a brief for a shift of analytical attention away from the work as an object to the response it draws, the experience it generates; but the shift is in Richards's theory preliminary to *severing* one from the other, whereas I would insist on their precise interaction. He does this by distinguishing sharply between scientific and emotive language:

A statement may be used for the sake of the *reference* true or false, which it causes. This is the *scientific* use of language. But it may also be used for the sake of the effects in emotion and attitude produced by the reference it occasions. This is the *emotive* use of language. The distinction once clearly grasped is simple. We may either use words for the sake of the references they promote, or we may use them for the sake of the attitudes and emotions which ensue. (p. 267)

But may we? Isn't it the case, rather, that in any linguistic experience we are internalizing attitudes and emotions, even if the attitude is the pretension of no attitude and the emotion is a passionate coldness? Richards's distinction is too absolute, and in his literary theorizing it becomes more absolute still. Referential language, when it appears in poetry, is not to be attended to as referential in any sense. Indeed, it is hardly to be attended to at all. This is in general the thesis of *Science and Poetry*:[17]

The intellectual stream is fairly easy to follow; it follows itself, so to speak; but it is the less important of the two. In poetry it matters only as a *means*. (p. 13)

A good deal of poetry and even some great poetry exists (e.g., some of Shakespeare's Songs and, in a different way, much of the best of Swinburne) in which the sense of the words can be *almost* entirely missed or neglected without loss. (pp. 22–23)

Most words are ambiguous as regards their plain sense, especially in poetry. We can take them as we please in a variety of senses. The sense we are pleased to choose is the one which most suits the impulses already stirred through the form of the verse . . . Not the strictly logical sense of what is said, but the tone of voice and the occasion are the primary factors by which we interpret. (p. 23)

It is never what a poem *says* which matters, but what it *is*. (p. 25)

Well, what is it? And what exactly is the "form of the verse" which is supposed to displace our interest in and responsibility to the sense? The answers to these questions, when they come, are disturbing: The cognitive structure of poetic (read literary) language is a conduit through which a reader is to pass untouched and untouching on his way to the *impulse* which was the occasion of the poem in the first place:

The experience itself, the tide of impulses sweeping through the mind, is the source and the sanction of the words . . . to a suitable reader . . . the words will reproduce in his mind a similar play of interests putting him for the while into a similar situation and leading to the same response.

Why this should happen is still somewhat of a mystery. An extraordinarily intricate concourse of impulses brings the words together. Then in another mind the affair in part reverses itself, the words bring a similar concourse to impulses. (pp. 26–27)

Declining to identify message with meaning, Richards goes too far and gives the experience of decoding (or attempting to decode) the message no place in the actualization of meaning. From feeling to words to feeling, the passage should be made with as little attention as possible to the sense, which is usually "fairly easy to follow" (that is, disposable, like a straw). In fact, attention to the sense can be harmful, if one takes it too seriously. Assertions in poetry are "pseudo-statements": A pseudo-statement is a form of words which is justified entirely by its effect in releasing or organizing our impulses and attitudes (due regard being had for the better or worse organizations of these *inter se*); a statement, on the other hand, is justified by its truth, i.e., its correspondence . . . with the fact to which it points" (p. 59).

This would be unexceptionable, were Richards simply warning against applying the criterion of truth-value to statements in poetry; but he seems to mean that we should not experience them as statements at all, even in the limited universe of a literary discourse. That is, very little corresponding to cognitive processes should be going on in our minds when we read poetry, lest the all important release of impulses be impaired or blocked. Contradictions are not to be noted or worried about. Logical arguments need not be followed too closely ("the relevant consequences are . . . to be arrived at by a partial relaxation of logic"). But while this may be the response called forth by some poetry (and prose), it is by no means universally true that in reading literature we are alwa-ֵֹ relieved of our responsibility to logic and argument. Very often, and even when the sense is "fairly easy to follow," cognitive processes—calculating, comparing, deducting—form the largest part of our response to a work, and any description of its effects must take this into account. Richards arbitrarily limits the range of meaningful response to feelings (impulses and attitudes) and of course here I cannot follow him. (In seventeenth century literature, for example, the impact of a work often depends on the encouragement and manipulation of ratiocinative patterns of response.)

The range of response is further narrowed when Richards argues for a hierarchy of experiences. What is the best life one can live, he asks? "The best life . . . which we can wish for our friend will be one in which as much as possible of himself is engaged (as many of his impulses as possible). The more he lives and the less he thwarts himself the better . . . And if it is asked, what does such life feel like . . . the answer is that it feels like and is the experience of poetry" (p. 33). The best poetry, then, is the poetry that gives the most impulses, with the greatest intensity and, presumably, with the least ratiocinative interference. It is hardly surprising, given this theory of poetic value, that Richards is not really interested in the sequence of the reading experience. His analysis of reading a poem (*Principles,* chap. 16) is spatial in terms of isolated word-impulse relationships, exactly what we might expect from an aesthetic which regards the ligatures of thought as a kind of skeletal container, holding the experience in but not forming any considerable part of it.

Richards's theories and his prejudices weigh heavily on his protocols and account, in part, for their miserable performance in *Practical Criticism*.[18] They begin not with a sense of responsibility to language in all of its aspects but with a license and, indeed, an obligation to ignore some of them. They are simply reporting on the impulses and attitudes they experience while reading, presumably under the influence of Richards's anticognitive bias. It is ironic and unfortunate that the case against analysis in terms of reader response is often made by referring to the example of a group of readers whose idea of response was disastrously narrow and whose sensitivity to language was restricted to only one of its registers. If *Practical Criticism* makes any case, it is a case for the desirability of my informed reader; for it shows what happens when people who have never thought about the language they use every day are suddenly asked to report precisely on their experience of poetry, and even worse, are asked to do so in the context of an assumption of poetic "difference."

In all of this, of course, I have been anticipated by Empson:

When you come down to detail, and find a case where there are alternative ways of interpreting a word's action, of which one can plausibly be called Cognitive and the other Emotive, it is the Cognitive one which is likely to have important effects on sentiment or character, and in general it does not depend on accepting false beliefs. But in general it does involve a belief of some kind, if only the belief that one kind of life is better than another, so that it is no use trying to chase belief-feelings out of the poetry altogether.

The trouble I think is that Professor Richards conceives the Sense of a word in a given use as something single, however "elaborate," and therefore thinks that anything beyond that Sense has got to be explained in terms of feelings, and feelings of course are Emotions, or Tones. But much of what appears to us as a "feeling" (as is obvious in the case of a complex metaphor) will in fact be quite an elaborate structure of related meanings. The mere fact that we can talk straight ahead and get the grammar in order shows that we must be doing a lot more rational planning about the process of talk than we have to notice in detail.[19]

Empson agrees with Richards that there are "two streams of experience in reading a poem, the intellectual and the active and emotional" but he objects to the suggestion that the inter-connection between them "had better be suppressed" (p. 11). In short, his position, at least on this point, is very close to (and is probably one of the causes of) my own. And his insistence that words carry with them discriminations of sense and feeling of which we are not always consciously aware goes a long way to making my case for the complexity, again largely unconscious, of the response these same words evoke.

We differ, however, in the scope and direction of our analy-ses. Empson does not follow the form of the reader's experience, but some form, usually arbitrary, which allows him to explore in depth isolated moments or potential moments in that experi-ence. (I say potential because his emphasis is often on what has gone into a word rather than an account of its effect.) Why *seven* types of ambiguity? I like the explanation offered recently by Roger Fowler and Peter Mercer: "Empson's categories are thrown off with a marvellous disbelieving *panache*—if there had been eight and not the magical seven we might have had to worry—but there are only as few or as many types as you want."[20] As you *need*, to write a book, that is, to generate a sufficient num-ber of categories to contain and at least keep physically separate the points you would like to make. The categories of *The Struc-ture of Complex Words* are to be taken no more seriously, that is, absolutely, than the seven types, and of course Empson never asks that you do. They are simply (or not so simply) containers and boundaries, artificial but necessary, if he is to manage the discussion (which is often a matter of keeping a great many balls in the air at once) and if we are to have the aid and comfort of some sort of ordering principle as we follow him.

The results, as Fowler and Mercer point out, are "scores of analyses probably unequalled in brilliance, if also at times, un-equalled in ingenuity, which proceed for the most part as frag-mented . . . imitations of the many-dimensional poetic object" (p. 58). In a word, the method tends to atomistic, in-depth analyses of lexical and semantic complexity without the re-straint imposed by the consideration of the mind's involvement

with the ligatures of thought. And if it is true, as some have
argued, that Empson equates value with this kind of complexity
(a standard not unlike Richards's intensity and frequency of impulse), one can see why he would avoid any methodological
strategy which would prevent him from fully attending to it.
(In my analyses, the range of associations and therefore of response is always being narrowed and directed by decisions made
or actions taken as a result of earlier events in the meaning experience.) Even when Empson considers whole poems—he is
more likely to subsume parts of poems under his various categories—the atomism and fragmentation is obvious. What he
always looks for, or constructs, is some classificatory mechanism
which relieves him of the responsibility for a sequential reading of the poem. The most obvious device is the emphasis on
a single word, for example, "all" in *Paradise Lost;* but even
here he does not follow the word through the poem but sets up
"classes" of occurrence ordered on the basis of certain emotions
(p. 102). In *Some Versions of Pastoral,* the categories of Bent-
leyan error serve the same purpose; and the thesis which later
becomes *Milton's God*—a book on the argument of *Paradise
Lost,* notable for the *absence* of semantic analysis—is developed
in the spaces *between* the explorations of verbal texture rather
than as a consequence of them.

The reading of Marvell's "Garden" displays the same characteristics. Here there is a gesture in the direction of considering the poem in the order of its stanzas, but at a certain point
Empson surrenders to his genius: "*Green* takes on great weight
here . . . .because it has been a pet word of Marvell's before. To
list the uses before the satires may seem an affectation of ped-
antry, but shows how often the word was used; and they are
pleasant things to look up."[21] Empson is off and running, from
Lawrence to Whitman to Wordsworth to Donne to Shakespeare
to Homer to Milton and even (or inevitably) Buddha, returning to "The Garden" only in a closing sentence whose impact
is derived from our awareness of its arbitrariness. It does not
conclude the essay or the reading of the poem; it merely *closes
off* this particular section of the lifelong dialogue Empson is
having with his language, its creations and their creators. And

who would want it otherwise? What Empson does, he does better than anyone else; but he does not analyze the developing responses of the reader to the words as they succeed one another in time.

Finally, I come to Michael Riffaterre, whose work has only recently been called to my attention. Riffaterre *is* concerned with the reader's developing responses, and insists on the constraints imposed on response by the left-to-right sequence of a temporal flow, and he objects, as I do, to methods of analysis that yield descriptions of the observable features of an utterance without reference to their reception by the reader. In a reply to a reading by Jakobson and Levi-Strauss of Baudelaire's "Les Chats," Riffaterre makes his position on these points very clear.[22] The systems of correspondences yielded by a structuralist analysis are not necessarily perceived or attended to by the reader; and the resulting data, encased as it often is in formidable spatial schematizations, often prevents us from looking at what is going on in the act of comprehension. The question, Riffaterre insists, is "whether unmodified structural linguistics is relevant at all to the analysis of poetry" (p. 202). The answer, it seems to me, is yes and no. Clearly we must reject any claims made for a direct relationship between structurally derived descriptions and meaning; but it does not follow for me, as it does for Riffaterre, that the data of which such descriptions consist is therefore irrelevant:

> The authors' method is based on the assumption that any structural system they are able to define in the poem is necessarily a poetic structure. Can we not suppose, on the contrary, that the poem may contain certain structures that play no part in its function and effect as a literary work of art, and that there may be no way for structural linguists to distinguish between these unmarked structures and those that are literarily active? Conversely, there may well be strictly poetic structures that cannot be recognized as such by an analysis not geared to the specificity of poetic language. (p. 202)

Here the basis for both my agreement and disagreement with Riffaterre is clear. He is a believer in two languages, ordinary and poetic, and therefore in two structures of discourse and two kinds of response; and he believes, consequently, that analysis should concern itself with "turning up" features, of language, structure and response that are specifically poetic and literary.

> Poetry is language, but it produces effects that language in every-day speech does not consistently produce; a reasonable assumption is that the linguistic analysis of a poem should turn up specific features, and that there is a causal relationship between the presence of these features in the text and our empirical feeling that we have before us a poem . . . In everyday language, used for practical purposes, the focus is usually upon the situational context, the mental or physical reality referred to . . . In the case of verbal art, the focus is upon the message as an end in itself, not just as a means. (p. 200)

This is distressingly familiar deviationist talk, with obvious roots in Jan Mukarovsky's distinction between standard language and poetic language and in Richards's distinction between scientific and emotive language. Riffaterre's conception of the relation between standard and poetic language is more flexible and sophisticated than most, but nevertheless his method shares the weakness of its theoretical origins, the *a priori* assumption that a great deal does not count. Deviation theories always narrow the range of meaningful response by excluding from consideration features or effects that are not poetic; and in Riffaterre's version, as we shall see, the range of poetic effects is disastrously narrow, because he restricts himself only to that which is called to a reader's attention in the most spectacular way.

For Riffaterre, stylistic study is the study of SDs or stylistic devices, which are defined as those mechanisms in the text that "prevent the reader from inferring or predicting any important feature. For predictability may result in superficial reading; unpredictability will compel attention: the intensity of reception will correspond to the intensity of the message."[23] Talking about style, then, is talking about moments in the reading experience when attention is compelled because an expectation has been disappointed by the appearance of an unpredictable element. The relationship between such moments and other moments in the sequence which serve to highlight them is what Riffaterre means by the "stylistic context":

The stylistic context is a linguistic *pattern suddenly broken by an element which was unpredictable,* and the contrast resulting from this interference is the stylistic stimulus. The rupture must not be interpreted as a dissociating principle. The stylistic value of the contrast lies in the relationship it establishes between the two clashing elements; no effect would occur without their association in a sequence. In other words, the stylistic contrasts, like other useful oppositions in language, create a structure.

(p. 171)

Riffaterre is more interesting than other practitioners of "contrast" stylistics because he locates the disrupted pattern in the context rather in any preexisting and exterior norm. For if "in the style norm relationship we understood the norm pole to be universal (as it would be in the case of the linguistic norm), we could not understand how a deviation might be an SD on some occasions and on others, not" ("Criteria," p. 169). This means, as he points out in "Stylistic Context,"[24] that one can have the pattern *Context-SD starting new context—SD:* "The SD generates a series of SDs of the same type (e.g., after an SD by archaism, proliferation of archaisms); the resulting saturation causes these SDs to lose their contrast value, destroys their ability to stress a particular point of the utterance and reduces them to components of a new context; this context in turn will permit new contrasts." In the same article (pp. 208–209) this flexible and changing relationship is redefined in terms of microcontext ("the context which creates the opposition constituting the SD") and macrocontext ("the context which modifies this opposition by reinforcing or weakening it"). This enables Riffaterre to talk about the relationship between local effects and a series of local effects which in its entirety or duration determines to some extent the impact of its members; but the principle of contextual norm, and its advantages, remains the same.

Those advantages are very real; attention is shifted away from the message to its reception, and therefore from the object to the reader. Indeed, in a later article Riffaterre calls for a "separate linguistics of the decoder" and argues that SF, the impact made on the reader, "prevails consistently over referential function," especially in fiction.[25] No fixed and artificial inventory of stylistic devices is possible, since in terms of contextual

norms anything can be a stylistic device. The temporal flow of
the reading experience is central and even controlling; it literally locates, with the help of the reader, the objects of analysis.
The view of language and of comprehension is nonstatic; the
context and SDs are moving and shifting; the reader is moving
with them and through his responses, creating them, and the
critic is moving too, placing his analytic apparatus now here, now
there.

All of this, however, is vitiated for me by the theory of language and style in the context (that word again) of which the
methodology operates. I refer of course to the positing of two
kinds of language and the resulting restriction of meaningful
or interesting response to effects of surprise and disruption. Riffaterre is very forthright about this:

> *Stylistic facts can be apprehended only in language, since that
> is their vehicle; on the other hand, they must have a specific char-
> acter, since otherwise they could not be distinguished from lin-
> guistic facts.*
>
> It is necessary to gather first all those elements which present
> stylistic features, and secondly, to subject to linguistic analysis
> only these, to the exclusion of all others (which are stylistically ir-
> relevant). Then and only then will the confusion between style
> and language be avoided. For this sifting, preliminary to analysis,
> we must find specific criteria to delineate the distinctive features
> of style.
>
> *Style* is understood as an emphasis (expressive, affective, or
> aesthetic) added to the information conveyed by the linguistic
> structure, without alteration of meaning. Which is to say that
> language expresses and that style stresses.[26]

"Stylistic facts," "Linguistic facts," "stylistically irrelevant,"
"distinctive features of style," "emphasis . . . added to the information . . . without alteration of meaning"—this is obviously
more than a distinction, it is a hierarchy in which the lower
of the two classes is declared uninteresting and, what is more
important, *inactive.* That is, the stress of style is doing something and is therefore the proper object of attention, while the
expression, the encoding and decoding of information, the meaning, is just there, and need not be looked into very closely. (Lan-

guage expresses, style stresses.) One could quarrel with this simply on the basis of its radical separation of style and meaning, and with its naive equation of meaning with information; but for my purposes it is enough to point out the implications for the specifying and analysis of response. Underlying Riffaterre's theorizing is the assumption that for long stretches of language, in both ordinary and literary discourse, there is no response worth talking about because nothing much is happening. (Minimal decoding, minimal response.)

This assumption is reflected at every level of his operation. It is the basis of his distinction between what is and what is not a literary structure. It is the basis too, of the context-SD relationship that obtains once a literary structure has been identified. That relationship is, as Riffaterre says, one of "binary opposition" in which "the poles cannot be separated."[27] Of course these are variable, not fixed, poles; but within their individual relationships one is always doing nothing but preparing the way (passively) for the other, for the "big moment" when the contextual pattern is disrupted and attention is compelled (that is, response occurs). And finally, it is the basis of Riffaterre's use of the reader as a locating device. Since all the features yielded by a linguistic analysis are not poetically active, there must be a way of isolating those features that are; and since these are the features that disrupt pattern and compel attention, we shall locate them by attending to the responses of actual readers, whether they are readers in our classroom-laboratory or readers who have left us a record of their experience in footnotes or articles. Riffaterre's reader is a composite reader (either the "average reader" or "super-reader"), not unlike my informed reader. The difference, of course, is that his experience is considered relevant only at those points where it becomes unusual or "effortful." "Each point of the text that holds up the superreader is tentatively considered a component of the poetic structure. Experience indicates that such units are always pointed out by a number of informants."[28]

I am less bothered by the idea of superreader than by what happens to his experience in the course of a Riffaterrian analysis. It too will become binary in structure, a succession of highlighted moments alternating with and created by intervals of contextual norm, more cyclical than linear; and, of course, in a large part of it, nothing will be happening. At one point in his reading of "Les Chats," Riffaterre comes upon the line "Ils cherchent le silence" and here is what he has to say: "Informants unanimously ignore *Ils cherchent le silence.* Undoubtedly *cherchent* is the poetic or high-tone substitute for *rechercher* or *aimer,* but this is no more than the normal transformation of prose into verse: the device marks genre, as do verse and stanza, setting the context apart from everyday contexts. It is expected and not surprising."[29] In other words, nobody noticed it or had any trouble with it; it's perfectly ordinary; therefore it's not doing anything and there's nothing to say about it.

Even when Mr. Riffaterre finds something to talk about, his method does not allow him to do much with it. This analysis of a sentence from *Moby Dick* is a case in point:

> "And heaved and heaved, still unrestingly heaved the black sea, as if its vast tides were a conscience . . ." We have here a good example of the extent to which decoding can be controlled by the author. In the above instance it is difficult for the reader not to give his attention to each meaningful word. The decoding cannot take place on a minimal basis because the initial position of the verb is unpredictable in the normal English sentence, and so is its repetition. The repetition has a double role of its own, independent of its unpredictability: it creates the rhythm, and its total effect is similar to that of explicit speech. The postponement of the subject brings unpredictability to its maximum point; the reader must keep in mind the predicate before he is able to identify the subject. The "reversal" of the metaphor is still another example of contrast with the context. The reading speed is reduced by these hurdles, attention lingers on the representation, the stylistic effect is created.[30]

"Stylistic effect is created." But to what end? What does one do with the SDs or with their convergence once they have been located by the informer-reader? One cannot go from them to meaning, because meaning is independent of them; they are stress. ("Stress" occupies the same place in Riffaterre's affections as does "impulse" in Richards's and they represent the same narrowing of response.) We are left with a collection of stylistic effects (of a limited type), and while Riffaterre does not claim transferability for them, he does not claim anything else either. And their interest is to me at least an open question. (I should add that Riffaterre's analysis of "Les Chats" is brilliant and persuasive, as is his refutation of the Jakobson–Levi-Strauss position. It is an analysis, however, which depends on insights his own method could not have generated. He will not thank me for saying so, but Riffaterre is a better critic than his theory would allow.)

The difference between Riffaterre and myself can be most conveniently located in the concept of "style." The reader may have wondered why in an essay subtitled "Affective Stylistics," the phrase has been so little used. The reason is that my insistence that everything counts and that something (analyzable and significant) is always happening makes it impossible to distinguish, as Riffaterre does, between "linguistic facts" and "stylistic facts." For me, a stylistic fact is a fact of response, and since my category of response includes everything, from the smallest and least spectacular to the largest and most disrupting of linguistic experiences, everything is a stylistic fact, and we might as well abandon the word since it carries with it so many binary hostages (style *and* ———).

This of course commits me to a monistic theory of meaning; and it is usually objected to such theories that they give no scope to analysis. But my monism permits analysis, because it is a monism of effects, in which meaning is a (partial) product of the utterance-object, but not to be identified with it. In this theory, the message the utterance carries—usually *one* pole of a binary relationship in which the other pole is style—is in its operation (which someone like Richards would deny) one more effect, one more drawer of response, one more constituent in the meaning experience. It is simply not *the* meaning. Nothing is.

Perhaps, then, the word "meaning" should also be discarded, since it carries with it the notion of message or point. The meaning of an utterance, I repeat, is its experience—all of it—and that experience is immediately compromised the moment you say something about it. It follows then that we should not try to analyze language at all. The human mind, however, seems unable to resist the impulse to investigate its own processes; but the least (and probably the most) we can do is proceed in such a way as to permit as little distortion as possible.

Conclusion

From controversy, I descend once more to the method itself and to a few final observations.

First, strictly speaking, it is not a method at all, because neither its results nor its skills are transferrable. Its results are not transferrable because there is no fixed relationship between formal features and response (reading has to be done every time); and its skills are not transferrable because you can't hand it over to someone and expect them at once to be able to use it. (It is not portable.) It is, in essence, a language-sensitizing device, and as the "ing" in sensitizing implies, its operation is long term and never ending (never coming to the point). Moreover, its operations are interior. It has no mechanism, except for the pressuring mechanism of the assumption that more is going on in language than we consciously know; and of course the pressure of this assumption must come from the individual whose untrained sensitivity it is challenging. Becoming good at the method means asking the question "what does that ——— do?" with more and more awareness of the probable (and hidden) complexity of the answer, that is, with a mind more and more sensitized to the workings of language. In a peculiar and unsettling (to theorists) way, it is a method which processes its own user, who is also its only instrument. It is self-sharpening and what it sharpens is *you*. It does not organize materials, but transforms minds.

For this reason I have found it useful as a teaching method, at every level of the curriculum. Characteristically I begin a course by putting some simple sentences on the board (usually "He is sincere" and "Doubtless, he is sincere") and asking my students to answer the question, "what does that ——— do?" The question is for them a new one and they always reply by answering the more familiar question, "what does ——— mean?" But the examples are chosen to illustrate the insufficiency of this question, an insufficiency they soon prove from their own classroom experience; and after a while they begin to see the value of considering effects and begin to be able to think of language as an experience rather than as a repository of extractable meaning. After that, it is a matter of exercising their sensitivities on a series of graduated texts—sentences of various kinds, paragraphs, an essay, a poem, a novel—somewhat in the order represented by the first section of this essay. And as they experience more and more varieties of effect and subject them to analysis, they also learn how to recognize and discount what is idiosyncratic in their own response. Not incidentally, they also become incapable of writing uncontrolled prose, since so much of their time is spent discovering how much the prose of other writers controls them, and in how many ways. There are of course devices—the piece-meal left-to-right presentation of texts via a ticker-tape method, the varying of the magic question (such as, what would have happened were a word not there or somewhere else?)—but again the area of the method's operation is interior and its greatest success is not the organizing of materials (although that often occurs) but the transforming of minds.

In short, the theory, both as an account of meaning and as a way of teaching, is full of holes; and there is one great big hole right in the middle of it which is filled, if it is filled at all, by what happens inside the user-student. The method, then, remains faithful to its principles; it has no point of termination; it is a process; it talks about experience and is an experience; its focus is effects and its result is an effect. In the end the only unqualified recommendation I can give it is that it works.[31]

2

What Is Stylistics and Why Are They Saying Such Terrible Things About It?

[THIS ESSAY was written for a session of the English Institute chaired by Seymour Chatman. The other panelists were Richard Ohmann, Frank Kermode, and Tzvetan Todorov. In the format of the institute, questions follow the presentation of each paper and the first question was put to me by Ohmann, who announced "My name is Louis Milic." The arguments of the paper were worked out in the graduate seminar on literary theory that I began to teach in 1970. I did not teach that seminar in the usual way, by choosing a text (*Hamlet,* "Lycidas") and then submitting it to a succession of methodologies in order to see if they would work, that is, in order to answer the question "Does it illuminate the text?" This question troubled me because of what it assumes and, by assuming, predecides. First of all, it assumes that texts are independent of theories, an assumption that is, at the least, arguable, and one I was in the process of challenging. Second, it assumes that theory is justified only in its relation to practice, whereas it seemed to me that theory is a form of thinking with its own goals and rules, and therefore that theories should be evaluated in terms of the coherence of their claims. Third, it assumes that it would be possible for a theory to *not* illuminate a text, whereas it was becoming clearer and clearer to me that the relationship between theory and practice is a secure one. That is, theories always work and they will always produce exactly the results they predict, results that will be immediately compelling to those for whom the theory's assumptions and enabling principles are self-evident. Indeed, the trick would be to find a theory that *didn't* work.

In my seminar, therefore, we did not concentrate on what theories can do (since they will always generate the texts demanded by their assumptions) but instead concentrated on the claims made for them as pieces of thinking. In the case of the stylisticians those claims included the elimination or control of interpretation by identifying a set of context-free elements or primes and building up from them to the determination of meaning. I found invariably that interpretation "infected" the procedure at every point, either because a meaning was preselected and (silently) guided the specification of formal features, or because it was imposed on formal features that had no necessary relationship to it at all. The impressionism or subjectivity of which the stylisticians characteristically complained was given free reign by an elaborate machinery that hid from them and from their readers what they were in fact doing. What they were doing, I asserted, was cutting the data off from the source of their value—the activity of readers who, rather than extracting significances, confer them. I counsel, then, not the end of stylistics but a new or "affective" stylistics "in which the focus of attention is shifted from the spatial context of a page and its observable regularities to the temporal context of a mind and its experience." I now believe that this shift is illusory, at least insofar as it involves (supposedly) a transfer of power from the text to the reader. Although the argument is mounted against the supremacy of the text and the assertion of Martin Joos that "text signals its own structure," it really extends that supremacy by adding the performance of the reader to what the text signals and, by signaling, controls.

In terms of the future shape of my work, the most significant thing about this article is the appearance in it of the names of Hubert Dreyfus and John Searle, two colleagues at the University of California. It was Searle who introduced me to speech-act theory, a theory of language first developed by J. L. Austin in which the unit of analysis is not the free-standing sentence but an utterance produced in a situation by and for intentional beings. It is therefore a theory that poses a direct challenge to the autonomy of the text and to the formalistic assumptions of stylistics. The same challenge is implicit in Dreyfus's argument that facts are the product of situations and cannot be independently specified. Although I cited this argument with approval, I did not see that it went much further than my own, for I did not yet understand Dreyfus's provocative characterization of human behavior as "orderly, but not rule governed."]

THE FIRST OF the questions in my title—what is stylistics?—has already been answered by the practitioners of the art. Stylistics was born of a reaction to the subjectivity and imprecision of literary studies. For the appreciative raptures of the impressionistic critic, stylisticians purport to substitute precise and rigorous linguistic descriptions and to proceed from these descriptions to interpretations for which they can claim a measure of objectivity. Stylistics, in short, is an attempt to put criticism on a scientific basis. Answering my second question—why are they saying such terrible things about it?—will be the business of this essay, and I would like to begin (somewhat obliquely, I admit) by quoting from the *New York Times Book Review* of April 23, 1972. On pages 18 and 19 of that issue we find the publishing firm of Peter Wyden,. Inc., proclaiming the merits of a new book by Tom Chetwynd. The book is entitled *How To Interpret Your Own Dreams (in One Minute or Less)*. The title appears on a reproduction of the book jacket and beneath it are the following descriptive claims: "Your key to 583 Dream Subjects with 1442 Interpretations," "An Encyclopedic Dictionary." These claims are supported and extended by a report of the author's researches and by a portion of the index. "What do *you* dream about?" the reader is asked, "Angels (see page 171), Babies (page 150), Bells (page 40), Cars, Collisions, Cooking, Death, Dogs, Doors, Exams, Falling, Hands, Hats, Illness, Monsters, Mother, Nudity, Sex, Teeth, Travel . . ." "And these," the blurb continues, "are just a few of the 583 dream subjects covered." "To compile this book," we are told, "the author spent 10 years analyzing the works of Freud, Jung, Adler and other dream authorities. Carefully indexed and cross indexed, each dream subject is rated in four ways: what it most likely means; what it could well mean; what it might mean; and what it might possibly mean . . . This remarkable dream dictionary enables you to look up any dream instantly . . . find complete clues to its meaning." Finally, and with typographic aids, the claims underlying these claims are put forward: in italics, *it really works,* and in large white letters against a black bar background, BASED ON SOLID SCIENCE.

However amusing one finds this advertisement, it would be a mistake to underestimate the desire to which it appeals: the desire for an instant and automatic interpretive procedure based on an inventory of fixed relationships between observable data and meanings, meanings which do not vary with context and which can be read out independently of the analyst or observer, who need only perform the operations specified by the "key." It is a desire as new as information theory and as old as the impulse to escape from the flux and variability of the human situation to the security and stability of a timeless formalism. It is also, I think, the desire behind stylistics, and in the first part of this essay I should like to examine some representative attempts to achieve it.

My first example is taken from the work of Louis Milic, author of *A Quantitative Approach to the Style of Jonathan Swift* and other statistical and computer studies. In an article written for *The Computer and Literary Style,* Milic attempts to isolate the distinctive features of Swift's style.[1] He is particularly interested in the Swiftian habit of piling up words in series and in Swift's preference for certain kinds of connectives. His method is to compare Swift, in these and other respects, with Macauley, Addison, Gibbon, and Johnson, and the results of his researches are presented in the form of tables: "Word-Class Frequency Distribution of All the Whole Samples of Swift, with Computed Arithmetic Mean," "Percentage of Initial Connectives in 2000-Sentence Samples of Addison, Johnson, Macauley and Swift," Total Introductory Connectives and Total Introductory Determiners as Percentages of All Introductory Elements," "Frequency of Occurrences of the Most Common Single Three-Word Pattern as a Percentage of Total Patterns," "Total Number of Different Patterns per Sample." It will not be my concern here to scrutinize the data-gathering methods of Milic or the other stylisticians (although some of them are challengeable even on their own terms), for my interest is primarily in what is done with the data after they have been gathered. This is also Milic's interest, and in the final paragraphs of his essay he poses the major question: "What interpretive inferences can be drawn from the material?" (p. 104). The answer comes in two parts and illustrates the two basic maneuvers executed by the stylisticians. The first is circular: "The low frequency of initial determiners, taken together with the high frequency of initial connectives, makes [Swift] a writer who likes transitions and made much of connectives" (p. 104). As the reader will no doubt have noticed, the two halves of this sentence present the same information in slightly different terms, even though its rhetoric suggests that something has been explained. Here is an example of what makes some people impatient with stylistics and its baggage. The machinery of categorization and classification merely provides momentary pigeonholes for the constituents of a text, constituents which are then retrieved and reassembled into exactly the form they previously had. There is, in short, no gain in understanding; the procedure has been executed, but it hasn't gotten you anywhere. Stylisticians, however, are *determined* to get somewhere, and exactly where they are determined to get is indicated by Milic's next sentence. "[Swift's] use of series argues [that is, is a sign of or means] a fertile and well stocked mind." Here the procedure is not circular but arbitrary. The data are scrutinized and an interpretation is *asserted* for them, asserted rather than proven because there is nothing in the machinery Milic cranks up to authorize the leap (from the data to a specification of their value) he makes. What does authorize it is an unexamined and highly suspect assumption that one can read directly from the description of a text (however derived) to the shape or quality of its author's mind, in this case from the sheer quantity of verbal items to the largeness of the intelligence that produced them.

The counterargument to this assumption is not that it cannot be done (Milic, after all, has done it), but that it can be done all too easily, and in any direction one likes. One might conclude, for example, that Swift's use of series argues the presence of the contiguity disorder described by Roman Jakobson in *The Fundamentals of Language;*[2] or that Swift's use of series argues an unwillingness to finish his sentences; or that Swift's use of series argues an anal-retentive personality; or that Swift's use of series argues a nominalist rather than a realist philosophy and is therefore evidence of a mind insufficiently stocked with abstract ideas. These conclusions are neither more nor less defensible than the conclusion Milic reaches, or reaches for (it is the enterprise and not any one of its results that should be challenged), and their availability points to a serious defect in the procedures of stylistics, the absence of any constraint on the way in which one moves from description to interpretation, with the result that any interpretation one puts forward is arbitrary.

Milic, for his part, is not unaware of the problem. In a concluding paragraph, he admits that relating devices of style to personality is "risky" and "the chance of error . . . great" because "no personality syntax paradigm is available . . . neither syntactic stylistics nor personality theory is yet capable of making the leap" (p. 105). Once again Milic provides a clear example of one of the basic maneuvers in the stylistics game: he acknowledges the dependence of his procedures on an unwarranted assumption, but then salvages both the assumption and the procedures by declaring that time and more data will give substance to the one and authority to the other. It is a remarkable *non sequitur* in which the suspect nature of his enterprise becomes a reason for continuing in it: a syntax personality may be currently unavailable or available in too many directions, but this only means that if we persist in our efforts to establish it, it will surely emerge. The more reasonable inference would be that the difficulty lies not with the present state of the art but with the art itself; and this is precisely what I shall finally argue, that the establishment of a syntax-personality or any other kind of paradigm is an impossible goal, which, because it is also an assumption, invalidates the procedures of the stylisticians before they begin, dooming them to successes that are meaningless because they are so easy.

Milic affords a particularly good perspective on what stylisticians do because his assumptions, along with their difficulties, are displayed so nakedly. A sentence like "Swift's use of series argues a fertile and well stocked mind" does not come along very often. More typically, a stylistician will interpose a formidable apparatus between his descriptive and interpretive acts, thus obscuring the absence of any connection between them. For Richard Ohmann, that apparatus is transformational grammar and in "Generative Grammars and the Concept of Literary Style" he uses it to distinguish between the prose of Faulkner and Hemingway.[3] Ohmann does this by demonstrating that Faulkner's style is no longer recognizable when "the effects of three

generalized transformations"—the relative clause transformation, the conjunction transformation, and the comparative
transformation—are reversed. "Denatured" of these transformations, a passage from "The Bear," Ohmann says, retains "virtu-
ally no traces of . . . Faulkner's style" (p. 142). When the same
denaturing is performed on Hemingway, however, "the reduced
passage still sounds very much like Hemingway. Nothing has
been changed that seems crucial" (p. 144). From this, Ohmann
declares, follow two conclusions: (1) Faulkner "leans heavily
upon a very small amount of grammatical apparatus" (p. 143),
and (2) the "stylistic difference . . . between the Faulkner and
Hemingway passages can be largely explained on the basis of
[the] . . . apparatus" (p. 145). To the first of these I would reply
that it depends on what is meant by "leans heavily upon." Is this
a statement about the apparatus or about the actual predilection
of the author? (The confusion between the two is a hallmark of
stylistic criticism.) To the second conclusion I would object
strenuously, if by "explained" Ohmann means anything more
than made formalizable. That is, I am perfectly willing to admit
that transformational grammar provides a better means of fingerprinting an author than would a measurement like the percentage of nouns or the mean length of sentences; for since the
transformation model is able to deal not only with constituents but with their relationships, it can make distinctions at
a structural, as opposed to a merely statistical, level. I am not
willing, however, to give those distinctions an independent
value, that is, to attach a fixed significance to the devices of
the fingerprinting mechanism, any more than I would be willing to read from a man's actual fingerprint to his character or
personality.

But this, as it turns out, is exactly what Ohmann wants to
do. "The move from formal description of styles to . . . interpretation," he asserts, "should be the ultimate goal of stylistics," and
in the case of Faulkner, "it seems reasonable to suppose that a
writer whose style is so largely based on just these three seman-
tically related transformations demonstrates in that style a certain conceptual orientation, a preferred way of organizing experience" (p. 143). But Faulkner's style can be said to be "based

on" these three transformations only in the sense that the submission of a Faulkner text to the transformational apparatus yields a description in which they dominate. In order to make anything more out of this, that is, in order to turn the description into a statement about Faulkner's conceptual orientation, Ohmann would have to do what Noam Chomsky so pointedly refrains from doing, assign a semantic value to the devices of his descriptive mechanism, so that rather than being neutral between the processes of production and reception, they are made directly to reflect them. In the course of this and other essays, Ohmann does just that, finding, for example, that Lawrence's heavy use of deletion transformations is responsible for the "driving insistence one feels in reading" him,[4] and that Conrad's structures of chaining reflect his tendency to "link one thing with another associatively,"[5] and that Dylan Thomas's breaking of selectional rules serves his "vision of things" of "the world as process, as interacting forces and repeating cycle";[6] in short, "that these syntactic preferences *correlate* with habits of meaning."[7]

The distance between all of this and "Swift's use of series argues a fertile and well stocked mind" is a matter only of methodological sophistication, not of substance, for both critics operate with the same assumptions and nominate the same goal, the establishing of an inventory in which formal items will be linked in a fixed relationship to semantic and psychological values. Like Milic, Ohmann admits that at this point his interpretive conclusions are speculative and tentative; but again, like Milic, he believes that it is only a matter of time before he can proceed more securely on the basis of a firm correlation between syntax and "conceptual orientation," and the possibility of specifying such correlations, he declares, "is one of the main justifications for studying style."[8] If this is so, then the enterprise is in trouble, not because it will fail, but because it will, in every case, succeed. Ohmann will always be able to assert (although not to prove) a plausible connection between the "conceptual orientation" he discerns in an author and the formal patterns his descriptive apparatus yields. But since there is no warrant for that connection in the grammar he appropriates, there is no constraint on the manner in which he makes it, and therefore his interpretations will be as arbitrary and unverifiable as those of the most impressionistic of critics.

The point will be clearer, I think, if we turn for a moment to the work of J. P. Thorne, another linguist of the generative persuasion. While Ohmann and Milic are interested in reading from syntax to personality, Thorne would like to move in the other direction, from syntax to either content or effect, but his procedures are similarly illegitimate. Thorne begins in the obligatory way, by deploring the presence in literary studies of "impressionistic terms."[9] Yet, he points out, these terms must be impressions of something, and what they are impressions of, he decides, "are types of grammatical structures." It follows from this that the task of stylistics is to construct a typology that would match up grammatical structures with the effects they invariably produce: "If terms like 'loose', or 'terse' or 'emphatic' have any significance . . . —and surely they do—it must be because they relate to certain identifiable structural properties" (pp. 188–189). What follows is a series of analyses in which "identifiable structural properties" are correlated with impressions and impressionistic terms. Thorne discovers, for example, that in Donne's "A Nocturnal upon St. Lucie's Day" selectional rules are regularly broken. "The poem has sentences which have inanimate nouns where one would usually expect to find animate nouns, and animate nouns . . . where one would expect to find inanimate nouns." "It seems likely," he concludes, "that these linguistic facts underlie the sense of chaos and the breakdown of order which many literary critics have associated with the poem" (p. 193). This is at once arbitrary and purposeful. The "breakdown of order" exists only within his grammar's system of rules (and strange rules they are, since there is no penalty for breaking them); it is a formal, not a semantic fact (even though the rules are semantic), and there is no warrant at all for equating it with the "sense" the poem supposedly conveys. That sense, however, has obviously been preselected by Thorne and the critics he cites and is, in effect, responsible for its own discovery. In other words, what Thorne has done is scrutinize his data until he discerns a "structural property" which can be made to fit his preconceptions. The exercise is successful, but it is also circular.[10]

It is not my intention flatly to deny any relationship between structure and sense, but to argue that if there is one, it is not to be explained by attributing an independent meaning to the linguistic facts, which will, in any case, mean differently in different circumstances. Indeed, these same facts—animate nouns where one expects inanimate and inanimate where one expects animate—characterize much of Wordsworth's poetry, where the sense communicated is one of harmony rather than chaos. Of course, counterexamples of this kind do not prove that a critic is wrong (or right) in a particular case, but that the search for a paradigm of formal significances is a futile one. Those who are determined to pursue it, however, will find in transformational grammar the perfect vehicle; for since its formalisms operate independently of semantic and psychological processes (are neutral between production and reception) they can be assigned any semantic or psychological value one may wish them to carry. Thus Ohmann can determine that in one of Conrad's sentences the deep structural subject "secret sharer" appears thirteen times and conclude that the reader who understands the sentence must "register" what is absent from its surface;[11] while Roderick Jacobs and Peter Rosenbaum can, with equal plausibility, conclude that the presence of relative clause reduction transformations in a story by John Updike results "in a very careful suppression of any mention of individual beings" as agents.[12] In one analysis the grammatical machinery is translated into an activity the reader must perform; in the other it prevents him from performing that same activity. This is a game that is just too easy to play.

It is possible, I suppose, to salvage the game, at least temporarily, by making it more sophisticated, by contextualizing it. One could simply write a rule that allows for the different valuings of the same pattern by taking into account the features which surround it in context. But this would only lead to the bringing forward of further counterexamples, and the continual and regressive rewriting of the rule. Eventually a point would be reached where a separate rule was required for each and every occurrence; and at that point the assumption that formal features *possess* meaning would no longer be tenable, and the enterprise of the stylisticians—at least as they conceive it—will have been abandoned.[13]

One can be certain, however, that it will not be abandoned, partly because the lure of "solid science" and the promise of an automatic interpretive procedure is so great, and partly because apparent successes are so easy to come by. For a final and spectacular example I turn to Michael Halliday and an article entitled "Linguistic Function and Literary Style."[14] Halliday is the proprietor of what he calls a category-scale grammar, a grammar so complicated that a full explanation would take up more space than I have. Allow me, however, to introduce a few of the basic terms. The number of categories is four: unit, structure, class, and system. Two of these, unit and structure, are categories of chain; that is, they refer to the syntagmatic axis or axis of combination. The category of unit relates the linear constituents of discourse to one another as they combine; representative units are morpheme, word, group, clause, and sentence. The category of structure is concerned with the syntagmatic relationships within units: subject, complements, adjunct, and predicator are elements of structure. The other two categories are categories of choice, of the paradigmatic axis or the axis of selection. The category of class contains those items which can be substituted for one another at certain points in a unit; classes include nouns, verbs, and adjectives. The category of system refers to the systematic relationships between elements of structure, relationships of agreement and difference, such as singular and plural, active and passive. Together, these categories make it possible for the linguist to segment his text either horizontally or vertically; that is, they make possible an exhaustive taxonomy.

This, however, is only part of the story. In addition, Halliday introduces three scales of abstraction which link the categories to each other and to the language data. They are rank, exponence, and delicacy. The scale of rank refers to the operation of units within the structure of another unit: a clause, for example, may operate in the structure of another clause, or of a group, or even of a word, and these would be first, second, and third degree rank shifts, respectively. Exponence is the scale by which the abstractions of the system relate to the data: it allows you to trace your way back from any point in the descriptive act to the actual words of a text. And finally the scale of delicacy is the degree of depth at which the descriptive act is being performed. While in some instances one might be satisfied to specify at the level of a clause or a group, in a more delicate description one would want to describe the constituents and relationships within those units themselves.

If this were all, the apparatus would be formidable enough; but there is more. Halliday also adopts, with some modifications, Karl Bühler's tripartite division of language into three functions —the ideational function or the expression of content; the inter-personal function, the expression of the speaker's attitudes and evaluations, and of the relationships he sets up between himself and the listener; and the textual function, through which language makes links with itself and with the extralinguistic situation.[15] Obviously these functions exist at a different level of abstraction from each other and from the taxonomic machinery of categories and scales, and just as obviously they create a whole new set of possible relationships between the items specified in that taxonomy; for as Halliday himself remarks, in a statement that boggles the mind with its mathematical implications, "each sentence embodies all functions . . . and most constituents of sentences also embody more than one function" (p. 334).

The result is that while the distinctions one can make with the grammar are minute and infinite, they are also meaningless, for they refer to nothing except the categories of the system that produced them, categories which are themselves unrelated to anything outside their circle except by an arbitrary act of assertion. It follows, then, that when this grammar is used to analyze a text, it can legitimately do nothing more than provide labels for its constituents, which is exactly what Halliday does to a sentence from *Through the Looking Glass:* "It's a poor sort of memory that only works backwards." Here is the analysis:

The word *poor* is a "modifier," and thus expresses a subclass of its head word *memory* (ideational); while at the same time it is an 'epithet" expressing the Queen's attitude (interpersonal), and the choice of this word in this environment (as opposed to, say, useful) indicates more specifically that the attitude is one of disapproval. The words *it's . . . that* have here no reference at all outside the sentence, but they structure the message in a particular way (textual), which represents the Queen's opinion as if it were an "attribute" (ideational), and defines one class of *memory* as exclusively possessing this undesirable quality (ideational). The lexical repetition in *memory that only works backwards* relates the Queen's remark (textual) to *mine only works one way* in which *mine* refers anaphorically, by ellipsis, to *memory* in the preceding sentence (textual) and also to *I* in Alice's expression of her own judgment *I'm sure* (interpersonal). Thus ideational content and personal interaction are woven together with, and by means of, the textual structure to form a coherent whole. (p. 337)

What, you might ask, is this coherent whole? The answer is, "It's a poor sort of memory that only works backwards." But that, you object, is what we had at the beginning. Exactly. When a text is run through Halliday's machine, its parts are first disassembled, then labeled, and finally recombined into their original form. The procedure is a complicated one, and it requires a great many operations, but the critic who performs them has finally done nothing at all.

Halliday, however, is determined to do something, and what he is determined to do is confer a value on the formal distinctions his machine reads out. His text is William Golding's *The Inheritors*, a story of two prehistoric tribes one of which supplants the other. The two tribes—the "people" and the "new people," respectively—are distinguished not only by their activities but by their respective languages, and these, in turn, are distinguishable from the language of the reader. Language A, the language of the "people," is, according to Halliday, dominant for more than nine-tenths of the novel. Here is a sample of it:

The man turned sideways in the bushes and looked at Lok along his shoulder. A stick rose upright and there was a lump of bone in the middle. Lok peered at the stick and the lump of bone

and the small eyes in the bone things over the face. Suddenly
Lok understood that the man was holding the stick out to him but
neither he nor Lok could reach across the river. He would have
laughed were it not for the echo of screaming in his head. The
stick began to grow shorter at both ends. Then it shot out to
full length again. The dead tree by Lok's ear acquired a voice.
"Clop." His ears twitched and he turned to the tree. By his face
there had grown a twig. (p. 360)

From this and other samples Halliday proceeds to a description
of the people's language, using the full apparatus of his category-
scale grammar; but what begins as a description turns very
quickly into something else:

> The clauses of passage A . . . are mainly clauses of action . . .
> location . . . or mental process . . . the remainder are attributive
> . . . Almost all of the action clauses . . . describe simple movements
> . . . and of these the majority . . . are intransitive . . . Even such
> normally transitive verbs as *grab* occur intransitively . . . More-
> over a high proportion . . . of the subjects are not people; they
> are either parts of the body . . . or inanimate objects . . . and of
> the human subjects half again . . . are found in clauses which are
> not clauses of action. Even among the four transitive action
> clauses . . . one has an inanimate subject and one is reflexive. There
> is a stress set up, a kind of syntactic counterpoint, between verbs
> of movement in their most active and dynamic form . . . and the
> preference for non-human subjects and the almost total absence
> of transitive clauses. (pp. 349–350)

Here, of course, is where the sleight of hand begins. To label a
verb "active" is simply to locate it in a system of formal differences and relationships within a grammar; to call it "dynamic"
is to semanticize the label, and even, as we see when the description continues, to moralize it:

> It is particularly the lack of transitive clauses of action with human
> subjects . . . that creates an atmosphere of ineffectual activity; the
> scene is one of constant movement, but movement which is as
> much inanimate as human and in which only the mover is affected
> . . . The syntactic tension expresses this combination of activity
> and helplessness. No doubt this is a fair summary of the life of
> Neanderthal man. (pp. 349–350)

This paragraph is a progression of illegitimate inferences. Halliday first gives his descriptive terms a value, and then he makes an ideogram of the patterns they yield. Moreover, the content of that ideogram—the Neanderthal mentality—is quite literally a fiction (one wonders where he got his information), and it is therefore impossible that these or any other forms should express it.

What happens next is predictable. The novel receives a Darwinian reading in which the grammatically impoverished "people" are deservedly supplanted by the "new people" whose fuller transitivity patterns are closer to our own: "The transitivity patterns . . . are the reflexion of the underlying theme . . . the inherent limitations of understanding of Lok and his people and their consequent inability to survive when confronted with beings at a higher stage of development" (p. 350). The remainder of the essay is full of statements like this; the verbal patterns "reflect" the subject matter, are "congruent" with it, "express" it, "embody" it, "encode" it, and at one point even "enshrine" it. The assumption is one we have met before—"syntactic preferences correlate with habits of meaning"—but here it is put into practice on a much grander scale: "The 'people's' use of transitivity patterns argues a Neanderthal mind."

In short, when Halliday does something with his apparatus, it is just as arbitrary as what Milic and Ohmann and Thorne do with theirs. But why, one might ask, is he arbitrary in this direction? Given the evidence, at least as he marshals it, the way seems equally open to an Edenic rather than a Darwinian reading of the novel, a reading in which the language of the "people" reflects (or embodies or enshrines) a lost harmony between man and an animate nature. The triumph of the "new people" would then be a disaster, the beginning of the end, of a decline into the taxonomic aridity of a mechanistic universe. There are two answers to this question, and the first should not surprise us. Halliday's interpretation precedes his gathering and evaluating of the data, and it, rather than any ability of the syntax to embody a conceptual orientation, is responsible for the way in which the data are read. There is some evidence that the interpretation is not his own (he refers with approval to the "penetrating critical study" of Mark Kinkead-Weakes and Ian Gregor), but whatever its source—and this is the second answer to my question—its attraction is the opportunity it provides him to make his apparatus the hero of the novel. For in the reading Halliday offers, the deficiencies of the "people" are measured by the inability of their language to fill out the categories of his grammar. Thus when he remarks that "in Lok's understanding the complex taxonomic ordering of natural phenomena that is implied by the use of defining modifiers is lacking, or . . . rudimentary" (p. 352), we see him sliding from an application of his system to a judgment on the descriptions it yields; and conversely, when the "new people" win out, they do so in large part because they speak a language that requires for its analysis the full machinery of that system. Not only does Halliday go directly from formal categories to interpretation, but he goes to an interpretation which proclaims the superiority of his formal categories. The survival of the fittest tribe is coincidental with a step toward the emergence of the fittest grammar. Whether Golding knew it or not, it would seem that he was writing an allegory of the ultimate triumph of Neo-Firthian man.

Is there, then, no point to Halliday's exercise? Are the patterns he uncovers without meaning? Not at all. It is just that the explanation for that meaning is not the capacity of a syntax to express it, but the ability of a reader to confer it. Golding, as Halliday notes, prefaces *The Inheritors* with an excerpt from H. G. Wells's discussion of Neanderthal man. As a result, we enter the story expecting to encounter a people who differ from us in important respects, and we are predisposed to attach that difference to whatever in their behavior calls attention to itself. It is in this way that the language of the "people" becomes significant, not because it is symbolic but because it functions in a structure of expectations, and it is in the context of that structure that a reader is moved to assign it a value. The point is one that Halliday almost makes, but he throws it away, on two occasions, first when he remarks that the reader's entrance into the novel requires a "considerable effort of interpretation" (p. 348), and later when he specifies the nature of that effort: "the difficulties of understanding are at the level of interpretation—or rather . . . of re-interpretation, as when we insist on translating 'the stick began to grow shorter at both ends' as 'the man drew the bow' " (p. 358). Here I would quarrel only with the phrase "we insist"; for the decision to reinterpret is not made freely; it is inseparable from the activity of reading (the *text* insists), and the effort expended in the course of that activity becomes the measure and sign of the distance between us and the characters in the novel. In other words, the link between the language and any sense we have of Neanderthal man is fashioned in response to the demands of the reading experience; it does not exist prior to that experience, and in the experience of another work it will not be fashioned, even if the work were to display the same formal features. In any number of contexts, the sentence "the stick grew shorter at both ends" would present no difficulty for a reader; it would require no effort of reinterpretation, and therefore it would not take on the meaning which that effort creates in *The Inheritors*. Halliday's mistake is not to assert a value for his data but to locate that value in a paradigm and so bypass the context in which it is actually acquired.

This goes to the heart of my quarrel with the stylisticians: in their rush to establish an inventory of fixed significances, they bypass the activity in the course of which significances are, if only momentarily, fixed. I have said before that their procedures are arbitrary, and that they acknowledge no constraint on their interpretations of the data. The shape of the reader's experience is the constraint they decline to acknowledge. Were they to make that shape the focus of their analyses, it would lead them to the value conferred by its events. Instead they proceed in accordance with the rule laid down by Martin Joos, "Text signals its own structure," treating the deposit of an activity as if it were the activity itself, as if meanings arose independently of human transactions.[16] As a result, they are left with patterns and statistics that have been cut off from their animating source, banks of data that are unattached to anything but their own formal categories, and are therefore, quite literally, meaningless.

In this connection it is useful to turn to a distinction, made by John Searle, between institutional facts—facts rooted in a recognition of human purposes, needs, and goals—and brute facts—facts that are merely quantifiable. "Imagine," says Searle,

> a group of highly trained observers describing a . . . football game in statements only of brute facts. What could they say by way of description? Well, within certain areas a good deal could be said, and using statistical techniques certain "laws" could even be formulated . . . we can imagine that after a time our observers would discover the law of periodic clustering: at regular intervals organisms in like colored shirts cluster together in roughly circular fashion . . . Furthermore, at equally regular intervals, circular clustering is followed by linear clustering . . . and linear cluster-ing is followed by the phenomenon of linear interpenetration . . . But no matter how much data of this sort we imagine our observers to collect and no matter how many inductive generaliza-tions we imagine them to make from the data, they still have not described football. What is missing from their description? What is missing are . . . concepts such as touchdown, offside, game, points, first down, time out, etc. . . . . The missing statements are precisely what describes the phenomenon on the field *as a game of football*. The other descriptions, the description of the brute facts can [only] be explained in terms of the institutional facts.[17]

In my argument the institutional facts are the events that are constitutive of the specifically human activity of reading, while the brute facts are the observable formal patterns that can be discerned in the traces or residue of that activity. The stylisti-cians are thus in the position of trying to do what Searle says cannot be done: explain the brute facts without reference to the institutional facts which give them value. They would specify the meaning of the moves in the game without taking into ac-count the game itself. Paradoxically, however, this gap in their procedures does not hamper but frees them; for while it is true, as Hubert Dreyfus has recently observed, that once the data have "been taken out of context and stripped of all significance, it is not so easy to give it back,"[18] the corollary is that it is *very* easy to replace it with whatever significance you wish to bring forward. The result is interpretations that are simultaneously fixed and arbitrary, fixed because they are specified apart from contexts, and arbitrary because they are fixed, because it is in contexts that meaning occurs.

The stylisticians, of course, have an alternative theory of meaning, and it is both the goal of, and the authorization for, their procedures. In that theory, meaning is located in the inventory of relationships they seek to specify, an inventory that exists independently of the activities of producers and consumers, who are reduced either to selecting items from its storehouse of significances or to recognizing the items that have been selected. As a theory, it is distinguished by what it does away with, and what it does away with are human beings, at least insofar as they are responsible for creating rather than simply exchanging meanings. This is why the stylisticians almost to a man identify meaning with either logic or message or information, because these entities are "pure" and remain uninfluenced by the needs and purposes of those who traffic in them. I have been arguing all along that the goal of the stylisticians is impossible, but my larger objection is that it is unworthy, for it would deny to man the most remarkable of his abilities, the ability to give the world meaning rather than to extract a meaning that is already there.

This, however, is precisely what the stylisticians want to avoid, the protean and various significances which are attached, in context and by human beings, to any number of formal configurations. Behind their theory, which is reflected in their goal which authorizes their procedures, is a desire and a fear: the desire to be relieved of the burden of interpretation by handing it over to an algorithm, and the fear of being left alone with the self-renewing and unquantifiable power of human signifying. So strong is this fear that it rules their procedures even when they appear to be taking into account what I accuse them of ignoring. Michael Riffaterre is a case in point. In every way Riffaterre seems to be on the right side. He criticizes descriptive techniques that fail to distinguish between merely linguistic patterns and patterns a reader could be expected to actualize.[19] He rejects the attempts of other critics to endow "formal . . . categories . . . with esthetic and . . . ethical values."[20] He insists that the proper object of analysis is not the poem or message but the "whole act of communication" (p. 202). He argues for the necessity of "following exactly the normal reading process" (p. 203), and it is that process he seeks to describe when he asks readers, or as he calls them, informants, to report on their experiences. Once the process is described, however, Riffaterre does something very curious: he empties it of its content.[21] That is, he discounts everything his readers tell him about what they were doing and retains only the points at which they were compelled to do it. That pattern that emerges, a pattern of contentless stresses and emphases, is then fleshed out by the interpretation he proceeds to educe.

Riffaterre does exactly what the other stylisticians do, but he does it later: he cuts his data off from the source of value and is then free to confer any value he pleases. The explanation for this curious maneuver is to be found in his equation of meaning with message or information; for if the message is the meaning, a reader's activities can only be valued insofar as they contribute to its clear and firm reception; anything else is simply evidence of an unwanted subjectivity and must be discarded. While the reader is admitted into Riffaterre's procedures, there is no real place for him in the theory and he is sent away after he has performed the mechanical task of locating the field of analysis. In the end, Riffaterre is distinguished only by the nature of his diversionary machinery. Like the other stylisticians, he introduces a bulky apparatus which obscures the absence of any connection between his descriptive and interpretive acts; the difference is that his is precisely the apparatus that would supply the connection (it is not taxonomic but explanatory); but after introducing it, he eviscerates it.

Richard Ohmann performs somewhat the same operation on an entire school of philosophy. In his most recent work, Ohmann has proposed literary applications to the speech-act theory of J. L. Austin (*How To Do Things with Words*) and John Searle,[22] a theory that turns traditional philosophy around by denying the primacy and even the existence of pure or context-free statements. All utterances, argue Austin and Searle, are to be understood as instances of purposeful human actions which happen to require language for their performance. Some of these are promising, ordering, commanding, requesting, questioning, warning, stating, praising, greeting, and so on. Even this abbreviated list should be enough to suggest the main contention of this school, which is captured in Searle's declaration that propositional acts do not occur alone.[23] What this means is that every utterance possesses an illocutionary force, an indication of the way it is to be taken (as a promise, threat, warning, or whatever) and that no utterance is ever taken purely, without reference to an intention in a context. Thus, for example, the string of words "I will come" may, in different circumstances, be a promise, a threat, a warning, a prediction; but it will always be one of these, and it will never be just a meaning unattached to a situation. What an older theory would have called the pure semantic value of the utterance is in this theory merely an abstraction, which, although it can be separated out for the sake of analysis, has no separate and independent status. The various illocutionary lives led by "I will come" are not different handlings of the same meaning, they are different meanings. In speech-act theory, there is only one semantic level, not two; detached from its illocutionary force, a sentence is just a series of noises. Illocutionary force *is* meaning. (This is obvious in the paradigm instances where the illocutionary force marker is explicit, that is, a part of the utterance, which certainly cannot be detached from itself.)

It is not my intention here to embrace this theory (although I am attracted to it) but to explain some of its terms, terms which Ohmann appropriates. He also distorts them, in two predictable directions. First of all, he takes the slice of the speech act that Searle insists cannot stand alone and gives it an independent status. He calls it the locutionary act—a designation he borrows from Austin—and endows it with a force of its own, the semantic force of logical and grammatical structures.[24] This locutionary act then becomes the basic level of a two-level system of significations. The second, and subsidiary, level is occupied by the inventory of illocutionary forces, which function more or less as a rhetoric of social conventions and intentions. Illocutionary force is thus dislodged from its primary position and reduced to a kind of emphasis, something that is added to a content which is detachable from it and survives its influence. Ohmann turns the major insight of the speech-act philosophers on its head, precisely undoing what they have so carefully done. It is in a way a remarkable feat: he manages to take a theory rooted in the recognition of human meaning and make it assert the primacy of a meaning that is specifiable apart from human activities. He succeeds, in the face of great odds, in preserving the context-free propositional core that is necessary if there is to be a rationale for the procedures of stylistics,[25] and it is only a measure of his success that he is then able to define literature impossibly as "discourse without illocutionary force."[26]

I do not mean to suggest conscious intention on Ohmann's part, any more than I would argue that the stylisticians consciously perform illegitimate acts of interpretation which they then deliberately disguise. Indeed, I take the performance of these acts as evidence of the extent to which they are unaware of their assumptions; for if they were true to their covert principles (as are, for example, the structuralists) they would be content with the description of formal patterns and admit that the value-free operation of those patterns has always been their goal.[27] But they are not so content and insist on leaping from those patterns to the human concerns their procedures exclude. The dehumanization of meaning may be the implication, as well as the result, of what they do; but it is not, I think, what they consciously *want* to do.

What we have, then, is a confusion between methodology and intention, and it is a confusion that is difficult to discern in the midst of the pseudo-scientific paraphernalia the stylisticians bring to bear. I return to my opening paragraph and to a final paradox. While it is the program of stylistics to replace the subjectivity of literary studies with objective techniques of description and interpretation, its practitioners ignore what is *objectively* true—that meaning is not the property of a timeless formalism but something acquired in the context of an activity—and therefore they are finally more subjective than the critics they would replace. For an open impressionism, they substitute the covert impressionism of anchorless statistics and self-referring categories. In the name of responsible procedures, they offer a methodized irresponsibility, and as a result, they produce

interpretations which are either circular—mechanical reshuf-
flings of the data—or arbitrary—readings of the data that are
unconstrained by anything in their machinery.

What makes this picture particularly disturbing is the un-
likelihood of its changing; for among the favorite pronouncements of the stylisticians are two that protect them from confronting or even acknowledging the deficiencies of their operations. The first is: "Stylistic studies are essentially comparative."
Properly understood, this article of faith is a covert admission
of the charges I have been making. What the stylisticians compare are the statistics derived from applying their categories to a
variety of texts; but since those categories are unattached to anything (are without meaning) the differences revealed by the
statistics are purely formal, and the only thing one can legitimately do with them is compare them with each other. The
weakness of the exercise is that it is without content, but this
is also its strength, since it can be endlessly and satisfyingly
repeated without hazarding assertions about meaning or value.
It is when such assertions are hazarded that the stylisticians get
into trouble, but at this point they are ready with a second article
of faith: the apparent unreliability of our procedures is a condition of insufficient data. Thus while Lúbomir Doležel (to cite
just one example) is forced to admit that "there are surprising
contradictions in the various interpretations of style characteristics," he manages to escape the implications of his admission
by hanging everything on a future hope: "All conclusions about
the properties and nature of style characteristics, about the
speaker type, and about stylistic differences, are to be considered
hypotheses that will be confirmed or refuted by the accumulation of vast empirical material."[28] But the accumulation of empirical material will make a difference only if the ability of
human begins to confer meaning is finite and circumscribable
within a statistical formula; if it is not, then the resulting data
will do nothing more than trace out more fully the past performance of that ability, rather than, as Doležel and others hope, make
its future performances predictable. In other words, the statistics
will never catch up with the phenomenon they seek to circumscribe. But one can avoid this realization simply by forever ad-

vancing the date when the availability of more data will make everything all right.[29] The failure of the basic assumption to prove itself is also the mechanism which assures its continuing life, and assures too that stylisticians will never come to terms with the theoretical difficulties of their enterprise.

If the enterprise is so troubled, if the things people say about stylistics are not terrible enough, what is the remedy? What is the critic who is interested in verbal analysis to do? The answer to this question would be the substance of another essay, but it has been more than anticipated here, especially in my counter-analysis of *The Inheritors.* I do not, the reader will recall, deny that the formal distinctions Halliday uncovers are meaningful; but where he assumes that they *possess* meaning (as a consequence of a built-in relationship between formal features and cognitive capacities), I would argue that they *acquire* it, and that they acquire it by virtue of their position in a structure of experience. The structure with which the stylisticians are concerned is a structure of observable formal patterns, and while such patterns do exist they are themselves part of a larger pattern the description of which is necessary for a determination of their value. Thus, for example, while it is certainly possible (as Halliday demonstrates) to specify the properties of the languages spoken by the tribes in *The Inheritors,* the significance of those properties is a function of their reception and negotiation by a reader who comes upon them already oriented in the direction of specific concerns and possessed of (or by) certain expectations. These concerns and expectations themselves arise in the course of a consecutive activity engaged in by a finite consciousness; and it is my contention that a characterization of that activity must precede, and by preceding control, the characterization of the formal features which become part of *its* structure. In short, I am calling not for the end of stylistics but for a new stylistics, what I have termed elsewhere an "affective" stylistics,[30] in which the focus of attention is shifted from the spatial context of a page and its observable regularities to the temporal context of a mind and its experiences.

Does this mean a return to the dreaded impressionism? Quite the reverse. The demand for precision will be even greater because the object of analysis is a process whose shape is continually changing. In order to describe that shape, it will be necessary to make use of all the information that formal characterizations of language can provide, although that information will be viewed from a different perspective. Rather than regarding it as directly translatable into what a word or a pattern *means,* it will be used more exactly to specify what a reader, as he comes upon that word or pattern, is *doing,* what assumptions he is making, what conclusions he is reaching, what expectations he is forming, what attitudes he is entertaining, what acts he is being moved to perform. When Milic observes that in Swift's prose connectives are often redundant and even contradictory—concessives cheek by jowl with causals[31]—we can proceed from what he tells us to an account of what happens when a reader is alternately invited to anticipate a conclusion and asked to qualify it before it appears. When Ohmann declares that the syntactical deviance of Dylan Thomas's "A Winter's Tale," breaks down categorical boundaries and converts juxtaposition into action,"[32] the boundaries, if they exist, take the form of a reader's expectations and their breaking down is an action *he* performs, thereby fashioning for himself the "vision of things" which the critic would attribute to the language. And when Halliday demonstrates that in the language of the "people" in Golding's *The Inheritors,* agency is given not to human but to inanimate subjects ("the stick grew shorter at both ends"), we can extrapolate from his evidence to the interpretive effort demanded of the reader who must negotiate it. In each case, a statement about the shape of the data is reformulated as a statement about the (necessary) shape of response, and in the kind of analysis I propose, a succession of such shapes would itself be given shape by the needs and concerns and abilities of a consciousness moving and working in time.

Information about language can be turned into information about response even when the formalizations are unattached to specific texts. Searle's analyses of questions, commands, promises, and so on, in terms of the roles they involve, the obligations they institute, and the needs they presuppose, allow us, indeed oblige us, to include these things in any account of what a reader of a question or command or promise understands. Thus when Joan Didion begins *Play It As It Lays* with the sentence "What makes Iago evil?," simply by taking the question in, the reader casts himself in the role of its answerer. Moreover, he is directed by the tense, aspect (frequentative), and semantic content of "makes" to play that role in the context of a continuing and public literary debate about causality and motivation (how different would it be were the question "Why is Iago evil?"); and he will respond, or so Didion assumes, with one or more of the many explanations that have been offered for Iago's behavior.[33] That same reader, however, will be made a little less comfortable in his role by the second sentence: "Some people ask." The effect of "some" is to divide the world into two groups, those who seek after reasons and causes and those who do not. The reader, of course, has already accepted the invitation extended by the prose to become a member of the first group, and moreover, he has accepted it in assumed fellowship with the first-person voice. That fellowship is upset by the third sentence—"I never ask" —which is also a judgment on what the reader has been (involuntarily) doing. Reader and narrator are now on different sides of the question originally introduced by the latter, and the tension between them gives point and direction to the experience of what follows.

Little of what I have said about this paragraph would emerge from a formal characterization of its components, but in my description of its experience I have been able to make use of formal characterizations—of a speech-act analysis of a question, of a logician's analysis of the properties of "some," of a philosopher's analysis of making something happen—by regarding their content as cues for the reader to engage in activities. What is significant about these activities is that they are interpretive; for this means that a procedure in which their characterization is the first order of business avoids the chief theoretical deficiency of stylistics as it is now practiced. I have repeatedly objected to the absence in the work of the stylisticians of any connection between their descriptive and interpretive acts. In the kind of stylistics I propose, *interpretive acts are what is being described;* they, rather than verbal patterns arranging themselves in space, are the content of the analysis. This is more than a procedural distinction; for at its heart are different notions of what it is to read which are finally different notions of what it is to be human. Implicit in what the stylisticians do is the assumption that to read is to put together discrete bits of meaning until they form what a traditional grammar would call a complete thought. In this view, the world, or the world of the text, is already ordered and filled with significances and what the reader is required to do is get them out (hence the question, "What did you get out of that?"). In short, the reader's job is to extract the meanings that formal patterns possess prior to, and independently of, his activities. In my view, these same activities are constitutive of a structure of concerns which is necessarily prior to any examination of meaningful patterns because it is itself the occasion of their coming into being. The stylisticians proceed as if there were observable facts that could first be described and then interpreted. What I am suggesting is that an interpreting entity, endowed with purposes and concerns, is, by virtue of its very operation, determining what counts as the facts to be observed;[34] and, moreover, that since this determining is not a neutral marking out of a valueless area, but the extension of an already existing field of interests, it *is* an interpretation.

The difference in the two views is enormous, for it amounts to no less than the difference between regarding human beings as passive and disinterested comprehenders of a knowledge external to them (that is, of an *objective* knowledge) and regarding human beings as at every moment creating the experiential spaces into which a personal knowledge flows. It is a difference in methodological responsibility and rigor, between a procedure which is from the very beginning organizing itself in terms of what is significant and a procedure which has no obligatory point of origin or rest. That is, if one sets out to describe in the absence of that which marks out the field of description, there is no way of deciding either where to begin or where to stop, because there is no way of deciding what counts. In such a situation, one either goes on at random and forever (here we might cite the monumental aridity of Jakobson's analyses of Baudelaire and Shakespeare) or one stops when the accumulated data can be made to fit a preconceived interpretive thesis. It has seemed to many that these are the only alternatives, and that, as Roger Fowler has declared, the choice is between "mere description" or description performed at the direction of a pre-formulated literary hunch.[35] I have been arguing for a third way, one which neither begs the question of meaning nor pre-decides it arbitrarily but takes as its point of departure the interpretive activity (experience) by virtue of which meanings occur.

This, then, is the way to repair the ruins of stylistics, not by linking the descriptive and interpretive acts but by making them one.[36] It is hardly necessary to say that this kind of analysis is not without problems, and the problems are for the most part a direct consequence of its assumptions about what it means to be human. It can have no rules in the sense of discovery procedures, since the contextualizing ability that characterizes being human is not circumscribed by its previous performances, performances which, while they constitute the history of that ability, do not constitute its limits. Thus the value a formal feature may acquire in the context of a reader's concerns and expectations is local and temporary; and there is no guarantee that the value–formal feature correlation that obtains once will obtain again (although an awareness that it has obtained once is not without interest or usefulness). All you have when you begin is a sense of this finite but infinitely flexible ability and a personal knowledge of what it means to have it. You then attempt to project the course that ability would take in its interaction with a specific text, using as the basis of your projection what you know, and at the same time adding to what you know by the very effort to make analytical use of it. There are other things that can help. Formal linguistic characterizations can help, if, as I have said, one views their content as potential cues for the performing acts. Literary history can help, if one views its conventions in the same way; a description of a genre, for example, can and should be seen as a prediction of the shape of response. Other minds can help, because they know what you know, but with the same lack of distance between themselves and their knowledge which makes the effort so difficult. Analyses of perceptual strategy can help,[37] because they acquaint us with the past performances of the ability we are trying to know. (Our trying is itself just such a performance.) Finally, however, you are left only with yourself and with the impossible enterprise of understanding understanding; impossible because it is endless, endless because to have reached an end is to have performed an operation that once again extends it beyond your reach. In short, this way lacks the satisfaction of a closed system of demonstration and is unable ever to prove anything, although, paradoxically, this makes rigor and precision more, not less, necessary; but these very deficiencies are the reverse side of its greatest virtue (in both the modern and Renaissance sense): the recognition that meaning is human.

3
How Ordinary Is Ordinary Language?

["ORDINARY LANGUAGE" is one of a number of terms used to designate a kind of language that "merely" presents or mirrors facts independently of any consideration of value, interest, perspective, purpose, and so on. Other such terms are "literal language," "scientific language," "propositional language," "logical language," "denotative language," "neutral language," "mathematical language," "serious (as opposed to fictional) language," "nonmetaphorical language," "representational language," "message-bearing language," "referential language," "descriptive language," and "objective language." Whatever the term, the claim is always the same: it is possible to specify a level at which language correlates with the objective world and from which one can build up to contexts, situations, emotions, biases, and finally, at the outermost and dangerous limits, to literature. The claim is a far-reaching one, because to make it is at the same time to make claims about the nature of reality, the structure of the mind, the dynamics of perception, the autonomy of the self, the ontology of literature, the possibility and scope of formalization, the stability of literary (and therefore of nonliterary) texts, the independence of fact from value, and the independence of meaning from interpretation. It is not too much to say that everything I write is written against that claim, in all of its consequences and implications. In this essay I challenge the ordinary-language/literary-language distinction, first by pointing out that it impoverishes both the norm and its (supposed) deviation, and second by denying that literature, as a class of utterances, is identified by formal properties. Literature, I argue, is the product of a way of reading, of a community agreement about what will count as literature, which leads the members of the community to pay a certain kind of attention and thereby to *create* literature. Since that way of reading or paying attention is not eternally fixed but will vary with cultures and times, the nature of the literary institution and its relation to other institutions whose configurations are similarly made will be continually changing. Aesthetics, then, is not the once and for all specification of essentialist literary and nonliterary properties but an account of the *historical* process by which such properties emerge in a reciprocally defining relationship. The writing of this aesthetics, of a truly new literary history, has hardly begun, and the essays in this volume do little more than sketch out its possibility.]

I T HAS BEEN more than twenty years since Harold Whitehall declared that "no criticism can go beyond its linguistics."[1] In that time linguistics itself has undergone a number of revolutions so that one of the terms in Whitehall's equation has been constantly changing. What has not changed, however, is the formulation of the difficulties involved in any attempt to marry the two disciplines. More often than not these difficulties have found expression in muted declarations of war which are followed by a series of journalistic skirmishes and then by uneasy, but armed, truces. Linguists resolutely maintain that literature is, after all, language, and that therefore a linguistic description of a text is necessarily relevant to the critical act; critics just as resolutely maintain that linguistic analyses leave out something, and that what they leave out is precisely what constitutes literature. This leads to an attempt, undertaken sometimes by one party, sometimes by the other, to identify the formal properties peculiar to literary texts, an attempt that inevitably fails, when either the properties so identified turn out to be found in texts not considered literary, or when obviously literary texts do not display the specified properties. In the end, neither side has victory, but each can point to the other's failure: the critics have failed to provide an objective criterion for the asserted uniqueness of their subject matter; the linguists have failed to provide the kind of practical demonstration that would support the claims they make for their discipline and its apparatus.

It seems to me that this state of affairs is unlikely to change so long as the debate is conducted in these terms, for what has produced the impasse between the linguists and the critics is not the points they dispute, but the one point on which both parties seem so often to agree. Let me illustrate by juxtaposing two statements. The first is by the linguist Sol Saporta and it was made in 1958 at the Indiana Conference on Style:

> Terms like *value, aesthetic purpose,* etc., are apparently an essential part of the methods of most literary criticism, but such terms are not available to linguists. The statements that linguists make will include references to phonemes, stresses, morphemes, syntactical patterns, etc., and their patterned repetition and co-occurrence. It remains to be demonstrated to what extent an analysis of messages based on such features will correlate with that made in terms of value and purpose.[2]

The second statement is dated 1970, and comes to us from the opposite direction. Elias Schwartz, a literary critic, is writing in the pages of *College English:*

> [Linguists] . . . have failed to distinguish clearly between . . . the structure of language and the structure of literature . . . From one point of view . . . a work of literature may be regarded as a piece of language. That . . . is the (proper) viewpoint of linguistics; but as soon as one so regards a literary work, it ceases to *be* a literary work and "becomes" a piece of language merely . . . Linguistic analysis is not, cannot be, literary criticism.[3]

Saporta and Schwartz can stand for all of those linguists and critics who have confronted each other in the past twenty years.[4] The linguist says, I have done the job of describing the language; you take it from here. The critic replies, I have no use for what you have done; you've given me at once too little and too much. Superficially, then, the two positions are firmly opposed, but only slightly beneath the surface one finds a crucial area of agreement: in their concern to characterize the properties of literary language, Schwartz and Saporta simply assume a characterization of nonliterary or ordinary language, and that characterization is also a judgment. In Schwartz's statement, the judgment is made with a single word, "merely"—"a literary work . . . ceases to *be* a literary work and 'becomes' a piece of language merely." Saporta delivers the same judgment indirectly. Terms like *value* and *purpose,* he says, are not available to linguists; what he means, of course, is that they are not available to language. By admitting that there *is* an ordinary language/

literary language split, the linguist anticipates and makes possible the tactics of the critic, who need merely agree with his
opponent's characterization of linguistics and then proceed to
find that discipline irrelevant to literary studies.

Saporta's statement is now fifteen years old, but the assumptions underlying it still provide the framework for discussions
of the question. "The task of the linguist," writes Gordon
Messing, "is limited to describing those formal components of
a literary text which are accessible to him . . . but the linguist
cannot judge the value of these various features; only the literary
critic can do that."[5] Messing is quoted approvingly by David
Hirsch, who then concludes that the "positivist orientation" of
transformational grammar circumscribes its usefulness for the
analyses of "poetic utterances."[6] Indeed, linguistics is positively
harmful when its procedures are applied to such utterances, and
it had best limit itself to the sphere of its competence, which is,
of course, ordinary language: "In our everyday utterances we
communicate meanings in one form that could as easily have
been communicated in another. But the language of poetry is
different. It communicates cognitive and emotive meanings in
a special way" (p. 88). The "special way" is not defined, but
clearly Hirsch's strategy is to declare it inaccessible to linguistics.

That same strategy is pursued by William Youngren in a
book-length argument. Youngren begins by accepting the semantic theory of Katz and Fodor, a theory that places severe restrictions on what is available to linguistic formalization.[7] He
then asks "whether or not the scientific study of meaning can be
of any help to the reader or critic of literature?" (p. 115). Since
the "scientific study of meaning" has already been identified with
a theory that refuses to go beyond "bare 'cognitive content'"
(p. 113), the answer to Youngren's question is necessarily "no"
and in due time it emerges:

> The explanatory adequacy . . . which a particular scientific theory
> possesses in its own sphere would seem to have nothing whatever
> to do with its inapplicability to criticism. (p. 164)

> The fact of the matter is that criticism . . . is an autonomous ac-
> tivity. (p. 173)

Once again the autonomy of criticism is achieved at the expense of a linguistic-literature interdependency. Linguistics is left with "its own sphere," that is, with the "scientific study of meaning," that is, with the study of "mere" language which will, presumably, be well served by a semantic theory whose goals are determinedly low.[8]

Examples could be multiplied indefinitely,[9] but the point, I trust, is clear: despite their apparent opposition, the critics and the linguists are collaborating to perpetuate the same disastrous model. By accepting the positivist assumption that ordinary language is available to a purely formal description, both sides assure that their investigations of literary language will be fruitless and arid; for if one begins with an impoverished notion of ordinary language, something that is then defined as a deviation from ordinary language will be doubly impoverished. Indeed, it is my contention that the very act of distinguishing between ordinary and literary language, because of what it assumes, leads necessarily to an inadequate account of both; and if I may put the matter aphoristically: *deviation theories always trivialize the norm and therefore trivialize everything else.* (Everyone loses.)

Let us take the two points of the aphorism in order. The trivialization of ordinary language is accomplished as soon as one excludes from its precincts matters of purpose, value, intention, obligation, and so on—everything that can be characterized as human. What, then, is left to it? The answers to this question are various. For some, the defining constituent of ordinary language, or language, is its capacity to carry messages; for others, the structure of language is more or less equated with the structure of logic, and the key phrase is cognitive or propositional meaning. Still others hold instrumental views: language is used to refer either to objects in the real world or to ideas in the mind; referential theories are also sometimes representational theories, ranging from the naive representationalism of so many words to so many things, to more sophisticated philosophical variations. But whatever the definition, two things remain constant: (1) the content of language is an entity that can be specified independently of human values (it is, in a word, pure) and (2) a need is therefore created for another entity or system in the context of which human values can claim pride of place. That entity is literature, which becomes by default the repository of everything the definition of language excludes.

At this point, however, something very curious happens. Once you've taken the human values out of the language, and yet designated what remains as the norm, the separated values become valueless, because they have been removed from the normative center. That is to say, every norm is also a morality, and whatever is defined in opposition to it is not merely different, but inferior and inessential. (This is reflected in the frequent characterization of literature as parasitic, deviational, and non- or un-grammatical.) It follows, then, that the area or sphere designated to receive the severed values immediately assumes a peripheral status; and, characteristically, those literary critics who work in this tradition are engaged in a frantic effort to find an honorific place for their subject. This then is the first result of the decision to distinguish between ordinary language and literature; both sides of the slash mark lose: ordinary language loses its human content, and literature loses its justification for being because human content has been declared a deviation. The inevitable end of the sequence is to declare human content a deviation from itself, and this is precisely what happens when Louis Milic asserts at the beginning of an article on literary style that "personality may be thought of as the reverse of humanity."[10] When I first read this statement, I was puzzled by it, as you may be now; but the puzzle is removed as soon as one sees it as the product of an inexorable logic. For if one is committed simultaneously to maintaining ordinary or message-bearing language as a norm and to preserving the link between language and humanity, humanity must be redefined so as to be congruent with the norm you have decided to maintain. Humanity must, like ordinary language, be thought of as a mechanism or a formalism, as the reverse of personality, as, and again these are Milic's words, "the uniformity of the human mass." The ultimate confusion involved in this theoretical sleight of hand, of making humanity a deviation from itself, is reflected in Milic's procedures; it is his avowed intention to identify the uniqueness that characterizes an author's style, but he is obliged to regard the uniqueness, when it is discovered, as a regrettable aberration. Thus, for example, Milic's analyses reveal that in Swift's prose connectives often function to suggest a logic the argument does not really possess; he then concludes— an inevitable conclusion, given his assumptions—that this is a tendency of which Swift must have been unaware, for had he been aware of it, it would have been curbed.[11]

I choose Milic for my example only because his statements reveal him to have the courage of his theoretical convictions. Other theorists are less open. Wimsatt and Beardsley, for instance, are engaged in precisely the same operation with their distinctions between explicit and implicit meaning, for in every case it turns out that the implicit meaning is admissible only when it is an extension of explicit meaning; otherwise it becomes an undesirable distraction which is to be deplored even as it is discovered. Wimsatt's stated intention is to rescue style from the category of superficies or scum, but the rescue operation is performed at the expense of the beneficiary, since style is honored only if it makes no claims for itself apart from the conveying of the message.[12]

My intention is not to criticize the work of the men, but to point out the extent to which the decision to separate ordinary and literary language dictates the shape of other decisions even before there is any pressure to make them. A distinction which assumes a normative value at its center is continually posing a choice between that value and anything else, and that choice will reproduce itself at every subsequent stage of the critical process. It reproduces itself preeminently in the only two definitions of literature that are now available, literature as either message-plus or message-minus. A message-minus definition is one in which the separation of literature from the normative center of ordinary language is celebrated; while in a message-plus definition, literature is reunited with the center by declaring it to be a more effective conveyor of the messages ordinary language transmits.[13] Thus for Michael Riffaterre, to cite just one example, literature, like language, communicates messages; the difference is that in literature, the reception of the message is assured by literary or stylistic devices whose function it is to compel attention.[14] This is no more than a strong form of the weaker classical definition of "what oft was thought, but ne'er so well expressed," where the message remains at the center, surrounded and decorated, as it were, by verbal patterns that make it more attractive and pleasing. In a message-minus definition, the priorities are reversed (these are the *only* possibilities) and preeminence is given to the verbal patterns; the message is either deemphasized, as it is in Richards's distinction between emotive and scientific meaning (that is, between literary and ordinary language), or it is completely overwhelmed, as it is for those who believe with Jakobson that in poetry, the principle of equivalence is projected from the axis of selection (lexical context free polysemy) into the axis of combination (the channel along which messages are built up and produced).[15]

What is common to both message-plus and message-minus definitions is the mechanism of exclusion each of them inescapably sets in motion. Message-minus theorists are forced to deny literary status to works whose function is in part to convey information or offer propositions about the real world. The difficulties and absurdities this leads to are illustrated by Schwartz's decision (p. 187) to include "A Modest Proposal" in the category "literature," but not Pope's *Essay on Man*, or by Richard Ohmann's doubt that Elizabeth Barrett Browning's "How do I love thee" was in fact literature when it was used to send Robert Browning a message.[16] Message-plus theorists, on the other hand, are committed to downgrading works in which the elements of style do not either reflect or support a propositional core. If there is a clash, declares Beardsley, there is a fault and it is a logical fault;[17] here again we see the *moral* force of the norm of ordinary language, its inevitable legislation of the ideal of logical clarity, even in contexts which are defined in opposition to that ideal. This hidden morality is even more strikingly operative when Wimsatt asserts flatly that *parataxis,* the absence of sequential relation, is "basically a wrong thing."[18] It is easy to see why message-plus theorists often have difficulty in dealing with works like *The Faerie Queene,* although of course they have the option either of declaring the offending work a failure or of finding a higher message in relation to which the wayward elements can be seen to cohere.

These, however, are the only possibilities, for the choice of either a message-plus or message-minus defintion of literature (which is the result of forcing a choice between ordinary and literary language) has built into it an evaluative criterion, the criterion of formal unity. In one context, the criterion is necessary because materials extraneous to the message can be tolerated only so long as they contribute to its expression or reception; in the other, the deemphasizing of the message leads to the requirement that these same materials cohere formally with each other. (What else could they do?) Either everything must converge on a center, or everything must converge in the absence of a center. As always, the alternatives are severely constrained, simultaneously reflecting and reproducing the choice between approving the separation of literature from life or reintegrating it with the impoverished notion of life implicit in the norm of ordinary language. Like everything else in the sequence, the criterion of formal unity is dictated, and it in turn dictates the setting up of a procedure designed to discover and validate it. Every time the procedure succeeds, it not only confers honorific status on a work, it also confirms the explanatory power of the evaluative criterion; and success is inevitable, since only ingenuity limits the ability of the critic to impose unity of either a cognitive or purely formal kind on his materials. (Witness the number of previously discredited works that are admitted into the canon when their "hidden" unity is uncovered.)

My point is not that characterizations of literature as message-plus or message-minus are inadequate (although I think they are) or that the criterion of formal unity is trivial (although I think it is), but that these and other positions have been determined by a decision that has often not even been consciously made. When Roman Jakobson declares that the chief task of literary theory is to discover "what makes a verbal message a work of art," whether he knows it or not he has delivered himself of an answer masquerading as a question.[19] What makes a verbal message a work of art? Whatever it is, it will presumably *not* be what makes it a verbal message. From this covert assumption follows necessarily the succession of entailments I have been describing: the reduction of language to a formal system unattached to human purposes and values; the displacement of those values to a realm that forever after has a questionable status; and the institution of procedures that extend the disastrously narrowing effect of the original distinction into every corner of the critical act. Or, in other words, deviation theories always trivialize the norm and therefore trivialize everything else.

What is the solution? How are we to break out of this impasse? Paradoxically, the answer to these questions lies in the repeated failure of those who have tried to define literary language. What has defeated them time and again is the availability in supposedly normative discourse of the properties they have isolated; and from this they have reluctantly come to the conclusion that there is no such thing as literary language. But to my mind the evidence points in another direction, to the more interesting, because it is the more liberating, conclusion that *there is no such thing as ordinary language,* at least in the naive sense often intended by that term: an abstract formal system, which, in John Searle's words, is only used incidentally for purposes of human communication.[20] The alternative view would be one in which the purposes and needs of human communication inform language and are constituent of its structure, and it is just such a view that a number of philosophers and linguists have been urging for some time, although literary critics have been characteristically slow to realize its implications.[21] Whatever the outcome of the quarrel between Chomsky and his revisionist pupils, it is clear that the point at dispute between them is the status of semantics, and that in work of Charles Fillmore, James MacCauley, George Lakoff, and others, the semantic component is not something added at a later stage to a fully formed and independent linguistic system, but is a motivating force in that system, influencing syntactic changes as much as syntactic changes influence it. Moreover, this new semantics is not simply a list of usages or an enumeration of features but an account of the philosophical, psychological, and moral concepts that are *built into* the language we use (that is to say, the language *we* use). When Fillmore sets out to investigate the "verbs . . . speakers use in speaking about various types of interpersonal relationships involving judgments of worth and responsibility," the relationships and judgments in question are the content of those words, and not the property of an extralinguistic context with which a structure of arbitrary noises interacts.[22] The significance of this is that the language system is not characterized apart from the realm of value and intention but begins and ends with that realm, and this is even more true of the theory of speech acts as it has been developed by a succession of Oxford philosophers. In this theory, utterances are regarded as instances of purposeful human behavior; that is to say, they refer not to a state of affairs in the real world but to the commitments and attitudes of those who produce them in the context of specific situations. The strongest contention of the theory is that all utterances are to be so regarded, and the importance of that contention is nicely illustrated by the argument of J. L. Austin's *How To Do Things with Words*.[23] In that book Austin develops an account of what he calls performatives, acts of speech the performance of which constitutes *doing* something—promising, warning, praising, ordering, greeting, questioning, and so on. These acts are subject to the criterion of felicity or appropriateness and they are opposed to constatives, the class of pure or context-free statements to which one may put the question, is it true or false. This distinction, however, does not survive Austin's exploration of it, for the conclusion of his book is the discovery that constatives are also speech acts, and that "what we have to study is not the sentence" in its pure or unattached form but "the issuing of an utterance in a situation" by a human being (p. 138). The class of exceptions thus swallows the normative class, and as a result the objectively descriptive language unattached to situations and purposes that was traditionally at the center of linguistic philosophy is shown to be a fiction. What takes its place, as Searle has explained, is a "language everywhere permeated with the facts of commitments undertaken and obligations assumed,"[24] and it follows then that description of that language will be inseparable from a description of those commitments and obligations.

What philosophical semantics and the philosophy of speech acts are telling us is that ordinary language is extraordinary because at its heart is precisely that realm of values, intentions, and purposes which is often assumed to be the exclusive property of literature. The significance of this for the relationship between literature and linguistics is enormous. I began by noting the critical objection to equating literature and language: "The literary work becomes a piece of language merely." But this objection loses much of its force—and the need for distinguishing between literature and language much of its rationale—if the adverb "merely" no longer applies. If deviation theories trivialize the norm and therefore trivialize everything else, a theory which restores human content to language also restores legitimate status to literature by reuniting it with a norm that is no longer trivialized.[25] (It levels *upward*.) At a stroke the disastrous consequences of the original distinction are reversed. No longer is the choice one of separating literature from life or reintegrating it with the impoverished notion of life that follows necessarily from an impoverished notion of language. No longer are works denied the designation "literary" by the exigencies which that choice creates. No longer are we bound to procedures that merely confirm and extend the narrowing of options implicit in the original distinction. Possibilities open up; alternatives can be freely explored, and the exploration will be aided by the formal, yet value-laden, characterizations of language which linguistics and linguistic philosophy are making increasingly available. The one disadvantage in all of this is that literature is no longer granted a special status, but since that special status has always been implicitly degrading, this disadvantage is finally literature's greatest gain.

Questions of course remain and the chief question is, what, after all, *is* literature? Everything I have said in this essay commits me to saying that literature is language (although not, of course, in the demeaning sense with which we began); but it is language around which we have drawn a frame, a frame that indicates a decision to regard with a particular self-consciousness the resources language has always possessed. (I am aware that this may sound very much like Jakobson's definition of the poetic function as the *set toward the message;* but his set is exclusive and aesthetic—toward the message *for its own sake*—while my set is toward the message for the sake of the human and moral content all messages necessarily display.) What characterizes literature then is not formal properties, but an attitude—always within our power to assume—toward properties that belong by constitutive right to language. (This raises the intriguing possibility that literary language may be the norm, and message-bearing language a device we carve out to perform the special, but certainly not normative, task of imparting information.) Literature is still a category, but it is an open category, not definable by fictionality, or by a disregard of propositional truth, or by a statistical predominance of tropes and figures, but simply by what we decide to put into it. The difference lies not in the language but in ourselves. Only such a view, I believe, can accommodate and reconcile the two intuitions that have for so long kept linguistic and literary theory apart—the intuition that there *is* a class of literary utterances, and the intuition that any piece of language can become a member of that class.

One obvious difficulty with this view is that it contains no room for evaluation. It can, however, explain the *fact* of evaluating by pointing out that the formal signals which trigger the "framing process" in the reader are also evaluative criteria. That is, they simultaneously *identify* "literature" (by signaling the reader that he should put on his literary perceiving set; it is the reader who "makes" literature) and *honor* (or validate) the piece of language so identified (that is, made). Of course, these signals change periodically, and when they do there is a corresponding change in the mechanism of evaluation. All aesthetics, then, are local and conventional rather than universal, reflecting a collective decision as to what will count as literature, a decision that will be in force only so long as a community of readers or believers (it is very much an act of faith) continues to abide by it. Thus criteria of evaluation (that is, criteria for identifying literature) are valid only for the aesthetic they support and reflect. The history of aesthetics becomes an empirical rather than a theoretical study, one that is isomorphic with the history of tastes.

It is in this light that the efforts of those committed to the ordinary language/literary language distinction should be viewed. They may say that they are trying to determine what literature is, but in fact they have already made that determination by deciding what it is not. This is true also of those for whom the distinction is between language and literature rather than between ordinary and literary language—those who, having concluded that there is no such thing as literary language, seek the difference (which they assume *must* be once and for all specifiable) elsewhere, rather than concluding that there is no such thing as ordinary language.[26] To characterize literature by, for example, fictivity is finally not at all different from characterizing it as a formal departure from normative speech. Both characterizations depend on the positivist assumption of an objective "brute fact" world and a language answerable to it on the one hand, and of an entity (literature) with diminished responsibility to that world on the other.

The same assumption underlies the attempt (often undertaken by the same people) to isolate style, which is usually defined either as a distinctive way of employing the rules of ordinary language (style as choice) or as a departure from those same rules (style as deviation).[27] Since the choice (between alternative expressions) does not affect the content of the utterance but merely puts a personal stamp—an emphasis—on it, and since the deviation is from that same content (even to the extent sometimes of obscuring and overwhelming it), the two notions depend on and leave intact the norm of ordinary language and are thus more or less parallel to the two definitions of literature (message-plus and message-minus) dictated by that same norm. The search for style, like the search for an essentialist definition of literature, proceeds in the context of an assumption that predetermines its shape. If one does not accept that (positivist) assumption, as I do not, the results of such inquiries will have only a limited *historical* interest; for even when they succeed (as they cannot help but do), it will be in the narrow sense of having been faithful to their constraining beginnings. It fol-

lows, then, that the attempt to specify once and for all the properties of literature and locate the boundaries of style should be
either abandoned (an event more to be hoped for than expected)
or recognized for what it is: not a disinterested investigation
but the reflection of an ideology; not a progress toward a theory
but the product of one; not a question but an answer.

4

What It's Like To Read L'Allegro *and* Il Penseroso

[ALONG WITH THE CHAPTER on Bacon in *Self-Consuming Artifacts,* this essay is the "purest" example of the reader-response analysis I was practicing between 1964 and 1976. First of all it is "pure," that is, absolute, in its claims: three hundred years of *L'Allegro–Il Penseroso* criticism are declared to have been in error because professional readers have insisted on interpreting a poem that is designed precisely to relieve us from the care and attention that interpretation requires. The claim, then, is that reader-response criticism is more objective than its predecessors because it recovers for us the experience of a text *before* it has been forgotten or distorted by critical presuppositions and misconceptions. In fact, however, the history I dismiss (the critical history of the poem) is responsible for what I have to say and for the force with which I can say it. It is only because so much effort has been expended in the interpretation of *L'Allegro* that there is any point to my characterization of the poem as one that protects us from interpretation, and there would have been little value in my assertion that *L'Allegro* and *Il Penseroso* stand for different modes of experience had there not already been so many other assertions of what they stand for. In the same way, the methodology itself gains a hearing in proportion to the challenge it poses to orthodox and commonplace ways of thought. The argument that a poem requires or allows inattention and thoughtlessness will fall strangely on formalist ears, especially when that argument is offered as praise. Perhaps that is why the reaction of audiences to the essay (surely innocuous in its subject matter) was often so hostile; it was a critical performance that seemed simply to fly in the face of much that was assumed about the properties a work must have in order to be considered literary. Of course, the hostility may well have been provoked by my title, insofar as many in the audience may have felt that what I was presuming to tell them (what it's like to read *L'Allegro* and *Il Penseroso*) was something they already knew, and knew in a way more immediate than any available to me. At any rate, I would still stand by the analysis (that is, I *believe* it) but I would no longer claim that it is not an interpretation. The distinction underlying this claim—between the experience of a poem and what one might say about it subsequently—will not hold because the characterization of the experience follows from a set of assumptions (about what one does when reading, about the inability of readers to withhold response, and so on) and is therefore itself an interpretation. In short, the way of reading which yields the "disconnective decorum" of *L'Allegro* is just that—a way of reading—and cannot properly be proclaimed (as I proclaim it) *the* way of reading in relation to which all others are interpretive distortions.]

I HAVE ONLY ONE POINT to make and everything else follows from it: *L'Allegro* is easier to read than *Il Penseroso*. This I assume is hardly news, but if one were a subscriber to the *Times Literary Supplement* in 1934, the matter might seem to be shrouded in considerable doubt, for on October 18 of that year J. P. Curgenven initiated a remarkable correspondence by asking and answering the question, "Who comes to the window in *L'Allegro,* line 46?" Curgenven is disturbed by those who construe "come" (45) as dependent on "hear" (41), which thus, he says, "gives the crude rendering: 'to hear the lark . . . to come, in spite of sorrow, and at my window bid good morrow." "Surely," he exclaims, " 'come' is dependent on 'admit' (38) and parallel to 'live' (39) and 'hear' (41), and thus it is L'Allegro who comes to his own window and bids good morrow" (p. 715). Curgenven attributes the alternative mistaken reading to two causes: "the expectation of finding inaccuracies in Milton's descriptions of natural phenomena" and the presence in earlier poetry of "some striking references to birds singing their good morrows" and among these, some larks. He duly cites these references, admitting in passing that Milton had no doubt read the poems in question. It is only the first of many curiosities in this exchange that Curgenven spends so much time marshaling evidence in support of the position he opposes.

One week later (October 25) the question is taken up again by T. Sturge Moore, who finds Curgenven's reading "unnatural." "Yet," he goes on, "I agree . . . that to make the lark come is absurd" (p. 735). Moore, it seems, has another candidate. "Surely [a word that appears often in this correspondence, but with a diminishing force], it is *Mirth* [who] is begged to come to the window. The poet has asked to be admitted of her crew . . . and runs on to enumerate advantages he hopes to gain . . . breaking off he resumes his petition: *Then*, as lark and sun rise, is the moment for the Goddess to come and bid him good morrow." A third week (November 1) finds Professor Grierson joining the fray to argue for the one reading that both Moore and Curgenven dismiss out of hand. It *is* the lark who comes, not in nature, but in the mind of the speaker who might well think, in spite of the natural error, that he was being wakened by the bird. A poet, Grierson reminds us, "is not a scientist, . . . he tells truth in his own way" (p. 755). On November 8, B. A. Wright becomes the first of several fence straddlers. He agrees with Curgenven that the syntax and the pronunciation of lines 39–48 are "perfectly clear" (a statement belied by the existence of his letter) and that the poet is himself the subject of the infinitive "come" as he is of the infinitives "live" and "hear." Noting, however, that Mr. Moore understands Mirth to be the subject of "come," Wright admits that this makes good sense and is grammatically typical of Milton. "Either of these interpretations," he concludes, "seems to me possible" (p. 775), although he "cannot with Professor Grierson imagine Milton imagining the lark first 'at his watch towre in the skies' and then still singing at his own bedroom window." (Notice that this assumes what is by no means certain, that it is the lark, not "dull night," who is "startled.") Grierson for his part continues to defend the lark (on November 15) but concedes that "if we are to judge by strict grammar then the most defensible meaning is that it is the cheerful man who comes to the window" (p. 795). "If I am in error," he continues, "I should prefer to take 'Then to come' as a bodily elliptical construction which leaves it quite indefinite who it is that comes." This retreat of course is more strategical than sincere, but it points toward the only conclusion the exchange will finally allow.

In the weeks that follow, old positions are restated and new ones put forward. Tillyard appears (November 15) to support Wright and the cheerful man by alluding, as he often did, to the *First Prolusion*. Joan Sargeaunt offers to remind us "of Bishop Copleston's sly dig at the literal seriousness of critics" (p. 795); presumably (although I am not sure) *she* intends some sly dig at the length and heat of the present correspondence and agrees with Grierson when he declares, "It is vain to argue these questions" (p. 795). Wright, however, will have none of that. It is a matter, he insists, of "Milton's poetic honour. Professor Grierson would seem to imply that any reader is entitled to his own interpretation of the lines," but no one, Wright thunders, is entitled to an interpretation which "makes Milton talk nonsense" (p. 840). Grierson's reading of the lines, he continues, is possible only "when they are isolated from their context." Grierson rather wearily replies, "I am afraid Mr. Wright is growing indignant with me which is a sign I should stop" (p. 855). He goes on long enough, however, to insist that "there remain some difficulties" (an understatement, I think) and to declare that where there is doubt, "surely [that word again] one may allow some freedom of interpretation." And indeed the limits of freedom had already been extended by B. R. Rowbottom, who on November 22 had proposed still another interpretation. "Neither 'Mirth' nor 'The Lark' nor 'The Cheerful Man' is 'then' to come and bid good-morrow at the window through the Sweet-Briar, or the Vine, or the twisted Eglantine, in spite of sorrow, but the 'Dawn' . . . while the Cock scatters the rear of darkness thin" (p. 840).

The controversy ends on November 29 with a letter from W. A. Jones, The County School, Cardiganshire, who reports that his classes of school children "invariably and without noticing any difficulty understand the lines" (p. 856). Whether or not the editors took this as a comment on the entire affair is a matter of conjecture, but at any rate they append a footnote to Jones' letter: "We cannot continue this correspondence."

The point, of course, is that this correspondence could have been continued indefinitely, but even in its abbreviated form, it allows us to make some observations.

(1) The proponent of each reading makes concessions, usually by acknowledging that there *is* evidence for the readings he opposes.

(2) Each critic is able to point to details which do in fact support his position.

(3) But in order fully to support his respective position every one of the critics is moved to make *sense* of the lines by supplying connections more firm and delimiting than the connections available in the text.

(4) This making of sense always involves an attempt to arrange the images and events of the passage into a sequence of logical action.

Thus V. B. Halpert, a latecomer to the controversy in 1963, argues for the lark on the basis of the temporal adverb "then," which, she says, signals a break from the simple infinitive construction of "to live" and "to hear" and therefore indicates the beginning of a new action with a new agent—the lark, who "after startling the dull night will then leave its watch tower and come to the poet's window."[1] "In other words," Halpert concludes, "the word *then* signifies a sequence of events." Perhaps so, but it is a sequence which Edith Riggs, who is also committed to making the lines "make perfect sense," finds "unhappy" and "dangerously close to *non*-sense."[2] She proposes a new sequence, one that puts "night" rather than the lark in the watchtower: "The lark, the first of day's forces, startles the enemy from his watch tower in the sky . . . Night is routed and forced to flee." Whether or not the routed night also stops at the poet's window to bid him good-morrow, Miss Riggs does not say (although nothing I can think of would debar her from saying it); she simply concludes on a note of triumph I find impossible to share: "The new reading thus rids the poem of a jarring image and replaces it by one . . . more meaningful within the total context of the passage."

What are we to make of all this? I find myself at least partly in Grierson's camp, and finally in the camp of Jones' children; for if the entire exchange proves anything, it is that Milton does not wish to bind us to any one of these interpretations. I do not mean (as Grierson seems to) that he left us free to choose whatever interpretation we might prefer, but he left us free *not* to choose, or more simply, that he left us free. As Brooks and Hardy observe, the reader of these lines "is hurried through a series of infinitives . . . the last of which is completely ambiguous in its subject."[3] I would only add that the ambiguity is *so* complete that unless someone asks us to, we do not worry about it, and we do not worry about it (or even notice it) because while no subject is specified for "come," any number of subjects —lark, poet, Mirth, Dawn, Night—are available. What is *not* available is the connecting word or sustained syntactical unit which would pressure us to decide between them, and in the absence of that pressure, we are not obliged to decide. Nor are we obliged to decide between the different (and plausible) sequences which choosing any one of these subjects would generate:

(1) If it is the lark who comes to the window, he does so while the cock "with lively din" scatters the rear of darkness thin, and the two birds thus perform complementary actions.

(2) If it is the dawn that comes to the window, she does so while the cock with lively din scatters the rear of darkness thin and is thus faithful to our understanding of the relation between cock's crowing and dawn.

(3) If it is the poet (L'Allegro) who comes to the window, he does so in response to lark, cock, and dawn, that is, while they are performing their related functions.

(4) And if it is Mirth who comes to the window, the action allies her with lark, cock, and dawn in the awakening of L'Allegro.

All of these readings hang on the word "while" in line 49, but since "while" is less time-specific than other temporal adverbs, it does not firmly call for any one of these and, more to the point, it functions equally well, that is, equally *loosely,* in all of them. Rather than insisting on a clear temporal relationship among the events it connects, "while" acts as a fulcrum around which those events swirl, supplying just enough of a sense of order to allow us to continue but not so much that we feel compelled to arrange the components of the passage into an intelligible sequence. In short, "while" neither directs nor requires choice; instead, it *frees* us from choice and allows us—and I mean this literally—to be careless. This is also the effect of the two "ors" in the preceding couplet: "Through the Sweet-Briar or the Vine, / Or the twisted Eglantine."[4] The "ors" divide alternative images, each of which registers only for a split second before it is supplanted by the next. We are neither committed to any one of them, nor required to combine them into a single coherent picture. The effect of the couplet extends both backward—softening the outline of the window and of *who*ever or *what*ever has come to it—and forward—removing the pressure of specificity from the weakly transitional "while."

I intend the phrase "weakly transitional" precisely, for it exactly captures the balance Milton achieves by deploying his connectives. If there were no transitions, the freedom of the poem's experience would become a burden, since a reader would first notice it and then worry about it; and if the transitions were firmly directing, a reader would be obliged to follow the directions they gave.[5] Milton has it both ways, just as he does with a syntax that is not so much ambiguous as it is loose. Twentieth-century criticism has taught us to value ambiguities because they are meaningful, but these ambiguities, if they can be called that, protect us from meaning by protecting us from working. They are there not to be noticed but to assure that, whatever track a reader happens to come in on, he will have no trouble keeping to it; no choice that he makes (of lark, poet, Goddess, and so on) will conflict with a word or a phrase he meets later. Anything fits with anything else, so that it is never necessary to go back and retrace one's effortless steps.

Rosemond Tuve has written that the pleasures enumerated in *L'Allegro* all have "the flat absence of any relation to responsibility which we sometimes call innocence."[6] What I am suggesting is that the experience of *reading* the poem is itself such a pleasure, involving just that absence; for at no point are we held responsible for an action or an image beyond the moment of its fleeting appearance in a line or a couplet. Moreover, it is a *flat* absence in the sense that we are not even aware of having been relieved of it. That is why Cleanth Brooks is not quite right when he declares that the unreproved pleasures of *L'Allegro* "can be had for the asking";[7] they can be had *without* the asking.

The result is an experience very much like that described by William Strode in "Against Melancholy," a poem that has been suggested by J. B. Leishman as a possible source for *L'Allegro:*[8]

> Free wandring thoughts not ty'de to muse
> Which thinke on all things, nothing choose,
> Which ere we see them come are gone.   (13–15)

"Take no care," Strode enjoins in line 18, but Milton goes him one better by *giving* no care, by not asking that we put things together, or supply connections, or make inferences, or do anything at all. Rather than compelling attention, the verse operates to diffuse attention, either by blurring the focus of its descriptions—the Sweet-Briar *or* the Vine *or* the twisted Eglantine—or by breaking off a description if its focus threatens to become too sharp, or by providing so many possible and plausible sequences that it finally insists on none. As a result we move from linguistic event to linguistic event with almost no hostages from our previous experience and therefore with no obligation to relate what we are reading to what we have read.

Critics have always been aware of the curious discreteness that characterizes *L'Allegro*, both as an object and as an experience, but in general they have responded either by downgrading the poem, so capable, as D. C. Allen observes, of "desultory rearrangement,"[9] or by attempting to rescue it from the charge of disunity and fragmentation. In 1958 Robert Graves went so far as to suggest that in the course of composing *L'Allegro* Milton misplaced sixteen lines, probably over the weekend. The lines beginning "Oft listening" (53) and ending with every shepherd telling his tale under the hawthorn in the dale (68) originally followed the account of the Lubber fiend as "Crop full out of the door he flings, / Ere the first cock his matins rings" (113–114). By restoring the original order, Graves asserts, we make the poem very much less of a "muddle," (that is, we make *sense* of it). Otherwise, he points out, we are left with this improbable sequence of events:

While distractedly bidding good-morrow, at the window, to Mirth, with one ear cocked for the hounds and horn . . . [he] sometimes, we are told, *"goes walking, not unseen, by hedgerow elms, on Hillock green."* Either Milton had forgotten that he was still supposedly standing naked at the open window—(the Jacobeans always slept raw)—or the subject of "walking" is the cock, who escapes from the barnyard, deserts his dames, ceases to strut, and anxiously aware of the distant hunt, trudges far afield among ploughmen and shepherds in the dale. But why should Milton give twenty lines to the adventures of the neighbor's wandering cock? And why, *"walking not unseen"?* Not unseen by whom?[10]

Graves is not unaware of the impression he is making. "Please do not think I am joking," he implores, and at least one critic has taken him seriously. Herbert F. West, Jr., admits that such an accident of misplacement is "possible" and that Graves' emendation "does little apparent danger to the text" and even seems to "smooth over some difficult spots."[11] And so it does. The poet now looks out of his window to say, quite naturally, "Straight mine eye hath caught new pleasures," and it is the Lubber fiend who walks not unseen on hillocks green where he is espied, one assumes, by plowman, milkmaid, mower, and shepherd. The sequence ends as he listens to each shepherd tell his tale under the hawthorn in the dale, making for a perfect transition to the next section, which begins with line 115: "Thus done the Tales, to bed they creep." Yet Graves' emendation should, I think, be rejected and rejected precisely *because* of its advantages; for by providing continuity to the plot line of the poem, it gives us something to keep track of, and therefore it gives us *care*. It is Milton's wish, however, to liberate us from care, and the nonsequiturs that bother Graves are meant to prevent us from searching after the kind of sense he wants to make. "Not unseen by whom?" he asks, and he might well have asked, why *not* unseen, a formula which neither relates the figure of the walker to other figures nor declares categorically the absence of such a relation, leaving the matter not so much ambiguous as unexamined. Or he might have asked (perhaps did ask) what precisely is the "it" that in line 77 "sees"? This question would only lead to another, for the pronoun subject is no

more indeterminate than the object of "its" seeing—the beauty
who is the cynosure of neighboring eyes. Is she there or is she
not? "Perhaps," answers Milton in line 79, relieving us of any
responsibility to her or even to her existence. This in turn removes the specificity from the adverbial of place which introduces the following line: "Hard by, a Cottage chimney smokes."
Hard by what? Graves might well ask. In this context or non-
context the phrase has no pointing function at all. It merely
gets us unburdened into the next line and into the next *discrete*
scene, where with Corydon and Thyrsis we rest in "secure delight" (91), that is, in delight *se cura*, delight without, or free
from, care.

It is the promise of "secure delight," of course, that is at the
heart of the pastoral vision, although it is the literary strength
of the pastoral always to default on that promise by failing to
exclude from its landscape the concerns of the real world. Milton, however, chooses to sacrifice that strength in order to secure
the peculiar flatness of effect that makes reading *L'Allegro* so
effortless. The details of this landscape are without resonance;
they refer to nothing beyond themselves and they ask from us no
response beyond the *minimal* and literary response of recognition. This lack of resonance is attributable in part to the swift
succession of images, no one of which claims our attention for
more than a couplet. Each couplet is self-enclosed by ringing
monosyllabic rhymes, and the enclosures remain discrete. Continuity is provided by patterns of alliteration and assonance
(mountains-meadows), which carry us along but do not move
us to acts of association or reflection. The "new pleasures"
which the eyes of both speaker and reader catch are new in the
sense of novel, *continually* new, following one another but not
firmly related to one another. From lawns to mountains to
meadows and then to towers, the sequence is so arranged as to
discourage us from extrapolating from it a composite scene,
the details of which would then be interpretable.[12] Neither
time's winged chariot nor anything else is at the back of these
shepherds, and the verse in no way compels us to translate them
into figures for the young poet or the weary courtier or the faithful feeder of a Christian flock. In other words, we know and

understand the quality of their untroubled (careless) joy because it is precisely reflected in the absence of any pressure on us to make more of their landscape than its surfaces present. (This introduces the interesting possibility that while *L'Allegro* is the easier of the two poems to read, it was the more difficult to write. In *Il Penseroso* Milton can exploit the traditions his verse invades; in *L'Allegro* he must simultaneously introduce them and denude them of their implications, employing a diction and vocabulary rich in complex associations without the slightest gesture in the direction of that complexity. In *L'Allegro* it is not so much what the images do, but what they do not do. The poem is a triumph of absence.)

There is then here, as elsewhere, a one-to-one correspondence between the pleasures celebrated in the poem and the pleasure of reading it, and this correspondence inheres in the careless freedom with which *any* activity, including the activity of reading, can be enjoyed. The tournaments of lines 119–124 belong in *L'Allegro* because the knights and barons bold who take part in them hazard nothing, not life or death or even honor. Their high triumphs are triumphs of style and involve a fidelity to forms which have no meaning beyond the moment of their execution. Like us they are engaged in an activity from which the consequences (hostages to time) have been carefully removed.

The activities of *L'Allegro* are consistently like this, without consequences as they are without antecedents. Only once is a consequence even threatened, when the Lydian airs are said to "pierce" the meeting soul—"Lap me in soft *Lydian* Airs / Married to immortal verse, / Such as the meeting soul may pierce" (136–138); but the first two words of the following line, "In notes," blunt the potential thrust of "pierce" exactly as the lances and swords of the knights and barons bold are blunted and rendered harmless. It has been suggested that Milton's conception of Lydian music is taken from Cassiodorus, who attributes to it the power to restore us with relaxation and delight, "being invented against excessive cares and worries."[13] Whether or not this is Milton's source, it is surely a description of the effect his music, *his* invention, has on us. We are delighted because we are relaxed, and we are relaxed because the cares to which other poems bind us—the care of attending to implications, the care of carrying into one line or couplet the syntax and sense of previous lines and couplets, the care of arranging and ordering the details of a poetic landscape, the care of rendering judgments and drawing conclusions, the care, in sum, of sustained (and consecutive) thought—these are here not present. The figure of Orpheus as he appears in lines 145–150 is thus a perfect surrogate for the reader; the music he hears calls him to nothing, as we have been called to nothing by the verse. He is enwrapped in its harmonies, resting on "heapt Elysian flow'rs" (147) as we rest, unexercised, on the heaped (not arranged) flowers of the poem's images and scenes, insulated from the resonances and complications which might be activated in another context (the context, in fact, of *Il Penseroso*). This music *merely* meets the ear and the ear it meets has no answering responsibility (of which there is the "flat absence") beyond the passive responsibility of involuntary delight. When Graves discovered that *L'Allegro* was "rather a muddle," it was after many years of reading the poem. He had, however, he explains, never before "read it carefully."[14] The point that I have been making is that no one asked him to, and that his period of *mis*reading began when he decided to accord the poem the kind of careful attention from which it was Milton's gift to set us free.

If I am right about *L'Allegro,* the other critics who have written on it are necessarily wrong; for to a man they have sought to interpret the poem, while it is my contention that interpretation is precisely what it does not invite, because its parts are arranged in such a way as to exert no interpretive pressures. Of course it would be easy to turn this argument into a criticism by saying that what I have demonstrated here is that *L'Allegro* lacks unity. This would certainly be true if unity were defined (narrowly) as the coherence of formal elements, but it is the absence of that coherence which is responsible for the unity I have been describing, a unity not of form but of experience. That is to say, what unifies *L'Allegro* is the consistency of the demands it makes, or rather declines to make, on the reader, who is thus permitted the freedom from care ("secure delight") which

is the poem's subject. It is this freedom which is banished when
Il Penseroso opens by declaring "Hence vain deluding joys."
"Vain" here is to be taken as fruitless or without purpose, and
it refers not to an abstraction but to a mode of experiencing, a
mode in which the brain is quite literally "idle" because it is
"possessed" by a succession of "gaudy shapes" and fancies "which
ere we see them come are gone." This is of course the experiential mode of *L'Allegro,* and it should not surprise us to find that
the experience of reading *Il Pensero* is quite different.

Like *L'Allegro, Il Penseroso* offers alternative genealogies in
its opening lines; but where in the first poem these are indifferently presented, in the second, one is specifically preferred to
the other; and the fact of the preference is rooted in a judgment
we are required to understand and in a distinction (or series
of distinctions) we are pressured to make. That pressure is felt
as soon as we hear, "Hail divinest Melancholy, / Whose Saintly
visage is too bright / To hit the sense of human sight" (12–14).
These lines turn on a paradox, and it is in the nature of a paradox that a reader who recognizes it is already responding to the
question it poses. What kind of light is so bright that it dazzles
and, in effect, darkens the sense of human sight? An answer to
this question is readily available in the Christian–neo-Platonic
opposition between the light of ordinary day and the "Celestial
light" which "shines inward" revealing "things invisible to mor-
tal sight" (*PL,* III, 52–55). There is no more familiar commonplace in Renaissance thought, but even so, in order to recall it,
a reader must reach for it; that is, he must *do* something, engage
in an activity, and it is an activity in which he is asked to continue as the passage unfolds:

> And therefore to our weaker view,
> O'erlaid with black staid Wisdom's hue.
> Black, but such as in esteem,
> Prince *Memnon's* sister might beseem,
> Or that Starr'd *Ethiop* Queen that strove
> To set her beauties praise above
> The Sea Nymphs, and their powers offended.
> Yet thou art higher far descended.   (15–22)

The single word "therefore" in line 15 can stand for every-thing that distinguishes the companion poems. It is a word that could never appear in *L'Allegro* because it operates to *enjoin* the responsibility (to backward and forward contexts) from which that poem sets us free.[15] The lines that follow "therefore" add to the responsibility, for in the course of reading them we are asked to do several things at once. First we must suspend one line of argument and attend to another, but that argument in turn unfolds in stages, so that we are continually revising our understanding of what we have just read; and, moreover, the effect of our revised understanding extends in every instance backward to the Goddess Melancholy, whose precise characteri-zation remains the goal of our consecutive attention. Obviously, that attention is not only consecutive but strenuous. A phrase like "Black, but" asks us simultaneously to recall the pejorative associations of black and to prepare ourselves for a more positive view of the color; but no sooner has that view been established than it too is challenged, first by the imputation to Cassiopeia of impiety and then (more directly) by the qualificatory "Yet" of line 22. In this context (the context not of the verse, but of our *experience* of the verse), there are at least three possible readings of that line: (1) the obvious literal reading: "Your lineage is more impressive than that of Memnon's sister or Cassiopeia." (2) The secondary literal reading: "You come to us from a loftier height than does Memnon's sister or Cassiopeia, that is, from the stars." (3) What we might call the moral reading: "You are higher precisely because you have descended, because you have been willing to accommodate yourself to our 'weaker view' by being black and low rather than bright and high ('starry')."

In *L'Allegro* the availability of alternative readings operates to minimize our responsibility to any one of them and therefore to any consecutive argument; here it is precisely because we have been following a consecutive argument that the alternative read-ings become available. In neither poem are we required to choose between the readings; but whereas in one the absence of choice is a function of the absence of interpretive pressure, in the other that pressure is so great that we are asked to choose every reading,

because each of them goes with one of the interpretive strains
we have been led to pursue and distinguish.

Here, then, is a way of answering the questions that have so
often been put to these two poems. Do they share patterns of
imagery, or is the presence in them of light and shadow consistently and meaningfully opposed? Are they to be read as the
hyperbolic rhetoric of their invocations suggests, or are those
invocations directed at the excess of the complementary means
they present? Is there mirth in *Il Penseroso's* melancholy and
melancholy in *L'Allegro's* mirth? So long as these (and other)
questions have been asked in the context of an examination of
the text, there has been no hope of answering them, for as the
history of the criticism shows, the observable evidence will support any number of answers. But if we turn our attention from
the text to the experience it gives, an unambiguous and verifiable answer is immediately forthcoming. Every point of contact
is a point of contrast, not in the poems (where the details could
be made to point in either direction) but in the nature of the
activities they require of their readers. The activities required
of us by *Il Penseroso* are consistently strenuous. Rather than
permitting us to move from one discrete unit to another, the
verse of the second poem insists that we carry into the present
context whatever insights we have won from previous contexts,
which are in turn altered or expanded retroactively. As a result,
our attention is not diffused but concentrated, and the distinction made in the opening lines—between an idle brain captive
to a succession of unrelated images and a mind that is "fixed"—
is precisely realized in the reading experiences of the two poems.

A fixed mind is one that keeps steadily before it an idea or a
project to which it relates whatever new particulars come into its
ken. Here the idea is the Goddess Melancholy and the project
is the understanding of the way of life she presents. It is of course
our project, and because it is ours, it gives interpretive direction
to our movement through the poem, providing us with ready-
made contexts—it is *we* who have made them—into which the
details of the verse are immediately drawn. Thus when the Goddess Melancholy materializes in the form of the "pensive Nun,"
the lines describing her habit and gait are resonant with sig-

nificance because we bring the significances with us. The Nun's "robe of darkest grain" (33) is capable of any number of interpretations, but the reader who has negotiated the preceding lines will immediately identify its color as the dark hue of staid Wisdom and distinguish it from the boasting blackness of Cassiopeia. Forgetting oneself to marble and gazing downward with an unseeing stare (41–44) is at the very least ambiguous behavior, but it is disambiguated when the same reader recalls that the dimming of natural vision and the stilling of bodily motion are preliminary to the descrying of a light that is too bright to hit the sense of human sight. As a figure in the landscape, the Nun displays less and less energy, but at the same time she is being energized from within by the meanings *we* attach to her dress and actions, until at line 45 she stands (frozen) before us as an embodiment of all the mythological and philosophical associations to which we have been called by the verse.

In a way I am simply giving body to an observation made by D. C. Allen. In *L'Allegro*, Allen points out, "there is an abrupt division between the invitation and the main body of the poem," while in *Il Penseroso*, the transition is "more fluid and skillful."[16] For Allen, however, abruptness and fluidity are properties of formal structures, and his distinction is a value judgment (presumably if the transitions of *L'Allegro* were more fluid, it would be a better poem). But in my terms, abruptness and fluidity are properties of experiences, and the distinction is not between a skillful and an unskillful arrangement but between the different experiences provided by arrangements that are indifferently skillful. The components of either poem offer ample possibilities for making connections (that is, for fluidity), but it is only while reading *Il Penseroso* that we are pressured to make them. The source of that pressure is the verse, and it is exerted both silently and explicitly: silently when we are asked to manage units of sense and syntax larger than the couplet, and explicitly when we are directed in line 49 to add ("And add to these retired Leisure"). What we are to add are Melancholy's companions, Peace, Quiet, Spare Fast, the Muses, retired Leisure, and first and chiefest (although last to be called) the Cherub Contemplation. Were this list in *L'Allegro,* we would receive its

items discretely ("Straight mine eye hath caught new pleasures");
but here we are asked to relate them both to each other and
to the master abstraction of which they are all manifestations.
Moreover, the point of relation is not something they share on
the surface—on its face the list is quite heterogeneous—but
something that is available only when we extrapolate from the
surface to an underlying pattern of significance. The content
of that pattern is a two-stage sequence—withdrawal from the
busy companies of men followed by an ascent to the realm of
pure and heavenly forms—and this of course is precisely the
sequence that has just been acted out by the pensive Nun, who
is herself a realization of the paradoxes exploited in the opening
lines. "The poetic components of *Il Penseroso*," declares Allen,
"seem to glide out of each other by brilliant acts of association."[17]
The point I have been making is that these acts are ours, and we
perform them with a self-consciousness that is repeatedly returning us to the first link in the associative chain, which in every
case is found to be isomorphic with the last. The Cherub Contemplation is the first and chiefest even though he brings up
the rear, because the values he declares explicitly, that is by
name, were present in the first and in every other of their in-
carnations.

We see then that the pattern of experience in *Il Penseroso*
is as consistent as the quite different pattern in *L'Allegro*. It is
a pattern of continually exerted pressure, and it moves us to a
set of sustained and related activities: generalizing, abstracting,
reflecting, recalling, synthesizing. Not only are these activities
sustained, but they have a single object, the precise elucidation
of the nature of melancholy; and this continues to be true when
the focus of the poem shifts to the speaker, for in his wanderings
he repeatedly acts out the sequence that joins the other figures
we have encountered. Three times he retires from the light of
day into an enclosure: first in some "removed place" (79) where
light is taught to counterfeit a gloom, later in twilight groves
(133) that have been sought specifically to escape the Sun's flar-
ing beams, and finally in the "Cloister's pale" (156) where the
light streaming through the windows is deemed religious *because* it is "dim." Three times as day's garish eye is shut out and

earthly sounds are stilled, Il Penseroso becomes physically inactive, sitting in some high and lonely tower (86), or sleeping
by a hallowed brook (139), or standing motionless as the pealing
organ blows to the full-voiced choir below (162). And three
times, as his body forgets itself to marble, his spirit soars, in the
company of Plato, as together they explore "what vast Regions
hold / The immortal mind that hath forsook / Her mansion
in the fleshly nook" (90–92); under the aegis of "some strange
mysterious dream" (147); and in response to the ecstasy-making
sounds of the "Service high and Anthems clear":

> With antic Pillars massy proof
> And storied windows richly dight,
> Casting a dim religious light.
> There let the pealing Organ blow,
> To the full voic'd choir below,
> In Service high and Anthems clear,
> As may with sweetness, through mine ear,
> Dissolve me into ecstasies,
> And bring all Heav'n before mine eyes.   (158–166)

   In this penultimate scene we are once again returned to the
master images whose exfoliation has been the stimulus to our interpretive efforts. The worshiper in the "Cloister's pale" assumes
exactly the position assumed earlier by the pensive Nun, and like
her he is the very embodiment of Peace, Quiet, Spare Fast, the
Muses, retired Leisure, and the Cherub Contemplation. Even
the pattern of word play is the pattern we experienced in the
opening lines, and we are moved by it to make the same distinctions we made then. The basic distinction is between two kinds
of perception, the physical and the spiritual. They share a vocabulary, but that vocabulary is so placed that we cannot help
but be aware of its two fields of reference. In line 160 the ruling
adjective is "dim," but line 163 ends with a strong stress on the
adjective "clear." The same apparent clash exists between the
adverb "below" in line 162, which refers to the spatial position-
ing of the organ and the choir, and the adjective "high" in line
163. The clash in both cases is only apparent, because as we come
upon them we understand "high" and "clear" to refer not to
spatial and sensible but to spiritual categories; but since that

understanding follows immediately upon a sequence in which spatial and sensible categories *are* operative, it signals a transference from outer to inner space. That transference is completed by the pointed juxtaposition in lines 164 and 166 of "through mine ear" and "before mine eyes." No word in the poem is more emphasized than "eyes"; it marks the end of a line, of a couplet, and of a section; and as we read it we know, with the full weight of everything we have learned, that it cannot be read literally, and that this is the eye of the mind which now opens, as it has opened so many times before, to a light that is too bright to hit the sense of human sight. Milton, the *Variorum Commentary* observes at this point, "is here summing up the whole process of self-education described in the poem";[18] but whatever has been described in the poem (and that has long been a matter of dispute), the process and the education have taken place in the reader.

Let me say, lest there be any misunderstanding, that I am not here offering an interpretation of *Il Penseroso* but arguing that interpretation is the activity to which the poem moves us and that it is this which distinguishes it from *L'Allegro*. In another sense, however, the poems are not to be distinguished; for in both there is a congruence of experience with thematic materials. The bards in *Il Penseroso* sing of "Trophies hung" (118) and therefore of tournaments in which something more than the applause of ladies is at stake. In place of a domesticated goblin who performs kitchen chores in return for a "cream bowl," the voice of *Il Penseroso* speaks to us of Daemons "Whose power hath a *true* consent / With Planet or with Element";[19] and it is precisely this "power" that Orpheus displays when he bests Pluto in a line whose stresses communicate and create a sense of urgency that is wholly alien to *L'Allegro:* "And made Hell grant what Love did seek" (108).

The singing of Orpheus, like everything else in *Il Penseroso,* has both purpose and consequence; and purpose and consequence are also what characterize our efforts as readers. There is here as in *L'Allegro* a one-to-one correspondence between the activities in the poem and the activity of reading it, and these activities merge in a single line: "Where more is meant than

meets the ear" (120). More is indeed meant by *Il Penseroso* than
meets the ear, and the responsibility for that meaning rests with
the ear that is met, an ear that is asked not only to take in a succession of sound but to relate them to each other and to a complex of significances in which they are implicated. It is just this
kind of sustained mental effort, the effort of synthesizing, generalizing, and abstracting, to which the pensive man pledges
himself in the poem's closing lines:

> Where I may sit and rightly spell
> Of every star that Heav'n doth shew,
> And every Herb that sips the dew;
> Till old experience do attain,
> To something like Prophetic strain.   (170–174)

To spell is to decipher, to puzzle out, to consider, to think—
to engage in just those actions the poem requires of its readers.
Here, then, is another point of contact between the two poems
that is finally a point of contrast. In both, the speaker and reader
are united by the kind of acts they do or do not perform. In *Il
Penseroso*, as Bridget Lyons has observed, we are continually
aware of a consciousness through which the phenomena of experience are being filtered.[20] In other words, we are aware of the
presence in the poem of a mind, and our awareness takes the
form of matching exertions. *L'Allegro*, on the other hand, is
striking for the absence of mind; there is, it would seem, no one
at home. The first-person pronoun only occurs once before the
final couplet, and it is followed immediately by the lines that
were the occasion of the *TLS* correspondence. They are in turn
so variously interpretable that any sense of a sustained and controlling presence is progressively weakened; nor is it reinforced
when the speaker appears again in line 69 as a disembodied eye:
"Straight mine eye hath caught new pleasures." Even this syn-
ecdochical identity is blurred when it is absorbed into a spec-
ulation about "neighboring eyes" (the progression is from "I"
to "eye" to "eyes") which may or may not be there. The same
imprecision of reference and sequence that removes the pressure
of consecutive thought also prevents us from finding in the poem
a consecutive thinker; and in the absence of a consciousness

whose continuing and active presence would give the poem unity, we are that much less inclined to unify it. If no one is at home, then we can be on holiday too.

In both poems, then, the speaker and the reader are to be identified, and this identification suggests a new answer to an old question: who or what are L'Allegro and Il Penseroso? L'Allegro and Il Penseroso are the reader; that is, they stand for modes of being which the reader realizes in his response to the poems bearing their names. The formal and thematic features of each poem are intimately related to its meaning, not because they reflect it but because they *produce* it, by moving the reader to a characteristic activity. In short, the poems *mean* the experience they give; and because they so mean, the conditionals with which they end are false:

> These delights if thou canst give,
> Mirth with thee I mean to live.   (151–152)

> These pleasures *Melancholy* give,
> And I with thee will choose to live.   (175–176)

These conditionals are false because the conditions they specify have already been met. The delights and pleasures of Mirth and Melancholy are even now ours, for in the very act of reading we have been theirs.

In conclusion, I would like to turn away from the poems to consider the larger implications of my analysis. More specifically, I would like to pose a question. What is it that a procedure focusing on the reader's experience can do? First of all it can deal with *L'Allegro,* which has, for the most part, been unavailable to other critical vocabularies. This is not to say that the experience of *L'Allegro* has been unavailable, but that the readers who have had that experience have been compelled by their theoretical assumptions either to allegorize it or to devalue it. In fact it is difficult to see how a formalist criticism, committed as it is to "care" both as a criterion for composition and as a condition of serious reading, could accept my description *of L'Allegro.* For the formalist, reading poetry is equivalent to noticing and *sharing in* the craft and labor that produced it.

A poem that asked for no such answering attention would therefore be suspect; and indeed when this paper was first read at a public meeting, a member of the audience rose to ask, with some indignation, why I was attacking *L'Allegro*. Presumably it was inconceivable to him that an account of the poem that did not tie up, but multiplied, loose ends could be praise. In this connection, the recently published *Variorum Commentary* is instructive. Time and again the editors note the presence in the poem of interpretive puzzles, and time and again the sifting of evidence leads to an indeterminate conclusion. The question of who comes to the window at line 46 is debated for a full four pages which end with the recording of a difference of opinion between the two editors. A discussion of alternative versions of line 104 breaks off with the admission that in either version the syntax is "somewhat obscure" and suggests a "degree of carelessness" (p. 295). (Carelessness indeed!) Even the simple phrase "tells his tale" in "every Shepherd tells his tale" (67) has had, we are told, "alternative explanations" (p. 287); but after a survey of those explanations, we read that "all that is certain is that the shepherds were sitting" (p. 288); anything else, "the reader must decide for himself" (p. 289).

The point of course is that he need not, and that these and other "obscurities" exist precisely so that he will not feel pressured to make the sense the editors seek. These same editors repeatedly turn up evidence for the reading offered in this essay (when for example they gloss "wanton" as "uncontrolled by plan or purpose" and "giddy" as "incapable of steady attention"), but they are unable to see the evidence for what it is because they are committed to a single criterion of formal unity (which is at base a criterion of cognitive clarity). At it turns out, however, that is exactly the wrong criterion to apply to a poem like *L'Allegro* which grows out of what Thomas Rosenmeyer has recently called the "disconnective decorum" of the Theocritan pastoral.[21] As Rosenmeyer describes it, this decorum is tied to "a perception of a world that is not continuous, but a series of discrete units, each to be savored for its own sake" (p. 46). A poem displaying this decorum will be "best analyzed as a loose combination of independent elements," since "the poet provides few if any clues ... for consolidation" (p. 47). The poem, Rosenmeyer continues, does not have a plot, so that it is protected "against the profundities and syntheses which ... plot ... is always on the verge of triggering" (p. 48). "Consequently," he concludes, "the artlessness of the poem is not there for a reason, but exists of itself, which also means that it is harder to explain" (p. 48). An analysis in terms of the reading experience has, I submit, been able to explain it, because it is not tied to an evaluative bias which both directs and crowns its procedures.

This success (if you will agree that it is one) is finally attributable to a large capability I would claim for experiential analysis: it provides a firm basis for the resolving of critical controversies. As I have argued elsewhere, formalist procedures are unable to settle anything because in the absence of constraints the observable regularities in a text can be made to point in any number of directions.[22] But if the focus of analysis is the reader's experience, a description of that experience will at the same time be an interpretation of its materials. Rather than two operations (description and interpretation) whose relationship is problematical, there is only one, and consequently many of the directions in which values might have been irresponsibly assigned are automatically eliminated.

As a final example, consider the question most often asked of *L'Allegro* and *Il Penseroso*. Is the mode of being that is presented in one poem to be preferred to the mode of being that is presented in the other? As it is usually posed, this is a spatial question which is to be answered by examining the two poems as objects and toting up the attitudes or judgments they contain. Not surprisingly, this procedure has led only to disagreement and dispute. If, however, we turn the spatial question into a temporal one, an unambiguous answer is immediately forthcoming because preference or choice is no longer an issue. The pressure for choice is the creation of the assumptions of the critics who make it. The experience of the poems, however, exerts no such pressure, because in the order of their reading, the faculties of judgment and discrimination come into play only in *Il Penseroso*.[23] Were that order reversed, the reflective self-consciousness encouraged by *Il Penseroso* would also encourage a critical attitude toward the flatness of implication characteristic of *L'Allegro,* and we would be unable to read that poem with the innocence (absence of responsibility) which is both its subject and its gift. The present order, the order Milton gave us, allows the pleasure of reading *L'Allegro* to be an "unreproved pleasure free," and only then does it introduce us to another pleasure (by giving us another experience) which does not so much reprove the first as remove it from memory. Allen ends his fine essay on the poems by speaking of "a ceaseless passing from one chamber of experience to the next."[24] It is that passing, rather than any after-the-fact judgment one could make on it, that I have tried to describe.

5

Facts and Fictions: A Reply to Ralph Rader

[RALPH RADER'S ESSAY in *Critical Inquiry* gave me an opportunity to defend and refine my version of reader-response analysis. I was particularly concerned to detach the structure of the reader's experience from the formal structure of the text, and I went so far as to assert that rather than proceeding from formal units, my analyses were responsible for bringing formal units into being. The trouble with this assertion is that it undercuts my criticism of Rader for allowing his assumptions to dictate what he is able to see, and in the concluding paragraph I am forced to acknowledge that everything I have said about his procedures applies as well to my own. In short, I was already in the process of giving up any claim to generality and objectivity, and substituting for it the weaker, and finally untenable, claim that mine was a superior fiction. I was thus flirting with a relativism that would be removed only when the notion of interpretive communities, grounded in a bedrock of belief, allowed me to preserve the distinction between the fictional and the true by understanding it as a conventional or community-specific distinction rather than as one rooted in nature and eternity.]

R ALPH RADER'S MODEL of literary activity is built up (or rather down) from a theory of intention. A literary work, he believes, embodies a "cognitive act,"[1] an act variously characterized as a "positive constructive intention" (*Fact,* p. 253), "an overall creative intention" (*Concept,* p. 86), and a "comprehensive intention" (*Concept,* p. 88). To read a literary work is to perform an answering "act of cognition" (*Fact,* p. 250), which is in effect the comprehension of this comprehensive intention, the assigning to the work of a "single coherent meaning" (*Concept,* p. 86).

136

Both acts—the embodying and the assigning—are one-time, single-shot performances. They are "ends" in two senses: the overall intention is the end to which everything in the work must be contributory, and its comprehension is something the reader does at the end (of a sentence, paragraph, poem).

Rader offers this model as if it were descriptive, as if it made explicit rules of behavior we unerringly follow, rules which underlie our "tacit or intuitive capacity" (*Fact,* p. 249) of intention producing and intention retrieving. But the model is, in fact, prescriptive since it quite arbitrarily limits this same capacity: authors are limited to no more than one positive constructive intention per unit, while readers or interpreters are limited to its discovery: whatever cannot be related to that discovery or interferes with it will either be declared not to exist (Rader will later say that such interferences "are not actively registered") or, if its existence cannot be denied, it will be labeled a defect, an *"unintended and unavoidable negative consequence* of the artist's positive constructive intention" (*Fact,* p. 253). The category of unintended negative consequences is a wonderful one. In every instance it will be filled by whatever does not accord with what Rader has decreed to be the positive constructive intention; it is a limbo for the safe disposal of everything his assumptions will not allow him to recognize or legitimize.

As a theory, this is, as Rader says, "inflexible" (*Fact,* p. 246), but the word is not so innocent as he would have us believe, because the inflexibility protects rather than tests his thesis by simply ruling out of court (or out of existence) anything that would challenge it. This is reflected in the words he himself uses: "Intelligibility . . . *overrides* any other interpretive consideration" (*Fact,* p. 252; my italics); incoherencies and ambiguities are to be *"eliminated"* (*Concept,* p. 86; my italics); to interpret is to "discover that meaning which renders the whole coherent and significant, to the *exclusion* of partial and incomplete meanings" (*Concept,* p. 85; my italics); it is the business of the interpreter "to *rule out* the assignment of meanings to a work of literature which cannot be pleasurably experienced within the tacit comprehension of the work" (*Fact,* p. 250; my italics). This last is a good instance of the way in which concepts that look as if they lend independent support to Rader's thesis are actually reformulations of it. As an abverb, "pleasurably" would seem to supply an additional reason for carrying through the program of ruling out meanings: to do so is, besides its other advantages, pleasurable in a sense independently defined. But for Rader pleasure is equivalent to the absence of interference or ambiguity in the course of reading and interpreting; that is, rather than justifying his program, the word is redefined so as to coincide with its aims: one experiences pleasure when and only when "irrelevant" meanings are ruled out. Any other definition of pleasure would presumably itself be ruled out, not because it had been shown to be incorrect but because it could be used to honor experiences other than the one Rader is prepared to recognize.[2] The system works because it cannot help but work, because its terms of praise and dispraise are implicit in and identical with the definitions which initiate its procedures. Rader himself declares as much in a characteristically full and careful statement of his assumptions:

> The understanding we have of literature and the pleasure we take in it . . . derive from . . . a comprehensive inferential grasp of an author's overall creative intention in a work, which allows us to eliminate in the act of reading any potential incoherencies and ambiguities which cannot be resolved within our appreciation of the coherence of the whole. (*Concept*, p. 86)

The only word which seems to me to ring falsely here is "allows"; the word should be "directs" or even "requires"; for this definition of pleasure is also a program (a set of marching orders) designed to generate only descriptions that satisfy it.

At several points, Rader characterizes my work as rigorous, and I must return the compliment. However, this rigor (or inflexibility) does not, as he would claim, result in an ever closer "approximation to the truth" (*Fact*, p. 246); rather, it maintains a picture of the truth as he would like it to be; it is a holding action, not a discovery procedure. It works, he says, "by extending a strong generalization over the widest possible range of fact toward potential refutation. The more disparate the in-

dependent facts that general premises can be shown logically
to entail, the more the premises may be assumed to reflect the
actual underlying structure of the fact" (*Fact*, p. 246). But the
potential refutation could never occur because the generalization is extended by recasting the "facts" in its own image; the
"general premises" entail nothing but themselves; the structure they uncover is the structure of their own formulations.
Consider for example Rader's discussion of what he calls the
"independently specifiable facts" (*Fact*, p. 246) of our literary
experience. These facts are of two kinds, direct and indirect (or
problematical) facts. Direct facts come to light in the range of
agreements that have emerged in the course of literary history,
agreements about what works mean, about the relative worth
of works and authors, about what is literary and nonliterary,
and about what constitutes the requirements for membership
in a genre.[3] Indirect facts are those implied by the range of disagreements, by what has been left "unexplained" (*Fact*, p. 246)
by previous interpretations. So far this could be a distinction of
two kinds of literary experiences, one that encourages the specification of a "single coherent meaning" or "overall creative intention" and one that does not; but Rader's model will only
tolerate the first of these, and we can predict that the other will
either be proven not to exist or be declared evil (a defect). This
happens almost immediately when the indirect facts are said
to be signs of "failure" (*Fact*, p. 247). Success, of course, would
be marked by their "elimination" (there is a perfect homology
between Rader's interpretive procedure and his picture of the
way we read, or *ought* to read), and this is achieved on page 253,
when they are revealed to be—you guessed it—"the unintended
and unavoidable negative consequence of the artist's positive
constructive intention." Once again the system has operated by
preserving itself, by rediscovering in a subsidiary set of terms
the biases that underlie it. To have allowed the "indirect facts"
to stand (either as evidence of a legitimately different experience
or as embarrassments to the theory) would have been to en-
danger Rader's picture of the way things are; and therefore they
are not allowed to stand.

Rader presents this picture as if it were objectively true; it

is made up out of the "independently specifiable facts" whose
existence he is supposedly proving; but in fact he is assuming
them, and with the same "logic" that characterizes his rejection
of the "revisionist view" of *Gulliver's Travels,* book 4: "The
obvious objection to the revisionist view is the absurdity of sup-
posing that Swift invented Gulliver's uniquely devastating views
only to undermine them" (*Fact,* p. 255). What is obvious about
this objection is its arbitrariness. Clearly one can argue with an
interpretation of *Gulliver's Travels* in which the Houyhnhnms
become the object of criticism, but just as clearly, to declare that
interpretation "absurd" is not to have conducted such an argument. In the same way one can surely put forward as a hypothesis
a model of reading and writing in which unambiguously embodied intentions are straightaway retrieved, but to put it forward is not to validate it as an objective account of our tacit experience (as an independently specified fact), and to proceed
from it to acts of interpretation and evaluation is not to discover
the truth but to continually *re*discover what you have arbitrarily
decided that the truth is going to be. The mechanism by which
the arbitrary decision is maintained and protected is the category
of "unintended consequence" which will accommodate (by
stigmatizing) whatever will not fit comfortably with what Rader
has declared to be the positive constructive intention. It is a
wonderful system, simultaneously inflexible and self-adjusting
(to the shape of its inflexibility), but it is by no means the reflection of a *fact*.

What then does it reflect? The answer, I think, is that it reflects a *desire,* a wish that a certain state of affairs (single intentions single-mindedly comprehended) obtain. This, I submit, is
the only "fact" in Rader's theory, the fact of the way he would
like things to be, and the related fact of his determination to re-
inscribe his desire—one might call it a fiction—at every stage
of the critical process.

I now come to Rader's criticism of my theory and practice,
although my defense (precisely the wrong word) is already implicit in the preceding pages. I have said that whatever will not
fit itself to Rader's assumptions is declared either a chimera or
a defect. Rather than dealing with counter-evidence he elimi-

nates it, if not by denying its existence, then by consigning it to the category of unintended negative consequences. One of the things he eliminates in this fashion is me.

The clearest example of Rader's strategy is his critique of my analysis of this sentence from Thomas Browne's *Religio Medici:*

> That Judas perished by hanging himself, there is no certainty in Scripture: though in one place it seems to affirm it, and by a doubt-ful word hath given occasion to translate it; yet in another place, in a more punctual description, it maketh it improbable, and seems to overthrow it.

Although I discuss the entire sentence, I am concerned mostly with the first two clauses: "That Judas perished by hanging him-self, there is no certainty in Scripture." I attempt to describe what it's like to read the sentence, and my description takes the following form: The reader is invited by the first clause to an interpretive act (which is also the inference of an intention), to wit, to assume that the proposition "Judas perished by hanging himself" is being affirmed. As a result, he stands in a certain rela-tionship to the proposition (he rests on it), but that relationship does not survive the discovery in the second clause that the status of the proposition is now in doubt (now you have it, now you don't). In other words, what the sentence does, I argue, is give the reader something (encourage him to settle into a stance) and then take it away (by making the stance he had settled into un-available); and as it continues, this "decertainizing" (a bar-barism for which I am heartily sorry) is repeated through the agency of a succession of maddeningly indefinite "its." I sup-port my analysis by pointing out what would happen if the sen-tence were reversed to read, "There is no certainty in Scripture that Judas perished by hanging himself." Since in this version the modal attitude we are to take toward the proposition is speci-fied *before* it appears, we do not commit ourselves to a position that will later have to be modified. That is to say, the status of the assertion is never in doubt because the reader knows from the beginning that it is doubtful; he is given a perspective on the state of affairs and that perspective is confirmed rather than challenged by what follows. Notice that the two sentences do not differ in syntax or semantics;[4] rather, what distinguishes them is the succession of deliberative acts to which their readers are moved. It is in the space of this difference that I perform my analyses (not only this one, but all of them), for what I call the structure of the reader's experience is nothing more or less than this succession of deliberative acts (see chap. 1, above).

Rader quite simply takes this space away from me. He begins wittily by declaring "That this analysis and conclusion are correct I do not believe," and goes on to offer the following counter-analysis:

> I do not believe that we read this or any other sentence in the piece-meal way Professor Fish suggests, taking the opportunity to go up as many semantic sidetracks toward dead ends as each segment of language considered independently might permit . . . Rather I believe that, even without a context, a reader reads this sentence (fairly easily) as he reads all sentences, by hypothesizing a comprehensive intention in terms of which the words make collective sense, to wit: "There is no certainty in Scripture that Judas perished by hanging himself. Though in one place it [Scripture] seems to affirm it [that he hanged himself] and by a doubtful word hath given occasion to translate it [that is, by a word of doubtful meaning in the original has prompted a translation which asserts that Judas hanged himself]; yet in another place, in a more punctual [that is, explicit] description, it [Scripture] makes it [the fact of hanging] improbable and seems to overthrow [that is, controvert] it [the fact of hanging]." With its meaning-oriented direction-finder, the mind gets through the tangle of references, emerging not with an experience of meaninglessness but with definite significance joined to a sense of inefficiency of expression. (We may notice, by the way, that the mind acutely attributes this inefficiency not to the ineptness of the writer, as it would with a sentence from a freshman composition, but to the development of English prose at the time the writer wrote.) (*Concept,* pp. 88–89)

This passage is made up of interdependent misunderstandings and agreements. The misunderstandings are concentrated in the word "piece-meal" and in the phrase "segments of language considered independently," which together imply that my unit of analysis is a formal unit of language (a word, a phrase, a clause) and that I conceive of reading as a "building up" of the discrete meanings these units contain. (It is this picture of what I do that leads Rader to call my method "a logical extension of the general New Critical Position.") In fact, my unit of analysis is interpretive or perceptual, and rather than proceeding directly from formal units of language, it determines what those units are. In the analysis of the Judas sentence it is true that the sequence of perceptual or interpretive acts I describe coincides with what grammarians would call the first and second clauses, but that is merely a coincidence: my unit of analysis is formed (or forms itself) at the moment when the reader hazards interpretive closure, when he enters into a relationship (of belief, desire, approval, disapproval, wonder, irritation, puzzlement, relief) with a proposition (that Judas perished by hanging himself); and that moment, while it may occur only once in the experience of a particular sentence, may just as well occur twice or three times or as many times as the preceding acts of closure and interpretation are modified or revised. There is no way to predict just how many times and in what ways this will occur by scanning the physical features of a text, because there is no regular invariant relationship between those features (which are in any case merely statistical) and the deliberative acts readers perform. Thus I could point to or write any number of sentences the reading of which would involve the sequence of commitment to a proposition followed by a questioning of its status, and none of these sentences would necessarily have the physical configurations of the one by Browne.[5]

Once this misunderstanding is cleared up, it becomes obvious that Rader and I are in some ways not so far apart after all. For his "hypothesizing a comprehensive intention" is exactly equivalent to my "hazarding perceptual or interpreted closure," to my deliberative act. Where we disagree is (1) in the number of times this occurs and (2) in the status of acts of hypothesizings preliminary to a final one. Rader would like to deny the existence of these preliminary acts,[6] but in the context of this particular example he can only do this with the first two clauses, which, he says, can be read easily by hypothesizing a comprehensive intention, to wit: "There is no certainty in Scripture that Judas perished by hanging himself." What Rader has done

of course is rewrite the sentence so that the comprehensive intention can be easily and immediately hypothesized; that is, he
pretends that the sentence always was the way it is when he figures it out at the end, and then he reverses the clauses in order
to eliminate all traces of the figuring out. Immediately the very
heart of my analysis—that moment when the reader, having settled into a stance, must resituate himself—disappears, is made
never to have happened. The rest of the sentence, however, does
not admit of so neat and final a solution, and Rader resorts to
bracketed interpolations in order to show how easily it can be
read. Of course it shows exactly the reverse (it is somewhat more
taxing than the bare text), marking out precisely those points at
which the reader must perform the adjustments I describe.
Rader, then, acknowledges those adjustments, both with the
brackets and in his description of the experience to whose complexity they testify ("With its meaning-oriented direction-finder,
the mind gets through the tangle of references"), but the acknowledgment is obviously dismissive; the "getting through"
has the wholly negative value of slogging through a swamp on
the way to the dry and promised land; it is both unfortunate and
(finally) inconsequential. In my model, it is everything. That is,
the getting throughs, the figuring outs, the false starts, the interpretations (as it turns out) prematurely hazarded are not in
my analyses regarded as the disposable machinery of extraction;
rather, they are the acts of structuring and restructuring, hypothesizing and dehypothesizing, stance taking and stance revising, the succession of which is the structure of the reader's experience. For Rader they are what the relentless operation of his
model—his desire—dictates they be, unintended and unavoidable negative consequences. In this case they are the negative
consequences not of an author's intention (which could only be
to communicate clearly and immediately) but of the inefficiency
of his medium. Rader, it seems, preaches not only a teleology of
the sentence but a teleology of the language. Not content with
limiting authors to a single intention (to communicate clearly
and immediately), he decrees that the achieving of that intention will be the only authorized goal of English prose.

"Goal" is the key word in the last sentence because it pinpoints the area of disagreement between Rader and me. In another critique he complains that my analysis of a three-line simile forces into undue prominence difficulties which "are not actively registered when the construction is understood" (*Fact*, p. 268); but it is clear that "when" means "after"; the difficulties *have* registered, but since they do not contribute to the "single coherent meaning," and indeed impede its realization, they are given no status except the predictable and negative status of unintended consequences. The same fate is accorded large sections of *Paradise Lost*. The "negative features" of the poem (the points at which the reader is made to feel distress or confusion) cannot be ignored—"they are quite definite and real" (*Fact*, p. 268)— but they can be explained (away) as the defects of Milton's intention to "pleasingly justify the ways of God to man" (*Fact*, p. 267). Notice how by adding "pleasingly" to Milton's statement, Rader arbitrarily limits the ways in which the intention can be achieved.) The pattern is always the same: everything the reader does which conflicts with or precedes the assigning of a final meaning either is made to disappear or is discarded as an imperfection. Rader calls his method the "polar opposite" of mine, but the situation is more complex. I believe, as he does, that as we read we hypothesize comprehensive intentions, get through tangles of references, eliminate ambiguities, exclude or rule out partial and incomplete meanings; but where he believes either that we do these things only once or that only one of the times we do them counts, I believe that we do them again and again (as many times as we are moved to perceptual closure) and that each instance of our doing them (not merely the last) has value. Rader asserts that until a construction is complete and its comprehensive intention "comes into focus," the words "cannot be said to have made sense at all" (*Fact*, p. 264); but we, as significance fabricating beings, have been making and remaking sense all the time, and I am in the business of describing not the sense but our persistent efforts to make it. It is a business Rader summarily closes down because his wish for a world whose only morality is univocal efficiency cannot tolerate it.

Of course everything I have said about Rader's procedures applies as well to my own. I too have assumptions which dictate the shape of my analyses and are inevitably confirmed by them. I assume that readers are always performing interpretive or structuring acts—variously characterized as pieces of deliberative reasonings, instances of perceptual strategies, specifications of authorial intentions, enterings into relationships with—and lo and behold I discover readers who are performing just those acts. There are, however, two differences: (1) I am aware that my model is an interpretation of reality rather than an approximation of it; and (2) my model is more generous than his because I can acknowledge his "reality" while he must exclude mine. In short, what Rader has demonstrated is not that I am wrong but that my fiction creates and honors facts which his fiction will not allow him to recognize. What I have demonstrated is that he is right.[7]

6
Interpreting the Variorum

[THIS ESSAY was written in three stages and, as it finally stands, is something of a self-consuming artifact. The original version was prepared in 1973 for a Modern Language Association forum organized by Frederic Jameson and was intended as a brief for reader-oriented criticism. I seized upon the publication of the Milton *Variorum* because it greatly facilitated what had long since become my method, the surveying of the critical history of a work in order to find disputes that rested upon a base of agreement of which the disputants were unaware. I then identified that base with the experience of a work, and argued that formalist criticism, because it is spatial rather than temporal in its emphasis, either ignored or suppressed what is really happening in the act of reading. Thus, in the case of three sonnets by Milton, what is really happening depends upon a moment of hesitation or syntactic slide, when a reader is invited to make a certain kind of sense only to discover (at the beginning of the next line) that the sense he has made is either incomplete or simply wrong. "In a formalist analysis," I complain, "that moment will disappear, either because it has been flattened out and made into an (insoluble) crux or because it has been eliminated in the course of a procedure that is incapable of finding value in temporal phenomena."

What I did not then see is that the moment that disappears in a formalist analysis is the moment that has been made to appear in another kind of analysis, the kind of analysis I was urging in this essay. This is the point of the second stage of the essay, which begins by declaring that formal features do not exist independently of the reader's experience and ends by admitting that my account of the reader's experience is itself the product of a set of interpretive assumptions. In other words, the facts that I cite as ones ignored by a formalist criticism (premature conclusions, double syntax, misidentification of speakers) are not discovered but *created* by the criticism I was myself practicing. The indictment of the first two

sections—that a bad (because spatial) model had suppressed what
was really happening—loses its force because of my realization that
the notion "really happening" is just one more interpretation. This
realization immediately presented me with the problem that led me
in the fall of 1975 to write the final section, the problem of accounting for the agreement readers often reach and for the principled
ways in which they disagree. It was at this point that I elaborated
the notion of interpretive communities as an explanation both for
the difference we see—and, by seeing, make—and for the fact that
those differences are not random or idiosyncratic but systematic and
conventional. The essay thus concludes with a perspective that is
not at all the perspective with which it began, and it is from that
perspective that the essays subsequent to this one are written.]

The Case for Reader-Response Analysis

THE FIRST TWO VOLUMES of the Milton
Variorum Commentary have now appeared,
and I find them endlessly fascinating. My inter-
est, however, is not in the questions they manage to resolve (although these are many) but in the theoretical assumptions
which are responsible for their occasional failures. These failures
constitute a pattern, one in which a host of commentators—separated by as much as two hundred and seventy years but contemporaries in their shared concerns—are lined up on either
side of an interpretive crux. Some of these are famous, even
infamous: what is the two-handed engine in *Lycidas?* what is
the meaning of Haemony in *Comus?* Others, like the identity
of whoever or whatever comes to the window in *L'Allegro,* line
46, are only slightly less notorious. Still others are of interest
largely to those who make editions: matters of pronoun refer-
ents, lexical ambiguities, punctuation. In each instance, however, the pattern is consistent: every position taken is supported
by wholly convincing evidence—in the case of *L'Allegro* and
the coming to the window there is a persuasive champion for
every proper noun within a radius of ten lines—and the editorial procedure always ends either in the graceful throwing up
of hands or in the recording of a disagreement between the two

editors themselves. In short, these are problems that apparently cannot be solved, at least not by the methods traditionally brought to bear on them. What I would like to argue is that they are not *meant* to be solved but to be experienced (they signify), and that consequently any procedure that attempts to determine which of a number of readings is correct will necessarily fail. What this means is that the commentators and editors have been asking the wrong questions and that a new set of questions based on new assumptions must be formulated. I would like at least to make a beginning in that direction by examining some of the points in dispute in Milton's sonnets. I choose the sonnets because they are brief and because one can move easily from them to the theoretical issues with which this paper is finally concerned.

Milton's twentieth sonnet—"Lawrence of virtuous father virtuous son"—has been the subject of relatively little commentary. In it the poet invites a friend to join him in some distinctly Horatian pleasures—a neat repast intermixed with conversation, wine, and song, a respite from labor all the more enjoyable because outside the earth is frozen and the day sullen. The only controversy the sonnet has inspired concerns its final two lines:

> Lawrence of virtuous father virtuous son,
> > Now that the fields are dank, and ways are mire,
> > Where shall we sometimes meet, and by the fire
> > Help waste a sullen day; what may be won
> From the hard season gaining; time will run   5
> > On smoother, till Favonius reinspire
> > The frozen earth; and clothe in fresh attire
> > The lily and rose, that neither sowed nor spun.
> What neat repast shall feast us, light and choice,
> > Of Attic taste, with wine, whence we may rise   10
> > To hear the lute well touched, or artful voice
> Warble immortal notes and Tuscan air?
> > He who of those delights can judge, and spare
> > To interpose them oft, is not unwise.[1]

The focus of the controversy is the word "spare," for which two readings have been proposed: leave time for and refrain from.

Obviously the point is crucial if one is to resolve the sense of the lines. In one reading "those delights" are being recommended—he who can leave time for them is not unwise; in the other, they are the subject of a warning—he who knows when to refrain from them is not unwise. The proponents of the two interpretations cite as evidence both English and Latin syntax, various sources and analogues, Milton's "known attitudes" as they are found in his other writings, and the unambiguously expressed sentiments of the following sonnet on the same question. Surveying these arguments, A. S. P. Woodhouse roundly declares: "It is plain that all the honours rest with" the meaning "refrain from" or "forbear to." This declaration is followed immediately by a bracketed paragraph initialled D. B. for Douglas Bush, who, writing presumably after Woodhouse has died, begins "In spite of the array of scholarly names the case for 'forbear to' may be thought much weaker, and the case for 'spare time for' much stronger, than Woodhouse found them."[2] Bush then proceeds to review much of the evidence marshaled by Woodhouse and to draw from it exactly the opposite conclusion. If it does nothing else, this curious performance anticipates a point I shall make in a few moments: evidence brought to bear in the course of formalist analyses—that is, analyses generated by the assumption that meaning is embedded in the artifact—will always point in as many directions as there are interpreters; that is, not only will it prove something, it will prove anything.

It would appear then that we are back at square one, with a controversy that cannot be settled because the evidence is inconclusive. But what if that controversy is *itself* regarded as evidence, not of an ambiguity that must be removed, but of an ambiguity that readers have always experienced? What, in other words, if for the question "what does 'spare' mean?" we substitute the question "what does the fact that the meaning of 'spare' has always been an issue mean"? The advantage of this question is that it can be answered. Indeed it has already been answered by the readers who are cited in the *Variorum Commentary*. What these readers debate is the judgment the poem makes on the delights of recreation; what their debate indicates is that the judgment is blurred by a verb that can be made to

participate in contradictory readings. (Thus the important thing
about the evidence surveyed in the *Variorum* is not how it is
marshaled but that it could be marshaled at all, because it then
becomes evidence of the equal availability of both interpretations.) In other words, the lines first generate a pressure for
judgment—"he who of those delights can judge"—and then
decline to deliver it; the pressure, however, still exists, and it is
transferred from the words on the page to the reader (the reader
is "he who"), who comes away from the poem not with a statement but with a responsibility, the responsibility of deciding
when and how often—if at all—to indulge in "those delights"
(they remain delights in either case). This transferring of responsibility from the text to its readers is what the lines ask us
to do—it is the essence of their experience—and in my terms
it is therefore what the lines *mean*. It is a meaning the *Variorum*
critics attest to even as they resist it, for what they are laboring
so mightily to do by fixing the sense of the lines is to give the responsibility back. The text, however, will not accept it and remains determinedly evasive, even in its last two words, "not unwise." In their position these words confirm the impossibility
of extracting from the poem a moral formula, for the assertion
(certainly too strong a word) they complete is of the form, "He
who does such and such, of him it cannot be said that he is unwise"; but of course neither can it be said that he is wise. Thus
what Bush correctly terms the "defensive" "not unwise" operates
to prevent us from attaching the label "wise" to any action, including *either* of the actions—leaving time for or refraining
from—represented by the ambiguity of "spare." Not only is the
pressure of judgment taken off the poem, it is taken off the activity the poem at first pretended to judge. The issue is finally
not the moral status of "those delights"—they become in
seventeenth-century terms "things indifferent"—but on the
good or bad uses to which they can be put by readers who are
left, as Milton always leaves them, to choose and manage by
themselves.

Let us step back for a moment and see how far we've come.
We began with an apparently insoluble problem and proceeded,
not to solve it, but to make it signify, first by regarding it as

evidence of an experience and then by specifying for that experience a meaning. Moreover, the configurations of that experience, when they are made available by a reader-oriented analysis, serve as a check against the endlessly inconclusive adducing
of evidence which characterizes formalist analysis. That is to
say, any determination of what "spare" means (in a positivist
or literal sense) is liable to be upset by the bringing forward of
another analogue, or by a more complete computation of statistical frequencies, or by the discovery of new biographical information, or by anything else; but if we first determine that
everything in the line before "spare" creates the expectation
of an imminent judgment then the ambguity of "spare" can be
assigned a significance in the context of that expectation. (It
disappoints it and transfers the pressure of judgment to us.) That
context is experiential, and it is within its contours and constraints that significances are established (both in the act of reading and in the analysis of that act). In formalist analyses the only
constraints are the notoriously open-ended possibilities and combination of possibilities that emerge when one begins to consult dictionaries and grammars and histories; to consult dictionaries, grammars, and histories is to assume that meanings
can be specified independently of the activity of reading; what
the example of "spare" shows is that it is in and by that activity
that meanings—experiential, not positivist—are created.

In other words, it is the structure of the reader's experience
rather than any structures available on the page that should be
the object of description. In the case of Sonnet 20, that experiential structure was uncovered when an examination of
formal structures led to an impasse; and the pressure to remove
that impasse led to the substitution of one set of questions for
another. It will more often be the case that the pressure of a spectacular failure will be absent. The sins of formalist-positivist
analysis are primarily sins of omission, not an inability to explain
phenomena but an inability to see that they are there because its
assumptions make it inevitable that they will be overlooked or
suppressed. Consider, for example, the concluding lines of another of Milton's sonnets, "Avenge O Lord thy slaughtered
saints."

Avenge O Lord thy slaughtered saints, whose bones
   Lie scattered on the Alpine mountains cold,
   Even them who kept thy truth so pure of old
   When all our fathers worshipped stocks and stones,
Forget not: in thy book record their groans   5
   Who were thy sheep and in their ancient fold
   Slain by the bloody Piedmontese that rolled
   Mother with infant down the rocks. Their moans
The vales redoubled to the hills, and they
   To heaven. Their martyred blood and ashes sow   10
   O'er all the Italian fields where still doth sway
The triple Tyrant: that from these may grow
   A hundredfold, who having learnt thy way
   Early may fly the Babylonian woe.

In this sonnet, the poet simultaneously petitions God and wonders aloud about the justice of allowing the faithful—"Even them who kept thy truth"—to be so brutally slaughtered. The note struck is alternately one of plea and complaint, and there is more than a hint that God is being called to account for what has happened to the Waldensians. It is generally agreed, however, that the note of complaint is less and less sounded and that the poem ends with an affirmation of faith in the ultimate operation of God's justice. In this reading, the final lines are taken to be saying something like this: From the blood of these martyred, O God, raise up a new and more numerous people, who, by virtue of an early education in thy law, will escape destruction by fleeing the Babylonian woe. Babylonian woe has been variously glossed;[3] but whatever it is taken to mean it is always read as part of a statement that specifies a set of conditions for the escaping of destruction or punishment; it is a warning to the reader as well as a petition to God. As a warning, however, it is oddly situated since the conditions it seems to specify were in fact met by the Waldensians, who of all men most followed God's laws. In other words, the details of their story would seem to undercut the affirmative moral the speaker proposes to draw from it. It is further undercut by a reading that is fleetingly available, although no one has acknowledged it because it is a function not of the words on the page but of the experience of the reader. In that experience, line 13 will for a moment be accepted as a complete sense unit and the emphasis of the line will fall on "thy way" (a phrase that has received absolutely no attention in the commentaries). At this point "thy way" can refer only to the way in which God has dealt with the Waldensians. That is, "thy way" seems to pick up the note of outrage with which the poem began, and if we continue to so interpret it, the conclusion of the poem will be a grim one indeed: since by this example it appears that God rains down punishment indiscriminately, it would be best perhaps to withdraw from the arena of his service, and thereby hope at least to be safely out of the line of fire. This is not the conclusion we carry away, because as line 14 unfolds, another reading of "thy way" becomes available, a reading in which "early" qualifies "learnt" and refers to something the faithful should do (learn thy way at an early age) rather than to something God has failed to do (save the Waldensians). These two readings are answerable to the pulls exerted by the beginning and ending of the poem: the outrage expressed in the opening lines generates a pressure for an explanation, and the grimmer reading is answerable to that pressure (even if it is also disturbing); the ending of the poem, the forward and upward movement of lines 10–14, creates the expectation of an affirmation, and the second reading fulfills that expectation. The criticism shows that in the end we settle on the more optimistic reading—it feels better—but even so the other has been a part of our experience, and because it has been a part of our experience, it *means*. What it means is that while we may be able to extract from the poem a statement affirming God's justice, we are not allowed to forget the evidence (of things seen) that makes the extraction so difficult (both for the speaker and for us). It is a difficulty we experience in the act of reading, even though a criticism which takes no account of that act has, as we have seen, suppressed it.

In each of the sonnets we have considered, the significant word or phrase occurs at a line break where a reader is invited to place it first in one and then in another structure of syntax and sense. This moment of hesitation, of semantic or syntactic slide, is crucial to the experience the verse provides, but in a formalist analysis that moment will disappear, either because it has been flattened out and made into an (insoluble) interpretive crux or because it has been eliminated in the course of a procedure that is incapable of finding value in temporal phenomena. In the case of "When I consider how my light is spent," these two failures are combined.

> When I consider how my light is spent,
>   Ere half my days, in this dark world and wide,
>   And that one talent which is death to hide,
>   Lodged with me useless, though my soul more bent   5
> To serve therewith my maker, and present
>   My true account, lest he returning chide,
>   Doth God exact day-labour, light denied,
>   I fondly ask; but Patience to prevent
> That murmur, soon replies, God doth not need
>   Either man's work or his own gifts, who best   10
>   Bear his mild yoke, they serve him best, his state
> Is kingly. Thousands at his bidding speed
>   And post o'er land and ocean without rest:
>   They also serve who only stand and wait.

The interpretive crux once again concerns the final line: "They also serve who only stand and wait." For some this is an unqualified acceptance of God's will, while for others the note of affirmation is muted or even forced. The usual kinds of evidence are marshaled by the opposing parties, and the usual inconclusiveness is the result. There are some areas of agreement. "All the interpretations," Woodhouse remarks, "recognize that the sonnet commences from a mood of depression, frustration [and] impatience."[4] The object of impatience is a God who would first demand service and then take away the means of serving, and the oft noted allusion to the parable of the talents lends scriptural support to the accusation the poet is implicitly making: you have cast the wrong servant into unprofitable darkness. It has also been observed that the syntax and rhythm of these early lines, and especially of lines 6–8, are rough and uncertain; the speaker is struggling with his agitated thoughts and he changes directions abruptly, with no regard for the line as a unit of sense. The poem, says one critic, "seems almost out of control."[5]

The question I would ask is "whose control?" For what these formal descriptions point to (but do not acknowledge) is the extraordinary number of adjustments required of readers who would negotiate these lines. The first adjustment is the result of the expectations created by the second half of line 6—"lest he returning chide." Since there is no full stop after "chide," it is natural to assume that this will be an introduction to reported speech, and to assume further that what will be reported is the poet's anticipation of the voice of God as it calls him, to an unfair accounting. This assumption does not survive line 7—"Doth God exact day-labour, light denied"—which, rather than chiding the poet for his inactivity, seems to rebuke him for having expected that chiding. The accents are precisely those heard so often in the Old Testament when God answers a reluctant Gideon, or a disputatious Moses, or a self-justifying Job: do you presume to judge my ways or to appoint my motives? Do you think I would exact day labor, light denied? In other words, the poem seems to turn at this point from a questioning of God to a questioning of that questioning; or, rather, the reader turns from the one to the other in the act of revising his projection of what line 7 will say and do. As it turns out, however, that revision must itself be revised because it had been made within the assumption that what we are hearing is the voice of God. This assumption falls before the very next phrase, "I fondly ask," which requires not one but two adjustments. Since the speaker of line 7 is firmly identified as the poet, the line must be reinterpreted as a continuation of his complaint—Is that the way you operate, God, denying light, but exacting labor?—but even as that interpretation emerges, the poet withdraws from it by inserting the adverb "fondly," and once again the line slips out of the reader's control.

In a matter of seconds, then, line 7 has led four experiential lives, one as we anticipate it, another as that anticipation is revised, a third when we retroactively identify its speaker, and a fourth when that speaker disclaims it. What changes in each of these lives is the status of the poet's murmurings—they are alternately expressed, rejected, reinstated, and qualified—and as the sequence ends, the reader is without a firm perspective on the question of record: does God deal justly with his servants?

A firm perspective appears to be provided by Patience, whose entrance into the poem, the critics tell us, gives it both argumentative and metrical stability. But in fact the presence of Patience in the poem finally assures its continuing instability by making it impossible to specify the degree to which the speaker approves, or even participates in, the affirmation of the final line: "They also serve who only stand and wait." We know that Patience to prevent the poet's murmur soon replies (not soon enough however to prevent the murmur from registering), but we do not know when that reply ends. Does Patience fall silent in line 12, after "kingly"? or at the conclusion of line 13? or not at all? Does the poet appropriate these lines or share them or simply listen to them, as we do? These questions are unanswerable, and it is because they remain unanswerable that the poem ends uncertainly. The uncertainty is not in the statement it makes—in isolation line 14 is unequivocal—but in our inability to assign that statement to either the poet or to Patience. Were the final line marked unambiguously for the poet, then we would receive it as a resolution of his earlier doubts; and were it marked for Patience, it would be a sign that those doubts were still very much in force. It is marked for neither, and therefore we are without the satisfaction that a firmly conclusive ending (in *any* direction) would have provided. In short, we leave the poem unsure, and our unsureness is the realization (in our experience) of the unsureness with which the affirmation of the final line is, or is not, made. (This unsureness also operates to actualize the two possible readings of "wait": wait in the sense of expecting, that is waiting for an opportunity to serve actively; or wait in the sense of waiting *in* service, a waiting that is itself fully satisfying because the impulse to self-glorifying action has been stilled.)

The question debated in the *Variorum Commentary* is, how far from the mood of frustration and impatience does the poem finally move? The answer given by an experiential analysis is that you can't tell, and the fact that you can't tell is responsible for the uneasiness the poem has always inspired. It is that uneasiness which the critics inadvertently acknowledge when they argue about the force of the last line, but they are unable to make analytical use of what they acknowledge because they have no way of dealing with or even recognizing experiential (that is, temporal) structures. In fact, more than one editor has eliminated those structures by punctuating them out of existence: first by putting a full stop at the end of line 6 and thereby making it unlikely that the reader will assign line 7 to God (there will no longer be an expectation of reported speech), and then by supplying quotation marks for the sestet in order to remove any doubts one might have as to who is speaking. There is of course no warrant for these emendations, and in 1791 Thomas Warton had the grace and honesty to admit as much. "I have," he said, "introduced the turned commas both in the question and answer, not from any authority, but because they seem absolutely necessary to the sense."[6]

Undoing the Case for Reader-Response Analysis

Editorial practices like these are only the most obvious manifestations of the assumptions to which I stand opposed: the assumption that there *is* a sense, that it is embedded or encoded in the text, and that it can be taken in at a single glance. These assumptions are, in order, positivist, holistic, and spatial, and to have them is to be committed both to a goal and to a procedure. The goal is to settle on a meaning, and the procedure involves first stepping back from the text, and then putting together or otherwise calculating the discrete units of significance it contains. My quarrel with this procedure (and with the assumptions that generate it) is that in the course of following it through the reader's activities are at once ignored and devalued. They are ignored because the text is taken to be self-sufficient—everything is *in* it—and they are devalued because when they are thought of at all, they are thought of as the disposable machinery of extraction. In the procedures I would urge, the reader's activities are at the center of attention, where they are regarded not as leading to meaning but as *having* meaning. The meaning they have is a consequence of their not being empty; for they include the making and revising of assumptions, the rendering and re-

gretting of judgments, the coming to and abandoning of conclusions, the giving and withdrawing of approval, the specifying
of causes, the asking of questions, the supplying of answers, the
solving of puzzles. In a word, these activities are interpretive—
rather than being preliminary to questions of value, they are at
every moment settling and resettling questions of value—and
because they are interpretive, a description of them will also
be, and without any additional step, an interpretation, not after
the fact but of the fact (of experiencing). It will be a description
of a moving field of concerns, at once wholly present (not waiting
for meaning but constituting meaning) and continually in the
act of reconstituting itself.

As a project such a description presents enormous difficulties, and there is hardly time to consider them here;[7] but it
should be obvious from my brief examples how different it is
from the positivist-formalist project. Everything depends on the
temporal dimension, and as a consequence the notion of a mistake, at least as something to be avoided, disappears. In a sequence where a reader first structures the field he inhabits and
then is asked to restructure it (by changing an assignment of
speaker or realigning attitudes and positions) there is no question of priority among his structurings; no one of them, even
if it is the last, has privilege; each is equally legitimate, each
equally the proper object of analysis, because each is equally an
event in his experience.

The firm assertiveness of this paragraph only calls attention
to the questions it avoids. Who is this reader? How can I presume
to describe his experiences, and what do I say to readers who report that they do not have the experiences I describe? Let me
answer these questions or rather make a beginning at answering
them in the context of another example, this time from Milton's
Comus. In line 46 of *Comus* we are introduced to the villain by
way of a genealogy:

> Bacchus that first from out the purple grape,
> Crushed the sweet poison of misused wine.

In almost any edition of this poem, a footnote will tell you
that Bacchus is the god of wine. Of course most readers already
know that, and because they know it, they will be anticipating

the appearance of "wine" long before they come upon it in the
final position. Moreover, they will also be anticipating a negative
judgment on it, in part because of the association of Bacchus
with revelry and excess, and especially because the phrase "sweet
poison" suggests that the judgment has already been made. At an
early point then, we will have both filled in the form of the
assertion and made a decision about its moral content. That
decision is upset by the word "misused"; for what "misused"
asks us to do is transfer the pressure of judgment from wine
(where we have already placed it) to the abusers of wine, and
therefore when "wine" finally appears, we must declare it innocent of the charges we have ourselves made.

This, then, is the structure of the reader's experience—the
transferring of a moral label from a thing to those who appropriate it. It is an experience that depends on a reader for whom
the name Bacchus has precise and immediate associations; another reader, a reader for whom those associations are less precise will not have that experience because he will not have rushed
to a conclusion in relation to which the word "misused" will
stand as a challenge. Obviously I am discriminating between
these two readers and between the two equally real experiences
they will have. It is not a discrimination based simply on information, because what is important is not the information
itself, but the action of the mind which its possession makes
possible for one reader and impossible for the other. One might
discriminate further between them by noting that the point at
issue—whether value is a function of objects and actions or of
intentions—is at the heart of the seventeenth-century debate
over "things indifferent." A reader who is aware of that debate
will not only *have* the experience I describe; he will recognize
at the end of it that he has been asked to take a position on one
side of a continuing controversy; and that recognition (also a
part of his experience) will be part of the disposition with which
he moves into the lines that follow.

It would be possible to continue with this profile of the op-
timal reader, but I would not get very far before someone would
point out that what I am really describing is the intended reader,
the reader whose education, opinions, concerns, linguistic competences, and so on make him capable of having the experience

the author wished to provide. I would not resist this characterization because it seems obvious that the efforts of readers are always efforts to discern and therefore to realize (in the sense of becoming) an author's intention. I would only object if that realization were conceived narrowly, as the single act of comprehending an author's purpose, rather than (as I would conceive it) as the succession of acts readers perform in the continuing assumption that they are dealing with intentional beings. In this view discerning an intention is no more or less than understanding, and understanding includes (is constituted by) all the activities which make up what I call the structure of the reader's experience. To describe that experience is therefore to describe the reader's efforts at understanding, and to describe the reader's efforts at understanding is to describe his realization (in two senses) of an author's intention. Or to put it another way, what my analyses amount to are descriptions of a succession of decisions made by readers about an author's intention—decisions that are not limited to the specifying of purpose but include the specifying of every aspect of successively intended worlds, decisions that are precisely the shape, because they are the content, of the reader's activities.

Having said this, however, it would appear that I am open to two objections. The first is that the procedure is a circular one. I describe the experience of a reader who in his strategies is answerable to an author's intention, and I specify the author's intention by pointing to the strategies employed by that same reader. But this objection would have force only if it were possible to specify one independently of the other. What is being specified from either perspective are the conditions of utterance, of what could have been understood to have been meant by what was said. That is, intention and understanding are two ends of a conventional act, each of which necessarily stipulates (includes, defines, specifies) the other. To construct the profile of the informed or at-home reader is at the same time to characterize the author's intention and vice versa, because to do either is to specify the *contemporary* conditions of utterance, to identify, by becoming a member of, a community made up of those who share interpretive strategies.

The second objection is another version of the first: if the

content of the reader's experience is the succession of acts he
performs in search of an author's intentions, and if he performs
those acts at the bidding of the text, does not the text then produce or contain everything—intention *and* experience—and
have I not compromised my antiformalist position? This objection will have force only if the formal patterns of the text
are assumed to exist independently of the reader's experience,
for only then can priority be claimed for them. Indeed, the claims
of independence and priority are one and the same; when they
are separated it is so that they can give circular and illegitimate
support to each other. The question "do formal features exist
independently?" is usually answered by pointing to their priority: they are "in" the text before the reader comes to it. The
question "are formal features prior?" is usually answered by
pointing to their independent status: they are "in" the text
before the reader comes to it. What looks like a step in an argument is actually the spectacle of an assertion supporting itself.
It follows then that an attack on the independence of formal
features will also be an attack on their priority (and vice versa),
and I would like to mount such an attack in the context of two
short passages from *Lycidas*.

The first passage (actually the second in the poem's sequence)
begins at line 42:

> The willows and the hazel copses green
> Shall now no more be seen,
> Fanning their joyous leaves to thy soft lays.

It is my thesis that the reader is always making sense (I intend
"making" to have its literal force), and in the case of these lines
the sense he makes will involve the assumption (and therefore
the creation) of a completed assertion after the word "seen," to
wit, the death of Lycidas has so affected the willows and the
hazel copses green that, in sympathy, they will wither and die
(will no more be seen by *anyone*). In other words, at the end of
line 43 the reader will have hazarded an interpretation, or performed an act of perceptual closure, or made a decision as to
what is being asserted. I do not mean that he has done four
things, but that he has done one thing the description of which

might take any one of four forms—making sense, interpreting, performing perceptual closure, deciding about what is intended. (The importance of this point will become clear later.) Whatever he has done (that is, however we characterize it), he will undo it in the act of reading the next line, for here he discovers that his closure, or making of sense, was premature and that he must make a new one in which the relationship between man and nature is exactly the reverse of what was first assumed. The willows and the hazel copses green will in fact be seen, but they will not be seen by Lycidas. It is he who will be no more, while they go on as before, fanning their joyous leaves to someone else's soft lays (the whole of line 44 is now perceived as modifying and removing the absoluteness of "seen"). Nature is not sympathetic, but indifferent, and the notion of her sympathy is one of those "false surmises" that the poem is continually encouraging and then disallowing.

The previous sentence shows how easy it is to surrender to the bias of our critical language and begin to talk as if poems, not readers or interpreters, did things. Words like "encourage" and "disallow" (and others I have used in this essay) imply agents, and it is only "natural" to assign agency first to an author's intentions and then to the forms that assumedly embody them. What really happens, I think, is something quite different: rather than intention and its formal realization producing interpretation (the "normal" picture), interpretation creates intention and its formal realization by creating the conditions in which it becomes possible to pick them out. In other words, in the analysis of these lines from *Lycidas* I did what critics always do: I "saw" what my interpretive principles permitted or directed me to see, and then I turned around and attributed what I had "seen" to a text and an intention. What my principles direct me to "see" are readers performing acts; the points at which I find (or to be more precise, declare) those acts to have been performed become (by a sleight of hand) demarcations *in* the text; those demarcations are then available for the designation "formal features," and as formal features they can be (illegitimately) assigned the responsibility for producing the interpretation which in fact produced them. In this case, the demarcation my interpretation calls into being is placed at the end of line 42; but of course the end of that (or any other) line is worth noticing or pointing out only because my model *demands* (the word is not too strong) perceptual closures and therefore locations at which they occur; in that model this point will be one of those locations, although (1) it need not have been (not every line ending occasions a closure) and (2) in another model, one that does not give value to the activities of readers, the possibility of its being one would not have arisen.

What I am suggesting is that formal units are always a function of the interpretative model one brings to bear; they are not "in" the text, and I would make the same argument for intentions. That is, intention is no more embodied "in" the text than are formal units; rather an intention, like a formal unit, is made when perceptual or interpretive closure is hazarded; it is verified by an interpretive act, and I would add, it is not verifiable in any other way. This last assertion is too large to be fully considered here, but I can sketch out the argumentative sequence I would follow were I to consider it: intention is known when and only when it is recognized; it is recognized as soon as you decide about it; you decide about it as soon as you make a sense; and you make a sense (or so my model claims) as soon as you can.

Let me tie up the threads of my argument with a final example from *Lycidas:*

> He must not float upon his wat'ry bier
> Unwept . . .   (13–14)

Here the reader's experience has much the same career as it does in lines 42–44: at the end of line 13 perceptual closure is hazarded, and a sense is made in which the line is taken to be a resolution bordering on a promise: that is, there is now an expectation that something will be done about this unfortunate situation, and the reader anticipates a call to action, perhaps even a program for the undertaking of a rescue mission. With "Unwept," however, that expectation and anticipation are disappointed, and the realization of that disappointment will be inseparable from the making of a new (and less comforting) sense:

nothing will be done; Lycidas will continue to float upon his wat'ry bier, and the only action taken will be the lamenting of the fact that no action will be efficacious, including the actions of speaking and listening to this lament (which in line 15 will receive the meretricious and self-mocking designation "melodious tear"). Three "structures" come into view at precisely the same moment, the moment when the reader having resolved a sense unresolves it and makes a new one; that moment will also be the moment of picking out a formal pattern or unit, end of line/beginning of line, and it will also be the moment at which the reader, having decided about the speaker's intention, about what is meant by what has been said, will make the decision again and in so doing will make another intention.

This, then, is my thesis: that the form of the reader's experience, formal units, and the structure of intention are one, that they come into view simultaneously, and that therefore the questions of priority and independence do not arise. What does arise is another question: what produces *them?* That is, if intention, form, and the shape of the reader's experience are simply different ways of referring to (different perspectives on) the same interpretive act, what is that act an interpretation *of?* I cannot answer that question, but neither, I would claim, can anyone else, although formalists try to answer it by pointing to patterns and claiming that they are available independently of (prior to) interpretation. These patterns vary according to the procedures that yield them: they may be statistical (number of two-syllable words per hundred words), grammatical (ratio of passive to active constructions, or of right-branching to left-branching sentences, or of anything else); but whatever they are I would argue that they do not lie innocently in the world but are themselves constituted by an interpretive act, even if, as is often the case, that act is unacknowledged. Of course, this is as true of my analyses as it is of anyone else's. In the examples offered here I appropriate the notion "line ending" and treat it as a fact of nature; and one might conclude that as a fact it is responsible for the reading experience I describe. The truth I think is exactly the reverse: line endings exist by virtue of perceptual strategies rather than the other way around. Historically, the strategy that we know as "reading (or hearing) poetry" has included paying attention to the line as a unit, but it is precisely that attention which has made the line as a unit (either of print or of aural duration) available. A reader so practiced in paying that attention that he regards the line as a brute fact rather than as a convention will have a great deal of difficulty with concrete poetry; if he overcomes that difficulty, it will not be because he has learned to ignore the line as a unit but because he will have acquired a new set of interpretive strategies (the strategies constitutive of "concrete poetry reading") in the context of which the line as a unit no longer exists. In short, what is noticed is what has been *made* noticeable, not by a clear and undistorting glass, but by an interpretive strategy.

This may be hard to see when the strategy has become so habitual that the forms it yields seem part of the world. We find it easy to assume that alliteration as an effect depends on a "fact" that exists independently of any interpretive "use" one might make of it, the fact that words in proximity begin with the same letter. But it takes only a moment's reflection to realize that the sameness, far from being natural, is enforced by an orthographic convention; that is to say, it is the product of an interpretation. Were we to substitute phonetic conventions for orthographic ones (a "reform" traditionally urged by purists), the supposedly "objective" basis for alliteration would disappear because a phonetic transcription would require that we distinguish between the initial sounds of those very words that enter into alliterative relationships; rather than conforming to those relationships, the rules of spelling make them. One might reply that, since alliteration is an aural rather than a visual phenomenon when poetry is heard, we have unmediated access to the physical sounds themselves and hear "real" similarities. But phonological "facts" are no more uninterpreted (or less conventional) than the "facts" of orthography; the distinctive features that make articulation and reception possible are the product of a system of differences that must be *imposed* before it can be recognized; the patterns the ear hears (like the patterns the eye sees) are the patterns its perceptual habits make available.

One can extend this analysis forever, even to the "facts" of grammar. The history of linguistics is the history of competing paradigms, each of which offers a different account of the constituents of language. Verbs, nouns, cleft sentences, transformations, deep and surface structures, semes, rhemes, tagmemes—now you see them, now you don't, depending on the descriptive apparatus you employ. The critic who confidently rests his analyses on the bedrock of syntactic descriptions is resting on an interpretation; the facts he points to *are* there, but only as a consequence of the interpretive (man-made) model that has called them into being.

The moral is clear: the choice is never between objectivity and interpretation but between an interpretation that is unacknowledged as such and an interpretation that is at least aware of itself. It is this awareness that I am claiming for myself, although in doing so I must give up the claims implicitly made in the first part of this essay. There I argue that a bad (because spatial) model had suppressed what was really happening, but by my own declared principles the notion "really happening" is just one more interpretation.

Interpretive Communities

It seems then that the price one pays for denying the priority of either forms or intentions is an inability to say how it is that one ever begins. Yet we do begin, and we continue, and because we do there arises an immediate counterobjection to the preceding pages. If interpretive acts are the source of forms rather than the other way around, why isn't it the case that readers are always performing the same acts or a sequence of random acts, and therefore creating the same forms or a random succession of forms? How, in short, does one explain these two "facts" of reading? (1) The same reader will perform differently when reading two "different" (the word is in quotation marks because its status is precisely what is at issue) texts; and (2) different readers will perform similarly when reading the "same" (in quotes for the same reason) text. That is to say, both the stability of interpretation among readers and the variety of interpretation in the career of a single reader would seem to argue for the existence of something independent of and prior to interpretive acts, something which produces them. I will answer this challenge by asserting that both the stability and the variety are functions of interpretive strategies rather than of texts.

Let us suppose that I am reading *Lycidas*. What is it that I am doing? First of all, what I am not doing is "simply reading," an activity in which I do not believe because it implies the possibility of pure (that is, disinterested) perception. Rather, I am proceeding on the basis of (at least) two interpretive decisions. (1) that *Lycidas* is a pastoral and (2) that it was written by Milton. (I should add that the notions "pastoral" and "Milton" are also interpretations; that is, they do not stand for a set of indisputable, objective facts; if they did, a great many books would not now be getting written.) Once these decisions have been made (and if I had not made these I would have made others, and they would be consequential in the same way), I am immediately predisposed to perform certain acts, to "find," by looking for, themes (the relationship between natural processes and the careers of men, the efficacy of poetry or of any other action), to confer significances (on flowers, streams, shepherds, pagan deities), to mark out "formal" units (the lament, the consolation, the turn, the affirmation of faith, and so on). My disposition to perform these acts (and others; the list is not meant to be exhaustive) constitutes a set of interpretive strategies, which, when they are put into execution, become the large act of reading. That is to say, interpretive strategies are not put into execution after reading (the pure act of perception in which I do not believe); they are the shape of reading, and because they are the shape of reading, they give texts their shape, making them rather than, as it is usually assumed, arising from them. Several important things follow from this account:

(1) I did not have to execute this particular set of interpretive strategies because I did not have to make those particular interpretive (pre-reading) decisions. I could have decided, for example, that *Lycidas* was a text in which a set of fantasies and defenses find expression. These decisions would have entailed the assumption of another set of interpretive strategies (perhaps like that put forward by Norman Holland in *The Dynamics of Literary Response*) and the execution of that set would have made another text.

(2) I could execute this same set of strategies when presented with texts that did not bear the title (again a notion which is itself an interpretation) *Lycidas, A Pastoral Monody*. I could decide (it is a decision some have made) that *Adam Bede* is a pastoral written by an author who consciously modeled herself on Milton (still remembering that "pastoral" and "Milton" are interpretations, not facts in the public domain); or I could decide, as Empson did, that a great many things not usually considered pastoral were in fact to be so read; and either decision would give rise to a set of interpretive strategies, which, when put into action, would *write* the text I write when reading *Lycidas*. (Are you with me?)

(3) A reader other than myself who, when presented with *Lycidas*, proceeds to put into execution a set of interpretive strategies similar to mine (how he could do so is a question I will take up later), will perform the same (or at least a similar) succession of interpretive acts. He and I then might be tempted to say that we agree about the poem (thereby assuming that the poem exists independently of the acts either of us performs); but what we really would agree about is the way to write it.

(4) A reader other than myself who, when presented with *Lycidas* (please keep in mind that the status of *Lycidas* is what is at issue), puts into execution a different set of interpretive strategies will perform a different succession of interpretive acts. (I am assuming, it is the article of my faith, that a reader will always execute some set of interpretive strategies and therefore perform some succession of interpretive acts.) One of us might then be tempted to complain to the other that we could not possibly be reading the same poem (literary criticism is full of such complaints) and he would be right; for each of us would be reading the poem he had made.

The large conclusion that follows from these four smaller ones is that the notions of the "same" or "different" texts are fictions. If I read *Lycidas* and *The Waste Land* differently (in fact I do not), it will not be because the formal structures of the two poems (to term them such is also an interpretive decision) call forth different interpretive strategies but because my predisposition to execute different interpretive strategies will *produce* different formal structures. That is, the two poems are different because I have decided that they will be. The proof of this is the possibility of doing the reverse (that is why point 2 is so important). That is to say, the answer to the question "why do different texts give rise to different sequences of interpretive acts?" is that *they don't have to,* an answer which implies strongly that "they" don't exist. Indeed, it has always been possible to put into action interpretive strategies designed to make all texts one, or to put it more accurately, to be forever making the same text. Augustine urges just such a strategy, for example, in *On Christian Doctrine* where he delivers the "rule of faith" which is of course a rule of interpretation. It is dazzlingly simple: everything in the Scriptures, and indeed in the world when it is properly read, points to (bears the meaning of) God's love for us and our answering responsibility to love our fellow creatures for His sake. If only you should come upon something which does not at first seem to bear this meaning, that "does not literally pertain to virtuous behavior or to the truth of faith," you are then to take it "to be figurative" and proceed to scrutinize it "until an interpretation contributing to the reign of charity is produced." This then is both a stipulation of what meaning there is and a set of directions for finding it, which is of course a set of directions—of interpretive strategies—for making it, that is, for the endless reproduction of the same text. Whatever one may think of this interpretive program, its success and ease of execution are attested to by centuries of Christian exegesis. It is my contention that any interpretive program, any set of interpretive strategies, can have a similar success, although few have been as spectacularly successful as this one. (For some time now, for at least three hundred years, the most successful interpretive program has gone under the name "ordinary language.") In our own discipline programs with the same characteristic of always reproducing one text include psychoanalytic criticism, Robertsonianism (always threatening to extend its sway into later and later periods), numerology (a sameness based on the assumption of innumerable fixed differences).

The other challenging question—"why will different readers execute the same interpretive strategy when faced with the 'same' text?"—can be handled in the same way. The answer is again that *they don't have to,* and my evidence is the entire history of

literary criticism. And again this answer implies that the notion "same text" is the product of the possession by two or more
readers of similar interpretive strategies.

But why should this ever happen? Why should two or more
readers ever agree, and why should regular, that is, habitual,
differences in the career of a single reader ever occur? What is
the explanation on the one hand of the stability of interpretation (at least among certain groups at certain times) and on the
other of the orderly variety of interpretation if it is not the
stability and variety of texts? The answer to all of these questions
is to be found in a notion that has been implicit in my argument, the notion of *interpretive communities*. Interpretive communities are made up of those who share interpretive strategies
not for reading (in the conventional sense) but for writing texts,
for constituting their properties and assigning their intentions.
In other words, these strategies exist prior to the act of reading
and therefore determine the shape of what is read rather than,
as is usually assumed, the other way around. If it is an article
of faith in a particular community that there are a variety of
texts, its members will boast a repertoire of strategies for making
them. And if a community believes in the existence of only one
text, then the single strategy its members employ will be forever
writing it. The first community will accuse the members of the
second of being reductive, and they in turn will call their ac-
cusers superficial. The assumption in each community will be
that the other is not correctly perceiving the "true text," but the
truth will be that each perceives the text (or texts) its interpretive
strategies demand and call into being. This, then, is the explanation both for the stability of interpretation among different
readers (they belong to the same community) and for the regu-
larity with which a single reader will employ different interpretive strategies and thus make different texts (he belongs to different communities). It also explains why there are disagreements
and why they can be debated in a principled way: not because
of a stability in texts, but because of a stability in the makeup
of interpretive communities and therefore in the opposing positions they make possible. Of course this stability is always temporary (unlike the longed for and timeless stability of the text).
Interpretive communities grow larger and decline, and indi-

viduals move from one to another; thus, while the alignments are not permanent, they are always there, providing just enough stability for the interpretive battles to go on, and just enough shift and slippage to assure that they will never be settled. The notion of interpretive communities thus stands between an impossible ideal and the fear which leads so many to maintain it. The ideal is of perfect agreement and it would require texts to have a status independent of interpretation. The fear is of interpretive anarchy, but it would only be realized if interpretation (text making) were completely random. It is the fragile but real consolidation of interpretive communities that allows us to talk to one another, but with no hope or fear of ever being able to stop.

In other words interpretive communities are no more stable than texts because interpretive strategies are not natural or universal, but learned. This does not mean that there is a point at which an individual has not yet learned any. The ability to interpret is not acquired; it is constitutive of being human. What is acquired are the ways of interpreting and those same ways can also be forgotten or supplanted, or complicated or dropped from favor ("no one reads that way anymore"). When any of these things happens, there is a corresponding change in texts, not because they are being read differently, but because they are being written differently.

The only stability, then, inheres in the fact (at least in my model) that interpretive strategies are always being deployed, and this means that communication is a much more chancy affair than we are accustomed to think it. For if there are no fixed texts, but only interpretive strategies making them, and if interpretive strategies are not natural, but learned (and are therefore unavailable to a finite description), what is it that utterers (speakers, authors, critics, me, you) do? In the old model utterers are in the business of handing over ready-made or prefabricated meanings. These meanings are said to be encoded, and the code is assumed to be in the world independently of the individuals who are obliged to attach themselves to it (if they do not they run the danger of being declared deviant). In my model, however, meanings are not extracted but made and made not by encoded forms but by interpretive strategies that call forms into being. It follows then that what utterers do is give hearers and readers the opportunity to make meanings (and texts) by inviting them to put into execution a set of strategies. It is presumed that the invitation will be recognized, and that presumption rests on a projection on the part of a speaker or author of the moves *he* would make if confronted by the sounds or marks he is uttering or setting down.

It would seem at first that this account of things simply re-introduces the old objection; for isn't this an admission that there is after all a formal encoding, not perhaps of meanings, but of the directions for making them, for executing interpretive strategies? The answer is that they will only *be* directions to those who already have the interpretive strategies in the first place. Rather than producing interpretive acts, they are the product of one. An author hazards his projection, not because of something "in" the marks, but because of something he assumes to be in his reader. The very existence of the "marks" is a function of an interpretive community, for they will be recognized (that is, made) only by its members. Those outside that community will be deploying a different set of interpretive strategies (interpretation cannot be withheld) and will therefore be making different marks.

So once again I have made the text disappear, but unfortunately the problems do not disappear with it. If everyone is continually executing interpretive strategies and in that act constituting texts, intentions, speakers, and authors, how can any one of us know whether or not he is a member of the same interpretive community as any other of us? The answer is that he can't, since any evidence brought forward to support the claim would itself be an interpretation (especially if the "other" were an author long dead). The only "proof" of membership is fellowship, the nod of recognition from someone in the same community, someone who says to you what neither of us could ever prove to a third party: "we know." I say it to you now, knowing full well that you will agree with me (that is, understand) only if you already agree with me.

7

Interpreting
"Interpreting the Variorum"

[THIS RESPONSE to a response to "Interpreting the *Variorum*" contains the most unfortunate sentence I ever wrote. Referring to affective criticism as a "superior fiction," I declare that "it relieves me of the obligation to be right (a standard that simply drops out) and demands only that I be interesting." I have long since repudiated this declaration along with the relativism is implies. The only thing that drops out in my argument is a standard of right that exists independently of community goals and assumptions. Within a community, however, a standard of right (and wrong) can always be invoked because it will be invoked against the background of a prior understanding as to what counts as a fact, what is hearable as an argument, what will be recognized as a purpose, and so on. The point, as I shall later write, is that standards of right and wrong do not exist apart from assumptions, but follow from them, and, moreover, since we ourselves do not exist apart from assumptions, a standard of right and wrong is something we can never be without.]

TOGETHER PROFESSOR BUSH and Mr. Mailloux present a problem in interpretation not unlike those that were the occasion of the essay they criticize: Professor Bush takes the first section of that essay more seriously (or at least with a different kind of seriousness) than I do, and Mr. Mailloux complains that I do not take it seriously enough. In their different ways they seem to miss or slight (or perhaps resent) the playfulness of my performance, the degree to which it is an attempt to be faithful to my admitted unwillingness to come to, or rest on, a point. Professor Bush seems to think that I am mounting an attack on the *Variorum*. Let me say at the outset that I intended no such attack, that I am sorry if anything I wrote gave that impression, and that I regret any offense that may have been taken. Professor Bush and I view the *Variorum* from different perspectives, both of which seem to me to be perfectly legitimate. He views it as a document, while I view it as a text. As a document, as a record and history of research and interpretation, it is a model of its kind, full, judicious, and, above all, honest. The editors pay us the compliment of not pretending to an impossible objectivity. They leave us the valuable record of their own occasional disagreements, and thus suggest (to me at least) that they know very well that theirs is an interim report. My inquiry is into the significance of that report; it is not a brief against the compiling of its materials but an attempt to put to them a question the editors quite properly do not ask: what does the history of the effort to determine the meaning of Milton's poems mean? In short, I am extending the scope of interpretation to include the interpreters themselves and, rather than attacking the *Variorum,* taking one step further the task it has so well begun.

Even in the context of our differing perspectives, however, Professor Bush and I may not be so far apart as he thinks. We both agree that in Milton's poetry one finds "complex, even contradictory feelings" and that the poet is "moving, at times, through doubt and struggle, to a positive resolution." It is just that while Professor Bush wishes to emphasize the resolution, I want to emphasize the doubt and struggles, to argue that they are ours as well as the poet's, and to assert that they do not lose their value (in the sense of being significance-bearing) simply because they give way to other "feelings." Like Ralph Rader, Professor Bush seems to believe that our final understanding (and I admit that we do in some cases achieve one) of what a poem means should be taken to be its meaning ("resolved sense"). It is my contention, however, that this understanding is no more to be identified with "the meaning" than the understandings which precede it and that an interpretation the reader entertains and then discards (or revises, or modifies, or extends, or forgets) has, in fact, been hazarded, and because it has been hazarded it involves commitments (to propositions, attitudes, assumptions, beliefs) which, even if they are only temporary, are nonetheless a part of the poem's experience. It is a question finally of whether perceptual strategies are regarded as instrumental, in the sense that they are preliminary to the determination of meaning, or as constitutive, in the sense that they are, at every moment, making meaning, and then, at every subsequent moment, making it again. It is a question, as Mr. Mailloux points out, of whether one's critical model is spatial or temporal.

Of course this is to do no more than restate the position to which Professor Bush is objecting, but what he does not seem to have realized is that I object to it too, or at least to the claims made for it in the first two sections of the paper. Those claims are withdrawn at the end of the third section, when I admit that in the course of defending my procedures I have given up the right to declare them superior to the procedures I had been criticizing. That is because the arguments in the later sections undercut the possibility of demonstrating that superiority (of providing evidence for it) and reduce it to an assertion. It is this that Mr. Mailloux sees and regrets, although apparently he believes that I have simply made a mistake. In fact what I have done is allowed two stances that had up to now been kept separate to come together within the (artificial) confines of a single essay. The result, as Mr. Mailloux observes, is a contradiction ("what Fish now appears to have given us is a self-consuming criticism"), and it is a contradiction which follows directly from an equivocation in my own theory and practice. At times, as in the first half of "Interpreting the *Variorum*" and in an earlier piece on "L'Allegro" and "Il Penseroso," my analyses are presented as if they were *descriptive*, as if I were in the business of making available to analytical consciousness the strategies readers perform, independently of whether or not they are aware of having performed them. When I am in this mood, my claim is similar to that sometimes made by linguists—to be telling people what it is they have always done, even though, as a consequence of their critical principles, they may be either unable or unwilling to acknowledge that they have been doing it. It is a claim, in short, that you read the way I say you do, and it won't do you any good to deny it because I can always explain away your denial as either a devaluation or a deliberate suppression of what has "really" happened. The other stance is no less arrogant, but it is arrogant in another direction. It is *prescriptive,* and it involves urging readers to read in a new or different way. When I am in this mood, I do not say "this is the way you read whether you know it or not," but, rather, "why don't you try it this way." "This way" means falling in with my assumption that the content of a reader's experience is a succession of deliberate acts (or perceptual strategies) and then monitoring the acts which are produced by (rather than discovered by) that assumption. The procedure will yield results, but they will have no necessary demonstrable relationship to a shared or normative reading experience.

Only if such a relationship obtains can the polemic stance of the first half of "Interpreting the *Variorum"* be justified, although the justification would depend on my ability to provide independent evidence for my analyses. But it is the very possibility of providing such evidence that is denied in the paper's second half, when, in a wholesale repudiation of formalism, I cut myself off from any recourse to evidentiary procedures. Mr. Mailloux says that "the claim of affective stylistics" ("that its description/interpretation reflects or dramatizes the way most readers actually read") is an empirical one "that can be tested against intuitive, psycholinguistic, and critical evidence." The case, however, is much less strong: intuitive, psycholinguistic, and critical evidence can be appropriated by affective stylistics, but it cannot serve as a test. By "critical evidence" I take Mr. Mailloux to be referring to the way I use previous criticism. Typically, I will pay less attention to the interpretations critics propose than to the problems or controversies that provoke them, on the reasoning that while the interpretations vary, the problems and controversies do not and therefore point to something that all readers share. If, for example, there is a continuing debate over whether Marlow should or should not have lied at the end of *Heart of Darkness,* I will interpret the debate as evidence of the difficulty readers experience when the novel asks them to render judgment. And similarly, if there is an argument over who is the hero of *Paradise Lost,* I will take the argument as an indication that, in the course of reading the poem, the identity of its hero is continually put into question. There will always be two levels, a surface level on which there seem to be nothing but disagreements, and a deeper level on which those same disagreements are seen as constituting the shared content whose existence they had seemed to deny. In short, critical controversies become disguised reports of what readers uniformly do, and I perform the service of revealing to the participants what it is they were really telling us.

As a strategy, however, this will be persuasive only if one accepts the assumption that criticism is a code that must be cracked rather than a body of straightforward reporting and opinion (the difference, again, between the *Variorum* as a text and as a document). Rather than citing evidence, I am manufacturing it by stipulating in advance that a scrutiny of the materials will reveal just the kind of activities that I claim readers to be performing. In short, for the "evidence" to be supporting, it requires the addition or superimposition of the very hypothesis it would test. This holds too for psycholinguistic evidence. It is true that the experiments of some psycholinguists have uncovered perceptual strategies that are similar to those I describe, but in their analyses these strategies are in the service of *processing* meaning, while it is my claim that they *have* meaning, not at one point, but at every point. Again, it is only by assuming what I would prove that the evidence becomes evidence, and indeed if we take as representative Frank Smith's definition of successful reading as the reduction of uncertainty, then the researches of psycholinguistics would seem to offer more comfort to Rader and to Bush than to me. All that remains to me is Mailloux's third category, intuitive evidence, by which he means the evidence provided by someone who, after hearing or reading me, nods in agreement. But this is evidence of a different kind than is required, for it is not available to a disinterested observer and therefore will compel assent only from those who have already assented. That is why the notion of an interpretive community is so important to my argument. It is at once objective, in the sense that it is the result of an agreement, and subjective, in the sense that only those who are party to that agreement (and who therefore constitute it) will be able to recognize it.

This last is a restatement of the final section of "Interpreting the *Variorum*," and it is an inevitable consequence of my gradual abandonment in that article of the descriptivist position. This is why it is curious to find Mr. Mailloux speculating that it may be a desire to preserve a "descriptive focus" that accounts for my retreat from the claim of priority, as if that claim would be easier to make in the absence of any descriptivist pretensions. The case, however, seems to me exactly the reverse: it is only by maintaining a descriptive focus that a claim of priority could be justified (at least theoretically), for without it there is no basis on which such a claim could be tested. In other words, it is because I have already done what Mr. Mailloux urges me to do—back off from the assertion of "descriptive power"—that I can no longer do what he wants me to do—hold on to the assertion of priority.

This does not mean, as he seems to fear, that I have given up the distinction between affective stylistics (not the happiest of designations) and the methodologies to which it originally stood opposed. It is just that the distinction cannot be maintained in its strongest form, as a distinction between what is true and what is not. Mr. Mailloux is right to point out that by virtue of a metacritical step I have put formalist and affective analyses on a par, but that is only in relation to the claim either of them might make to objectivity; and it is also only in relation to that claim that the distinction between reading strategies and critical strategies is collapsed. With respect to other levels of comparison the differences remain. The chief difference, as Mailloux observes, is between a method which assigns value to the temporal reading experience and a method which either denies that experience or regards it as merely instrumental. The difference is not, however, one of fidelity to that experience, since the act of reading which is the object of affective criticism is also its creation. Even so, a case for the superiority (if not the priority) of affective criticism can still be made. First of all, it is more coherent in its own terms than formalist criticism, which is vitiated, as I have argued, by the absence of any connection between its descriptions and its interpretations. Either the interpretation precedes the description and is then made (illegitimately) to appear as its consequence, or a description is scrutinized until, as if by magic, an interpretation which fills its spaces emerges. In either case, the procedure is arbitrary. Of course there is arbitrariness in my procedure too, but it enters at the beginning, when a set of assumptions is adopted which subsequently directs and generates the analyses. Affective criticism is arbitrary only in the sense that one cannot prove that its beginning is the right one, but once begun it unfolds in ways that are consistent with its declared principles. It is therefore a superior fiction, and since no methodology can legitimately claim any more, this superiority is decisive. It is also creative. That is, it makes possible new ways of reading and thereby creates new texts. An unsympathetic critic might complain that this is just the trouble, that rather than following the way people actually read I am teaching people to read differently. This is to turn the prescriptive claim into a criticism, but it will be felt as a criticism only if the alternative to different reading is right reading and if the alternative to the texts created by different reading is the real text. These, however, are the fictions of formalism, and as fictions they have the disadvantage of being confining. My fiction is liberating. It relieves me of the obligation to be right (a standard that simply drops out) and demands only that I be interesting (a standard that can be met without any reference at all to an illusory objectivity). Rather than restoring or recovering texts, I am in the business of making texts and of teaching others to make them by adding to their repertoire of strategies. I was once asked whether there are really such things as self-consuming artifacts, and I replied: "There are now." In that answer you will find both the arrogance and the modesty of my claims.

8
Structuralist Homiletics

[THIS ESSAY was originally published in 1973 as "Sequence and Meaning in Seventeenth-Century Narrative" and was written for a seminar on narrative organized by Earl Miner and held at the William Andrews Clark Library Memorial, University of California at Los Angeles. The other participants in the seminar were Miner, Paul Alpers, Richard Lanham, Robert Scholes, and Robert M. Adams. The essay extends the arguments of *Self-Consuming Artifacts* to the sermons of Lancelot Andrewes by finding in them (or at least in one of them) a continual undermining of the rational and discursive structures of which they are supposedly instances. At the same time, I assert a parallel between Andrewes's theologically motivated dislodging of the self as the originator of meaning and the structuralist elimination of the subject in favor of discursive systems that in some sense "speak it." The title "Structuralist Homiletics" is obviously an allusion to Jonathan Culler's *Structuralist Poetics,* and indeed some sentences from that book could well be seen as describing the "plot" of Andrewes's sermon as it is characterized in my analysis: "Once the conscious subject is deprived of its role as source of meaning . . . the self can no longer be identified with consciousness. It is 'dissolved' as its functions are taken up by a variety of interpersonal systems that operate through it" (p. 28). In Andrewes's theology the self is constituted not by a system but by the indwelling presence of Jesus Christ; but the effect of the two ways of thinking is the same, to deny the distinction between the knower and the object of knowledge that is so crucial to a positivist epistemology. In general it seems to me that structuralist and poststructuralist insights and positions have been anticipated by theological modes of reasoning even though "theological" is a term of accusation in structuralist and poststructuralist rhetoric.]

IF, AS PAUL RICOEUR has said, "structuralism is Kantianism without a transcendental subject," then Christianity is structuralism *with* a transcendental subject.¹ This one difference of course finally makes all the difference, but in what they oppose the two systems are very much alike, and what they oppose is what Roland Barthes calls variously "classical language," the ideology of the referent, and, most, suggestively, the language of "bad faith." The faith is bad because it is a faith in the innocence and transparency of language, which is in turn a faith in the innocence and transparency of the mind and in its ability to process and elucidate a meaning of which it is independent. To this Barthes and others oppose a view of language which makes it at once more and less, less because it is no longer the privileged conveyer of meaning, more because it becomes, in the true sense of the phrase, meaning-*full*. In this view, meaning is not the product of our operations but that which makes our operations possible; it does not lie waiting for us at the end of every disposable utterance but encloses us, includes us, speaks us; and it is the substance and source of all our attempts to apprehend it. "My heart," cries Herbert in *Love II*, "pants thee," rather than pants *after* thee; by deleting the preposition the poet removes the distance between his words and their putative object, that is, he removes the "bad faith attaching to any language which is ignorant of itself" by being ignorant of its origin.²

Removing the bad faith is the program of the literature Barthes admires, modern poetry since Mallarmé and the novel since Flaubert, and the distinctive feature of this literature is the transgression of the flow of sequential discourse. This is necessary because it is the apparent self-sufficiency and internal coherence of discourse which is responsible for the illusion of its independence, and by interrupting the progress of a sentence or a line we free its components from the chain of a meaning into which they are combined and return them to the already constituted meaning that is their source. Thus, as Barthes writes in his most recent publication, we pass "from simple readability, characterized by a stringent irreversibility of actions . . . to a complex readability (precarious), subject to the forces of dispersion and to the reversibility of symbolic elements which destroy both time and logic."[3] The result is a literature of multiple signifiers, in which, as Bathes explains in *Writing Degree Zero*, "the spontaneously functional nature of language" is destroyed and "only its lexical basis" is left standing.

> The Word shines forth above a line of relationships emptied of their content; grammar is bereft of its purpose, it becomes prosody and is no longer anything but an inflection which lasts only to present the Word. Connections are not properly speaking abolished, they are merely reserved areas, a parody of themselves, and this void is necessary for the density of the Word to rise out of a magic vacuum . . . Thus under each Word in modern poetry there lies a sort existential geology, in which is gathered the total content of the Name, instead of a chosen content . . . the consumer . . . encounters the Word frontally and receives it as an absolute quantity, accompanied by all its possible associations.[4]

I shall not comment on this remarkable passage, nor on its historical assumptions, except to point out that in its every appearance the word Word is capitalized (as it is in the French); perhaps there is something in that "magic vacuum" after all. Let us see.

On the sixteenth of April in the year of our Lord sixteen hundred and twenty Lancelot Andrewes preached a sermon before the King's Majesty. It was Easter day and Andrewes took his text from the twentieth chapter of the gospel of John, verses 11–17:

> But Mary, stood by the Sepulcher weeping; and as she wept, she stooped, and looked into the Sepulcher,
> And saw two Angels, in white, sitting, the one at the head, the other at the feet, where the Body of JESUS had lyen.
> And they said to her, Woman, why weepest thou? Shee said to them,
> They have taken away my **LORD** and I know not where they have laid Him.
> When she had thus said, she turned her selfe about, and saw JESUS standing, and knew not that it was JESUS.
> JESUS saith to her, Woman, why weepest thou? Whom seekest thou?
> Shee (supposing He had been the gardiner) said to Him, Sir if

thou have borne Him hence, tell me where thou hast laid Him, and I will take Him thence.

JESUS saith to her, Mary. She turned herselfe, and said to Him, Rabboni; that is to say, Master.

JESUS said to her, Touch Me not; for I am not yet ascended to My Father: But, goe to My brethren, and say to them, I ascend to my Father and to your Father, and to my GOD and your God.[5]

This text is appropriate not only to that day in 1620 but to our purposes here, for it is very obviously a narrative, answerable in every way to Aristotle's criteria for a well constructed plot, "a whole . . . which has beginning middle and end":

A beginning is that which does not itself follow anything by causal necessity, but after which something else naturally is or comes to be. An end, on the contrary, is that which itself naturally follows some other thing, either by causal necessity or as a rule, but has nothing following it. A middle is that which follows something as some other thing follows it. Plots that are well planned, therefore, are such as do not begin or end at haphazard, but conform to the types just described. (*Poetics* vii, 1450b)[6]

Aristotle's terms, as one commentator has observed, "connote not space and structure but time and causal movement, a sense of progress to completion."[7] The assertion is that in a good plot, sequence, rather than chance or haphazard arrangement, is revelatory of meaning; that event follows event in a probable and inevitable manner; and that this is a condition not only of the action as it is formally describable, but of our *reception* of the action, whose full meaning is revealed to us even as the characters discover it, *in time*. What is discovered in the course of this action is Christ, who is first sought and then, as we might reasonably expect, found. There is, however, at least one sentence in the sermon which suggests something altogether different:

> He is found of them that seeke Him
> not
> but
> of them that seeke Him
> never
> but
> found.   (538)

What interests me in this sentence (as some of you will have guessed) is the number of adjustments required to negotiate it. No adjustment would be necessary at all were it to end as it might well have, at the first point of natural closure—"he is found of them that seeke him"—for this unit is both superficially and deeply satisfying: superficially satisfying because the stresses of sense and rhythm coincide ("He is *found* of them that *seeke* Him"), and deeply satisfying because in its unfolding the sequence is answerable to several of our expectations: (1) the expectation of empirical cause and effect (that is, you are more likely to find something if you look for it), (2) the expectation of finding this empirical causality reflected in the relational logic of discourse, and (3) the *moral* expectation that, if he is to be found by anyone, it should be by those who seek him, for as the scriptures tell us, "Seek and ye shall find." Every one of these expectations falls before the word "not," for we are forced by it not only to revise our understanding of the sequence but to give up the assumptions which had made that understanding both probable and attractive.

As a result, we are for a moment without bearings, but only for a moment, since the very next word invites us to stabilize the sentence by predicting a new direction for it. As an adversative conjunction, "but" signals an antithesis and it helps us to domesticate the reversal of the relationship between seeking and finding by allowing us to anticipate its extension to those who *do* seek him. It is not ideas that make the mind uncomfortable but the difficulty of managing them, and we adjust to the unexpected and unwanted complication of "not" by making it the basis of a new projection of the shape the sentence will finally take. That shape very quickly becomes the shape of a chiasmus, one of the most firmly directing of schematic figures, and with every succeeding word the reader is more securely (in two senses) locked into the pattern of the figure and therefore into the sense that pattern is encouraging him to make. Both sense and pattern hold through the word "never" where suddenly we are met with another complication in the form of a second "but." This "but" does not perform a clearly adversative function, nor can it be handled by simply reversing direction, for this only precipitates a clash between the two "buts," one so obligingly orienting, the other so egregiously *dis*orienting. The only option that remains, then, is to go forward, not in confidence but in the hope of finding some help in what remains of the sentence. What we find is "found," the word we least expect precisely because it was so firmly expected after "never." Had it appeared then, "found" would have completed the contrast of the chiasmic pattern—"He is found of them that seeke Him not, but of them that seek Him *never* found"—but placed as it is after "but," "found" subverts that pattern and makes the sentence and its experience circular.

Some of you may want to object that my analysis of the sentence is more tortuous and torturing than the reader's experience of it. And you would be right. For although the experience does, I think, involve the disruptions I have described, it is itself not disrupting but satisfying, and it is satisfying because in the end the sentence gives you exactly what you want and once had, the comfort of the assumptions which led you to welcome its opening words. That is to say, by leaving its discursive track and leaving you to stumble into its conclusion, the sentence returns you to the security of its first clause, but only after you have forsaken that security—o ye of little faith—for the problems raised by the syntax. What this means is that while you finally get what you want, it is not what you expect or when you expect it; you expect "found" to appear after "never," even though its appearance there, while locally satisfying, would be ultimately disconcerting (but those who seek him *should* find him); but you get "found" after "but" where it is locally disconcerting but ultimately satisfying. That is, while you find "found," you find it independently of the discursive operations you have been performing, and therefore it could be more truly said that *found finds you*.

This is exactly what happens in the sermon, not only to Mary Magdalene but to Andrewes and his parishioners, all of whom spend a great deal of time looking for something that has already found them. What Andrewes is looking for are things that fit together, correspondences, agreements, and he begins by commenting with satisfaction on the appropriateness of the day to

the text: "It is *Easter-day* abroad: And it is so in the Text. We
keep *Salomons* rule" (531). The keeping of Solomon's rule ("on
the day of the Word, so this day") is not only a point of honor
for Andrewes but a source of security, for by Solomon's rule
at least the first step of his exegetical exercise can be validated.
In another sermon it occurs to him that he is *not* keeping
Solomon's rule—his text, he admits, comes "a little too soone,
before the time and should have staied till the day it was spoken
on rather than on this day"—and he is at pains to find a rationale
for thus proceeding out of order. Like any other interpreter,
then, Andrewes worries about his method of analysis and exposition, and in the early stages of the sermon he is very careful
both to introduce the machinery of his exposition and to continually point out to us that it is processing the meaning he seeks:

> To look a little into it. 1. *Mary* is the name of a woman: 2. *Mary
> Magdalene,* of a sinful woman. That, to a woman first, it agreeth
> well, to make even with *Eve;* that as by a woman came the first
> newes of death; so by a woman also might come the first notice of
> the Resurrection from the dead. And the place fits well, for, in a
> garden, they came, both. That to a sinful woman first; that also
> agrees well. To her first that most needed it, and so first sought it.
> And it agrees well, He be first found of her that first sought Him.
> (532)

What kind of agreements are these? First of all they are exclusive agreements, in the sense that for the phrase "it agrees
well" one might substitute "it is fitting," and this in turn implies that were it otherwise, were Mary Magdalene neither sinful
nor a woman, it would not be fitting. In the second place (for
we are now exegetes of the exegesis) these are agreements which
agree with our common sense of the way the world is and should
be. Andrewes here sounds curiously like the Puritan preachers
for whom he and Donne were the evil exemplars of a self-
glorying virtuosity; the style is plain; what repetitions there are
support the unfolding of the argument, the argument is easy
to follow, and it is itself followed by an application or "use":
"In which two, there is opened unto us *a gate of hope* . . . one,
that no infirmity of sex . . . the other, that no enormity of sinne
. . . shall debarre any to have their part in CHRIST" (532). In

short, one thing is succeeding another in a meaningful and meaning-producing order, and both Andrewes and his parishioners are finding what they want which is also what they expect. And then something very curious happens; the schemes or divisions which are to serve as a framework for the sermon proliferate; first there is the division of the three parties. Mary, the Angels, and Christ, each of whom is further divided into his or her parts; these divisions are followed immediately by a fourfold division of the favor vouchsafed unto Mary this day, and that in turn by a tenfold division of the love by which she merited that favor. One division is helpful, two are complicating, four are impossible, and as these succeed one another without interruption and without exposition, they operate to inhibit rather than facilitate the forward progress of the sermon; rather than providing direction for the listener (as the handbooks claim) they give him more directions than he can comfortably manage.

This change in the pace and mode of the sermon coincides with a change in its language, which is now more recognizably the language of Lancelot Andrewes:

> We cannot commend her faith; her love, wee cannot but commend; and so doe: Commend it in her, commend it to you. Much it was, and much good proofe gave she of it. Before, to *him* living, now, to *Him dead*. To Him dead, there are diverse; 1. She was last at His crosse, and first at His grave; 2. Staied longest there, was soonest here; 3. Could not rest, till she were up to seeke Him; 4. Sought Him, while it was yet darke, before she had light to seeke Him by. (533)

There are in this passage two organizational forces, one represented by the sequence of numbers and the other *created* by the patterned repetition of words and phrases. While earlier these two were mutually reinforcing, they here compete for the attention of the reader or listener. Moreover, the competition is short-lived, for it is not long before the order provided by the numbers becomes secondary to the multiple and nonlinear orderings of the proliferating verbal patterns. These are too many to be listed here, and of course their listing would be a distortion of the geometric manner of their apprehension; but one can point at least to the more obvious patterns of alliteration and assonance: good, gave, living; good, proof, before; dead, Dead, divers; divers, Last, Cross, first; first, stayed, longest, soonest, rest, seek, sought; sought, til, while, light. Notice that these patterns are both discontinuous and overlapping and that their components are themselves involved in other patterns of schematic point and contrast (that is, "Before to *him* living, now to *Him* dead'). To a large extent, then, the listener is not following any one pattern but allowing multiple and multiplying patterns to register. The only constant element in all of these is the pronoun Him, which thus draws to itself all the separate significances of the structures in which it momentarily operates.

What happens in this passage can be described by returning to the language of Roland Barthes: "the word shines forth above a line of relationships emptied of their content; grammar is bereft of its purpose, it becomes prosody, and is no longer anything but an inflection which lasts only to present the Word." Or, in more formal but hardly less formidable terms (they are Roman Jakobson's): "the principle of equivalence [is projected] from the axis of selection into the axis of combination."[8] That is to say, the axis on which semantic units are combined into a meaning that is available only at the end of a chain becomes instead a succession of equivalent spaces in which independent and immediately available meanings are free to interact with each other, unconstrained by the subordinating and distinguishing logic of syntax and discourse. Sequence is no longer causal but additive; it no longer processes a meaning but provides an area in which meanings separately constituted are displayed and equated. This comes about in one of two ways: either the relational links which make discourse progressive and linear are simply omitted (as they are in much of Andrewes's extraordinarily compressed and elliptical prose), or they remain but cease to function because they are overwhelmed by the logic of equivalence:

And as she wept, she stooped, and looked in, ever and anon. That is, she did so *weepe,* as she did *seeke* withall. *Weeping* without *seeking,* is but to small purpose. But, her *weeping* hindred not her *seeking,* Her sorrow dulled not her diligence. And, diligence is a character of love, comes from the same roote, *dilectio* and *diligentia* from *diligo,* both. *Amor diligentiam diligens.* (534)

We begin with the narrative situation and with the assertion of a clash between weeping and seeking; but of course even as the two are separated by the argument (" *weeping* without *seeking,* is but to small purpose") they are joined by the likeness of sound, and, as Andrewes continues, likeness *becomes* the argument, repeated and extended in the transformation of seeking into sorrow and sorrow into diligence and diligence into love. In short, the axis of combination, the syntagmatic axis, becomes the vehicle for enlarging the axis of selection, the paradigmatic axis, and, as the sermon proceeds, the paradigmatic axis is enlarged to include *everything;* that is, everything is transformed into a character of love.

Now if the paradigmatic axis, the storehouse of equivalent and interchangeable meanings, includes everything, choice is less crucial than it would be in a world of real differences, and arrangement and order (the Aristotelian bywords) become matters of indifference, not because we are indifferent to meaning but because meaning is available independently of our structures which, rather than generating it, simply display it. Thus the correspondences which Andrewes seeks and we expect are found not at the end of his sentences or paragraphs or sections but in the equivalencies already existing in the materials at his disposal; and while these sentences and paragraphs and sections cannot help but bring meaning to light, we do not feel that they are producing it. Ftting together is in the nature of things; agreement is a condition of the universe rather than the product of our procedures. It is not that you cannot find meaning but that you cannot help but find it; indeed, it finds you or you stumble into it as we do in the sentences of this sermon long before they come to *their* point.

What I am suggesting is that in the universe of the sermon, a universe which includes the reader and the preacher as well as the characters, it is impossible to make a mistake, or to fail to find what you are seeking (he is found of them that seek him not, but of them that seek him, never but found), but this also means that is is impossible to be right; you cannot seek successfully precisely because your success is always assured. And in this at least the sermon is not a gloss on the story of Mary Magdalene, but rather the story of Mary Magdalene is a gloss on the sermon, for she makes mistake after mistake and looks everywhere but in the proper place, and yet she finds what she is looking for even as she looks past it:

> For *they* (but she knew not who) *had carryed Him* (she knew not whither) *laid Him* (she knew not where) there to doe to *Him* (she knew not what). (536)

At each point where the question is asked—by who, whither, where, what—it is answered in an exactly parallel position by *Him, Him, Him, Him.* Even in her verbal seeking—and seeking is what a question does—Mary is found by what she seeks. What she seeks of course is Christ, and at the most dramatic yet anticlimactic moment in the sermon, anticlimactic because it is so prolonged, she fails to recognize him. "And so, CHRIST she saw, but knew *Him* not. Not only not knew *Him,* but misknew *Him, tooke Him for the Gardiner* (538)." But even as this mistake is reported it is explained away, first because it is understandable—"it fitted well the time and place . . . The time, it was the Spring; the place, it was a Garden (that place is most in request at that time)"—and then because it is no mistake at all— "though she might seeme to erre in some sense, yet in some other she was in the right. For, in a sense, and in a good sense, CHRIST may well be said to be a *Gardiner,* and indeed is one. For our rule is CHRIST, as he appears, so *He* is ever: No false semblant in *Him.* A *Gardiner* He is then." The sense in which she is right is the sense Christ makes possible, for since he made the world it is proper to find him—and only Him—in its *every* appearance. Nothing can be miscalled in his name, for everything bears the imprint of his signature, and is a character of love, as Andrewes proceeds to discover by looking a little into the word gardener:

> The first, the fairest garden that ever was (Paradise) He was the *Gardiner,* it was of His planting . . . So, a *Gardiner* in that sense. But not in that alone . . . Hee it is that gardens our soules . . .

sowes and plants them with true roots and seeds of righteousnesse, waters them with the dew of His grace . . . besides all these, nay over and above, all these, this day (if ever) most properly He was a *Gardiner* . . . who made such an herbe grow out of the ground this day, as the like was never seene before, a dead body, to shoot forth alive out of the grave . . . I aske, was He so this day alone? No . . . For, He it is, that by vertue of this mornings act, shall garden our bodies, too: turne all our graves into garden-plots. (538–539)

(Dare I hope for a pun?) This amazing sequence ends not merely by clearing Mary Magdalene of error but by implying that she would have been in error had she done otherwise: "So then: He appeared no other, than He was; a *Gardiner* Hee was, not in shew alone, but *opere et veritate,* and so came in His owne like-nesse." Of course, this would have been the case no matter what or whom she had mistaken him for; the operation performed on this word could have been performed on any other. Christ's own likeness is everything in the world he has created and, just as his omnipresence makes it impossible not to find him, so it is impossible to say anything of him that is not true. One can even charge him, as Mary does, with being "a breaker up of graves, a carryer away of Corses." Her "if thou have borne him hence," as Andrewes observes, "implies as much." And yet he marvels, "see how GOD shall direct the tongue! In thus charging Him . . . She sayes truer than she was aware. For indeed, if any *tooke Him away,* it was Hee did it. So, shee was not much amisse. Her *si tu,* was true, though not in her sense . . . This was true, but this was no part of her meaning" (540).

Here we come to the crux of the matter, not only with respect to Mary and her seeking but with respect to the expository machinery of the sermon: both succeed but through no fault of their own and both are overtaken by the meaning they seek, Mary when she looks past what she has already found, and the sermon when its sentences yield what they are seeking (and what we expect) before their linear course is run. Her inability to say amiss is matched by the inability of the language to refrain from displaying correspondences; both succeed accidentally in the sense that they have access to what they find not because they elucidate it but because they are a part of it and involuntarily trace out what *it* has inscribed in *them*. They do not find a meaning but live in it and so declare it in everything they do.

For Mary Magdalene, for Andrewes, and for us the moral is the same: if the paradigmatic axis, the storehouse of already constituted and interchangeable meanings, includes everything, it also includes the structures by means of which we validate and assert our independence; we, no less than the words we speak, are meant, stipulated, uttered by another. In our postures as seekers, after meaning or after Christ (they are of course the same), we place ourselves outside a system and presume to make sense of it, to fit its parts together; what we find is that the parts are already together and *that we are one of them,* living in the meaning we seek—"in him we live and move and have our meaning"—not as its exegetes but as its bearers. We are already where we want to be and our attempts to get there—by writing, by reading, by speaking—can do nothing else but extend through time the "good news" of our predetermined success.

The sequence of our lives, then, in the life of the reading experience, is exactly like the sequence of this sermon, proceeding from point to point, but in a progression that is not generating meaning but merely creating new spaces into which the meaning that is already there expands. The syntagmatic axis, in all of its manifestations—in discourse, in history, in time itself—is simply a succession of areas in which the paradigmatic equivalences are made manifest. Every "but" is an "and," every "however" an "also," and every transition is nothing more than an opportunity to take a breath. In Aristotelian terms, *everything is middle,* even where there are, as there are in this sermon, all the formal signs of a beginning and an end.

In this sermon those signs suffer the fate reserved for all relational links in seventeenth-century antinarrative: they become irrelevant. You will recall that in the opening paragraphs a great deal of emphasis is placed on the manner of the division or divisions, and it might have occurred to you, and it is certainly occurring to you now, that I have paid no attention to those divisions at all. This omission is precisely true to the experience of the sermon, for the life of that experience inheres in the proliferation and cross-indexing of innumerable and interrelated patterns, and that life flows independently of the numbers which regularly but irrelevantly interrupt and segment it. This is not an irrelevance we bother about, because we are aware of it only at two points. The first is immediately after Mary Magdalene has been praised for being right despite herself: "This was true, but this was no part of *her* meaning." Andrewes then pauses to say, "I can not here passe over two more Characters of her love, that so you may have the full ten I promised" (540). This aside is gratuitous exactly in the measure that we have long since ceased to expect the full ten or any other number.

That is to say (and I have said it before), we have been getting what we want rather than what we expected, and what we expected is no longer controlling or even remembered. The organization of the sermon, the arrangement of its parts, is no more responsible for the meanings that have been brought to light than Mary is responsible for the meaning her words find. Indeed, the relationship is even more oblique, for what she finds at least validates her intention if not her perception, while what the structure of the sermon finds is simply what is there in any case. Ten is an arbitrary number signaling the end of an arbitrary sequence; any number would have done, any order would have served; it is a matter of indifference, an indifference Andrewes displays openly when he closes or rather stops by remarking: "I see, I shall not be able to goe further than this verse" (542). Here we see exactly how time is at once everything and nothing; presumably the bell has rung and he must give over, but while time has run out, the sermon is nevertheless complete, for the meaning it offers is found not at the end of it, in the *fullness* of time, but at every point in its temporal succession. Am I then arguing that the parts of the sermon could be rearranged with no loss of coherence or power? Not at all, for, paradoxically, it is the sequence of the sermon as it stands that leads us to affirm the irrelevance of sequence. The experiential point is realized only through the agency of the structure it subverts, which becomes, in effect, the vehicle of its own abandonment.

When I was asked to write this essay I worried a great deal because it seemed to me that there weren't very many narratives in the seventeenth century to be theoretical about, but of course this has long since become my point. A good plot, Aristotle tells us, is a series of irreversible actions leading to a conclusion that has been determined by the intersection of character and choice with circumstance, a chain of events each of which is significant by virtue of its relationship to a *developing* meaning. But a Christian plot, in the sense that there is one, is haphazard, random in its order, heedless of visible cause and effect, episodic, inconclusive, consisting of events that are both reversible and interchangeable. This is more, however, than an incompatability of aesthetics; for the logic of narrative, of sequential causality, is the logic of human freedom and choice: the freedom to take a step that is determining and the choice to be a character in an action that is either fortunate or unfortunate. Within a Christian framework, however, the plot is fortunate by divine fiat, and one reaches a point not because he chooses but because he has been chosen, that is, redeemed. The price we pay for this redemption is the illusion of self-sufficiency and independence, the illusion of moving toward a truth rather than moving by virtue of it and within it, the illusion that destiny and meaning are what we seek rather than what has sought, and found, us. It is finally, of course, a question of epistemology, and I return once more to Lancelot Andrewes: "The *Apostle* saith, *Now we have knowne* GOD, (and then correcteth himself) *or rather have been known of* GOD For till He know us, we shall never know Him aright" (541).

This anatomy of knowing is exactly the opposite of what we naturally assume, and our natural assumptions are reflected in the flow of discursive and sequential thought which implicitly claims for itself, and therefore for us from whom it issues, the responsibility for making and elucidating meaning. If we are to disengage ourselves from these claims, they must not only be raised to the level of consciousness but their supports in language must be made spectacularly nonfunctional. This is why in Andrewes's sermons, and in the other great monuments of seventeenth-century prose, temporal structures—the signs of connection and relation—are not omitted but exaggerated, emptied of their explanatory and organizing powers but remaining nevertheless as "merely reserved areas, a parody of themselves."[9] The bad faith of referential language is removed by making the forms of that language—logic, subordination, definition, sequence—conspicuously irrelevant to the meaning which overwhelms them, a meaning of which they are not independent, although it is independent of them, a meaning which is found no matter where or how or with what indifferent means it is sought; for he is found of them that seek him not, but of them that seek him, never but found.

9
How To Do Things with Austin and Searle: Speech-Act Theory and Literary Criticism

[THIS ARTICLE is written in three parts. In the first part I present a speech-act analysis of Coriolanus in order to demonstrate what speech-act theory can do when it is taken up by literary criticism. In the second part I turn on the analysis, first by arguing that Coriolanus is a special case and therefore not generalizable, and second by pointing out the distressing consequences of any attempt to extend the theory beyond the explanatory limits it declares. This leads, in the third part, to a consideration of the distinction between serious and fictional discourse, a distinction which, I argue, cannot be maintained if the implications of speech-act theory are clearly and steadily seen. I am thus in the position of insisting on a version of the theory stronger than any that would be accepted by those most responsible for its development, J. L. Austin and John Searle.

   In the penultimate chapter of *How To Do Things with Words,* J. L. Austin presents a sentence and asks us to consider it. The sentence is "France is hexagonal," and the question he puts to it is a very familiar one in analytical philosophy: Is it true or false? The answer, however, is not so familiar. It depends, says Austin: "I can see what you mean by saying that it is true for certain intents and purposes. It is good enough for a top-ranking general, perhaps, but not for a geographer" (p. 142). It other words, the truth or falsehood of the sentence is a function of the circumstances within which it is uttered, and since it is always uttered within some set of circumstances or other, it is not in and of itself either true or false, accurate or innaccurate, precise or imprecise. "It is essential," Austin concludes, "to realize that 'true' and 'false' . . . do not stand for anything simple at all but only for a general dimension of being a right and proper thing to say as opposed to a wrong thing in these circumstances, to this audience, for these purposes and with these intentions" (p. 144). That "general dimension" is later named by Austin the "dimension of assessment," and his point is that it is only

197

in relation to dimensions of assessment that judgments of truth and falsity, adequacy and inadequacy, are possible.

In the drama of *How To Do Things with Words,* this discussion of France and its hexagonality marks the final overturning of the distinction with which Austin begins, the distinction between constative and performative language. Constative language is language that is, or strives to be, accountable to the real or objective world. It is to constatives—to acts of referring, describing, and stating— that one puts the question "Is it true or false?" in which true and false are understood to be *absolute* judgments, made independently of any particular set of circumstances. Performative language, on the other hand, is circumstantial through and through. The success of a performative depends on certain things being the case when it is uttered; performatives therefore are appropriate or inappropriate in relation to conditions of utterance rather than true or false in relation to a reality that underlies all conditions. One kind of language is responsible to what John Searle calls brute facts—facts that exist prior to any linguistic report of them—and the other is responsible to institutional facts, facts that are facts only with reference to some social or conventional human practice (that is, promising, marrying, apologizing, appointing, and so on).

On its face, the sentence "France is hexagonal" is a perfect example of a constative utterance—an utterance that merely refers or describes or reports—and France is a perfect example of a brute fact, a fact that exists independently of anything that is said about it; but what Austin discovers at the end of *How To Do Things with Words* is that all utterances are performative—produced and understood within the assumption of some socially conceived dimension of assessment—and that therefore all facts are institutional, are facts only by virtue of the prior institution of some such dimension. This means not only that statements about an object will be assessed (as right, wrong, relevant, or irrelevant) according to the conditions of their utterance, but that the object itself, insofar as it is available for reference and description, will be a *product* of those conditions. There are a great many things one can say about France, including that it is or is not hexagonal, but the felicity of whatever one says will be a function of its relation to some dimension of assessment or other—whether that dimension is military, geographical, culinary, or economic—and moreover, the France one is saying it about will be recognizable, and therefore describable, *only* within that dimension. In short, the one thing you can never say about France is what it is *really* like, if by "really" you mean France as its exists independently of any dimension of assessment whatsoever. The France you are talking about will always be the product of the talk about it, and will *never* be independently available.

What the example of France shows is that all facts are discourse specific (since no fact is available apart from some dimension of assessment or other) and that therefore no one can claim for any language a special relationship to the facts as they "simply are," unmediated by social or conventional assumptions. This, however, is precisely the claim traditionally made for "serious" or "real-world" language as opposed to literary language, and it is this distinction that I challenge in the third section of this essay. In order to forestall the charge that by so arguing I make everything literary and therefore weightless, I introduce the notion of the standard story, a story in relation to which we are not tellers (and therefore free to approve or reject it) but characters, simultaneously enabled and limited by the ways of thinking and seeing it constrains. While the world given by the standard story is no less a constructed one than the world of a novel or play, for those who speak from within it (and indeed as extensions of it) the facts of that world will be as obvious and inescapable as one could wish. In short, the standard story and the world it delivers rest on a bedrock of belief, and even if that bedrock were challenged, it would be so from the vantage point of a belief (and a world) that had already taken its place.

Of course, not everyone believes the same thing or, to be more precise, not everyone's perceptions are a function of the same set of beliefs, and so there will not be one but many standard stories in relation to which the world will be differently constituted, with different facts, values, ways of arguing, evidentiary procedures, and so on. As a result, what may be fiction for the characters in one standard story will be obvious and commonsense truth for characters in another. The distinction between what is true and what is fictional will always be made, but it will be made from *within* a story (or dimension of assessment) and therefore will always be a distinction between what is true and what is not from the vantage point of that story. Moreover, it is a distinction that will always be in dispute because the distinction could never be settled by the invocation of story-independent facts. This line of argument is somewhat obscured in the essay by the use of words like "popular" and "prestigious," which suggest that there is only one standard story at a time, one that is determined by a vote or a survey. There are as many standard stories as there are systems of belief (and that is not as many as one might think), and the contests between them are not decided by shows of hands but by acts of persuasion, as a result of which persons find themselves telling, and being told by, a new story.

There is at least one other large mistake in the essay, and it concerns the claims made for the analysis of *Coriolanus*. I say, finally, that speech-act theory works for *Coriolanus* because it is a speech-act play, that is, a play about speech acts. I am thus in the position of arguing for a special relationship between an interpretive system (speech-act theory) and a play as it "really is." But by my own (often) declared principles, the play as it really is is the play as it appears obviously to be from the perspective of some interpretive system or other. *Coriolanus* is a speech-act play for me because it is with speech-act theory in mind that I approached the play in the first place, and that approach seemed a reasonable one because the kinds of things that had been said about *Coriolanus* before (by D. J. Gordon and others) had given the play a shape that seemed answerable to the shape of the theory. The form of my analysis, therefore, is the product of two interpretive gestures, one performed over a long period of time by a succession of Shakespeare critics and the other performed largely by Austin and Searle in the course of developing their theory. If any reader is persuaded by the analysis it will not be because it accords with the facts of the play but because he will have first been persuaded to the interpretive assumptions in the light of which the facts as I cite them seem inescapable.]

I Banish You!

IN THE SECOND SCENE of the second act of *Coriolanus*, the tribunes Brutus and Sicinius decide that in order to bring about the hero's downfall they need only leave him to his own (verbal) devices. They know that he cannot be named consul until he asks the citizens for their votes and they are sure that, faced with this situation, he will perform badly. "He will," says Sicinius, "require them, / As if he did contemn what he requested should be in them to give" (159).[1] This is not only an accurate prediction of what Coriolanus does in fact do (and not do), it is also an astonishing anticipation of the formulation in speech-act theory of the preparatory conditions on requesting. Here is John Searle's analysis of that act (where S = Speaker, H = Hearer, and A = Act):

		Request
Types	Propositional Content	Future act *A* of *H*
of		
	Preparatory	1. *H* is able to do *A*. *S* believes *H* is able to do *A*.
Rule		2. It is not obvious to both *S* and *H* that *H* will do *A* in the normal course of events of his own accord.
	Sincerity	*S* wants *H* to do *A*
	Essential	Counts as an attempt to get *H* to do *A*.[2]

According to Searle, the rules governing the making of a request (and of any other illocutionary act) are not regulative but constitutive: that is, they do not regulate an antecedently existing behavior but define the conditions under which that behavior can be said to occur. If those conditions are unfulfilled, that behavior is either defective or void (some conditions are more centrally constitutive than others); the speaker will have done something (one cannot help but do things with words), but he will not have performed the act in question. This would be true even if the name of the act were part of the utterance. "I promise to flunk you," is not in normal circumstances a promise because "a promise is defective if the thing promised is something the promisee does not want done" (p. 58). What Sicinius predicts (correctly) is that Coriolanus will void his request by making it in such a way as to indicate that he does not accept the conditions on its successful performance. He does not, for example, believe that *H* (the hearer or requestee) is able to do *A* (render a judgment by voting). Indeed, in his very first appearance on the stage, he attacks the citizens on just this point. "You!" he tells them, "are no surer, no, / Than is the coal of fire upon the ice." Not only are you fickle ("With every minute you do change a mind, / And call him noble that was now your hate"), but your judgments are true readings of value only if they are reversed:

> Who deserves greatness
> Deserves your hate; and your affections are
> A sick man's appetite, who desires most that
> Which would increase his evil. He that depends
> Upon your favor swims with fins of lead.   (I, i, 177–181)

Thus Coriolanus judges those to whose judgment he is supposed
to submit, finding them incapable of playing their part in the
ceremony enjoined by custom. In so finding, however, he sets
aside the conditions governing that ceremony and substitutes
for them conditions of quite another kind. The ability of the
citizens to bestow their votes cannot legitimately be an issue
because it is stipulated by the rules of the game, that is, by the
conventions that define (or constitute) the workings of the state.
In the context of those rules the citizens are the only ones who
"are able to do A"; and they have that ability by virtue of their
position, and not because they have been certified by some test
outside the system of rules. One can complain about their performance, but one cannot challenge their right to perform without challenging the institution that gives them their role. (Similarly one can argue with an umpire, but one cannot ignore or
set aside his decisions and still be said to be playing the game.)
This is in fact what Coriolanus does when he at first disdains to
ask for their votes because he considers them incompetent to
bestow them. He rejects the public (conventional) stipulation of
competence and substitutes for it his own private assessment. He
declares himself outside (or, more properly, above) the system
of rules by which society fixes its values by refusing to submit to
the (speech-act) conditions under which its business is conducted.

The citizens, on the other hand, do submit to those conditions even though they know as well as he does that in one sense
they are free to disregard them. They discuss the point in Act
II, scene iii, immediately after Sicinius makes his prediction.
The first citizen states the general rule: "Once if he do require
our voices, we ought not to deny him." The "ought" here is not
moral but procedural; they incur the obligation because they
have bound themselves ahead of time to the system of conventions. The formula is, if he does x, then we are obliged, because
he has correctly invoked the procedure, to do y. Immediately,

the second citizen reminds them that the obligation may be repudiated at any time: "We may, sir, if we will." The word "will"
has particular force, because it indicates how fragile are the
bonds that hold a civil society together: in fact men break those
bonds whenever they like. The third citizen acknowledges as
much, but then goes on to explain what restrains them from
exercising this freedom. (Were it not for the dialogue and the
dramatic situation, this might well be a textbook discussion of
the force and necessity of constitutive rules.)

> We have power in ourselves to do it, but it is a power that we have
> no power to do; for if he show us his wounds and tell us his deeds,
> we are to put our tongues into these wounds and speak for them;
> so if he tell us his noble deeds, we must also tell him our noble ac-
> ceptance of them.

The reasoning is admirably clear and the distinctions precise:
true, we may do anything we like, but if we consider ourselves
members of a state rather than discrete individuals, then we are
bound to the mechanism by which the state determines value,
and must comport ourselves accordingly, even when the determination does not sort with our private judgments. The
"nobility," both of Coriolanus' deeds and the citizens' acceptance of them, is pro forma. It is not that they personally regard
his deeds as noble (although some of them may) but that they
are noble by virtue of their position in the procedure. Similarly,
we are not to imagine that they really feel gratitude; rather,
they engage in a form of behavior which counts as an expression
of it.

"Counts as" is the important phrase in this last sentence because it gets at the heart of the speech-act position on intention.
Intention, in the view of that theory, is a matter of what one
takes responsibility for by performing certain conventional
(speech) acts. The question of what is going on inside, the question of the "*inward performance*" is simply bypassed; speech-
act theory does not rule on it. This means that intentions are
available to anyone who invokes the proper (publicly known
and agreed upon) procedures, and it also means that anyone who
invokes those procedures (knowing that they will be recognized

as such) takes responsibility for having that intention. Were it otherwise, then the consequences would be disastrous. Were intention solely a matter of disposition in relation to which words were merely a report, then formulas like "I'm sorry" and "thank you" would not be accepted as expressions of regret and gratitude unless it could be proven, by some independent test, that the speaker was actually so disposed. (The things one does with words would never get done.) And were we not responsible for the conventional acts we perform, then one would forever be at the mercy of those who make promises, give permissions, render verdicts, and so on, and then tell us that they didn't mean it. (The things one does with words would have no status in law.) J. L. Austin's elaboration of this point is classic:

> We are apt to have a feeling that their [the words] being serious consists in their being uttered as (merely) the outward and visible sign, for convenience or other record or for information, of an inward and spiritual act: from which it is but a short step to go on to believe or to assume without realizing that for many purposes the outward utterance is a description, *true or false,* of the occurrence of the inward performance. The classic expression of this idea is to be found in the *Hippolytus* (1.612) where Hippolytus says . . . "my tongue swore to, but my heart (or mind or other backstage artiste) did not." Thus "I promise to. . . ." obliges me—puts on record my spiritual assumption of a spiritual shackle.
>
> It is gratifying to observe in this very example how excess of profundity, or rather solemnity, at once paves the way for immorality. For one who says "promising is not merely a matter of uttering words! It is an inward and spiritual act!" is apt to appear as a solid moralist standing out against a generation of superficial theorizers: we see him as he sees himself, surveying the invisible depths of ethical space, with all the distinction of a specialist in the *sui generis.* Yet he provides Hippolytus with a let out, the bigamist with an excuse for his "I do" and the welsher with a defence for his "I bet." Accuracy and morality alike are on the side of the plain saying that *our word is our bond.*[3]

It is a question finally of what is considered real and therefore of what we are to be faithful to. Austin is suggesting that, at least in terms of legal and moral obligation, reality is a matter of its public specification. In the alternative view, reality is essen-

tial and substantial; it exists independently of any identifying
procedures which can only relate to it as they are more or less
accurate. (The implicit analogy is always to a mirror which is
either clear or distorting.) It is this latter view (scorned by Austin) that Coriolanus espouses when he refuses to accept the procedures by which the state identifies merit because they do not
suspend themselves in recognition of his inherent, that is, obvious, superiority. It is on this opposition that the action (such as
it is) of the play turns: on the one hand, the state demands
adherence to the values its conventions define and create; on
the other, Coriolanus invokes values that (he claims) exist independently of any conventional formula. When he stands before
the citizens and is asked "what hath brought you to't" (II, iii, 67),
he answers "mine own desert." The correct answer is "to ask
for your votes, to gain your approval," but his point is that he
doesn't need it; his desert validates itself and they should acknowledge it without even being asked, as one acknowledges any
natural phenomenon. (He is claiming that a request is unneces-
sary because the nonobvious condition—"it is not obvious to
both S and H that H will do A in the normal course of events of
his own accord"— doesn't or shouldn't obtain.) The second citizen is puzzled. Things are not going as they were supposed to.
He queries, "Your own desert?" The reply is devastating: "Ay,
not mine own desire." With this statement Coriolanus explicitly
violates the sincerity condition on requests—S wants H to do A
—and he indicates that he will default on the essential condition
by not uttering a sentence that "counts as an attempt to get H
to do A." (As we have seen, he has been denying the principal
preparatory condition—S believes H is able to do—from the very
beginning.) Coriolanus knows as well as Austin does that having
an intention *is* "merely a matter of uttering words," and he is
determined to avoid invoking the proper formula. The citizens,
however, are no less tenacious than he. (Sicinius has already declared that they will not "bate / One jot of ceremony.") "If we
give you anything," they remind him, "we hope to gain by you."
Or, in other words, you're not going to get something (our votes)
for nothing. "Well then," replies Coriolanus, "I pray, your
price o'th' consulship?" This is at once taunting and daring.

Coriolanus gives them the *form* of a request, but he uses it simply to ask a question (the force of "pray" is diminished so that it is merely a politeness marker). The citizens, however, are through playing: "The price is, to ask it kindly." "Kindly" is ambiguous, but in a single direction: it means both properly and in accordance with nature, with kind. He is to ask it according to the conventional rules, that is, in such a way as to acknowledge his kinship with other men. This is precisely what he finally does by adopting the citizens' "kindly" and by repeating the formula "I pray," but this time with the full force of a genuine (that is, properly executed) request: "Kindly, sir, I pray let me ha't."

The wire-tight dialectic of this scene underscores the reason for Coriolanus' reluctance. By discharging the custom of request (the phrase is Sicinius'—II, iii, 148) he submits himself to the judgment of others, admitting, in effect, that his merit does not have its own self-validating existence but requires a public finding to certify it. In a word, he acknowledges (or at least seems to; the felicity of his act will later be challenged) his dependence on the community and its evaluative processes. It is exactly the position he least likes to be in, for as Brutus observes to him, "You speak o' th' people / As if you were a god, to punish, not / A man of their infirmity" (III, i, 80–82). Later this statement is confirmed by no less an authority than Coriolanus himself. "I'll stand," he declares, "As if a man were author of himself / And knew no other kin" (V, iii, 34–37). This is always his desire, to stand alone, without visible or invisible supports, as a natural force. He wants to be independent of society and of the language with which it constitutes itself and its values, seeking instead a language that is the servant of essences he alone can recognize because he alone embodies them. As Menenius says, "His heart's his mouth / What his breast forges, that his tongue must vent" (III, i, 256–257). In Searle's terms, this defines the "direction of fit": his language is (or tries to be) true not to publicly acknowledged realities but to the absolute values he bears in his breast. ("I will not do't; / Lest I surcease to honor mine own truth.") "Would you have me / False to my nature?" (III, ii, 14–15), he asks his mother. "Must I / With my base tongue give to my noble heart / A lie?" (99–101). It is the choice of the world he complains "rather to have my hat than my heart" (II, ii, 103), that is, to have my recognition of its meanings rather than my loyalty to my own. His choice, as Volumnia notes, is to be always speaking by his own instruction and to the "matter" which his "heart prompts" (III, ii, 53–54). Unfortunately, language is wholly and intractably conventional; it is a space already occupied by the public, "everywhere permeated," as Searle says, "with the facts of commitments undertaken, obligations assumed" (p. 197), and Coriolanus spends much of the play trying desperately to hold himself clear of those commitments and obligations. This is why he cannot for a time bring himself to utter the illocutionary formula: "What, must I say 'I pray, sir' . . . I cannot bring my tongue to such a pace!" (II, iii, 53–55).

Coriolanus reveals himself not only in the critical scene, where the stakes are high and obvious, but in every aspect of what we might call his illocutionary behavior. It is not simply that he cannot bear to request something of his avowed enemies and social inferiors; he cannot bear to request something of anyone. As Cominius' nominal underling he must twice ask him for favors, and on both occasions he has great difficulty. On the first occasion he begins conventionally enough: "I do beseech you" (I, vi, 55), but in the space between this illocutionary-force-indicating phrase and the propositional content (future act *A* of *H*), Coriolanus interposes a series of reasons for Cominius to grant the not yet specified request: "By all the battles wherein we have fought, / By th' blood we have shed together, by th' vows / We have made to endure friends." The effect of this is to limit Cominius' supposedly free power to do or not to do what Coriolanus will ask. The force of the utterance changes from "will you please do this?" to something like "you really are obliged to do this," and when the request is finally made it is clear that Cominius has no choice: "that you directly / Set me against Aufidius." It is the form of a request, but it has the force of a command, as Cominius well knows. "Dare I never / Deny your asking."

On a second occasion, Cominius grants Coriolanus' request before it is made, thereby taking away its sting as an admission of dependence. "Tak't; 'tis yours. What is't?" he declares, saying in effect, "you don't have to ask" (I, ix, 81). Even so, Coriolanus does have to ask, and he resents it: "I that now / Refused most princely gifts, am bound to beg / Of my lord general." The word "bound" precisely locates his discomfort; bonds of any kind are intolerable to the free-standing man. Yet for once Coriolanus chooses to put them on:

> I sometimes lay here in Corioles
> At a poor man's house; he used me kindly.
> He cried to me; I saw him prisoner:
> But then Aufidius was within my view,
> And wrath o'erwhelmed my pity. I request you
> To give my poor host freedom.   (I, ix, 82–87)

"He used me kindly." That of course is just the trouble. By using him kindly, this "poor man" makes Coriolanus his debtor (and implies that he is his equal). This is why Coriolanus is willing to execute a proper request, without in any way qualifying it: he will put himself under an obligation (to a man who has already assured him that it will not be considered so) in order to get out from under a more burdensome one; he asks a favor only to be relieved of owing one. Any doubt that this rather than gratitude or compassion is his motive is removed by the exchange that follows:

> Cominius: Deliver him Titus.
> Lartius: Marcius, his name?
> Coriolanus: By Jupiter, forgot!   (I, ix, 89–90)

The man himself is not important; he is less someone to be remembered than a shackle to be thrown off.

If Coriolanus has difficulty with requests, he is literally beside himself in the face of praise. He cannot bear to hear it, and he is unable to accept it, from anyone. Lartius merely suggests that it is too soon for Coriolanus to reenter the battle, and he is told (does the gentleman protest too much?) "Sir praise me not" (I, v, 16). Later Coriolanus spends an entire scene turning away praises, and he is careful to explain that his is no army-camp gesture: "My mother, / Who has a charter to extol her blood, / When she does praise me grieves me" (I, ix, 13–15). Why grieves? Surely that is an excessive reaction. The reason for it becomes clear when we allow a speech-act analysis to tell us what is involved both in praising and in accepting praise:

	Praise	Accepting Praise
Propositional content	Some act, property, quality, etc., *E* related to *H*	Past act *A* done by *H*
Preparatory	*E* reflects creditably on *H* and *S* believes that it does.	A benefits *S* and *S* believes *A* benefits *S*.
Sincerity	*S* values *E* positively.	*S* feels grateful or appreciative for *A*
Essential	Counts as a positive valuation of *E*.	Counts as an expression of gratitude or appreciation.

The analysis of praising is my own; the analysis of accepting praise is Searle's analysis of thanking for, because that is what the acceptance of praise is. Together they show that if Coriolanus were to thank his praisers he would be admitting their right to evaluate him, to determine what in his actions was creditable; he would be acknowledging that he received addition from the praise. In short, he would be receiving from others what he thinks can only be bestowed by himself on himself. That is what grieves him, the ignominy (even if its form is benign) of submitting himself to the judgment of anyone. Cominius says as much when he protests the protesting. "You shall not be / The grave of your deserving; Rome must know / The value of her own" (I, ix, 19–21). That is, you must not be so jealous of your merits as to allow no one but yourself to confirm them. He urges Coriolanus (still Marcius) to accept one tenth of the horses and treasure "In sign of what you are" (26). Such a sign, however, would be a public recognition of just the kind Coriolanus wishes to avoid, lest it appear that because his desert was for hire, it required external verification. I cannot, he declares, "make my heart consent to take / A bribe to pay my sword. I do refuse it" (37–38). He wants no third parties interfering (claiming a part) in the transactions between himself and himself. It is hard, however, to keep the public out (short of setting up a state of one, something he will later come to); the

LIBRARY ST. MARY'S COLLEGE

soldiers make of his disavowing of praise and treasure an occasion for new praise, drawing from the hero still another refusal: "No more, I say . . . / You shout me forth / in acclamations hyperbolical; / As if I loved my little should be dieted / In praises and sauced with lies" (47, 50–53). This is naked. To accept these praises would be to admit that he courted them, wanted them, needed them; even worse, it would be to imply that he was fed by them instead of by the approval he bestows on himself and would reserve *to* himself. This is too much for Cominius, who comes close to telling Coriolanus what his modesty really signifies:

> Too modest are you;
> More cruel to your good report than grateful
> To us that give you truly.   (53–55)

This may be gracefully turned, but it is unmistakably a complaint, bordering on a criticism. In your concern to protect your modesty, to hold yourself aloof from "good report," you neglect the reciprocal courtesies that make a society civil; you withhold gratitude and thereby imply that we are unable to perform an act that would draw it. Cominius tries once again, offering Marcius a new name, "Caius Marcius Coriolanus" (65). This too is a sign, but because it is a sign of himself (of *his* action), the power to bestow it is severely limited. In a sense, then, he bestows it on himself. The acceptance is curt and graceless—"Howbeit, I thank you"—but it is made. The contest is over.

In this scene Coriolanus parries with his friends; in Act II, scene iii, he faces his enemies; but the structure of both scenes is exactly the same: a determined effort by the hero to keep himself clear of all obligations and bonds, except for those he himself nominates, is resisted by those who perceive, however dimly, what his illocutionary behavior means. His reluctance to make a request and his inability to accept praise have a single source in a desire for total independence.

There are speech acts he is good at. He is fine at refusing and even better at promising. Both make sense. Refusing is saying "I can do (in the fullest sense of agency) without it"; and while promising involves undertaking an obligation, it is an obligation the promiser both creates and discharges; when he keeps his promise, he is being true to *his own word,* not to the word of another. It is Coriolanus' favorite speech act, the one by which he defines himself. When news of war reaches Rome, he is urged to "attend upon Cominius," who reminds him, "It is your former promise" (I, i, 239). "Sir, it is," he says, "and I am constant." Later he meets Aufidius on the battlefield, and, reaching for the worst thing he can think of, declares, "I do hate thee / Worse than a promise-breaker" (I, viii, 1–2). When he is asked to take back his word to the tribunes ("Repent, what you have spoke"), he cries, "I cannot do it to the Gods, / Must I then do't to them?" (III, ii, 38–39). When the citizens take back theirs, he asks in contempt, "Have I had children's voices?" (III, i, 30). The tribunes base their entire strategy on a pledge they have heard him make:

> I heard him swear,
> Were he to stand for consul, never would he
> Appear i' th' marketplace, nor on him put
> The napless vesture of humility;
> Nor, showing, as the manner is, his wounds
> To th' people, beg their stinking breaths.
>
> (II, i, 238–242)

"It was his word," says Brutus and Sicinius wishes "no better / Than to have him hold that purpose and to put it / In execution." They know their man (Brutus replies "'Tis most like he will"), and as he goes off to "discharge the custom of request" they predict his behavior in the passage with which this essay began:

> Brutus: You see how he intends to use the people.
> Sicinius: May they perceive's intent. He will require them,
>   As if he did contemn what he requested
>   Should be in them to give.

It might seem from this that they are counting on him to be insincere, to say one thing and mean another. But in fact it is exactly the reverse—they are counting on him to mean exactly what he says and they count on him to do it by making void the speech act he purports to be performing. The surest way to avoid a speech act is to violate the essential condition, to say in the case of promises, "I promise to do *x*, but I don't intend to" or in the case of requests, "I am asking you to do this, but I don't want you to." When Sicinius says, "May they perceive's intent," he doesn't mean "may they see through his language to the motion of his heart," but "may they correctly (by attending to the performance or nonperformance of stipulated procedures) read his language." (In fact, it is hard to see what it would mean to make an insincere request if the specification were other than conventional. If I execute the proper procedures and ask you to do something, and later, after you've done it, I tell you that I didn't want you to, you have a perfect response in "well, you shouldn't have *said* that." Notice that you will not say, "You shouldn't have intended that" because it is assumed that intention is a function of what is said. Part of Coriolanus' tragedy is that he is forever seeking a level of intention deeper—more essential or more real—than that stipulated by the public conventions of language.)

The tribunes' laissez-faire strategy almost doesn't work, precisely because for a time the citizens do not "perceive's intent," even though, as we have seen, he systematically violates every one of the conditions on the request he is supposedly making.[4] It is only later that they open their copy of *Speech Acts* and begin to analyze the infelicities of his performance:

Second Citizen: ... To my poor unworthy notice,
He mocked us when he begged
our voices.
Third Citizen: Certainly,
He flouted us downright.
First Citizen: No, 'tis his kind of speech—he did
not mock us.
Second Citizen: Not one amongst us, save yourself, but says
He used us scornfully.

(II, iii, 163–168)

The tribunes need only guide the discussion, which ends in the determination that he "did not ask, but mock" (II, iii, 213). Again, the finding is a procedural, not a moral, one. It is not that Coriolanus did not keep his word, but rather that he did, and in a way altogether typical, by botching a procedure which, if properly executed, would have tied him to the word of another.

It becomes possible to write a speech-act history of Coriolanus, the play and the man: he cannot make requests or receive praise; he is most himself when he is either putting things by or promising. In slightly different ways requesting and accepting praise are acts which place their performer in a position of dependence (hence the force of "I wouldn't ask you for the time of day" as a way of asserting that you don't want or need my help); promising and rejecting, on the other hand, are transactions that leave the self inviolate. Coriolanus' every illocutionary gesture is one that declares his disinclination to implicate himself in the reciprocal web of obligations that is the content of the system of conventional speech acts. To put it simply, Coriolanus is always doing things (with words) to set himself apart.

He finally succeeds. The most spectacular illocutionary act performed in *Coriolanus* is the double banishing of III, iii. In any production, the scene is the centerpiece, the climax to which everything before it has been building; but in a way that speech-act theory can explicate, it is anticlimactic. It is anticlimactic because the explicit act merely confirms or ratifies what Coriolanus has been doing all the while, setting himself apart from the community. He cuts the last tie before he is banished, when in response to the pleas of Cominius and Menenius ("Is this the promise you made to your mother"), he declares, "I would not buy / Their mercy at the price of one fair word. / Nor check my courage for what they can give, / To hav't with saying 'Good morrow' " (III, iii, 90–93). It is no accident that "greeting" is cited as the smallest price he might be expected to pay. Here is Searle's analysis of it:

	Greet
Propositional content	None
Preparatory	*S* has just encountered (or been introduced to, etc.) *H*.
Sincerity	None
Essential	Counts as courteous recognition of *H* by *S*.

What strikes us immediately is how little, relative to other speech acts, greeting commits us to. One who greets commits himself neither to a proposition, nor to a desire, nor to a position in a line of authority and dependence, but simply to being a member of the (speech-act) community whose conventional means of expressing courtesy he is now invoking. Greeting is the bottom line of civility; it has no content except the disposition to *be* civil; it is an act we perform even in the company of our enemies, signifying that the differences dividing us finally depend on something we share. We can say of someone, "I'll never ask him for anything again," or "I'll never rely on his promises," and still be understood to have commerce with him; but if we say "I will not even say 'hello' to that man," it is understood that we will have nothing to do with him at all. Coriolanus says that to the Roman citizens, and when, in the very next instant they banish him, they merely say it back: "Let him away! / He's banished" (III, iii, 106–107).

What happens next, however, does not take place within the precincts of speech-act conventions; rather, it subverts them and along with them the institutions with which they exist in reciprocal support. Coriolanus turns around and says, "I banish you":

> You common cry of curs, whose breath I hate
> As reek o' the rotten fens, whose loves I prize
> As the dead carcasses of unburied men
> That do corrupt my air, I banish you.   (III, iii, 120–123)

The disruptive force of this is a function of the kind of act banishing is. Following Searle's taxonomy, we would label it a declarative, a class that has two defining characteristics:

(1) The successful performance of one of its members brings about the correspondence between the propositional content and reality. . . . Declarations bring about some alteration in the status or condition of the referred to object or objects solely in virtue of the fact that the declaration has been successfully performed.

(2) The mastery of those rules which constitute linguistic competence by the speaker and hearer is not in general sufficient for the performance of a declaration. In addition there must

exist an extralinguistic institution and the speaker and hearer must occupy special places within this institution. It is only given such institutions as the church, the law, private property, the state and a special position of the speaker and hearer within these institutions that one can excommunicate, appoint, give and bequeath one's possessions or declare war.[5]

The first point can be captured in the phrase "saying makes it so." Other speech acts are attempts either to get the words to match a state of affairs in the world (reports, assertions, explanations) or to get the world to match the words (promises, requests): but, with a declarative, the direction of fit goes both ways, for the words are made to fit the world at the same instant as the world is made to fit the words. This is because declaratives create the conditions to which they refer. More obviously than any other class of speech acts, they testify to the power of language to constitute reality. Searle's second point is that this power depends on the speaker's occupying a position of authority in an extralinguistic institution; in the absence of that institution and the speaker's position in it, a so-called declarative utterance would have no force (as when a fan yells "strike three").

What Coriolanus' counterbanishing suggests is that this can be turned on its head. It is not that words are in force only so long as the institutions are, but that institutions are in force only so long as the words are, so long as hearers perform in the stipulated way when words are uttered (the batter returns to the dugout, the armed forces mobilize, the defendant is released from custody). If, on the other hand, hearers simply disregard a declarative utterance, it is not that they have ceased to pay attention to the words (which still bear the perfectly ordinary and understood meanings of commands that are not being obeyed) but that they have ceased to recognize—and assist in the constitution of—the institution. The moral of this is chastening, even disturbing: institutions are no more than the (temporary) effects of speech-act agreements, and they are therefore as fragile as the decision, always capable of being revoked, to abide by them. This becomes obvious if one reflects a bit on the ontological status of declaratives (a reflection not usually encouraged because so much hangs on the implicit claim of authority to be

eternal): if declarative utterances, when they have their intended
force, alter states of affairs, what brings about the state of affairs
in which a declarative utterance is endowed with its intended
force? The answer is, another declarative utterance, and it is an
answer one would have to give no matter how far back the
inquiry was pushed. The conclusion is inescapable: declarative
(and other) utterances do not merely mirror or reflect the state;
they *are* the state, which increases and wanes as they are or are
not taken seriously.

   It might be objected that to reason in this way is to imply that
one can constitute a state simply by declaring it to exist. That of
course is exactly what happens: a single man plants a flag on a
barren shore and claims everything his eye can see in the name
of a distant monarch or for himself; another man, hunted by
police and soldiers, seeks refuge in a cave, where, alone or in the
company of one or two fellows, he proclaims the birth of a revolutionary government. In the case of Coriolanus, the declaration
of independence is more public, but it has the same content. We
can see this by imagining him doing something else: had he said,
"You can't banish me because I hereby renounce my citizenship"
(on the model of "You can't fire me; I resign"), his act would be
a recognition of the state and of his position in it; but by saying
"I banish you," he reduces the state to a counterdeclaration and
brings about the very condition he had warned against earlier:

> my soul aches
> To know, when two authorities are up,
> Neither supreme, how soon confusion
> May enter 'twixt the gap of both and take
> The one by th'other.   (III, i, 108–112)

The case is worse even than that: if two authorities, why not
three or four or four hundred? What Coriolanus does opens the
way for anyone who feels constrained by the bonds of a society
to declare a society of his own, to nominate his own conventions,
to stipulate his own obligations; suddenly there is a possibility
of a succession of splinter coalitions, each inaugurated by the
phrase Coriolanus hurls at those whom he has cast behind him:
"There is a world elsewhere."

It would be a mistake, however, to think of Coriolanus simply as a revolutionary. He would not agree with my analysis of what he does because in his mind banishing is not a political act (and therefore finally dependent on the vagaries of circumstance) but an act which derives (or should derive) its authority from the natural merit of its performer. The world elsewhere he seeks is not another state (for then he would simply be trading one system of conventional ties for another) but a world where essences are immediately recognized and do not require for their validation the mediation of public procedures. For a time, the Volsci seem to offer him such a world. He is given command without having to ask for it. Aufidius hands over his prerogatives as if they were his natural right ("no questions asked him by any of the senators but they stand bald before him"); soldiers obey him and even preface their prayers with his name; towns fall to him even before they are besieged ("All places yield to him ere he sits down"). And all of this seems to transpire, as Aufidius says, "by sovereignty of nature" (IV, vii, 35). He is, in short, exactly what he always wanted to be, a natural force whose movement through the world is independent of all supports except those provided by his own virtue. He is complete and sufficient unto himself. He is a God.

It is as a God (and as a machine) that Menenius reports him:

> When he walks, he moves like an engine and the ground shrinks before his treading. He is able to pierce a corselet with his eye, talks like a knell, and his hum is a battery. He sits in his state as a thing made for Alexander. What he bids be done is finished with his bidding. He wants nothing of a god but eternity and a heaven to throne in. (V, iv, 18–25)

"What he bids be done is finished with his bidding." A more concise account of declaratives could not be imagined. Coriolanus is in that happy state where his word is law, and not because he is the spokesman for an institutional authority but because he is the source of law itself. His is the declarative of divine fiat, the logos, the *all*-creating word.

This, however, is an illusion, mounted by Aufidius with the inadvertent complicity of the Volsci, and believed in only by

Coriolanus. The truth is that there is no world elsewhere, at least not in the sense Coriolanus intends, a world where it is possible to stand freely, unencumbered by obligations and dependencies. There are only other speech-act communities, and every one of them exacts as the price of membership acceptance of its values and meanings. Coriolanus is paying that price, even as he is supposedly moving toward independence and Godhead. He no sooner enters Antium before he performs the very acts he disdained in Rome. He greets ("Save you, sir"); he requests, and with full acknowledgment of the position it puts him in ("Direct me, if it be your will," "Which is his house, beseech you?"); and he thanks ("Thank you, sir: farewell").[6] A greater ignominy follows: when he gains admission to Aufidius' house, no one knows him; in a gesture intended to be revelatory, he unmuffles, expecting, Satan-like, to be announced simply by the transcendant brightness of his visage. Nothing happens, and Aufidius keeps asking "What is thy name?" as Coriolanus feeds him more and more clues. Finally he is reduced to telling his name: "My name is Caius Marcius" (IV, 4, 69). The man who would strip down to essences and be recognized simply by "sovereignty of nature" is forced to cover himself with public identification (name, rank, and serial number) before he has enough substance even to be addressed.

In a footnote to *Speech Acts,* Searle makes a point that is relevant here: "Standing on the deck of some institutions one can tinker with constitutive rules and even throw some other institutions overboard. But could one throw all institutions over-board? . . . One could not and still engage in those forms of behavior we consider characteristically human" (p. 186n). Coriolanus tries to throw over all institutions at the same time that he is engaging in activities that are characteristically human. It is a contradiction that he tries to mediate by acting as if his contacts with human beings were accidental, as if he were a meteor or comet whose unconstrained way just happened to take it through places where men lived together in mutual interdependence. That is why he answers to no name: "Coriolanus / He would not answer to; forbade all names; / He was a kind of nothing, titleless" (V, i, 11–13). He wants to be a nothing in the sense of a substance not made, a substance that might for a moment take up community space but would abide long after the community and its names had passed away. But his ability even to strike such a pose is a function of the power a community, the Volscian community, has given him. He may stand "As if a man were author of himself / And knew no other kin," but the "as if" precisely locates the weakness of his stance; it is rooted in a fiction, in the illusion that a man can be a man and still be totally alone.

It is, however, his fiction, no less real in its consequences than the fictions of society; and even if he is the only one who lives by it, he is still subject to its rules and penalties. There is, finally, only one rule: the word is from Coriolanus and it is the law; it acknowledges no other authority; it recognizes no obligations that it does not itself stipulate ("Away . . . Wife, mother, child"); it hears no appeals; it is inexorable, or, to use a word several times aplied to Coriolanus, "absolute." Once set in motion, it is like the machine he is said to have become: nothing can stand against it.

It follows, then, that when Coriolanus stands against it, he is destroyed. It is his own word that convicts him and it is able to convict him because he has pledged his loyalty to it and to nothing else. Had he not made a religion of keeping to his word, then his breaking of it could not have been cited by Aufidius as a capital crime: "perfidiously / He has betrayed your business . . . / Breaking his oath and resolution, like / A twist of rotten silk" (V, vi, 95–96). What he stands accused of is being human; he has listened to his mother, wife, and child; but since it has been his claim and his desire to stand apart from human ties, he cannot now acknowledge them without paying the penalty demanded by the abstraction—the totally autonomous self—he has set up in their place. Yet at the very moment that he pays the penalty, Coriolanus exposes that abstraction as a fiction. The speech-act community reclaims him as inescapably its own when he provides the strongest possible evidence that he is neither a God nor a machine. He dies.

It is evidence the significance of which always escapes him. Unlike some of Shakespeare's heroes, Coriolanus never learns anything: even as his "world elsewhere" reveals itself to be baseless, he defiantly reasserts its constitutive first principle: "Alone I did it." The final comment on this and on his every other claim of independence is made by the play's closing words: "He shall have a noble memory." The irony is unrelenting. The man who scorned the word of the community ("You common cry of curs whose breath I hate"), even to the extent of disdaining its names, now depends on that word (and on those breaths) for the only life he has.

What Not To Do with Speech-Act Theory

I want to make it clear what it is that I am and am not claiming for this analysis of *Coriolanus*. I am not claiming that it is exhaustive. Nor am I claiming that what it says is wholly new. What I am claiming is that it doesn't cheat; by that I mean that the stages in the argument follow one another without ever going outside the definitions and descriptions of speech-act theory. Thus, simply by paying attention to the hero's illocutionary behavior and then referring to the full dress accounts of the acts he performs, it is possible to produce a speech act "reading" of the play:

(1) In his reluctance to make a request or accept praise, he declares his independence of conventional (that is, public) procedures for confirming merit or desert.

(2) When he goes so far as to refuse to greet, his setting himself apart from the community is complete, and he stands alone.

(3) By banishing him, the citizens simply ratify and confirm what he has already done; by banishing them, he makes explicit his rejection of the community and his intention to stand alone, as a society of one, as a state complete in himself, independent of all external supports and answerable only to the laws he himself promulgates. In short, he decides to be a God.

(4) As a God, he demands absolute obedience to his word (the sacred text), establishing his promises and pledges as the law against which no other considerations or loyalties can stand ("Thou shalt have no other Gods before me").

(5) By going back on his pledge, he stands against it and is struck down accordingly. Dying, he acknowledges involuntarily his

necessary involvement in the community from whose conventions he sought to be free. In the end, the fiercely private man exists only by virtue of the words of others ("He shall have a noble memory").

To the extent that this reading is satisfying, it is because *Coriolanus* is a speech-act play. That is to say, it is *about* what the theory is "about," the conditions for the successful performance of certain conventional acts and the commitments one enters into or avoids by performing or refusing to perform those acts; indeed, as we have seen, these conditions and commitments *are* what the characters discuss, so that at times it is almost as if they were early practitioners of Oxford or "ordinary language" philosophy. That is why we seem to have gotten somewhere by putting scenes from the play side by side with the analyses of the theory: the questions it is able to ask and answer—what is involved in a request? what is one doing when one greets? what enables one to banish?—are the questions about which the action revolves.

There are of course questions the theory does not even touch, and it is when its terms are stretched to include such questions that cheating occurs. Like transformational grammar before it, speech-act theory has been sacrificed to the desire of the literary critic for a system more firmly grounded than any afforded him by his own discipline. The career of this desire always unfolds in two stages: (1) the system or theory is emptied of its content so that the distinctions it is able to make are lost or blurred, and (2) what remains, a terminology and an empty framework, is made into a metaphor. A spectacular instance of this process has recently been provided by Wolfgang Iser,[7] who begins by allegorizing the term "performative," taking it to mean that part of an utterance which produces something as opposed to that (constative) part which asserts something; illocutionary force, in his account, refers to a "quality of productiveness" (p. 11). But the only thing that performative or illocutionary acts produce is recognition on the part of a hearer that the procedures constitutive of a particular act have been invoked: illocutionary force is not something an illocutionary act exerts but something it has (by virtue of its proper execution); it refers to the way an utterance is taken (as a promise, command, request) by some-one who knows the constituting procedures and their value. It is simply wrong to think of an illocutionary act as producing meaning in the sense of creating it. Indeed, the meaning the act produces (a better word would be presents, as in he presents a compliment) necessarily preexists it; or, to put it another way, in speech-act theory, meaning is prior to utterance.

Iser's confusion is such that one mistake not only leads to but makes inevitable another. The notion of productiveness, once having been produced (out of thin air as it were), proceeds to rule his argument. Literature, he says, "imitates the illocu-tionary speech act, but what is said does not produce what is meant" (p. 12). What Iser wants to say, I suppose, is that in literature illocutionary acts do not have their usual consequences (a position that Austin does in fact hold), but this is quite dif-ferent from saying that illocutionary acts in literature don't produce what they produce in serious or everyday discourse, be-cause in both contexts what illocutionary acts produce is recogni-tion that they have been produced. If Iser wants a basis for distinguishing literary from ordinary language, he won't find it here. Nor will he find it where he seeks it next, in conventions and the possibility of "reorganizing" them: "For Austin, literary 'speech' is void because it cannot invoke conventions and ac-cepted procedures" (p. 13). But Austin's point is precisely that the conventions and procedures *have* been invoked, but that there is nothing for them to hook up to (no one to receive the command or hear the question). Indeed, if the conventional pro-cedures were not invoked what we would have is not "void" speech but no speech. If there is a distinction between literary and nonliterary speech, it is not one between illocutionary acts and some other kind but between illocutionary acts put to differ-ing uses. By the same argument, the conventions (or rules) that define those acts cannot be said to be present in one kind of dis-course and absent (or uninvoked) in another; for they are the procedures which make all discourse possible, and any distinc-tion one might want to draw must be drawn at a level of gen-erality below that at which they operate. Iser avoids this realiza-tion because he equivocates between two senses of "convention":

the stricter sense by which illocutionary acts are constitutive rather than regulative, and the looser sense (roughly equivalent to "accepted practice") employed by literary critics when they talk, for example, of the conventions of narrative. The equivocation is important to Iser (I am not ascribing an intention to him) because he wants to assert a parallel between a violation of speech-act conventions and a violation of the conventions of literature or society. But the parallel will not hold because in one case a violation amounts to nonperformance, while in the other the convention (which, rather than constituting the activity, is merely a variation on it) is either replaced or modified.

Iser, then, is able to conduct his argument only because there is so much shift and slippage in its principal terms. The shift and slippage is in one direction, away from the strictness of definition required by the theory, and toward the metaphorical looseness that makes it possible for him to say anything he likes. In the end, the words he is using have no relationship to the theory at all. It is this, paradoxically, that makes Iser's performance less distressing than it otherwise might have been. The connection between what he is saying and the concerns of the theory is finally so slight that there is no possibility of anyone's following him. This is not the case, however, with Richard Ohmann, who is a responsible and informed student of the subject and a respecter of theories. With respect to this particular theory, however, I believe that he is confused. His confusion can be located at his use of a single word: felicity. Here for example, is what he has to say about *King Lear:* "King Lear ceremonially measures out his lands in geometric correspondence to his daughters' professions of love. The terrible infelicity of his acts corresponds to the depth of his error about what sort of human reality an old king inhabits."[8] Apparently, Ohmann thinks that he is making a speech-act judgment here, but he isn't. The criterion of felicity has to do with the execution of conventional procedures; an act is felicitous if certain specified conditions are met: it must be performed by the proper person (a private cannot give an order to a general); it must be possible (one cannot promise to have done something yesterday); and so on. These conditions will differ with different acts, but my point is

that in the case of Lear's act (we might call it the act of appor-
tioning) they are all met, and the act is, in terms of the theory,
perfectly felicitous. That is, there is a procedure, he invokes it,
and he is the proper person to have done so. In fact, he is the
only person who could have done so. What then does Ohmann
mean when he calls this act infelicitous? Obviously, that it
turned out badly (and indeed it has), but this has nothing to
do with its having been properly executed. As Austin says (his
example is of advice that would have been better not followed),
"That an act is happy or felicitous in all our ways does not
exempt it from all criticism."[9]

   The case is even clearer with another of Ohmann's examples.
He is discussing the scene in *Major Barbara* in which Lord
Saxmundham (Bodger the distiller) is reported to have promised
to contribute five thousand pounds to the Salvation Army if five
other "gentlemen" will give a thousand each. Undershaft promises to help, much to Mrs. Baines's delight and Barbara's con-
sternation. Ohmann comments:

> The promiser's moral character and intentions bear on the felicity
> of his *promise,* and in fact determines whether she [Barbara]
> would be party to it—agrees to accept the gift and so bring the
> promise to completion. As clearly, for Mrs. Baines this is ir-
> relevant . . . The dramatic irony here rests precisely in the am-
> bivalence of Undershaft's act—felicitous for Mrs. Baines and
> seemingly, but not really, for him; infelicitous for Barbara. (p. 87)

Again, this blurs the distinction (which gives the theory whatever force it has) between two different kinds of felicity. Undershaft's promise is complete as soon as his intention to make it
is recognized. That is what distinguishes conventional acts from
others; they are performed by invoking procedures that are
agreed on in advance to *count as* their proper execution. Barbara does not need to accept the gift in order to complete the
promise; it is complete as soon as it is understood to be one. The
word for this understanding is "uptake" ("ah, so that's what he's
doing"); what Ohmann is talking about is reaction and it is a
reaction to an act already, and felicitously, performed. Were it
otherwise, then the reaction would be impossible. The strongest

evidence for the completeness of Undershaft's promise is Barbara's recoiling from it. (Similarly, a breach-of-promise suit is possible only if a promise has been successfully made; if the promise could be shown to be infelicitous the suit would fail.)

In both instances Ohmann is doing the same thing: he is sliding over from illocutionary acts to perlocutionary effects and trying to include the latter in the felicity conditions of the former. Moreover, this confusion is a matter of principle as he himself declares in another article: "The notion of felicity is itself distinctly social. A felicitous act is one that 'takes,' one whose legitimacy is acknowledged by all the participants and all those affected, and whose performance changes, however slightly, the social connectedness among people."[10] But in speech-act theory the notion of felicity isn't social but conventional; the scope of "takes" as Ohmann uses it is much larger than the theory of illocutionary acts allows; for by his criterion an act would not be considered felicitous until a series of follow-up interviews had been conducted and the behavior of the participants had been monitored; it might even be necessary for the speaker and his hearers to undergo therapy so that their "true" intentions or responses could be determined. But we have recourse to conventions precisely in order to get the world's verbal business done without going through the time and effort (both endless) of checking everything out. The notion of felicity is social only in the narrow sense that it is tied to conditions specified by a society, and not in the larger sense that we must wait for social circumstances to *emerge* before it can be affirmed.

Again, when Ohmann declares, "I won't felicitously say to you, 'that's a phoebe' unless I have greater expertise than you in classifying birds" (p. 130), his condition refers to the confidence one might have in the act (of reference) and not to the question of whether or not it has been performed. (Actually there are all kinds of circumstances in which I can say that to you irrespective of my expertise: for example, I have been asked by you to be on the lookout for phoebes.) Once an illocutionary act has been performed, there are all kinds of questions or objections you can put to it—what gives you the right to say that? do you really want me to? you didn't have to order, you could have asked; you should never make a promise you might not be able to keep—but you will be able to frame those objections only because the proper procedures have been invoked and up-take has been secured. According to Ohmann, "If six month delays are my standard operating procedure, I can't felicitously apologize for one of them" (p. 131). But one apologizes when one produces an utterance that in the circumstances counts as an expression of regret. You may not accept my apology and you may be wary of regarding it as a guarantee of my future behavior, but you will be able to do these and other things only because I have in fact made it. (You don't say, I failed to apologize because he didn't accept it, but, rather, I apologized, *and* he didn't accept it.)

What is important about Ohmann's errors is that they are always honorable and attractive; that is, they are made in an effort to stretch the theory so that it will do things we would like it to do: talk about the trains of events that illocutionary (and other) acts set in motion, distinguish in dramatic situations the different effects the performance of a particular act will have, speculate as to the reasons why a request or an order or a warning hasn't done what the speaker had hoped it would. Speech-act theory can point to these matters—they are perlocutionary effects—but it cannot explicate them because they lie outside the area of its declared competence. Illocutionary effects are conventional; they occur simply by virtue of speakers and hearers being members of the same community and therefore parties to the same agreements about what finite and ordered procedures "count as" the performance of what acts. Perlocutionary effects, on the other hand, are contingent; they cannot be predicted because there is no way of knowing what will certainly bring them off. This is not to say that one can't calculate them with probability; but that probability will be natural, not conventional. Austin puts it this way: "for clearly *any* or almost any perlocutionary act is liable to be brought off, in sufficiently special circumstances, by the issuing, with or without calculation, of any utterance whatsoever" (p. 109).

Obviously this does not mean that perlocutionary effects don't occur or that we shouldn't be interested in them when doing literary criticism, but that speech-act theory can offer us no special help in dealing with them, apart from telling us that they are what it cannot handle. And if we insist on asking the theory to do what it cannot, we will end up by taking from it the ability to do what it can. What it can do is tell us what is conventional and what is not and provide analyses of conventional performances. But if we ignore the distinction between the conventional and the contingent and call everything we meet an illocutionary act or its consequences, then the terms we are using will have no cutting force; they will tell us nothing, or, what is the same thing, they will tell us anything.

Ohmann courts this danger when he assumes that almost any verb that appears in a sentence is the name of an illocutionary act. (This is an inevitable consequence of his thinking that a classification of illocutionary acts is a classification of verbs; for a persuasive refutation of this view, see Searle, *A Classification of Illocutionary Acts,* forthcoming.) Among his lists of illocutionary verbs we find "lament," "rejoice," "assume," and "wish" (as in "May you have a long life"). None of these are names of illocutionary acts although they can all be used in sentences that have an illocutionary force. If I say "I rejoice in your happiness," I don't perform some act of rejoicing; I express my feelings. If I say, "I wish you a long life," I am not making a wish but expressing good will. If I say, "I assume that it's raining," I am not making an assumption but expressing one. In each of these cases (and in the case of "lament") the verb is not a performative one because the act it refers to is a motion of the mind or heart and does not require the invoking of previously specified procedures for its occurrence. Here is another instance where the abuse of speech-act theory is also a comment on its limitations: just as it stops short of claiming knowledge of what happens after the performance of an illocutionary act, so is it silent on the question of what (if anything; the whole world may be conventional) preceded it. No one would deny that these are matters for a literary critic to inquire into, but they are the province of rhetoric (the art of persuasion, a perlocutionary art) and psychology. Speech-act theory can tell us nothing about them.

Neither can it tell us what is involved in telling a story. In another instance of stretching the theory out of its proper shape and usefulness, Ohmann invents "the general speech act of telling a story"[11] and goes on to talk about narrative conventions which include the condition "that the teller knows, having invented, all the facts and all the sentences contained in that story," and the rule that "the teller always endorses the fictive world of the story for its duration, and again, by convention, does not acknowledge that it *is* a fiction" (pp. 251, 247). But if these are rules they are regulative; that is, they are imposed on an antecedently existing form of behavior. One can vary and even ignore them and still be engaging in that behavior. Speech-act rules, on the other hand, are constitutive; they do not regulate behavior but enumerate the procedures which define it. If you practice creative story telling, you are likely to end up in an anthology. If you practice creative promising, you will not be understood as having promised at all. This is not to deny that there are conventions of storytelling (many of which are mutually exclusive and yet indiscriminately felicitous), but that they are not on all fours with the illocutionary acts for which speech-act theory has provided descriptions.

What is perhaps Ohmann's most troubling distortion of the theory concerns the vexed question of style. He believes that in "the distinction between the activated meaning and the fully launched illocutionary act we have the kind of split required for style to exist."[12] Of course style can only exist in a binary opposition with content or meaning. In Ohmann's account, meaning is identified with the locutionary act, that is, the act of saying something with a particular sense and reference. To this basic meaning one adds illocutionary force, much as one might add an intensifier to a sentence or flavoring to a piece of meat: "The indicator or indicators of illocutionary force implant the meaning in the stream of social interaction; they are what makes speech take hold." This suggests that "the meaning" exists independently of, and prior to, the application of illocutionary force, and that the full speech act is built up from a kernel of pure semantic value. But as Searle points out, propositional acts do not occur alone;[13] that is, you don't build up from the proposition to the act, but down from the act to the proposition which could not even be picked out were the act not fully launched. Ohmann says, "a speaker may assign different illocutionary forces to the same meaning" (p. 18), but in fact what a speaker may do is perform different illocutionary acts with the same sentence. The mistake is to think that the sentence without illocutionary force is "an unactivated meaning"; rather it is just a series of noises, a dead letter with no more "content" than a list of words. If this seems counterintuitive, just try to utter a sentence without its being an assertion, a question, a command, and so on, and just try to think of a meaning that is available independently of one or other speech act in which it is *already* imbedded.

To be sure, illocutionary acts which share a sentence also share something else, predication. Thus the sentence "I will leave" may, in different circumstances, be a promise, a threat, a warning, or a prediction, and in each of those illocutionary lives the question of my leaving will have been raised or put on the table. It would be wrong, however, to conclude that this raising or putting on the table of the question is the basic meaning of these acts and that the illocutionary force indicators represent "stylistic choices that a speaker of English can make in issuing his meanings" (p. 119); for, as Searle explains, "One cannot just raise the question without raising it in some form or another, interrogative, assertive, promissory, etc. . . . And . . . this mirrors the fact that predication is not an act which can occur alone" (p. 124). Another way of putting this is to say that predication and the uttering of propositions are not separate acts; they are slices from the illocutionary act, and as in the serving of a pie, they cannot be sliced, or even be said to be available for slicing, until the illocutionary act has been baked. If I were to say to you, "As to my leaving . . . ," you could not even think in an anticipatory way about the predication without casting it in some or other illocutionary mode. Indeed, to be consistent Ohmann would have to turn his terminology around and identify meaning with illocutionary force and style with propositional or predicational content, since the distinction between meaning and style is always a distinction between the essential and the not-so-essential (and in hard-line formulations, the dispensable). In short, the notion of illocutionary style makes no sense except as the result of mistaking an analytic account of the speech act for a genetic one. Whatever style is (an issue I will not engage), it varies independently of illocutionary force.

But for the sake of argument, let us suppose that one could talk of "illocutionary style" as Ohmann wants to. How would we proceed? It would seem from Ohmann's analyses that we would first calculate the incidence of various illocutionary acts in a stretch of text and then on the basis of this evidence draw conclusions about an author and/or his characters. The trouble is that this evidence is not interpretable, or to put the case more sharply, it is interpretable in any direction one likes. Suppose that someone in a novel were constantly asking questions. What would this mean? Well, it depends: it might mean that he is disoriented and doesn't know how to move about in the situation; it might mean that he was constantly testing those he met; it might mean that he wanted to make people feel nervous and defensive; or it might simply mean that there were things he didn't know. Of course, a consideration of the context would in a particular case pin the significance down, but the more context is brought in, the less the significance is attributable to the incidence of questions or of any other illocutionary act. That is to say, there will be no regular relationship between a particular illocutionary act and the determined significance, which in another context, would not need that act to emerge. There is simply no principled way to complete a sentence of the type, the man who characteristically performs act x will indicate thereby . . . On the other hand, if a character or an author is continually talking about the acts he does or does not perform, and debating the conditions for their successful performance and the commitments they entail (if questioning as an act became a subject of discussion *in* the novel), then speech-act analysis will help us understand what he is doing because he is doing what it is doing. *Illocutionary style* is a notion unattached to anything and will always remain merely statistical (unless it is given an arbitrary significance), but *illocutionary behavior* is a notion one can work with because it is what speech-act theory is all about.

I have been belaboring this point because I believe that by misconstruing it Ohmann turns the major insight of the speech-act philosophers on its head, precisely undoing what they have so carefully done. In *How To Do Things with Words*, Austin begins by making a distinction between "constatives"—utterances whose business "can only be to 'describe' some state of affairs, or to 'state some fact' which it must do either truly or falsely" (p. 1)—and "performatives"—utterances the issuing of which constitutes "the performing of an action" (p. 6). This distinction does not survive Austin's exploration of it, for the conclusion of his book (which is in many ways a self-consuming artifact) is the discovery that constatives are also "doings," and that "what we have to study is not the sentence" in its pure unattached form but "the issuing of an utterance in a situation" by a human being (p. 138). The class of exceptions thus swallows the supposedly normative class, and as a result the objectively descriptive language unattached to situations and purposes that was traditionally at the center of linguistic philosophy is shown to be a fiction. By reifying the locutionary act and making it an independently specifiable meaning to which human purposes and intentions are added (in the form of illocutionary forces) Ohmann reinstates that fiction in its old position of ontological privilege.[14]

Fact and Fiction

Ontological privilege, however, is one position philosophy is reluctant to leave empty, and it is not surprising that a theory which substitutes for the principle of verification the notion of appropriateness conditions would attempt to put those conditions in its place. This is the most popular thing that literary people try to do with Austin and Searle, and they do it by using speech-act theory to arrive at definitions of literature and/or fiction. Such an enterprise necessarily begins with an attempt to specify what is *not* literature and fiction, or, in a word, what is normative. According to most of those who have worked on this problem, what is normative is language that intends to be or is held to be responsible to the real world. Here are three representative statements:

> The aesthetic distance of the hearer or reader is an essential ingredient in the aesthetic experience he has in hearing or reading a fictional story as a fictional story. But he can have aesthetic distance only if there is something he is distant from, that being the practical responses that are typically or appropriately brought about by nonfictive uses of the sentences comprising the story. It is only because language has the practical role of helping us come to grips with the real, workaday world that there can be an aesthetically pleasurable "holiday" use of it.[15] (R. Gale)

> Writing (or speaking) a literary work is evidently an illocutionary performance of a special type, logically different from the seeming acts that make it up. The contract between poet and reader or hearer does not put the poet behind the various statements, rejoinders, laments, promises, or whatever, that he seemingly voices. His word is not his bond, in just this way. Perhaps the *only* serious condition of good faith that holds for literary works and their authors is that the author not give out as fact what is fiction . . . Literary works are discourses with the usual illocutionary rules suspended. If you like, they are acts without consequences of the usual sort, sayings liberated from the usual burden of social bond and responsibility.[16] (R. Ohmann)

> Now what makes fiction possible, I suggest, is a set of extralinguistic, nonsemantic conventions that break the connection between words and the world established by the rules mentioned earlier. Think of the conventions of fictional discourse as a set of horizontal conventions that break the connections established by the vertical rules. They suspend the normal requirements established by these rules. Such horizontal conventions are not meaning rules; they are not part of the speaker's competence. Accordingly, they do not alter or change the meanings of any of the words or other elements of the language. What they do rather is enable the speaker to use words with their literal meanings without understaking the commitments that are normally required by those meanings.[17] (J. Searle)

These statements are not on all fours with one another. While Searle and Gale oppose workaday or normal discourse

to fiction, Ohmann oposes it to literature, a point Searle takes
up when he asserts that because literature, unlike fiction, "is
the name of a set of attitudes we take toward a stretch of discourse, not a name of an internal property of the stretch of discourse" (p. 320), one cannot make a clean break between the
literary and the nonliterary. (I have argued for this position elsewhere.)[18] Ohmann also implies that the speech acts found in
literature and ordinary discourse differ in kind, where for
Searle and Gale the difference is one of degree: the acts are the
same (else one would have to learn a whole new set of meaning
rules in order to read fiction), but they entail fewer commitments. These, however, are family quarrels and they leave a
large and central area of agreement. For Searle, Ohmann, and
Gale (and many others) there are two kinds of discourse: one
that in various ways (or modes) hooks up with the real world,
and another that operates with diminished responsibility to that
world; the first is basic and prior, the other derivative and dependent. Again, the classic formulation is Austin's:

> A performative utterance will, for example, be *in a peculiar way*
> hollow or void if said by an actor on the stage, or if introduced
> in a poem . . . Language in such circumstances is in special ways
> —intelligibly—used not seriously, but in ways *parasitic* upon its
> normal use—ways which fall under the doctrine of the *etiolations*
> of language. All this we are *excluding* from consideration. Our
> performative utterances, felicitous or not, are to be understood as
> issued in ordinary circumstances.[19]

That there are different kinds of discourse and that they are
distinguished (in part) by the commitment one assumes by engaging in them seems to me to be obvious. I am not convinced,
however, that one of them is ontologically prior to the others,
and it is this assumption I would like to challenge by inquiring
into the status of phrases like "normal use" and "ordinary circumstances." My argument will engage Searle's, because it seems
to me to be fuller and more rigorous than any I have seen.

Everything Searle says devolves from his juxtaposition of two
passages, one an excerpt from an article in the *New York Times*,
written by Eileen Shanahan, and the other from a novel by
Iris Murdoch:

Washington, Dec. 14—A group of federal, state, and local government officials rejected today President Nixon's idea that the federal government provide the financial aid that would permit local governments to reduce property taxes.

Ten more glorious days without horses! So thought Second Lieutenant Andrew Chase-White recently commissioned in the distinguished regiment of King Edwards Horse, as he pottered contentedly in a garden on the outskirts of Dublin on a sunny Sunday afternoon in April nineteen-sixteen.[20]

The first passage Searle labels "serious," the second "fictional," and he insists that he intends nothing disparaging by this distinction: "this jargon is not meant to imply that writing a fictional novel or poem is not a serious activity, but rather that for example if the author of a novel tells us that it is raining outside he isn't seriously committed to the view that it is actually at the time of writing raining outside. It is in that sense that fiction is nonserious" (pp. 320–321). This gets to the heart of Searle's central point: in a "normal" assertion, such as Shanahan's, the speaker is held responsible for the way his (or her) utterance relates or does not relate to the world: he commits himself to the truth of the expressed proposition; he must be ready with evidence or reasons if the truth of the expressed proposition is challenged; he will not assert something that is obviously true to both himself and his hearer; and so on. Moreover, these rules or felicity conditions establish what counts as a mistake, and in law, what is actionable. If Shanahan's assertion is shown to be without substance or proof, she is likely to be thought (at least on this occasion) a bad reporter (the title fits perfectly with the illocutionary act involved) and she is vulnerable to a suit for libel. The case, insists Searle, is exactly the reverse for Murdoch. "Her utterance is not a commitment to the truth of the proposition that on a sunny Sunday afternoon in April of nineteen-sixteen a recently commissioned lieutenant . . . Furthermore, as she is not committed to its truth she is not committed to being able to provide evidence for its truth" (pp. 321–323). The test for what is "serious" and what is fictional is the "internal canons of criticism" peculiar to each mode of discourse. The question in every case is, what counts as a mistake?

If there never did exist a Nixon, Miss Shanahan (and the rest of us) are mistaken. But if there never did exist an Andrew Chase-White, Miss Murdoch is not mistaken. Again, if Sherlock Holmes and Watson go from Baker Street to Paddington Station by a route which is geographically impossible, we will know that Conan Doyle blundered even though he has not blundered if there never was a veteran of the Afghan campaign answering to the description of John Watson, M.D. (p. 331)

It is typical of Searle to be scrupulous even at the expense of the distinction (between serious discourse and a work of fiction) he would maintain. It would seem from this example that what counts as a mistake in "real life" can also count as a mistake in a novel, and it is not hard to think of novels in which the assertion and descriptions are held responsible to all the rules that apply to articles in the *New York Times*. In certain historical novels, for example, every detail would be subject to the scrutiny of readers and critics who would at every opportunity be looking for the chance to say, "but that's not the way it was (or is)." One might reply that when that happens, we are no longer dealing with fiction, but with history, but this would simply embroil us in a new argument about what is and is not history. Are those passages in Herodotus and Sallust where historical personages deliver speeches of which there could not possibly be a record history or fiction? Are Herodotus and Sallust "bad" historians because they indulge in such practices? Even to ask such questions is to cast doubt on the utility of the distinction which forces them. One who is committed to the distinction can hold on to it by admitting the existence of "mixed modes," a course Searle takes when he acknowledges that "not all of the references in a work of fiction will be pretended acts of referring; some will be real references as in the passage from Miss Murdoch where she refers to Dublin" (p. 330). But, once this door is opened, it cannot be closed: an author is free to import whatever real world references he likes, and there will be no rules regarding the proportions. It is precisely this freedom of mix and proportion that makes a taxonomy of genres both possible and uninteresting. "Fictional genres," Searle declares, are in part "defined by the nonfictional commitments involved

in the work of fiction. This difference, say, between the natural-
istic novel, fairy tales, works of science fiction, surrealistic stories,
is in part defined by the extent of the author's commitment to
represent facts" (p. 331). The trouble with this is that the differences can be endlessly refined. As Searle admits, "As far as the
possibility of the ontology is concerned, anything goes." He tries
to put the brake on by invoking a criterion that can be applied
within any of the worlds that novelists create: "As far as the
acceptability of the ontology is concerned, coherence is a crucial
consideration" (p. 331). By coherence he means consistency, the
degree to which an author honors the contract made with his
reader "about how far the horizontal conventions of fiction break
the vertical connections of serious speech." But the contract can
be broken at will without any loss of acceptability; the reader
will simply (or not so simply) adjust and enter into a new
contract whose life may be no longer than the first.[21] In other
words, coherence is a possibility, but not an absolute value and
as a notion it doesn't help us to define or circumscribe anything.

The truth is that Searle protects his distinction between fictional and serious utterances at the expense of its *literary* interest. That is, the category "work of fiction" finally has no content; one can say of it what Searle says of literature: there is no
trait or set of traits which all works of fiction have in common
and which could constitute the necessary and sufficient conditions for being a work of fiction. Searle himself says as much
when at the end of the article he feels "compelled" to make a
"final distinction: that between a work of fiction and fictional
discourse. A work of fiction need not consist entirely of, and in
general will not consist entirely of, fictional discourse." At this
point the hope of isolating fiction is abandoned: "real world" or
serious discourse can be found in novels, and fictional discourse
is often engaged in by persons operating in the "real world," by
philosophers who say, "Let us suppose that a man hammers a
nail," and by sales managers who say, "Men, let's assume you
run into someone who has never seen an encyclopedia . . ." In
short, "fictional discourse" and "work of fiction" are not co-
extensive categories because "fictional discourse" is a rigorous
notion in a way that "work of fiction" is not. Therefore one can

make and hold on to a distinction between fictional discourse and serious discourse without in any way helping us to answer questions like what is a novel or a story and how do we tell it from a laundry list?[22]

Yet, even if the distinction isn't much help to the literary critic, it still stands. There is, I think we would all be willing to say, a kind of discourse that is characterized by the suspension of the rules to which speech acts are normally held accountable. The real question is the status of those rules when they are not suspended. What do they enforce? The answer implicit in Searle's work is that they enforce a responsibility to the facts. As far as it goes, this is unexceptionable and true, but it still leaves room for another question: responsibility to what facts? Insofar as he is committed to the priority of "serious" discourse Searle would have to say to the facts as they really are, but I would say to the facts as the conventions of serious discourse stipulate them to be. I am not claiming that there are no facts; I am merely raising a question as to their status: do they exist outside conventions of discourse (which are then more or less faithful to them) or do they follow from the assumptions embodied in those same conventions? "If there never did exist a Nixon," say Searle, "Miss Shanahan (and the rest of us) are mistaken." But suppose someone with a philosophical turn of mind were to declare that Nixon as a free and independent agent whose actions can be reported and assessed did not exist; that "in fact" the notion of his agency was a bourgeois myth (one might say a fiction) by means of which a repressive society evaded responsibility for its own crimes and tyrannies. It would follow from such a view that any sentence in which the name Nixon were attached to a finite preterite transitive verb (Nixon said, Nixon rejected, Nixon condemned) would be false to the way things really are, would be mistaken; and any evidence brought forward to substantiate Nixon's existence (birth certificate, photographs, witnesses to his actions) would be inadmissible because the rules of evidence (the procedures for its stipulation) were derived from (or constituted by) the same myth. In the face of such a challenge, the *New York Times* and Shanahan could reply that in normal circumstances persons are assumed to exist as independent

agents and that it is in the context of this assumption that reporters function and are held accountable for their mistakes.
This would be a proper and powerful reply, one that could
be answered only by a wholesale rejection of "normal circumstances" along with all the "facts" that its assertion entails. No
doubt such a rejection would fail, but the failure would only
confirm the persuasiveness and coherence of the "normal picture"; it would say nothing about the claim of that picture to
be objective. Of course the press is often criticized precisely because it is not objective; it reads, some complain, as if it were
fiction; but the greater fiction is indulged in when it is read
as if it were objective fact, as if the standard of fact to which it
strove to be faithful were natural and not something made.
Searle makes a great deal of the "internal canons of criticism"
governing an utterance. I am only insisting that these canons are
indeed internal, and that what counts as a mistake is a function of
the universe of discourse within which one speaks, and does not
at all touch on the question of what is ultimately—that is, outside of and independent of, any universe of discourse—real. In
short, the rules and conventions under which speakers and hearers "normally" operate don't demand that language be faithful
to the facts; rather, they specify the shape of that fidelity (what
Gale calls the "real workaday world"), creating it, rather than
enforcing it.

At this point it might be helpful to recall P. F. Strawson's
notion of "story relative" identification. Consider, says Strawson, "the following case:"

> A speaker tells a story which he claims to be factual. It begins:
> "A man and a boy were standing by a fountain," and it continues:
> "The man had a drink." Shall we say that the hearer knows which
> or what particular is being referred to be the subject expression
> in the second sentence? We might say so. For, of a certain range
> of two particulars, the words "the man" serve to distinguish the
> one referred to, by means of a description which applies only to
> him . . . I shall call it . . . a *story-relative,* or, for short, a *relative*
> identification. For it is identification only relative to a range of
> particulars (a range of two members) which is itself identified
> only as the range of particulars being talked about by the speaker

. . . The identification is within a certain story told by a certain speaker. It is identification within his story; but not identification within history.[23]

What I have been suggesting is that identification (or specification of facts) is *always* within a story. Some stories, however, are more prestigious than others; and one story is always the standard one, the one that presents itself as uniquely true and is, in general, so accepted. Other, nonstandard, stories will of course continue to be told, but they will be regarded as nonfactual, when, in fact, they will only be nonauthorized.

Searle is right, then, to distinguish between serious and fictional discourse on the basis of internal canons of criticism, but it does not follow, I think, that this is a distinction between the real and the not-so-real; rather, it is one between two systems of discourse conventions (two stories) which certainly can be differentiated, but not on a scale of reality. Of course the conventions of "serious" discourse include a *claim* to be in touch with the real (that is, what being the standard story means), and therefore it comes equipped with evidentiary procedures (routines for checking things out) to which members of its class must be ready to submit. But these procedures (which fictional discourse lacks, making it different, not less "true") inhere in the genre and therefore they cannot be brought forward to prove its fidelity to some supraconventional reality. The point may be obscured by the fact (I do not shrink from the word) that the fiction of this genre's status as something natural (not made) is one to which we "normally" subscribe; but this only means that of the realities constituted by a variety of discourse conventions it is the most popular. That is why we give it the names we do— "real workaday world," "normal circumstances," "ordinary usage," etc.—and why Searle's arguments are so persuasive: he speaks to us from within it. But these names are attempts to fix (or reify) something, not proof that it *is* fixed, and indeed the notion of normal or ordinary circumstances is continually being challenged by anyone (Freud, Marx, Levi-Strauss) who says to us, "Now the real facts of the matter are . . ." Even in the real-workaday (as opposed to the philosopher's) world, where the operative assumption is that the facts are stable and once-and-for-all specifiable, we very often subscribe to different versions of what those facts are. "Ordinarily" we hold a man responsible for what he does, "does" being defined by a rather crude standard of "eyeballing," but in the law, which is dedicated to the finding (what a wonderfully ambiguous word) of facts, responsibility is attenuated in two directions. A man who participates in a felony may be found guilty of a murder even though he did not wield or even see the weapon, and conspiracy can be proven even in the absence of any overt action. On the other hand, acts that, according to our "usual" ways of thinking, have indisputably been performed by a single individual, are excused by "mitigating circumstances" or even denied because the agent is said not to have been responsible. Lawyers have had a limited success arguing that the crime of which their client stands accused has "in fact" been committed by society. To be sure, that argument has not been generally accepted, but it could happen, although if it did, the judicial system would have to soften the claims usually made for its processes.

A judge in Massachusetts rules that under the law only women can be prosecuted for prostitution; a woman in California promptly opens a male bordello, at once upholding and challenging the reality the law has created. For Searle this would be an instance of the way in which institutions bring facts into being. Institutional facts, by his definition, are distinguished from brute or natural facts because there is "no simple set of statements about physical or psychological properties of states of affairs to which the statements of facts such as these are reducible" (*Speech Acts*, p. 51). "They are indeed facts; but their existence, unlike the existence of brute facts, presupposes the existence of certain human institutions. It is only given the institution of marriage that certain forms of behavior constitute Mr. Smith's marrying Miss Jones." What I am saying is that the facts Searle would cite as "brute," the facts stipulated by the standard story, are also institutional, and that the power of the law to declare a man and woman husband and wife is on a par with the (institutional) power of the standard story to declare that Richard Nixon exists. Moreover, nothing in the theory of speech acts directs us to distinguish these declarations from one another or from the declaration by Iris Murdoch of the existence of Lieutenant Andrew Chase-White. Of course there are distinctions to be made, and we do, in fact, make them, and that is why Searle's argument seems at first so obviously right. But its rightness is a function of the *extra-theoretical* stipulation of the standard story as uniquely true. That is, I am not denying that what will and will not be accepted as true is determined by the standard story. I am only pointing out that its being (or telling; it amounts to the same thing) the truth is not a matter of a special relationship it bears to the world (the world does not impose it on us) but of a special relationship it bears to its users.

In large part, my argument follows from Wittgenstein's notion of a "language game" in which words are responsible not to what is real but to what has been laid down as real (as pickoutable) by a set of constitutive rules; the players of the game are able to agree that they mean the same things by their words not because they see the same things, in some absolute phenomenal sense, but because they are predisposed by the fact of being in the game (of being parties to the standard story) to "see them," to pick them out. Interestingly enough, there is more than a little support for this view in Searle's own writings, and especially in his theory of reference. In *Speech Acts* Searle inquires into "the necessary conditions for the performance of the speech act of definite reference." By one account, a successful reference is "a kind of disguised assertion of a true uniquely existential proposition, i.e., a proposition asserting the existence of one and only one object satisfying a certain description" (p. 83). But this, Searle argues, is to confuse referring with describing. The aim of a description is to characterize an object so that it can be distinguished from all other objects in the world; the aim of a reference is to characterize an object in such a way as to identify it to a person (or persons) with whom you share a situation. Thus, in a referring expression the definite article "the" is a "conventional device indicating the speaker's intention to refer to a single object, not an indication that the descriptor which follows is true of only one object" (p. 84). In other words the descriptor does not look to the object as it might exist neutrally in space but to the object as it exists in a context; the "facts which one must possess in order to refer" are context specific; they are not facts "about some independently identified object."

This account of reference could be cited in support of my position were it not firmly attached by Searle to the axiom of existence: "There must exist an object to be referred to." What this means is that the identifying capacity of a referring expression ultimately depends on (even if it is not in the business of asserting) the existence of one and only one object satisfying a certain description. In other words, the "context" in Searle's theory is ultimately the real world (all referring expressions have to link up to it sooner or later), although it seems to me that little is lost if the context is thought of as a story that has been told *about* the real world. The emended account would then be indistinguishable from Searle's theory of fictional reference:

> But how is it possible for an author to "create" fictional characters out of thin air, as it were? To answer this let us go back to the passage from Miss Murdoch. The second sentence begins, "So thought Second Lieutenant Andrew Chase-White." Now in this passage Murdoch uses a proper name, a paradigm-referring expression . . . One of the conditions on the successful performance of the speech act of reference is that there must exist an object to be referred to. To the extent that we share in the pretense, we will also pretend that there is a lieutenant named Andrew Chase-White living in Dublin in 1916. It is the pretended reference which creates the fictional character and the shared pretense which enables us to talk about the character. ("Logical Status," pp. 329–330)

This seems to me to be exactly right not only for fiction but for discourse in general. "Shared pretense" is what enables us to talk about anything at all. When we communicate, it is because we are parties to a set of discourse agreements which are in effect decisions as to what can be stipulated as a fact. It is these decisions and the agreement to abide by them, rather than the availability of substance, that make it possible for us to refer, whether we are novelists or reporters for the *New York Times*. One might object that this has the consequence of making all discourse fictional;

but it would be just as accurate to say that it makes all discourse serious, and it would be better still to say that it puts all discourse on a par. One cannot term the standard story a pretense without implying that there is another story that is not. The very words "pretense," "serious," and "fictional" have built into them the absolute opposition I have been at pains to deny, between language that is true to some extra-institutional reality and language that is not. This is not, however, to deny that a standard of truth exists and that by invoking it we can distinguish between different kinds of discourse: it is just that the standard is not brute, but institutional, not natural, but made. What is remarkable is how little this changes: facts, consequences, responsibilities, they do not fall away, they proliferate and make the world—every world—alive with the significances our stories (standard and otherwise) create.

In all of this I take Searle several steps further than he would want to go. Characteristically his arguments rest on a basic opposition: brute facts vs. institutional facts, regulative rules vs. constitutive rules, serious discourse vs. fictional discourse, the natural vs. the conventional. In each case, the left-hand term stands for something that is available outside of language, something with which systems of discourse of whatever kind must touch base—Reality, the Real World, Objective Fact. What I am suggesting is that these left-hand terms are merely disguised forms of the terms on the right, that their content is not natural but made, that what we know is not the world but stories about the world, that no use of language matches reality but that all uses of language are interpretations of reality.

It follows necessarily that speech-act theory is one of those interpretations (or stories), and that it is a description not of the truth but of one attempt to make it manageable, or, more properly, to make it. As an interpretation, however, it has a special status, since its contents are the rules that make all other interpretations possible. That is, the fiction it embodies and therefore presupposes (it is removed from examination) is intelligibility itself. Speech-act rules do not regulate meaning but constitute it. To put it another way, the ideology of speech-act theory is meaning, the assumption of sense and of the possibility of its transmission. Of course that assumption is correct (I am now depending on it), but it is correct because as members of speech-act communities we are parties to rules that enforce it, rules that make sense rather than merely conform to it. Once sense is made it becomes possible to forget its origins, and when that happens the myth of ordinary language has established itself, and established too the inferior and subsidiary status of whatever departs from it.

Conclusion

If speech-act theory is itself an interpretation, then it cannot possibly serve as an all purpose interpretive key. And indeed the emphasis of this essay seems to have shifted from the abuses of the theory to an enumeration of all the things it *can't* do (they of course imply one another): it can't tell us anything about what happens after an illocutionary act has been performed (it is not a rhetoric); it can't tell us anything about the inner life of the performer (it is not a psychology); it can't serve as the basis of a stylistics; it can't be elaborated into a poetics of narrative; it can't help us to tell the difference between literature and non-literature; it can't distinguish between serious discourse and a work of fiction, and it cannot, without cheating, separate fiction from fact. The question forces itself: what can it do? Well, one thing it can do is allow us to talk with some precision about what is happening in *Coriolanus*, although after the arguments of the past few pages, one may wonder how that is possible. The explanation is simple: *Coriolanus*, as I have said before, is a speech-act play. By this I don't mean that it is full of speech acts (by definition this is true of any play, or poem, or essay, or novel) but that it is about speech acts, the rules of their performance, the price one pays for obeying those rules, the impossibility of ignoring or refusing them and still remaining a member of the community. It is also about what the theory is about, language and its power: the power to make the world rather than mirror it, to bring about states of affairs rather than report them, to constitute institutions rather than (or as well as) serve them. We see this everywhere, but most powerfully in III, iii when in frenzied unison the citizens cry again and again "It shall be so."

Finally, *Coriolanus* is a speech-act play in its narrowness. The course of its action turns on the execution or misexecution of illocutionary acts; the consequences that befall the characters are the consequences of those acts; they follow necessarily and predictably; they are not contingent and therefore they are not surprising. (Indeed it is a feature of the play that everyone knows what will happen in advance.) So rigorous is the play's movement, so lacking in accident, coincidence, and contingency, that it is questionable whether or not it is a true tragedy or even, in the usual sense, a drama.

One might say then that the power of the play is a function of its limitations, and these are point by point the limitations of speech-act theory: the stopping short of perlocutionary effects (the banishing is not a response to what Coriolanus does but another name for it), the silence on the question of the inner life (a space Coriolanus finds already occupied by a public language), the exclusive focus on acts that can be performed simply (and only) by invoking a conventional (that is, specified in advance) procedure. This fit between the play and the theory accounts for whatever illumination the present analysis has been able to provide, and it is also the reason why we should be wary of concluding from the analysis that we are in possession of a new interpretive key. Speech-act theory is an account of the conditions of intelligibility, of what it means to mean in a community, of the procedures which must be instituted before one can even be said to be understood. In a great many texts those conditions and procedures are presupposed; they are not put before us for consideration, and the emphasis falls on what happens or can happen after they have been met and invoked. It follows that while a speech-act analysis of such texts will always be possible, it will also be trivial (a mere list of the occurrence or distribution of kinds of acts), because while it is the conditions of intelligibility that make all texts possible, not all texts are *about* those conditions. *Coriolanus* is about those conditions, and it goes the theory one better by also being about their fragility. It does not hide from us the fact that its own intelligibility rests on nothing firmer than an agreement (forever being renewed) to say "Good Morrow."[24]

10

What Is Stylistics and Why Are They Saying Such Terrible Things About It? Part II

[THIS ESSAY was first presented as a talk at a conference on style held at the Graduate Center of the City University of New York in April 1977. To some extent the occasion dictated my strategy: E. L. Epstein was the organizer of the conference; S. J. Keyser was one of the principal speakers; and Donald Freeman was the chairman of the session in which the essay was delivered. I was thus in the position of attacking my host, my chairman, and my fellow panelist, and, more to the point, in the position of attacking the enterprise to which they gave their energies. The challenge to that enterprise is much more serious in this essay than it had been in 1972, when my complaint was simply that the move from the description of formal features to their interpretation was illegitimate. Here I assert that the act of description is itself interpretive and that therefore at no point is the stylistician even within hailing distance of a fact that has been independently (that is, objectively) specified. Indeed, the very formalism that supposedly grounds his analysis—the system of rules and definition that constitutes grammar—is no less an interpretive construct than the poem it is brought in to explain: and in the more compelling of the analyses I discuss, the building up of the interpretation and the building up of the grammar are one and the same activities.

To say this is not only to challenge the claims of stylistics but to challenge the very project of linguistics itself, at least as Chomsky describes it in the opening paragraphs of *Aspects of the Theory of Syntax:* "Linguistic theory is concerned primarily with an ideal speaker-listener, in a completely homogenous speech community, who knows its language perfectly and is unaffected by such grammatically irrelevant conditions as memory limitations, distractions, shifts of attention and interest, and errors (random or characteristic) in applying his knowledge of the language in actual performance" (p. 3). For Chomsky, to know the language perfectly is to know it as it is *before* it is inserted into any particular situation with its network of interests, purposes, and goals. But if the conclusions of this essay can be generalized (and I think they can), a language is neither known nor describable apart from the conditions that Chomsky labels "irrelevant." That is, any account of the language would proceed, whether the linguist knew it or not, under the aegis of some set of contextual circumstances, or, to put it another way, any so-called competence grammar is really a performance grammar in disguise, a grammar that has already assumed the knowledge (of the world or, to be more precise, of *some* world) from which its mechanisms are supposedly abstracted. That is why the history of linguistics in the Chomsky era is a history of counterexamples to what are offered as general or algorithmic rules: the counterexamples follow from a set of interpretive assumptions other than the ones assumed by the rulemakers; in effect, a different world is generating a different grammar, and since there is no grammar that does not proceed from some world or other, there is no hope of ever specifying a linguistic system that has the formal purity Chomsky desires.]

I INTEND TODAY to continue what Barbara Smith has recently characterized as my "saturation bombing" of stylistics.[1] As before, the focus of the discussion will be on the relationship between description and interpretation. In "What Is Stylistics and Why Are They Saying Such Terrible Things About It?" I found that in the practice of stylisticians of whatever school that relationship was always arbitrary, less a matter of something demonstrated than of something assumed before the fact or imposed after it.[2] Five years later, the situation has changed somewhat, but in terms of the claims traditionally made for and by stylistics, it is no more satisfactory, merely unsatisfactory in a different way. Charting that way will be the business of this essay, and I will begin by rehearsing my conclusions in advance:

(1) Stylistic analysis is of two kinds, but those who practice the art do not distinguish between them, even though the assumptions underlying them are contradictory.

(2) One kind of stylistics is incoherent, even on its own terms;

the other *is* coherent on its own terms, but they are not terms
which the stylisticians can comfortably acknowledge, because
to acknowledge them would be to admit that the goal of
stylistics—an objective account of form and meaning—is an
impossible one.

The first point to be made, then, is that the proponents of
stylistics literally don't know what they are doing, although,
typically, they preface their analyses with programmatic statements that suggest a clear-eyed understanding of both purpose
and method. Here are excerpts from the opening paragraphs of
what Roger Fowler has dubbed essays in the "new stylistics."

This paper starts from what might be called the Ohmann
Hypothesis . . . "stylistic preferences reflect cognitive preferences."[3]

It is a commonplace of literary criticism to observe that form
and content in a poem are closely related . . . Four poems by Wallace Stevens will be analyzed from a formal standpoint. Then an
attempt will be made to show how the formal analysis is closely related to what the poem is about.[4]

In the model of language production that is assumed for the
purposes of this paper, a speaker or writer first constructs a lexical
constellation which mimes a state of affairs.[5]

These paragraphs share a vocabulary, and in particular a set
of related verbs: "reflect," "relate," "mime," and, in later appearances, "embody," "correlate with," and "express." Together
they point to the central assertion of stylistics as it is forthrightly
stated by Fowler: "It is possible to say the same thing in different
words."[6] It is an assumption that, as Fowler says, one *must* make
given the two-stage procedure it authorizes. First, formal features
patterns are discovered by the application of some descriptive
apparatus, and then they are found to be expressive of or reflect
or mime a meaning or a content which stands apart from them
and which could have been expressed (or reflected or mimed by)
some other pattern, or which could have been packaged in formal
patterns that did not reflect it at all, but merely presented it. As
Samuel Keyser observes, the "demonstration of a form–content
correlation will be significant only if it is logically possible for
the formal structure encountered in a poem to bear *no* relation

to the poem's content" (*WS*, p. 597), that is, only if it is possible to point to a formal structure without already having invoked some interpretive principle.

It is here at the heart of stylistics that one feels the contradictory pull of two demands. Only if forms are separable from the meanings they encase and adorn can there be said to be a choice between them, and a question for stylistics to answer (what is the relationship between this form and that meaning?). But only if the relationship of the form to the meaning can be shown to be necessary (indeed inevitable) will its demonstration escape the charge of being arbitrary, of being capable of assertion in any number of directions.

E. L. Epstein's analysis of "Lycidas," line 167, is a small but instructive case in point. The line reads, "Sunk though he be beneath the watry floar," and it exhibits, he says, "a remarkable degree of objective mimesis through a combination of syntactic and phonological structures" (*SRA*, p. 54). The most important of these involves the "movements of the tongue and lower jaw," which by accomplishing "the stressed vowels of this line mime a motion from *mid central* to *high front* to *back*." One wonders what Epstein means here by "mime"; as he typically uses it the verb indicates a relationship of distance, that is, different *from*, but imitative *of*; but there is no distance between the movements of the tongue and jaw and the central, front, and back positions which those movements successively occupy; those movements do not *mime* a motion, they perform it. The equivocation is of no consequence, except insofar as it is evidence of Epstein's desire to assert mimesis even in a case where he could have had the real thing. What *is* important, however, is what this motion (be it mimetic or performative) is itself said to mime: "The motion in turn mimes the relationship *low-high-low* expressed in the lexis—the body of Edward King on the sea floor (low) and the surface of the sea (high). The high front vowels mime the notion 'the watery floor' far beneath which King has sunk." This is arbitrary in so many directions that one suspects it must be a parody. In the first place the two patterns—one phonological, the other lexical—are not parallel in a way that would allow the first to be mimetic of the second. The movement

low-high-low occurs on a vertical plane, while the movement
mid central-high front-back occurs on the horizontal or curvi-
linear plane of the roof of the mouth (itself a metaphor which
if taken seriously—and why not?—would at the very least complicate the problem of mimesis and give it a different shape than
Epstein proposes.)

The only genuine parallel between the two patterns would
seem to be the presence in each of three successive and alternating states or stages; but even this parallel will not bear examination, because Epstein's description of the "lexical constellation"
(that is, of what the line is saying) is open to challenge. It is by no
means obvious that the line expresses the relationship low-high-
low; indeed it would make equal and better sense (and one in
accord with Milton's practice elsewhere) to say that the movement described is from low (sunk) to lower (beneath) to lower
still. In order to give the phrase "watry floar" the value of "high,"
Epstein has to treat it as a surface (a word he uses), but the effect
of joining the two words (in what is almost an oxymoron) is to
call attention to the way in which this particular floor does not
have the properties of a surface (it is "watry"). The other or
"low" pole in Epstein's pattern is provided by a genuine surface,
the floor of the sea, but nowhere is it asserted that King rests
there or anywhere else; indeed, for many the poignancy of the
poem derives from that fact that the location of his body is
unknown.

Of course this is a matter of interpretation, and I am not
arguing for a particular reading of "Lycidas." My point is that
Epstein's reading is no less an interpretation, and that rather
than standing in an independent and confirming relationship
to a structural pattern, it is produced by the exigencies of that
pattern. Epstein asserts that the phonological structure is worth
noticing only because of the "polar situation" it mimes; but in
fact the dependency is the other way around: the line is read as
it is because a structural pattern already discerned needs a meaning that it can be said to mime, and the critic is determined to
provide one. (It could have been the other way around.) It is
not that what Epstein does cannot be done, but that it cannot
not be done because there are no constraints on the manufacture

of the correlations his method uncovers. Is there a line whose articulation does not involve some back and forth movement of the tongue, and is there a sense which could not be brought into some relation (of expression, counterpoint, opposition, irony) with that movement? Even those verses which Epstein cites as instances of nonmimesis could be shown to be mimetic by someone sufficiently committed to the principle. All you need is a meaning and a formal pattern (any meaning and any formal pattern will do) and the pressure of the question "how do they relate?" and a relation will always be found.

It is certainly found by Keyser in his analysis of Stevens's "Anecdote of a Jar." He begins by declaring that "the immediate impression one receives upon reading this poem is that it is akin in some way to a painting" (*WS*, p. 586). This curious judgment is delivered as if it were a truth universally acknowledged, one that required neither defense nor explanation. Once delivered, however, it is abandoned as abruptly as it was introduced, and Keyser proceeds to a discussion of the poem's formal features. The most prominent of these, we are told, involves a succession of variations on the syllable *round:* "round," "surround," "around," "round" again, and "ground." Between the second and third stanzas *round* is replaced as an organizing principle by a series of *air* rhymes: "air," "everywhere," and "bare," and by the alliteration in the penultimate line of "bird" and "bush." An unexceptionable conclusion follows: "There is, then, a nonoverlapping succession of rhyming devices which appear in a serial fashion . . . beginning with variations on *round,* moving to end-rhyme, then to alliteration and terminating with identical rhyme between the first and last lines" (*WS*, p. 587). As always, the question is where does one go from here, and Keyser, who is nothing if not forthright, tells us: "If . . . there exists a relationship between form and meaning in this poem, it should be possible for us to find an interpretation congenial to the structure that we have already established . . . the successive nonoverlapping series of rhyming devices" (*WS*, p. 588).
My point is that given this kind of determination it would be impossible *not* to find an interpretation that was congenial in

the sense that it is available for correlation with the poem's structural properties. In less than a page and one half it is duly found, and then summarized: "A property of the jar is mentioned and the relationship of the property to the environment is specified. With respect to the property round, the jar made the wilderness surround the hill. With respect to the property tall and of a port in air, the jar dominated the wilderness. With respect to the property gray and bare, the jar contrasted its own barrenness to the implied life of the wilderness" (*WS*, p. 588). Basically, this is an expansion into a stilted language of the phrase "took dominion everywhere." It is followed by the promised relation of the poem's structural properties to its now discovered meaning. Keyser recalls that his formal analysis had uncovered a succession of variations on the syllable "round," which therefore dominates the first two stanzas of the poem just as the jar dominates the wilderness. Or in his inflated account: "The actual phonological shape of the property of the jar which, in English, takes the form of the word *round* imposes an order, just as the semantic property 'round,' which the jar possesses, imposes an order on the wilderness. Using the shape of the word *round* to impose an order on the poem parallels using the actual shape of the object to impose an order on the wilderness" (*WS*, p. 589). This relation, he continues, also "exists with respect to the second property, namely *tall and of a port in air*. Once again, the physical shape of a word used to describe the property, i.e., *air*, imposes a new rhyming order on the poem . . . and this parallels the imposition of a new perception on the wilderness by the semantic content of the phrases of which the word is part" (*WS*, p. 589).

The first thing to say about this is that Keyser cheats, even on his own terms, when he extends his argument from the syllable "round" to the syllable "air." Unlike "round," "air" does not describe that property of the jar which imposes an order on the wilderness. Only if the repeated sound were "all" (as in "tall") would the syllable function as he says it does, in an intimate relationship with the specified property. This, however, is an internal criticism of the procedure. The more serious criticism is that it is trivial because its shape is in no way constrained.

Having decided that the poem is about the imposition of order, and having also decided that it would be desirable to find a formal pattern that mimes or parallels that imposition, it would be impossible not to succeed (just as it would be impossible not to find a theme which an already observed formal pattern might mime). Some pattern or other—alliterative, assonantal, consonantal—will always be uncovered and designated as the dominating one, and in the unlikely absence of a suitable pattern, that absence could itself be interpreted as an ironic and deliberate (and therefore mimetic) nonmimesis which expressed or reflected the absence of a relationship between language and reality.

In other words, the exercise is an arbitrary one, ruled by the determination to *have* a relation rather than by a procedure which demonstrates it. The phonological shape of "round" imposes an order on the poem only if you have already decided that the poem is about order. That is, the pattern emerges under the pressure of an interpretation and does not exist as independent evidence of it. In the event of a different interpretation, the pattern would be seen differently and be evidence in another direction. One might decide, for example, that the poem was about the many ways of viewing a jar (as in the thirteen ways of looking at a blackbird); it would then be a series of puns: the jar is round; it is also a round; it is a superround (*super* is the Latin for "sur" and means over, above, and on top of); and as the focus of attention it functions as a g-round. In the context of this reading, the pattern of sound would reflect difference and variation rather than similarity and order. Or alternately, one's reading might pay particular attention to the first person pronoun and regard the poem as the utterance of a limited persona, someone who is seeking the meaning of his experience, and fails to recognize it in the patterns of his own language: the repetition of "round," a syllable hidden in words which pay no particular attention to it, would then mime the psychological state of unawareness.

Of course it is not necessary that an interpretation be involved with the syllable "round" at all. Phonological patterns do not announce themselves naturally; they are picked out by an interested perception, and a perception otherwise interested will pick out another pattern. It is possible, for example, to read the poem as a meditation on nature in its benign and threatening forms. This distinction could then be seen in the migration of the syllable "ill" from "h*ill*" to "w*ill*derness," back to "h*ill*" and then to "w*ill*derness" again, and finally ending in the triumph of threatening nature when the sound is transformed into "w*ill*d." My little phonological drama has the same status as Keyser's: his sounds dominate and order, mine migrate and oppose, but in both cases the pattern as perceived is the product of an interpretation and not independent confirmation of it. As I have said elsewhere, this is a game that is just too easy to play.

Keyser himself shows how easy it is when in a final paragraph he reinterprets his formal patterns as evidence for his impression that the poem is akin to a still-life painting: "The apparent framing of this poem between the repeated phrases *in Tennessee* which appear in the opening and the closing line of the poem provides a verbal counterpart of a frame to the still life in words" (*WS*, p. 589). Somehow Keyser doesn't see that his conviction that the poem is like a painting is what leads him first to see a repetition, then to characterize it as a frame, and pretends instead that the homology is between two independently existing systems. In the next paragraph he does it again (and he could have done it forever) when he succeeds (it is an assured success) in seeing in the phonological order an allegory of the poetic act. Here at least he has the right word, although it is applied in the wrong place. Whether or not the poem is an allegory, his performance surely is, in the discredited Ruskinian sense of reading a prefabricated meaning into patterns that have no necessary relationship to it whatsoever.

Allegory is also the mode of his analysis of "The Snowman." Here the formal description is of a syntax that has continually to be revised: while "the opening stanza constitutes what appears at first sight to be a complete sentence . . . the beginning of the next stanza indicates that an ellipsis has occurred and that the sentence which apparently terminated at the end of the first stanza is, in fact, the first member of a coordinate sentence" (*WS*, p. 590). The sequence repeats itself in the relationship between the second and third stanzas, when a "new ellipsis shows that once again we have been mistaken in our syntactic analysis, and we must now go back and reanalyze" (*WS*, p. 591). The pattern is varied somewhat in the last stanza, for "whereas the second stanza paralleled the first and the third paralleled the second, each time within a conjoined sentence, we now find that the last stanza parallels the first four, itself in a conjoined sentence." As a result, Keyser concludes, the poem consistently "demands that we analyze and then reanalyze yet again as we pass linearly and in time from one point to another in the structure" (*WS*, p. 595).

It is at this point that Keyser makes his characteristic move. Let us, he says, "look at the relationship between the formal device described above and the meaning of the poem." What he means, of course, is let us look for a meaning of the poem that can stand in an iconic relationship to the formal pattern we have discerned. That meaning is immediately found when Keyser decides, with some help from Stevens and Frank Kermode, that the poem is about the "need to perceive reality in a 'clear fashion" (*WS*, p. 596). In the course of the poem "we find that in the implied regimen needed to move toward a clear perception of reality, there is a constant change of perspective. Thus Stevens observes that to begin with, one must have a mind of winter, i.e. a particular state of mind in order to regard the frost. However, this state of mind is not in itself reliable for one must have had it for a long time in order to behold the junipers shagged with ice and not think of misery" (*WS*, p. 596). The conclusion can be seen coming from half a mile away, and in due time it arrives: "We saw that . . . the poem consists of a syntactic pattern whose main characteristic is that its structure at any one time seems clear but which, at the next moment, requires a complete reanalysis . . . This designed need to change syntactic perspective cannot more closely parallel the sense of the poem which is to change one's outward perspective in order to more accurately understand reality" (*WS*, pp. 596–597).

In this wholly uninteresting reading the poem becomes a "how-to" manual, a developing set of directions for achieving a clear understanding of reality. Curiously, the reading would have been much more interesting if Keyser were more aware of what he is doing. He thinks that he is discerning an independent formal pattern and relating it to a content, but in fact he is eviscerating a pattern that is not, at least as he first comes upon it, formal. This is because his description is not, as he claims, of a syntax but of a mind in the act of doing something; and it is therefore a description that follows upon a set of psychological assumptions about what people do when they read. What Keyser is assuming that they do is revise, and a complete description, one that was responsible to the principles that made it possible, would trace the career of that revising and not merely note it as preliminary to allegorizing it.

In other words, while in the analysis of "Anecdote of a Jar" there is no legitimate, that is, constrained, direction in which one might go after pointing out the appearances of "round," here the direction in which one might go is built into the initial observation, but Keyser refuses to take it. This does not, however, prevent *us* from taking it, if only in order to see what kind of reading Keyser could have produced if he had seen what his own vocabulary so clearly implies: that the act of revising has as its object not merely a syntactic structure, but the structure of the reader's understanding. That is, each time we revise or reanalyze, what changes is not only our understanding of the syntax but our understanding of what is required to regard the frost and the junipers; and the shape of that change is a complicating of what it means to "have a mind of winter." At first it seems to mean no more than that one's mind should be full of wintry thoughts or be unsympathetic in some undefined way; the phrase, in short, seems to be metaphorical. But then, with each realization that the syntax, and therefore the unit of sense, is not complete, comes the realization that the requirements for a clear and undistorting perception have grown tighter. They grow wiretight in stanza three, where the newly specified requirement is "not to think / Of any misery in the sound of the wind." "Wintry thoughts," then, are precisely what must be avoided, and if we pause at the end of the line—"and not to think"—the injunction becomes even more sweeping: one must not have any thoughts at all, that is, one must efface oneself completely and become an observer so pure that he adds nothing to a reality which will be unmediated because he as a medium—as something obstructing—is no more. Only then, when he is nothing himself, will his self not be interposed between him and the nothing—the thing that is not an object of human thought— that is. But the reader who understands that this is what it means to have a mind of winter purchases that understanding at the price of being able to have one, since the act of understanding, of apprehending from a distance, is precisely what must be given up. What we finally discover is that what is required is a mind not active in the way it must be for the discovery to be made. The demand that the reader reanalyze does not parallel a program for the achieving of a pure perception; rather it is inseparable from the realization that such a perception is forever unavailable.

Now I am not claiming for this hypothetical reading that it is truer to the poem or to Stevens's intention than the reading Keyser actually performs; but that it is more likely to convince someone of its trueness because there is a clear line of argument from its uncovering of a formal structure to the stipulation of that structure's meanings. That is to say, given the assumptions already imbedded in the notion of revising, a reading which follows the career of that revising will have an immediate, persuasive force. There is no point in the reading where the analyst must stop in order to cast around for a meaning that can be related to his forms, because the description of those forms is at the same time a stipulation of their meanings. The assumption (it is Keyser's) that what a reader does is revise leads necessarily to an account of that revising, and that account is already involved with the determination and redetermination of sense. In short, in the second reading, the formal description is already an interpretation, and, in fact, the so-called formal elements come into view only because an interpretive assumption (about what readers do) is already in force. What Keyser does is detach his own formal patterns from the interpretive act which made them available, and then he proceeds to find for them an interpretation with which they have nothing, necessarily, to do. There is nothing inevitable about his analysis because at the crucial moment (when you would ask why *that*) the relationship be-

tween his form and his content is simply asserted. He would have
achieved inevitability if he had only read out of his formal pattern the content it already, implicitly, had. And, indeed, this is
what he does in the first of his analyses, although for reasons
that should now be clear, he won't admit that he is doing it.

The poem is "The Death of a Soldier," and in it Keyser discerns three significant formal choices. Stevens has:

1. . . . selected verbs which can under no circumstances take agents.
2. He has selected the nonagentive use of verbs which can but
   need not take agents.
3. In the two instances where he has selected the agentive sense
   of a verb . . . he has displayed the verbs in a syntactic construction which requires that the agent be deleted from the surface
   of a poem. (*WS*, p. 582)

It is important to realize that these formalizations are different
in kind from the others we have encountered, from the back and
forth movement of the tongue, or the variation of a single syllable, or a syntax whose description becomes more and more complex. These patterns, at least as they are presented by Epstein
and Keyser, are *purely* formal, and they acquire a semantic value
only by being made icons of a meaning independent of them.
Here the meaning is built into the formalization, and when the
time comes all you have to do is read it out. Thus, when Keyser
asks himself "whether there is a relationship between the suppression of . . . agency and the meaning of the poem?" the question is a rhetorical one because the suppression of agency *is*
the meaning of the poem. I don't mean that it truly is, in some
indisputable way, but that in the context of this formal description the specification of that meaning is inevitable, and this is
enough to distinguish the analysis from those in which the specification of meaning is an act of prestidigitation. That is, Keyser
can legitimately claim for this analysis what he claims for all the
others (and if he doesn't claim it, it's hard to know what he *is*
claiming): that the parallel between form and meaning could not
be drawn in any other direction; and the claim can be made
because it is *not* a parallel between form and meaning but a
spelling out of the meaning that has from the very beginning
been the content of this formal category.

The curious thing is that Keyser feels obliged to assert the contrary and to deny the real coherence—a persuasive coherence —his analysis has. His conclusion makes that clear: "The manipulation of syntax and semantics to remove all vestiges of an agent . . . corresponds to the world of the poem in which there are no initiators" (*WS*, p. 583). The key word here is "corresponds," which is in the same line of work as correlates with, parallels, mimes, and reflects; it implies distance, but in this case there is none, because the notion of a world in which there are no initiators is derived directly (and not by way of correspondence) from a grammar without any visible agency. Keyser claims to have shown that "the form of his poem reflects its content" (*WS*, p. 584); but his formal description merely yields up the content it has always had. He refuses to see this because he is committed to keeping the two levels of his system separate. But in this example, at least, there is only one level; we can call it formal or we can call it semantic; what we cannot do is maintain the fiction of a distinction.

That distinction, however, is essential to the stylistician's enterprise, since it is the availability of a purely formal component—of formal features that one can pick out independently of any interpretation of them—that allows him to claim objectivity for his analyses. We can now see clearly the choice that confronts the stylistician. Either he engages in an activity that is incoherent in its own terms because its assignment of significances is arbitrary; or he engages in a coherent activity whose terms do not allow him the claims he would like to make for it because the coherence is itself interpretive. In his analysis of Blake's "The Tyger" Epstein manages to engage in both activities at the same time. He first decides on the meaning of the poem:" 'Tyger' seems to record a moment of illumination, the moment when the nature of the fundamental energy of the universe became clear. There are, therefore, two aspects of this experience—memory of the sensation of mystic illumination, and awe before the object of perception" (*SRA*, p. 53). It is no surprise to find the assertion that "both of these aspects are reflected in syntactic structures . . . that communicate this moment with great power to the reader." Apparently, however, these syntactic structures are not available on the surface, since Epstein finds it necessary to create them.

His strategy illustrates something extremely important about this kind of analysis. When one interrogates a text with a grammar, one populates the text with the entities the grammar is able to recognize, that is, with entities that are a function of the grammar's categories; and if one of your categories is syntactic ambiguity, the question "is this text ambiguous?" will always be answered in the affirmative. Epstein puts that question to the lines "Tyger, Tyger, burning bright, / In the forests of the night." The first line, he discovers, can be read as either "The Tyger is burning," or "The Tyger is bright"; while the second line is ambiguous in several directions. The tyger could be burning or bright against the background of the forests of the night, or in the forest of the night, or within the forests of the night, and the phrase "forests of the night" could be predicating either thickness of the night or darkness of the forest. By the time he has finished, Epstein is able to speak of "this octuply ambiguous expression," and if we recall that each ambiguity exists in multiple relationships with the other seven, his mathematics are conservative. Now, having created this structure by means of a grammatical apparatus specifically *designed* to create it, Epstein declares that the information provided in the second, third, and fourth stanzas dissolves it by removing the ambiguities, so that when the first two lines reappear in the final stanza, they are "completely unambiguous," or in terms more appropriate to the art here being practiced: "Now you see it; now you don't."

I find this argument very strange. It asserts that in this last stanza contextual pressures are operating in such a way that the ambiguities noted in the first stanza don't arise; but those same or other pressures could just as easily have been operating in the first place. That is to say, one could have argued for historical or biographical or other contextual circumstances that would have removed the potential ambiguities of the lines before a reader ever came to them. What is Epstein's warrant for assuming that lines one and two of the poem are without context (not, in fact, a possible assumption), and are therefore available for an unconstrained quarrying by a grammatical apparatus? The question contains its own answer: the assumption of a-contextual circumstances is necessary if Epstein is to be free to "discover" a formal pattern that can stand in an iconic (mimetic) relationship to a sense already selected. In this case the process of fabricating such a pattern is so complicated that one tends to forget (as you may have forgotten) what the preselected sense is. In a triumphant conclusion, Epstein reminds us: "The movement from eightfold syntactic ambiguity to single structure provides syntactic mimesis for the feeling of universal understanding with which the reader finishes the poem" (*SRA*, p. 67). The sleight of hand is transparent; the movement of the poem is entirely the creation of his analytic strategy; and that in turn is dictated by an interpretation which, rather than being mimed by a formal pattern, produces it. In short, the formal pattern is not there, in the independent sense claimed by the analysis, and even if it were, there would be no exclusive relationship between it and this particular interpretation. The movement from the complex to the simple could mime the change from a questioning of the divine mystery to its unthinking (that is, nonunderstanding) acceptance. Or it could mime an interpretation that Epstein specifically rejects: that the poem is spoken by a limited observer whose attempts to preconceive a reality too complex for him are finally given up. The point is that unless his interpretation is the only one that fits the "formal facts" (and remember that they are not really formal facts in the way he would have them be), the claim of mimesis is empty because there are no formal patterns or interpretations that could not be made into components of a mimetic relationship. In short, everything about this procedure is arbitrary: the interpretation is arbitrary; the formal pattern is arbitrary; the link between them is arbitrary.

Epstein, however, is not yet done, and in the second half of his essay he produces an analysis as compelling in its own terms as this one is bizarre. The subject is still Blake's "Tyger," but the formalism is now speech-act theory and the doctrine of illocutionary forces. Epstein distinguishes between yes/no questions, answerable by a single assent or negation, and questions "to which the answer cannot be 'yes' or 'no' but which must be a phrase, a substitute for an interrogative pronominal, and whose syntactic class is strictly governed by the choice of interrogative pronominal," that is, where, when, why, what (*SRA*, p. 70). The questions headed by some of these interrogatives are simple in form—"Where did you go?"—while others are more complex. An example would be "Whose hat is missing?" which assumes a situation previously ordered and understood. (There is a hat and no one has claimed it.) A given question may assume several prior levels of ordered understanding, and thus be a tertiary or even higher question. Such a question always implies that either the questioner or answerer "has already advanced beyond the point of confronting an unordered situation." Epstein finds that in lines like "What immortal hand or eye, / Could frame thy fearful symmetry," Blake proposes secondary and tertiary questions which are not preceded by the appropriate primary question. The result is "to rob the questions of the power to elicit information of which the questioner is ignorant." They are "not really questions at all, but disguised exclamations." The situation of the reader is thus uneasy; he listens to the form of questions, but is aware at some level that they are disguised exclamations, and therefore questions that he cannot even begin to answer. In stanza five, however, the questions are in "perfect canonical form"—"Did he smile his work to see?"—and they come as a great relief because "the construction of an answer can at least begin for them. Thus the 'true' questions in stanza five act to release tension previously created by the asking of questions subtly false in form" (*SRA*, p. 73).

Now one can quarrel with this, but the quarrel would be with the account of the different kinds of questions and their effects on readers; but given that account, Epstein's conclusions follow. If there is any magic in the sequence, it is at the beginning, where the formal apparatus is introduced. Two points should be made about that apparatus: 1. It isn't formal in the strictest sense since it contains information about responses and takes into account not only the situation of utterance, but the situations prior to utterance. 2. It is not a finished thing, but is in the process of being constructed. Epstein is forthright about this, noting that he is depending to some extent on rules not yet formulated and labeling his approach, quite properly as "tentative." These two points will allow us to make a third by way of a question. What would happen if Epstein were to come up with a new formulation of the rules governing questions? One is tempted to answer that the description of the poem would change, but when the categories in dispute are as basic as the structure of questions or the properties of verbs, there is literally nothing to describe. That is, if descriptive categories are themselves interpretive (because they are open to challenge) they are constitutive of their object rather than being faithful (or unfaithful) to it; and when one system of formal rules gives way to another, the result is not a new description of the same poem but a new poem. Epstein's analysis of the questions in "The Tyger" is not persuasive because it matches up to the poem but because it produces the poem: one interpretive structure— a theoretical account of interrogatives—leads inevitably to another—the poem he proceeds to "describe." There is certainly a coherence to the procedure, but it is a coherence that begins and ends in interpretation, without ever touching base with a fact or a pattern that is *independently* specifiable.

Another way of putting this is to say that in the more coherent (and therefore more persuasive) of these analyses, the construction of the grammar and the construction of the poem are going on at the same time. Indeed, they are the same activities. This is especially clear in Donald Freeman's analysis of Keats's "To Autumn."[7] Freeman's exposition is subtle and complex, but basically it is an argument about the verbs "load," "bless," "bend," "fill," "swell," and "plump" as they appear in the following lines:

> Conspiring with him how to load and bless
> With fruit the vines that round the thatch-eves run;
> To bend with apples the moss'd cottage-trees,
> And fill all fruit with ripeness to the core;
> To swell the gourd, and plump the hazel shells,
> With a sweet kernel . . .

Freeman notes that in the surface structure all of these verbs are transitive, and are to some extent causative, while in their underlying forms "plump" and "swell" are intransitive, and "fill" has at least one intransitive reading. It is possible, he continues, to argue that "load," "bless," and "bend" also have underlying intransitive readings. One need only add the suffix "en" to them to see that they denote states in the process of coming about. "Just as *the ice thickened . . .* underlies *John thickened the sauce,* so does *the hazel shells plump[en]* underlie to *plump the hazel shells,*" and similarly with "bend*en*" "load*en*," and "bless*en*" (*TA*, p. 6). Freeman concludes that by embedding these basically inchoative verbs in a surface structure marked "transitive," Keats achieves an effect basic to the meaning of the poem. The underlying subjects of natural and apparently independent states —the trees which bend, the shells which plump—are made into the objects of Autumn's all-powerful agency. Rather than the fruit filling with ripeness (where "ripely" is the answer to the question, "in what manner does the fruit fill?"), the fruit is filled by Autumn, who *uses* ripeness in the accomplishing of her work. Normally, "with fruit," "with apples," "with ripeness," and "with a sweet kernel" would not be instrumentals, but in this construction they become the means by which Autumn loads, blesses, bends, fills, swells, and plumps. Each of these instrumental phrases, rather than being the result of a verb's action (the vine is loaded—with what?—with fruit), becomes the object of Autumn's action (Autumn loads the vines and she loads the vines with fruit.) The overriding agency of Autumn, by making everything her object, makes everything her instrument, even the sun. She conspires with him in the sense of using him; she conspires, and the instrument of her conspiring is him, and the complements of his instrumentality are all the subsidiary instrumental actions: loading, blessing, bending, and so on. Thus as instrument, the sun "becomes a part of the objects upon which it is employed (the fruit, the apples, the ripeness, the sweet kernel) just as they in turn become . . . a part of the objects upon which they are employed as instruments the vines, the trees, the fruit, the hazel shells.)" "On this reading," Freeman concludes, "the sun can be seen . . . as a meta-instrument for Autumn, the ultimate agent of all the natural forces in the poem" (*TA*, p. 10).

I find this all elegant and persuasive, but it is also interpretive from the very first word to the last. Like Keyser, Freeman believes otherwise. He sees his reading of "To Autumn" as a demonstration of "syntactic mimesis, the imitation by the poem's syntactic structure of its subject matter" (*TA*, p. 12); but this is to give himself less credit than he is due. The syntactic structure and the poem's subject matter are not brought together in the analysis; they are created by the analysis as the building of the one produces an account of the other. Freeman admits as much in a footnote where he attempts to argue that the pattern he discerns represents options chosen by Keats from alternatives in the deep structure. But the enterprise, as he himself says, founders, because linguists disagree about what is in the deep structure, and therefore about what would be alternative derived structures. Nevertheless, he remains convinced that the inchoative-causative pattern in "To Autumn" reflects a preference, although, as he says, a preference over what is a question he cannot answer. The answer is obvious. The preference of one grammar over the other is not the author's but the critic's, and what it reflects in his reading of the poem, a reading which is the very content of his formal categories. The point has been made by J. P. Thorne, who acknowledges that his grammatical analysis of a poem follows rather than precedes his understanding of it, and therefore cannot stand in a relationship of confirmation to that understanding: "The whole point of constructing a grammar [for a poem] . . . is that it provides a way of stating clearly the interpretation that one finds."[8] Just so. Freeman's specifying of the inchoative-causative pattern is not an act preliminary to interpretation; it is itself an interpretive act, and the specifying of the poem's "subject" matter is nothing more than a transposition of that act into a more discursive and less technical vocabulary. In short, when Freeman chooses one grammar rather than another he is choosing one meaning rather than another and is therefore choosing one poem rather than another. Eugene Kintgen has remarked that given the number of competing grammars and the disputes concerning their basic categories, "two stylistic analyses of the same text written at different times may . . .

associate different phenomena, and make apparently different claims about the text.''[9] I would go even further: the two grammars would be making different texts.

With that statement I come to the end of my argument and can return to its beginning and to my conclusions. There are two varieties of stylistics and neither of them will support the stylisticians' strongest claims. The one falls apart in the middle because there is no legitimate way (and every illegitimate way) to relate its formal and semantic components. In the other the formal and semantic components are so perfectly related that the distinction between them is lost: its stages are interpretive from the first to the last. The stylisticians often perform these two kinds of analysis without seeing the difference between them, because they remain committed to a form/meaning distinction even when they have in their practice abandoned it. That is, they begin by assuming that a form can express many meanings and that a meaning can be clothed in many forms, and it is an assumption that they persist in even when demonstrating how much semantic content—how much meaning—their formal categories have. In short, they refuse to acknowledge their dilemma. Either they can continue in an activity that is wholly illegitimate, or engage in an activity which, while legitimate, is not, in the sense they desire, formal. They can still claim rigor and precision, but it will be rigor in the unfolding of an interpretation, and precision in the stating of that interpretation.

Some of you will have noted that this same dilemma is writ larger in the history of transformational grammar. On the one hand there are those who have argued for an independently motivated syntax to which a semantic component must then be added in some ad hoc or artificial way; and on the other, those whose syntactic categories are already so laden with semantic content that the distinction between them finally disappears. The lesson to be drawn from the plight of stylistics is a hard one, especially for those who still dream of a criticism, or even of a linguistics, that begins with free-standing and independent formal facts and builds up from those facts to the larger world of discourse: the dream, in short, of an analysis that moves in a principled way from the objective description of a text to its interpretation. What I have been saying is that every description is always and already an interpretation, and that therefore the first act of any criticism, and especially of a linguistically based criticism, is to constitute the text.

Finally, I should point out that the argument of this essay differs considerably from that of its predecessor. In "What Is Stylistics and Why Are They Saying Such Terrible Things About It?" the focus is on the arbitrary relationship between the specification of formal patterns and their subsequent interpretation. Here my thesis is that formal patterns are themselves the products of interpretation and that therefore there is no such thing as a formal pattern, at least in the sense necessary for the practice of stylistics: that is, no pattern that one can observe before interpretation is hazarded and which therefore can be used to prefer one interpretation to another. The conclusion, however, is not that there are no formal patterns but that there are always formal patterns; it is just that the formal patterns there always are will always be the product of a prior interpretive act, and therefore will be available for discerning only so long as that act is in force. Or, to end with an aphorism: there always is a formal pattern, but it isn't always the same one.

11

Normal Circumstances, Literal Language, Direct Speech Acts, the Ordinary, the Everyday, the Obvious, What Goes without Saying, and Other Special Cases

[THIS ESSAY is an attempt to disassociate myself from a certain characterization (actually a caricature) of the poststructuralist or Derridian position. In that characterization (represented, for example, by the writings of M. H. Abrams) the denial of objective texts and determinate meanings leads to a universe of absolute free play in which everything is indeterminate and undecidable. In the view I put forward, determinacy and decidability are always available, not, however, because of the constraints imposed by the language or the world—that is, by entities independent of context—but because of the constraints built into the context or contexts in which we find ourselves operating. Thus I pursue a double strategy in the manner indicated by my title. I want to argue for, not against, the normal, the ordinary, the literal, the straightforward, and so on, but I want to argue for them as the products of contextual or interpretive circumstances and not as the property of an acontextual language or an independent world. In six short sections written from wholly different perspectives (religion, sex, baseball, literature, the law, speech-act theory, ambiguity) I make essentially the same point: language does not have a shape independent of context, but since language is only encountered in contexts and never in the abstract, it always has a shape, although it is not always the same one. The problem with this formulation is that for many people determinacy is inseparable from stability: the reason that we can specify the meaning of a text is because a text and its meanings never change. What I am suggesting is that change is continually occurring but that its consequence is *never* the absence of the norms, standards, and certainties we desire, because they will be features of any situation we happen

268

to be in. This means that while we can never specify value once and for all—that is, label a sentence ambiguous or unambiguous *in itself* —we can always specify value within the circumstances informing our perception—that is, perceive sentences as ambiguous or unambiguous in context. This is to say in another way what I said in "How To Do Things with Austin and Searle": there always is a standard story, and as characters who are embedded in it, we are never without a conviction of facts, consequences, responsibilities—of everything that comprises our sense of being in a world.

The writing of this essay was attended with a certain serendipity. It was first given as a talk in a seminar conducted by Edward Said at Columbia University. As I boarded the train for New York I happened to glance at the sports pages of the *Baltimore Sun* to find the exploits of Pat Kelly celebrated in large headlines. By the time I reached New York, the talk had a new beginning, one that focused for the first time in my work on the issue of belief. Pat Kelly continues to prosper. He played an important role in the improbable success of the 1979 Orioles, and midway through the season he demonstrated that he had lost none of his interpretive abilities. It had been a confirming feature of his heroic home runs that they were usually hit on Sunday. On one occasion, however, he won a game by hitting a dramatic home run on a Wednesday night. Asked if this did not upset his theory of providential agency, he thought for a moment and replied that it was all right because there had been a prayer meeting earlier in the day, and so this Wednesday was the same as Sunday. What would be perceived as an absolute difference under one set of assumptions— the difference between Wednesday and Sunday—is perceived as no difference at all under the set of assumptions in relation to which Kelly sees the world as already organized. He knew, with certainty and without reflection, that any day on which he hit a home run must be the Lord's day, and it was no trick at all for him to see this day as an instance of what he already knew.]

O N MAY DAY, 1977, Pat Kelly, an outfielder for the Baltimore Orioles, hit two home runs in a game against the California Angels. The *Baltimore Sun* devoted three columns to the story, in part because Kelly had rarely displayed such power (he had hit only five home runs in the entire previous season) but largely because of the terms in which he saw his accomplishment. In fact, Kelly didn't see it as his at all but as the working through him of divine Providence. Two years previously he had experienced a religious conversion. As he reports it, "I had been like a normal ballplayer. I was an extreme party-er, hanging around in bars and chasing all the women. But then this change came over me, and I have dedicated myself to Him." The effects of this change are described by the *Sun* reporter, Michael Janofsky, whose comments betray some understandable exasperation: "It is not even possible to discuss [with Kelly] the events of yesterday's game— or any game—on strictly a baseball level. He does not view his home runs as merely a part of athletic competition. They are part of his religious existence." One assumes that Janofsky had tried to discuss the events of yesterday's game and found that Kelly simply did not recognize the facts to which sports writers' questions routinely refer. These are the facts that exist on "strictly a baseball level," a wonderful phrase that can serve to identify the subject of this essay, a level of observation or discourse at which meanings are obvious and indisputable, the level of the ordinary, the normal, the usual, the everyday, the straightforward, the literal. From Janofsky's point of view it is this level that Kelly has lost, but from Kelly's point of view it has simply been redefined: as Janofsky reports, he now *literally* sees everything as a function of his religious existence; it is not that he allegorizes events after they have been normally perceived but that his normal perception is of events as the evidence of supernatural forces. Kelly played on May 1st only because the regular right fielder came down with conjunctivitis, and "even that," Janofsky exclaims, "he interpreted as divine intervention." "Interpreted" is not quite right because it suggests an imposition upon raw data of a meaning not inherent in them, but for Kelly the meaning is prior to the data which will always have the same preread shape. The effort that Janofsky must make before he can read providential design into everyday occurrences is *natural* for the born-again Christian, who would now have to make an effort wholly *un*natural in order once again to see a "mere athletic competition."

What this suggests is that categories like "the natural" and "the everyday" are not essential but conventional. They refer not to properties of the world but to properties of the world as it is given to us by our interpretive assumptions. In the world in which Janofsky is situated as an independent agent amidst equally independent phenomena, Kelly is an anomaly (and therefore noteworthy) because rather than accepting that world as it is, he populates it with the invisible presences demanded by his belief. That is, Janofsky assumes (without being aware of the assumption) that he speaks from a position above or below or to the side of belief, but in fact he speaks from within an *alternative* belief, one that gives him his world of "natural" causes as surely as Kelly's belief gives him a world alive with divine interventions. At stake here is the status of the ordinary. It would never occur to Janofsky to explain or defend the basis on which he describes events on a "strictly baseball level" (as he asks Kelly to explain and defend his point of view); he is simply describing what is there. That is what the ordinary is, that which appears to be there independently of anything we might say or think about it. It does not require comment (one doesn't write news stories about it) because it is obvious, right there on the surface; anyone can see it. But what anyone sees is not independent of his verbal and mental categories but is in fact a product of them; and it is because these categories, rather than being added to perception, are its content that the entities they bring into being seem to be a part of the world in the sense that they were there before there was anyone to perceive them. In other words, while the ordinary and the obvious are always with us because we are always in the grip of some belief or other, they can change. They have changed for Kelly and that is why his story can bear the weight I am putting on it. "I had," he says, "been like a normal ballplayer," by which he means that he saw what normal ballplayers see. Now what he just as normally sees are divine interventions. His conversion follows the pattern prescribed by Augustine in *On Christian Doctrine*. The eye that was in bondage to the phenomenal world (had as its constitutive principle the autonomy of that world) has been cleansed and purged and is now capable of seeing what is really there, what is obvious, what anyone who has the eyes can see: "to the healthy and pure internal eye He is everywhere."[1] He is everywhere not as the result of an interpretive act self-consciously performed on data otherwise available, but as the result of an interpretive act performed at so deep a level that it is indistinguishable from consciousness itself.

I have lingered over this example because it seems to me to bear (however indirectly) on the question most frequently debated in current literary discussions: What is in the text? That question assumed that at some (perhaps molecular) level what is in the text is independent of and prior to whatever people have said about it, and that therefore the text is stable, even though interpretations of it may vary. I want to argue that there always is a text (just as there always is an ordinary world) but that what is in it can change, and therefore at no level is it independent of and prior to interpretation. My literary example is Milton's *Samson Agonistes,* a text whose history has a surprising relationship to Pat Kelly's conversion.

Like Milton's other major works, *Samson Agonistes* has received many readings. Among the readings now considered acceptable is one in which Samson's story is seen in relationship to the life of Christ. In its starkest form, the argument for this reading has the air of a paradox: *Samson Agonistes* is about Christ because he is nowhere mentioned. Such an argument seems to fly in the face of the rules of evidence, but in fact it illustrates something very important about evidence: it is always a function of what it is to be evidence for, and is never independently available. That is, the interpretation determines what will count as evidence for it, and the evidence is able to be picked out only because the interpretation has *already* been assumed. In this case, the evidence is evidence for a typological interpretation, and that is why it *is* evidence even if, in some sense, it is not there. Typology is a way of reading the Old Testament as a prefiguration or foreshadowing of events in the life of Christ. It is not, at least in its Protestant version, allegorical because it insists on respecting the historical reality of the type who is unaware of his significance as an anticipation of one greater than he. In *Paradise Lost,* this significance can be pointed out by the narrator, who stands outside the consciousnesses of the characters and therefore can look forward to the new dispensation without violating typological decorum. In *Samson Agonistes,* however, there is no narrator, and the consciousnesses of the characters mark the limits of allowable awareness. It follows (given a disposition to read typologically) that the absence of any reference to Christ, rather than being evidence that he is not being referred to, is evidence of Milton's intention to respect typological decorum. As William Madsen puts it, "Instead of collapsing Samson and Christ, [Milton] is concerned with measuring the distance between the various levels of awareness . . . possible to those living under the old dispensation and the level of awareness revealed by Christ."[2] Once this characterization of Milton's intention has been specified, the text will immediately assume the shape that Madsen proceeds to describe: "If . . . Samson is viewed first of all as a concrete individual living in a concrete historical situation, then his significance for the Christian reader lies primarily in his inability to measure up to the heroic norm delineated in *Paradise Regained*" (pp. 201–202). The fact that this significance is unavailable to the characters is precisely what makes it inescapable for the Christian reader. Moreover, it is not a figurative significance, one that is imposed on the text's literal level; rather it is built into the text as it is *immediately* seen by anyone who operates within Madsen's interpretive assumptions. A reader who was innocent of those assumptions would not see that significance, but he would see some other, and that other would be similarly the product of the assumptions within which *he* was operating. In either case (and in any other that could be imagined) the resulting meaning would be a *literal* one that followed directly upon a determination of what was in the text. The category "in the text" is usually thought to refer to something that is irreducibly there independently of and prior to all interpretive activities. The example of *Samson Agonistes* suggests that what is perceived to be "in the text" is a *function* of interpretive activities, although these activities are performed at so primary a level that the shapes they yield seem to be there before we have done anything. In other words, the category "in the text," like the category of the "ordinary," is always full (because there is never a point at which a set of interpretive assumptions is not in force), but what fills it is not always the same. For some present-day readers Christ is "in the text" of *Samson Agonistes,* for others he is not, and before the typological interpretation of the poem was introduced and developed by Michael Krouse in 1949, he was not "in the text" for anyone. Again, it is important to see that the question of what is in the text cannot be settled by appealing to the evidence since the evidence will have become available only because some determination of what is in the text has already been made. (Otherwise it would be impossible to read.) Indeed the same piece of evidence will not be the same when it is cited in support of differing determinations of what is in the text. Thus for one reader the fact that Christ is not mentioned "proves" that he is not in the text, while for another the same "fact" (really not the same) proves that he is. Nor can one descend to a lower level of description and assert that at least *that* fact about the text (that Christ is not mentioned) is beyond dispute; for the two readers I posit would be stipulating two different notions of "mention," and indeed the second reader would be claiming that the mention of Samson *includes* Christ and that thus He is no less mentioned than his Old Testament prefiguration. This does not mean that the text of *Samson Agonistes* is ambiguous or unstable; it is always stable and never ambiguous. It is just that it is stable in more than one direction, as a succession of interpretive assumptions give it a succession of stable shapes. Mine is not an argument for an infinitely plural or an open text, but for a text that is always set; and yet because it is set not for all places or all times but for wherever and however long a particular way of reading is in force, it is a text that can change.

Perhaps a shorter example, one taken neither from the sports pages nor from literature but from (if you will pardon the expression) life, will make the point clearer. I have in mind a sign that is affixed in this unpunctuated form to the door of the Johns Hopkins University Club:

PRIVATE MEMBERS ONLY

I have had occasion to ask several classes what that sign means, and I have received a variety of answers, the least interesting of which is, "Only those who are secretly and not publicly members of this club may enter it." Other answers fall within a predictable and narrow range: "Only the genitalia of members may enter" (this seems redundant), or "You may only bring in your own genitalia," or (and this is the most popular reading, perhaps because of its Disney-like anthropomorphism) *"Only* genitalia may enter." In every class, however, some Dr. Johnson-like positivist rises to say, "But you're just playing games; everyone knows that the sign really means, 'Only those persons who belong to this club may enter it.' " He is of course right. Everyone does know (although, as we shall see, everyone does not always know the same thing), but we can still inquire into the source of that knowledge. How is it that a text so demonstrably unstable can be stabilized to such a degree that a large number of people know immediately what it means? The answer can be found in the exercise performed by my students. What they did was move the words out of a context (the faculty club door) in which they had a literal and obvious meaning into another context (my classroom) in which the meaning was no less obvious and literal and yet was different. What they did not do was move away from a meaning that was available apart from a context to the various meanings contexts confer. Paradoxically the exercise does not prove that the words can mean anything one likes, but that they always and only mean one thing, although that one thing is not always the same. The one thing they mean will be a function of the shape language *already has* when we come upon it in a situation, and it is the knowledge that is the content of being in a situation that will have stabilized it. In the case of PRIVATE MEMBERS ONLY, the knowledge is the knowledge of what to do with signs on faculty club doors. Those who enter the club do not first perceive the sign in some uninterpreted or acontextual form and *then* construe it so as to conform with the situation; rather, being in the situation means that they have already construed it, even before they see it. That is, to know what to do with signs on faculty club doors is already to have done it because that knowledge will already have been organizing perception.

This is not to say that the knowledge of what to do with the signs on faculty club doors is itself stable, but that in whatever form it takes, it is always stabilizing. In many municipalities a business will incorporate as a club in order to secure certain tax advantages, and in some "dry" states incorporation is a way of circumventing laws that prohibit the public sale of liquor. In such situations the word "private" means "public" (it is not restrictive at all, except in the sense that any business establishment is restrictive), and the sign PRIVATE MEMBERS ONLY would be immediately understood to mean "anyone who has the price may enter." That would then be as literal a reading as "Only those persons who belong to this club may enter it" because, to those whose understandings were an extension of the situation they were already in, the words could mean nothing else. It may seem confusing and even contradictory to assert that a text may have more than one literal reading, but that is because we usually reserve "literal" for the single meaning a text will always (or should always) have, while I am using "literal" to refer to the different single meanings a text will have in a succession of different situations. There always is a literal meaning because in any situation there is always a meaning that seems obvious in the sense that it is there independently of anything we might do. *But that only means that we have already done it,* and in another situation, when we have already done something else, there will be another obvious, that is, literal, meaning. The stronger sense of literal, in which "single" is inseparable from "once and for all," would itself make sense only if there were a meaning that was apprehensible apart from any situation whatsoever, a meaning that was not the product of an interpretation but was available independently. Every literal meaning comes to us with that claim, but it is a claim that seems to be supportable only because an interpretive act is already in force but is so embedded in the situation (its structure *is* the structure of the situation) that it doesn't seem to be an act at all. We are never not in a situation. Because we are never not in a situation, we are never not in the act of interpreting. Because we are never not in the act of interpreting, there is no possibility of reaching a level of meaning beyond or below interpretation. But in every situation some or other meaning will appear to us to be uninterpreted because it is isomorphic with the interpretive structure the situation (and therefore our perception) already has. Therefore, there always will be a literal reading, but (1) it will not always be the same one and (2) it can change.

In this newly defined sense, a literal reading can even be plural, as it is for my students when they are asked, "What does PRIVATE MEMBERS ONLY mean?" Constituting *their* perception is not the knowledge of what to do with signs on faculty club doors but the knowledge of what to do with texts written on blackboards by professors of English literature. That is, professors of English literature do not put things on boards unless they are to be examples of problematic or ironic or ambiguous language. Students know that because they know what it means to be in a classroom, and the categories of understanding that are the content of that knowledge will be organizing what they see before they see it. Irony and ambiguity are not properties of language but are functions of the expectations with which we approach it. If we expect a text to be ambiguous, we will in the act of reading it imagine situations in which it means first one thing and then another (there is no text with which this cannot be done), and those plural meanings will, in the context of that situation, be that text's literal reading. That is, in a situation in which the obvious (immediately apprehensible) reading is a plural one, meaning more than one thing will be the one thing a text means.

In summary, then, there are two things I do not want to say about PRIVATE MEMBERS ONLY: that it has a literal meaning, and that it doesn't. It does not have a literal meaning in the sense of some irreducible content which survives the sea change of situations; but in each of those situations one meaning (even if it is plural) will seem so obvious that one cannot see how it could be otherwise, and that meaning will be literal.

If the question of what is literal is important in literary discussions, it is the central question in the law, where determining what a text (contract, statute, case, precedent, ruling) *says* is the business everyone is in. A close examination of the way that business is conducted will reveal a pattern that should by now be familiar. My example is a case that deals with the probating of wills, *Riggs* v. *Palmer,* New York, 1889.[3] The decision is prefaced by a rehearsal of the facts: "On the thirteenth day of August, 1880, Francis B. Palmer made his last will and testament, in which he gave small legacies to his two daughters, Mrs. Riggs and Mrs. Preston, the plaintiffs in this action, and the remainder to his grandson, the defendant Elmer E. Palmer." In 1882 the elder Palmer married one Mrs. Bressee, and there was some indication that he would alter the will so as to make his new wife the principal beneficiary. It was then that Elmer acted: "He knew," says the court "of the provisions made in his favor . . . and that he might prevent his grandfather from revoking such provisions, which he had manifested some intention to do, and to obtain the speedy enjoyment and immediate possession of his property, he willfully murdered him by poisoning him. He nows claims the property and the sole question for our determination is, Can he have it? The defendants say that the testator is dead; that his will was made in due form, and has been admitted to probate, and that, therefore, it must have effect according to the letter of the law." It is with this last phrase—"the letter of the law"—that this example falls into line with the others. Elmer's lawyers have presented the court with a dilemma: either it must decide in favor of the client or it must go against what the law plainly says. The law in this case is a statute that reads as follows: "All persons, except idiots, persons of unsound mind and infants, may devise their real estate, by a last will and testament, duly executed, according to the provisions of this article." In effect Elmer and his counsel are arguing that there is nothing in the statute that bars a murderer from inheriting or a victim from bequeathing his property to a murderer, and that therefore his act is irrelevant to the question of probate.

The court begins rather badly by conceding Elmer's basic claim: "It is quite true that statutes regulating the making, proof, and effect of wills, and the devolution of property, if

literally construed, and if their force and effect can in no way
and under no circumstances be controlled or modified, give
this property to the murderer." This would be a damaging admission were it not that as the decision unfolds the court proceeds to take it back. It does this by introducing the notion
of purpose and by insisting that the statute be read in its light:
"The purpose of the statutes was to enable testators to dispose
all of their estates to the objects of their bounty at death . . .
and in considering and giving effect to them, this purpose must
be kept in view. It was the intention of the law-makers that
the donees in a will should have the property given to them.
But it never could have been their intention that a donee who
murdered the testator to make the will operative should have
any benefit under it." Why could it "never have been their intention"? The court answers that question by invoking as one
of the "general fundamental maxims of the common law" the
principle that "no one shall be permitted to profit by his own
fraud, or take advantage of his own wrong, or found any claim
upon his own iniquity, or to acquire property by his own crime."
At this point the court's strategy becomes clear. It wants to find
a way of reading the statute so that it bars Elmer from inheriting, and the way it finds is to assert that something goes without
saying (that is why it is a matter of common, that is, unwritten,
law) and therefore has been said. The reasoning is the same that
yields the typological reading of *Samson Agonistes:* just as the
mention of Samson is understood to include a reference to
Christ, so is the text of a statute understood (at least under this
interpretive assumption) to include a proviso disallowing any
claim founded upon the commission of a wrong.

It is a very good argument, and the court errs only in thinking that in order to make it, the literal reading must be set aside.
That is, the court apparently believes that only *it* is reading the
statute with "a purpose in view" while the defendant is urging
a reading of what the words literally express. The truth of the
matter is that both are pointing to what the words literally express but in the light of two different purposes. The opposition between a literal and a nonliteral reading could be maintained only if it were possible to conceive of a reading that did

not follow from the assumption of some purpose or other, but as Kenneth Abraham observes, "A statute without a purpose would be meaningless . . . to speak of the literal meaning of a statute . . . is already to have read it in the light of some purpose, to have engaged in an interpretation."[4] In other words, any reading that is plain and obvious in the light of some assumed purpose (and it is impossible not to assume one) is a literal reading; but no reading is *the* literal reading in the sense that is available apart from any purpose whatsoever. If it is assumed that the purpose of probate is to ensure the orderly devolution of property at all costs, then the statute in this case will have the plain meaning urged by the defendant; but if it is assumed that no law ever operates in favor of someone who would profit by his crime, then the "same" statute will have a meaning that is different, but no less plain. In either case the statute will have been literally construed, and what the court will have done is prefer one literal construction to another by invoking one purpose (assumed background) rather than another.

· It is not that we first read the statute and then know its purpose; we know the purpose first, and only then can the statute be read. This is exactly the sequence the court follows, and at one point the principle underlying its procedure is articulated: "It is a familiar canon of construction that a thing which is within the intention of the makers of a statute is as much within the statute as if it were within the letter; and a thing which is within the letter of the statute is not within the statute, unless it be within the intention of the makers." The rhetoric of this sentence insists upon the distinction between what is intended and what is literally there, but the argument of the sentence takes the distinction away. It is your specification of the makers' intention that tells you what is in the statute, not your literal reading of the statute that informs you as to its makers' intention. This would seem to suggest that one need only recover the makers' intention in order to arrive at the *correct* literal reading; but the documents (including even *verbatim* reports) that would give us that intention are no more available to a literal reading (are no more uninterpreted) than the literal reading it would yield. However one specifies what is in a statute—

whether by some theory of strict constructionism or by some construction of an original intention—that specification will have the same status as the specification of what is in *Samson Agonistes* or of what PRIVATE MEMBERS ONLY means. It can always be made, but as situations and the purposes which inform them change, it will have to be made again.

I could imagine someone objecting to the previous pages in the following way: "Aren't you in each of these examples simply talking about ambiguous language, language that can mean more than one thing?" My answer is that the objection would have force only if there were a kind of language to which ambiguous language could be opposed. That is, to label a sentence "ambiguous" will be to distinguish it only if there are sentences that always and only mean one thing, and I would contend that there are no such sentences. I am not saying that sentences always have more than one meaning, but that the sentence which is perceived as having only one meaning will not always have the same one. In other words, I am as willing to say that all sentences are straightforward as I am to say that all sentences are ambiguous. What I am not willing to do is say that any sentence is by right either one or the other. That is, I wish to deny that ambiguity is a property of some sentences and not of others.

Typically, the division of sentences into two classes (ambiguous, nonambiguous) is not defended; it is simply assumed in the course of presenting strings that are asserted to be obviously members of one or the other class. In a recent introduction to transformational grammar the following sentence is offered as an example of one that is ambiguous on its face: "The suit is light."[5] As the authors point out, the reference can be either to the suit's weight or its color, and the situation is not helped, they observe, when the sentence is expanded to read: "The suit is too light to wear." The additional material is not sufficiently disambiguating because the words do not combine in such a way as to make one reading inescapable; but when the sentence is further expanded to read "The suit is too light to wear on such a cold day," the ambiguity, we are told, disappears. In the new sentence, the "semantic environment" specified by "cold day" blocks one of the possible readings of "light," and the result is a perfectly straightforward utterance.

It is an elegant argument, but unfortunately it won't work. It takes only a moment of reflection to imagine a situation in which this sentence would have the reading that is now supposedly blocked. It so happens that I have a weakness for light-colored suits, and I have several that are heavy enough to wear on a cold day. My wife, however, is more conscious of the proprieties of fashion than I am and is likely to say to me, "That suit is too light to wear on such a cold day," and be immediately understood as meaning that the suit is too light in color. M. F. Garrett offers a similar counterexample to a supposedly unambiguous sentence put forward by Katz and Postal: "The stuff is light enough to carry." It is not ambiguous, Katz and Postal say, because "light enough to carry" cannot be understood to mean "light enough in color to be carried." But, objects Garrett, "it does not take an especially tortured context to make this the preferred reading:

> Scene: Highway patrolman lecturing to 3rd grade class.
> Patrolman: "When you are walking on a highway at night, it is important to wear light colored clothing or carry a light colored flag so that you will be visible to oncoming cars. For instance (holds up flag), this stuff is light enough to carry."[6]

Katz and Postal might reply that what the counterexample shows is that the original sentence was not sufficiently explicit. If we were to add more information to it and write (let us say) "This stuff is light enough to carry even for a small child," it will be capable of one reading and of no other. But if this sentence were uttered by a manufacturer's representative, the word "carry" would be understood to mean "stock in inventory," and the speaker would be reminding a potential buyer that small children do not normally wear the darker colors. One could imagine counterexample following upon counterexample, but the result would always be the same; for no degree of explicitness will ever be sufficient to disambiguate the sentence if by disambiguate we understand *render it impossible to conceive of a set of circumstances in which its plain meaning would be other than it now appears to be.*

The conclusion that Garrett draws from this and other examples is that all sentences are ambiguous, but then he is faced with the problem of explaining the fact that "we simply don't notice most of the ambiguities that we encounter" (p. 50). It is a problem because Garrett has moved away from one version of an error only to embrace another. He correctly sees that no sentence always means the same thing, but this leads him to affirm that every sentence has more than one meaning. What he does not realize is that these positions are the same position in that they both assume a stage in the life of sentences *before* they are perceived in a context. It is just that in one position that stage is characterized by a timeless stability (means only one thing), in the other by a timeless instability (means more than one thing). The truth is that there is no such stage. A sentence is never apprehended independently of the context in which it is perceived, and therefore we never know a sentence except in the stabilized form a context has *already* conferred. But since a sentence can appear in more than one context, its stabilized form will not always be the same. It follows then that while no sentence is ambiguous in the sense that it has (as a constitutive property) more than one meaning, every sentence is ambiguous in the (undistinguishing) sense that the single meaning it will always have can change. Now, it is sometimes the case that we are asked to imagine first one and then another context in which a sentence will have different single meanings. In that case, we are in a *third* context in which the single meaning the sentence has is that it has more than one single meaning. The insight which makes perfect sense of these apparent paradoxes is firmly articulated by Garrett: "We must, I believe, always assume that any sentence is interpreted with respect to some context" (p. 51). Garrett then immediately demonstrates how easy it is to slip away from that insight by declaring that if "a sentence is ambiguous, it is the context which determines what reading will be assigned." In the interval of a typographical space, the context-less utterance has been revived since, presumably, no context at all has determined that the sentence is ambiguous in the first place. But by Garrett's own axiom, there is no "first place" in the sense of a state in which the natural (acontextual) properties of a sentence can be observed and enumerated. In order for the sentence to be perceived as ambiguous (or to be perceived at all), it must already be in a context, and the context, rather than any natural property, will be responsible for the ambiguity the sentence will then (in a limited sense) have.

A sentence is never not in a context. We are never not in a situation. A statute is never not read in the light of some purpose. A set of interpretive assumptions is always in force. A sentence that seems to need no interpretation is already the product of one. These statements have made my single point from a variety of perspectives, and I am about to make it again with another statement. No sentence is ever apprehended independently of some or other illocutionary force. Illocutionary force is the key term in speech-act theory. It refers to the way an utterance is taken—as an order, a warning, a promise, a proposal, a request and so on—and the theory's strongest assertion is that no utterance is ever taken purely, that is, without already having been understood as the performance of some illocutionary act. Consider, as an example, the sentence "I will go." Depending on the context in which it is uttered, "I will go" can be understood as a promise, a threat, a warning, a report, a prediction, or whatever, but it will always be understood as one of these, and it will never be an unsituated kernel of pure semantic value. In other words, "I will go" does not have a basic or primary meaning which is then put to various illocutionary uses; rather, "I will go" is known only in its illocutionary lives, and in each of them its meaning will be different. Moreover, if the meaning of a sentence is a function of its illocutionary force (the way it is taken), and if illocutionary force varies with circumstances, then illocutionary force is not a property of sentences but of situations. That is, while a sentence will always have an illocutionary force (because otherwise it would not have a meaning), the illocutionary force it has will not always be the same.

My authority for much of the preceding paragraph is John Searle, and therefore it is surprising to find that Searle, along with other speech-act theorists, is committed to a distinction between direct and indirect speech acts. A direct speech act is defined as one whose illocutionary force is a function of its meaning, and the best example of a direct speech act would be an explicit performative, that is, "I promise to pay you five dollars." An indirect speech act is one whose illocutionary force is something other than its literal meaning would suggest. "Can you reach the salt?" is literally a question about the hearer's abilities, but in normal circumstances it is heard as a request. The distinction then is between utterances that mean exactly what they say and utterances that mean something different or additional. As Searle puts it, "In indirect speech acts the speaker communicates to the hearer more than he actually says by way of relying on their mutually shared background information . . . together with the general powers of rationality and inference on the part of the hearer."[7] This assumes, of course, that in the performance of direct speech acts speaker and hearer do *not* rely on their mutually shared background information because what is actually said is available directly (hence the distinction). It is with this assumption that I would like to quarrel, if only because it reinstates what J. L. Austin in *How To Do Things with Words* was at such pains to dislodge, a class of utterances (constative utterances) that mean independently of situations, purposes, and goals. It seems to me that *all* utterances are understood by way of relying on "shared background information" and that therefore the distinction between direct and indirect speech acts, as it is usually formulated, will not hold.

What I have to show, then, is that the acts cited as direct are, in fact indirect, at least according to the theory's definition of the terms. My argument will take up Searle's as it appears in his first full example. Searle begins by imagining a conversation between two students. Student X says, "Let's go to the movies tonight," and student Y replies, "I have to study for an exam." The first sentence, Searle declares, "constitutes a proposal in virtue of its meaning," but the second sentence, which is understood as a rejection of the proposal, is not so understood in virtue of its meaning because "in virtue of its meaning it is simply a statement about Y" (pp. 61, 62). It is here, in the assertion that either of these sentences is ever taken in the way it is "in virtue of its meaning," that this account must finally be attacked. For if this were the case, then we would have to say that there is something about the meaning of a sentence that makes it more available for some illocutionary uses than for others, and this is precisely what Searle proceeds to say about "I have to study for an exam": "Statements of this form do not, in general, constitute rejections of proposals, even in cases in which they are made in response to a proposal. Thus, if Y had said *I have to eat popcorn tonight* or *I have to tie my shoes* in a normal context, neither of these utterances would have been a rejection of the proposal" (p. 62).

At this point my question would be "Normal for whom?" Or, to put it another way: is it possible to imagine a set of circumstances in which "I have to eat popcorn tonight" would immediately and without any chain of inference be heard as a rejection of X's proposal? It is not only possible; it is easy. Let us suppose that student Y is passionately fond of popcorn and that it is not available in any of the local movie theaters. If student X knows these facts (if he and student Y mutually share background information), then he will hear "I have to eat popcorn tonight" as a rejection of his proposal. Or, let us suppose that student Y is by profession a popcorn taster; that is, he works in a popcorn manufacturing plant and is responsible for quality control. Again if student X knows this, he will hear "I have to eat popcorn tonight" as a rejection of his proposal because it will mean "Sorry, I have to work." Or, let us suppose that student Y owns seventy-five pairs of shoes and that he has been ordered by a dormitory housemother to retrieve them from various corners, arrange them neatly in one place, and tie them together in pairs so that they will not again be separated and scattered. In such a situation "I have to tie my shoes" will constitute a rejection of student X's proposal and will be so heard. Moreover, it is not just "I have to eat popcorn" and "I have to tie my shoes" that could be heard as a rejection of the proposal; given the appropriate circumstances *any* sentence ("The Russians are coming," "My pen is blue," "Why do you behave like that?") could be so heard. This does not mean than any sentence is potentially a proposal (that would be the mistake of ascribing properties to sentences) or that it doesn't matter what sentence a speaker utters, but that for any sentence circumstances could be imagined in which it would be understood as a proposal, and as nothing but a proposal.

The objection to these examples (which could easily be multiplied) is obvious: they have reference to *special* contexts, while Searle is talking about what sentences mean in a *normal* context. But for those who are in the contexts I describe, the meanings I specify would be the normal ones because they would be the only ones. Searle's argument will hold only if the category "normal" is transcendental, if what fills it is always the same, whatever the circumstances. But what is normal (like what is ordinary, literal, everyday) is a *function* of circumstances in that it depends on the expectations and assumptions that happen to be in force. Any other sense of normal would require that the circumstances not be circumstantial but essential (always in force), and that would be a contradiction in terms. In other words, "normal" is context specific and to speak of a normal context is to be either redundant (because whatever in a given context goes without saying *is* the normal) or incoherent (because it would refer to a context whose claim was not to be one).

In short, I am making the same argument for "normal context" that I have made for "literal meaning," "straightforward discourse," "the letter of the law," and the category of what is "in the text." There will always be a normal context, but it will not always be the same one. This means that if it becomes possible to see how "I have to eat popcorn" could be heard as a rejection of a proposal, it is not because we have imagined a set of special circumstances but because we have imagined an appropriate set of *normal* circumstances. The point can just as well be made from the opposite direction. Having to study for an exam is no more normal (in the sense that it is a state of which everyone has an implicit knowledge) than having to eat popcorn is special (in the sense that it is a departure from what everyone normally does). To be in either situation is to have already organized the world in terms of certain categories and possibilities for action (both verbal and physical), and in either situation the world so organized, along with the activities that can transpire within it, will be perceived as normal. Once again the moral is clear, even though it has the form of a paradox: a normal context is just the special context you happen to be in, although it will not be recognized as special because so long as you are in it whatever it permits you to see will seem obvious and inescapable.

From this perspective, Searle's argument falls apart. This first example, as he presents it, is intended to distinguish between:

(1) "I have to study for an exam" when it is "simply a statement about *Y*," that is, when it means what it says and is therefore a direct speech act;

(2) "I have to study for an exam" when it is a rejection of Y's proposal, that is, when by virtue of shared background it means more than it says and is an indirect speech act; and

(3) "I have to eat popcorn tonight," which cannot be a rejection of the proposal "without some special stage setting."

If what I have been saying is true, these distinctions cannot be maintained (at least as they are here formulated) because given different sets of special or differently normal circumstances, the three speech acts are equally direct or indirect. They are direct because in each case the illocutionary force they have will be immediately perceived; and they are indirect because their immediately perceived illocutionary force will have been a function of mutually shared background information (that is, of some or other special stage setting). The trick is to see that when Searle moves from "I have to study for an exam" as a statement about Y to "I have to study for an exam" as a rejection of a proposal, he has not moved from a literal meaning to a meaning that emerges in a set of circumstances, but from one meaning that emerges in a set of circumstances to another meaning that emerges in another set of circumstances. Both meanings are then equally circumstantial (indirect) and equally literal (direct), and in both cases the utterance means exactly what it says because what it says is a function of shared background information.

The argument will also hold for "Let's go to the movies to-night," although, for reasons that will become clear, it is harder to make. Here what has to be shown is the reverse of what had to be shown in the case of "I have to eat popcorn." Rather than having to imagine a situation in which an utterance ("I have to eat popcorn") could possibly count as the performance of a certain speech act, we have to imagine a situation in which an utterance ("Let's go to the movies tonight") could count as something *other* than the performance of a certain speech act. The problem is that the examples that first come to mind make Searle's point rather than mine. That is, they are examples in which the perceived illocutionary force is perceived only because a "more normal" illocutionary force is seen to be inappropriate. Thus if speakers X and Y are trapped in some wilderness, and one says to the other, "Let's go to the movies tonight," it will be heard not as a proposal but as a joke; or if student X is confined to his bed or otherwise immobilized, and student Y says, "Let's go to the movies tonight," it will be heard not as a proposal but as a dare. But in either case the dare or joke will be heard *only* because the circumstances rule out the possibility of a proposal, a possibility whose absence (and therefore whose presence) must be recognized for the effect to be secured. What we need are examples in which "Let's go to the movies tonight" is heard *immediately* as a dare or a joke (or as anything but a proposal) and which do not involve the two stage inferential procedure specified by Searle. And what we need too is an explanation of why such examples are relatively difficult to come by; that is, why it is so much harder to think oneself *out of* a necessary association between "Let's go to the movies tonight" and a proposal than it is to think oneself *into* a necessary association between "I have to eat popcorn" and the proposal's rejection.

First of all, Searle's analysis depends on the assumption of a generalized relationship between the use of "let's" and the performing of a proposal: "in general, literal utterances of this form will constitute a proposal, as in . . . 'Let's eat pizza tonight.' "[8] But in this very same paragraph Searle provides an example of an exception to his own generalization when he says, "Let us begin by considering a typical case. . . ." In the context of his discourse, it is not really open to a reader (or, in the case of a lecture, to a hearer) to suggest another beginning or to counterpropose that he not begin at all. Moveover, a hearer who responded in either of these ways would be thought to have misunderstood the illocutionary force of "Let us," which is here not so much a proposal as it is the laying down of a plan. Similarly, when a quarterback leads his team out of the huddle by saying "Let's do it" or "Let's go," he is not proposing, but exhorting. It would be inappropriate for one of his linemen to answer "I have to study for an exam" or even to answer at all, just as it would be inappropriate if a member of a congregation were to demur when the minister said (here he would be announcing, not proposing) "Let us pray."

In each of these cases, "let's" does not introduce a proposal because in the situation as it is imagined the speaker is understood to be concluding or forestalling an exchange rather than initiating one. Notice that in Searle's example the understanding is exactly the reverse: "Let's go to the movies tonight" is assumed to be the first utterance in an exchange that has no antecedents, and that is why it is heard as a proposal. Placed differently, at the end rather than at the beginning of a conversation, the same utterance would be heard as an assent to a proposal that had already been made. (It would be equivalent to "OK, let's go to the movies tonight.") The point is that neither placement is intrinsically the more natural or normal one, and that the stage has to be set no less for "Let's go to the movies tonight" to be heard as a proposal than for "I have to eat popcorn" to be heard as its rejection.

Why then does Searle spend so little time setting that stage in relation to the time that I must spend to dismantle it? The answer is that it is already set for him by the habitual (not inevitable) practices of an entire society and that he need do nothing more than assume those practices in order to secure the benefit of their continuing operation. When someone is asked to assign an illocutionary force to an utterance, he does so in the context of the circumstances in which that utterance has been most often heard or spoken. For most of us those circumstances are the ones presupposed by Searle, and therefore it appears that the relationship between "Let's go to the movies tonight" and its stipulated force is natural when, in fact, it is a function of a context so widely shared that it doesn't seem to be one at all. It is just such contexts that produce the felt continuity of life by allowing us to rely on and assume as normative the meanings they make available; and it is because Searle invokes such a context (by failing to realize or point out that it is one) that so much effort is required to see around his example.

In a sense, then, the circumstances that lead us to assign the force of a proposal to "Let's go to the movies tonight" *are* normal in that they occur more frequently than do circumstances that would lead to a different assignment. But they remain circumstances still (statistically, not inherently, normal), and because they do, the main assertion of this section is intact: there is no distinction between direct and indirect speech acts because all speech acts are understood by way of relying on mutually shared background information. All speech acts are direct because their meanings are directly apprehended, and all speech acts are indirect because their directly apprehended meanings are functions of the situations in which they are embedded.

It is important to realize what my argument does *not* mean. It does not mean that a sentence can mean anything at all. In their discussion of indirect speech acts Herbert and Eve Clark point out that "under the right circumstances" any one of a number of sentences could be "used as a request to open the window; yet," they warn, "not just any sentence can serve this purpose," for "if so, communication would be chaotic" because "listeners would never know what speech act was being performed."[9] But the chaos the Clarks fear would be possible only if a sentence could mean anything at all *in the abstract*. A sentence, however, is never in the abstract; it is always in a situation, and the situation will already have determined the purpose for which it can be used. So it is not that any sentence can be used as a request to open the window, but that given any sentence, there are circumstances under which it would be heard as a request to open the window. A sentence neither means anything at all nor does it always mean the same thing; it always has the meaning that has been conferred on it by the situation in which it is

uttered. Listeners *always* know what speech act is being performed, not because there are limits to the illocutionary uses to
which sentences can be put but because in any set of circumstances the illocutionary force a sentence may have will already
have been determined.

The Clarks can stand for all those who think that it is necessary to anchor language in some set of independent and formal
constraints, whether those constraints are given the name of
literal meaning, or straightforward discourse, or direct speech
acts, or the letter of the law, or normal circumstances, or the
everyday world. The question that is always being asked is "Are
there such constraints and, if so, how can we identify them?"
Behind that question, however, is the assumption that the constraints must be specifiable once and for all, and that if they are
not so specifiable at *some* level, we live in a world of chaos where
communication is entirely a matter of chance. What I have been
saying again and again is that there are such constraints; they do
not, however, inhere in language but in situations, and because
they inhere in situations, the constraints we are always under
are not always the same ones. Thus we can see how it is neither
the case that meanings are objectively fixed nor that the meanings one construes are arbitrary. To many these have seemed
the only alternatives, and that is why the claims for objectivity
and subjectivity have been continually debated. It is because
the position elaborated here is neither subjective nor objective
(nor a combining of the two) that it can reconcile the two facts
cited again and again by the respective combatants: (1) that
there are no inherent constraints on the meanings a sentence
may have, and (2) that, nevertheless, agreement is not only possible but commonplace.

It may interest you to know that, after hitting two home runs
in a single game, Pat Kelly went on to hit three more in the same
week, thus equaling his entire total for 1976. At the end of the
week a teammate was heard to say, "Maybe there's something
in that religion stuff after all."

12
A Reply to John Reichert

READING JOHN REICHERT'S objections to "Normal Circumstances . . . and Other Special Cases" is a curious experience because he is often on the verge of embracing the position that so distresses him. Consider for example his discussion of my discussion of *Samson Agonistes*. Reichert's point is that the assumptions we hold "about the context in which the poem was 'uttered'" constrain the range of meanings that we are likely to accept. This of course is also my point: because William Madsen believes that Milton wrote *Samson Agonistes* from a typological perspective, Samson will appear to him to be acting in ways that are either like or unlike Christ. I do not mean that Madsen first reads the text and *then* decides that its facts fit a typological interpretation; the assumption of a typological interpretation informs his reading *from the first* and is responsible for the facts as he then proceeds to describe them. The interpretation constrains the facts rather than the other way around and also constrains the kinds of meanings that one can assign to those facts. That is to say, those who agree in principle with Madsen might debate with him or among themselves the significance of certain facts, but the course of that debate would be constrained by the same perspective that had led to the production of those facts. Once it had been determined, for example, that at certain points in the play Samson despairs (a determination which is only possible within the prior assumption that the play is Christian and that therefore despairing is something that its characters can reasonably be suspected of doing or not doing), there could be an argument as to whether or not his despairing speeches prefigure Christ's words on the cross ("My God, my God, why hast thou forsaken me"). If it were decided that they did not and that some other significance was more apt, that significance would also be theological and would present itself as a possible one only because the religious framework was so firmly assumed. Thus both the area of agreement—what the "facts" of the text are presumed to be—and the shape of any subsequent disagreement over the significance of those facts are determined by a set of overarching interpretive principles that are not themselves the object of dispute because they set the terms within which disputes can occur.

I suspect that Reichert would be in substantial agreement with the previous paragraph but that he would point out, as he does in his article, that we can always decide that such principles are wrong and that the possibility of so deciding means that interpretation must finally rest on something besides itself. This argument, however, will hold only if such decisions (and I acknowledge that we make them) are made independently of interpretive assumptions, and this I would deny. Let us continue with the example of *Samson Agonistes* and ask under what circumstances might Madsen renounce his typological reading. There are of course many, but I can think immediately of at least three: (1) he might be persuaded by newly discovered biographical evidence (in a letter, perhaps) that Milton did not write with a typological intention; (2) he might be persuaded by the absence in contemporary responses to *Samson Agonistes* of any reference to typological significances; and (3) he might be persuaded by a demonstration that in Milton's other works Samson is always treated as a political rather than a theological example. In each case, however, the evidence that would constitute a challenge to Madsen's assumptions would *be* evidence only in the light of other assumptions which could in their turn be challenged. The force of something found in a letter depends on the privileged status of authorial statement, which in turn depends on a theory of intention that many (psychoanalysts, for example) would reject as naive. The weight of contemporary responses would be conclusive only if you were committed to an historical view of poetry's production and reception; to someone whose view of interpretation was progressive, the comments of seventeenth-century readers would seem primitive and insufficiently literary. And quarrying Milton's other works would only be to the point if one believed that an author's *oeuvre* was everywhere informed by the same concerns; to a genre critic the exercise would prove little because it would not have respected essential distinctions between, say, epics, odes, closet dramas, and masques. In short, the "solid arguments" in the face of which Madsen might decide that his interpretation was wrong would not be received *as* arguments if he did not already hold certain beliefs about what is a relevant thing to say in a literary debate. One is reminded of the final scene in Billy Wilder's *Some Like It Hot* when Jack Lemmon is trying to convince Joe E. Brown that it would be wrong for them to marry. "But I'm a *man*," he finally says, thinking that he has found a "knock down" argument. "Nobody's perfect," Brown replies (it is the film's last line), demonstrating for all time that one man's reason is another man's irrelevance.

The moral is not that no one can ever demonstrate to someone else that he is wrong but that the parties to a dispute must already be agreed as to what will count as a demonstration. Reichert thinks that the "wrongness" of a position is determined by procedures (evidentiary, logical) that are themselves uninvolved in any position; but it is only *from* a position that one argues, and the arguments one makes will only be convincing to someone who is, at least in part, in that same position. The present exchange is a case in point. Reichert and I both agree that it would be damaging to a theory if it were unable to account for the possibility of being wrong, and it is *because* we agree that I have been trying to show, first, that my theory is not open to that criticism and, second, that the means by which one can be shown to be wrong follow from my assumptions rather than from Reichert's. If, however, I were the kind of critic who welcomed and even celebrated the proliferation of indifferently authorized interpretation (let a hundred flowers bloom), I would not even bother to reply to Reichert because what he put forward as a criticism I would receive as a compliment. The logic that leads me to take his point seriously is not a logic whose opera-

LIBRARY ST. MARY'S COLLEGE

tions are independent of belief but one which follows upon a belief that he and I share, the belief that it would be wrong not to be able to say that someone is wrong.

The point is that standards of right or wrong do not exist apart from assumptions but follow from them; they are standards that are decided upon, not standards that decide—notions *in* dispute rather than notions that settle disputes. That is why there could be no *independent* determination of whether Janofsky or Kelly was correct about the agency of the latter's home runs. The evidence either would be willing to admit would be a function of his assumptions and therefore could not be used to confirm or disconfirm them; and the evidence adduced by a third party (Reichert or me or anyone else) would be a function of *his* assumptions, and Kelly and Janofsky would have to share them if they were to be at all swayed. Assumptions do not stand in an independent relationship to verifying procedures, they determine the shape of verifying procedures, and if you want to persuade someone else that he is wrong you must first persuade him to the assumptions within which what you say will be convincing.

One might object that such an act of persuasion could succeed only if some assumption were already in place, for otherwise there would be no basis for distinguishing between what was persuasive and what was not. The question, then, is where would these assumptions come from when it is assumptions themselves that are in dispute? The answer is that assumptions are not all held at the same level and that a challenge to one proceeds within the precinct of others that are, at least for the time being, exempt from challenge. Thus, for example, one reader might attempt to persuade another to his view of *Samson Agonistes* by invoking a characterization of Milton's career and intentions with which they both agree; points would be recognized as relevant and evidence as telling insofar as they were in accord with, and did not contradict, that characterization. At some other time that characterization might itself become the subject of dispute, and the course of that dispute would be determined by some unexamined notions of the intentions a poet might properly have and of the means by which they might be determined. Of course, those notions could in their turn be questioned, but if they were it would be within the framework of still other notions (of the specificity of poetry and the possibility of identifying it) that were not being questioned at all. It might seem that, at some point, the layers of interpretive assumptions will have been peeled away and we would find ourselves at last on the uninterpreted ground from which everything has been built up; but in fact we would find that the ground was barren. If the constitutive and enabling assumptions of the literary institutions were all dismantled and discarded, there would be nothing to talk about because it is the conventional categories of literary discourse (which include poets, poems, genres, styles, periods, and so on) that make available the entities about which we can both agree and disagree.

Another way of putting this is to say that in any situation there are always assumptions so deeply held that the entities they make available are perceived as part of the world and not as the products of assumptions at all. One feels about such entities that they are being apprehended *directly*, without the mediation of interpretive activity, and that it is on their foundation that acts of interpretation build. This is true not only of objects and texts but of meanings and, in particular, of what Searle and others call literal meanings, the meanings sentences possess by virtue of their linguistic and semantic structure *before* they are inserted into any context or situation. It is these meanings that Searle identifies with direct speech acts, and it is my argument that since there are no such meanings (meanings that are specifiable in the abstract) the distinction between direct and indirect speech acts will not hold. Reichert claims that by so arguing I show myself to be "unaware of the role of inference in interpreting the meaning of a remark" (p. 168) and that I do not understand Searle's assertion that "an indirect speech act is one that is performed *by means of* a direct speech act." The fact is, however, that I agree with Reichert when he points out that we often apprehend an utterance by reasoning from a more familiar or "normal" meaning to the meanings it acquires in a context. It is just that the more familiar meaning is no less contextually produced than the indirect meaning to which it gives rise. True, it is apprehended *directly*, in the sense that it appears to us

without our having to make any inferences, but that is because
we have already made them. Any meaning that is obviously and
immediately accessible is so because it follows from (emerges by
inference from) a contextual setting that has become so much a
part of the background (within which we perceive and read) that
it is invisible. That is why the examples of direct speech acts offered by Searle and Reichert are so forceful; they come embedded in contexts of which we are unaware and therefore they can
be plausibly presented as utterances whose meanings are independent of any context whatsoever. The characteristic gesture
here (one performed by both Searle and Reichert) is what we
might call the "table-thumping gesture"; you do it by throwing
your sentence on the table and daring anyone to say that it
means anything but what it so obviously means and then you
conclude that since you specified no context for it, the obvious
meaning it has must be acontextual. It is a convincing gesture
because in the absence of an overtly specified context your readers will hear the sentence as already embedded in the context in
which it has been most often produced (and understood). In
short, the context is always there, but like the nose in front of
our face we don't always see it and when we don't the meanings
it makes available will appear to stand without any visible means
of support. Those meanings, then, will stand in relation to others
as direct to indirect speech acts, but the relation will really be
between speech acts whose indirectness is hidden from us and
speech acts of whose indirectness we are actively conscious.

I could go on in this way, replying to Reichert's reply, point
by point, but the pattern of my replies is already set: he charges
that my position entails certain undesirable consequences and
flies in the face of some of our most basic intuitions; I labor to
show that none of those consequences (the lack of a basis for
deciding that something is wrong, for example) follow and that
our basic intuitions are confirmed (albeit in a new light) rather
than denied by what I have to say. This of course is exactly what
I was doing in the article to which he takes exception. I am not,
however, optimistic that Reichert will ever become a convert
because the fears that impel his argument are so basic to his
beliefs. I take the key sentence in his article to be this one:

"Since I would like to think that I read the same *King Lear* that Dr. Johnson read, and am therefore free to disagree with his interpretation of it, I would like to find a way out of Fish's formulation of the reader's situation" (pp. 164–65). Reichert's commitment to what he would like to be able to do and his conviction that if what I say is true he will be unable to do it make it impossible for him to regard my position as anything but perverse and dangerous. Even if I could demonstrate in his own terms (as I think I have) that his fears are unfounded—that he is still free to disagree with Dr. Johnson or anyone else— any argument I might make would be received within the belief that it *had* to be wrong, and within that belief he could only hear it as wrong. (Of course I am equally open to this characterization; when Reichert, or anyone else identifies something—an object, a text, an intention—as being available independently of interpretation, I know in advance that it could not be so and I look immediately for ways to demystify or deconstruct it. I always succeed.) To this Reichert would probably reply that arguments are either good or bad, irrespective of beliefs, and that mine are bad; but it is my contention that arguments are forceful only *within* a set of beliefs and that unless someone is willing to entertain the possibility that his beliefs are wrong, he will be unable even to hear an argument that constitutes a challenge to them. That is why the fact that Reichert is likely to remain unconvinced by my argument is its strongest confirmation.

Interpretive Authority in the Classroom and in Literary Criticism

13
Is There a Text in This Class?

[THESE ESSAYS have a double origin, in the incident that gave them their title, and in Meyer Abrams's recently published paper "How To Do Things with Texts," a forthright attack on the work of Jacques Derrida, Harold Bloom, and me. I was present when Abrams delivered the paper at the Lionel Trilling Seminar of 1978, and I remember laughing very hard when he took on Bloom and Derrida and trying very hard to laugh when he turned his attention to me. Abrams's arguments are familiar; they are essentially the same he deployed against J. Hillis Miller in the "pluralism" debate. Specifically, he accuses each "Newreader" of playing a double game, of "introducing his own interpretive strategy when reading someone else's text, but tacitly relying on communal norms when undertaking to communicate the methods and results of his interpretations to his own readers" (*Partisan Review*, 1979, no. 4, p. 587). Miller, Derrida, and the others write books and essays, and engage in symposia and debates, and in so doing use the standard language in order to deconstruct the standard language. The very presumption that they are understood is an argument against the position they urge.

As a counterargument this has a certain prima facie plausibility, if only because it imagines as its object a theory that renders understanding impossible. But in the theory of this Newreader, understanding is always possible, but not from the outside. That is, the reason that I can speak and presume to be understood by someone like Abrams is that I speak to him *from within* a set of interests and concerns, and it is in relation to those interests and concerns that I assume he will hear my words. If what follows is communication or understanding, it will not be because he and I share a language, in the sense of knowing the meanings of individual words and the rules for combining them, but because a way of thinking, a form of life,

shares us, and implicates us in a world of already-in-place objects, purposes, goals, procedures, values, and so on; and it is to the features of
that world that any words we utter will be heard as necessarily
referring. Thus Abrams and I could talk about whether or not a
poem was a pastoral, advance and counter arguments, dispute evidence, concede points, and so forth, but we could do these things only
because "poem" and "pastoral" are possible labels of identification
within a universe of discourse that also includes stipulations as to
what would count as an identifying mark, and ways of arguing that
such a mark is or is not there. It would be within the assumption
of such ways, stipulations, and classifications that Abrams and I
would proceed, and we could not proceed at all if either of us were
someone for whom they were not already assumed. Nor would it be
enough to give someone "on the outside" a set of definitions (of the
order "a poem is . . . ," "a genre is . . .") because in order to grasp the
meaning of an individual term, you must already have grasped
the general activity (in this case academic literary criticism) in relation to which it could be thought to be meaningful; a system of intelligibility cannot be reduced to a list of the things it renders intelligible. What Abrams and those who agree with him do not realize
is that communication occurs only *within* such a system (or context,
or situation, or interpretive community) and that the understanding
achieved by two or more persons is specific to that system and determinate only within its confines. Nor do they realize that such an
understanding is enough and that the more perfect understanding
they desire—an understanding that operates above or across situations—would have no place in the world even if it were available,
because it is only in situations—with their interested specifications
as to what counts as a fact, what it is possible to say, what will be
heard as an argument—that one is called on to understand.

These essays were originally delivered as the John Crowe Ransom
Memorial Lectures, and were given at Kenyon College from April 8
through 13, 1979. In effect, I was engaged in a week-long seminar
consisting of some three hundred members, and I found the experience both exhilirating and exhausting. Apparently, some of the same
feelings were shared by the audience, for in an editorial written for
the college newspaper (entitled "Fish Baits Audience") generous
praise of my "intellectual skill" was immediately qualified by the
observation that, needless to say, "it was not always the skill of a
gentleman."]

O N THE FIRST DAY of the new semester a colleague at Johns Hopkins University was approached by a student who, as it turned out,
had just taken a course from me. She put to him what I think
you would agree is a perfectly straightforward question: "Is there
a text in this class?" Responding with a confidence so perfect
that he was unaware of it (although in telling the story, he refers
to this moment as "walking into the trap"), my colleague said,
"Yes; it's the *Norton Anthology of Literature,*" whereupon the
trap (set not by the student but by the infinite capacity of language for being appropriated) was sprung: "No, no," she said,
"I mean in this class do we believe in poems and things, or is it
just us?" Now it is possible (and for many tempting) to read this
anecdote as an illustration of the dangers that follow upon listening to people like me who preach the instability of the text and
the unavailability of determinate meanings; but in what follows
I will try to read it as an illustration of how baseless the fear of
these dangers finally is.

Of the charges levied against what Meyer Abrams has recently called the New Readers (Derrida, Bloom, Fish) the most
persistent is that these apostles of indeterminacy and undecidability ignore, even as they rely upon, the "norms and possibilities" embedded in language, the "linguistic meanings" words
undeniably have, and thereby invite us to abandon "our ordinary realm of experience in speaking, hearing, reading and
understanding" for a world in which "no text can mean anything in particular" and where "we can never say just what
anyone means by anything he writes."[1] The charge is that literal
or normative meanings are overriden by the actions of willful
interpreters. Suppose we examine this indictment in the context
of the present example. What, exactly, is the normative or literal or linguistic meaning of "Is there a text in this class?"

Within the framework of contemporary critical debate (as it
is reflected in the pages, say, of *Critical Inquiry*) there would
seem to be only two ways of answering this question: either there
is a literal meaning of the utterance and we should be able to
say what it is, or there are as many meanings as there are readers

and no one of them is literal. But the answer suggested by my little story is that the utterance has *two* literal meanings: within the circumstances assumed by my colleague (I don't mean that he took the step of assuming them, but that he was already stepping within them) the utterance is obviously a question about whether or not there is a required textbook in this particular course; but within the circumstances to which he was alerted by his student's corrective response, the utterance is just as obviously a question about the instructor's position (within the range of positions available in contemporary literary theory) on the status of the text. Notice that we do not have here a case of indeterminacy or undecidability but of a determinacy and decidability that do not always have the same shape and that can, and in this instance do, change. My colleague was not hesitating between two (or more) possible meanings of the utterance; rather, he immediately apprehended what seemed to be an inescapable meaning, given his prestructured understanding of the situation, and then he immediately apprehended another inescapable meaning when that understanding was altered. Neither meaning was imposed (a favorite word in the anti–new-reader polemics) on a more normal one by a private, idiosyncratic interpretive act; both interpretations were a function of precisely the public and constituting norms (of language and understanding) invoked by Abrams. It is just that these norms are not embedded in the language (where they may be read out by anyone with sufficiently clear, that is, unbiased, eyes) but inhere in an institutional structure within which one hears utterances as already organized with reference to certain assumed purposes and goals. Because both my colleague and his student are situated in that institution, their interpretive activities are not free, but what constrains them are the understood practices and assumptions of the institution and not the rules and fixed meanings of a language system.

Another way to put this would be to say that neither reading of the question—which we might for convenience's sake label as "Is there a text in this class?"$_1$ and "Is there a text in this class?"$_2$ —would be immediately available to any native speaker of the language. "Is there a text in this class?"$_1$ is interpretable or readable only by someone who already knows what is included under the general rubric "first day of class" (what concerns animate students, what bureaucratic matters must be attended to before instruction begins) and who therefore hears the utterance under the aegis of that knowledge, which is not applied after the fact but is responsible for the shape the fact immediately has. To someone whose consciousness is not already informed by that knowledge, "Is there a text in this class?"$_1$ would be just as unavailable as "Is there a text in this class?"$_2$ would be to someone who was not already aware of the disputed issues in contemporary literary theory. I am not saying that for some readers or hearers the question would be wholly unintelligible (indeed, in the course of this essay I will be arguing that unintelligibility, in the strict or pure sense, is an impossibility), but that there are readers and hearers for whom the intelligibility of the question would have neither of the shapes it had, in a temporal succession, for my colleague. It is possible, for example, to imagine someone who would hear or intend the question as an inquiry about the location of an object, that is, "I think I left my text in this class; have you seen it?" We would then have an "Is there a text in this class?"$_3$ and the possibility, feared by the defenders of the normative and determinate, of an endless succession of numbers, that is, of a world in which every utterance has an infinite plurality of meanings. But that is not what the example, however it might be extended, suggests at all. In any of the situations I have imagined (and in any that I might be able to imagine) the meaning of the utterance would be severely constrained, not after it was heard but in the ways in which it *could,* in the first place, be heard. An infinite plurality of meanings would be a fear only if sentences existed in a state in which they were not already embedded, and had come into view as a function of, some situation or other. That state, if it could be located, would be the normative one, and it would be disturbing indeed if the norm were free-floating and indeterminate. But there is no such state; sentences emerge only in situations, and within those situations, the normative meaning of an utterance will always be obvious or at least accessible, although within another situation that same utterance, no longer the same, will have another normative meaning that will be no less obvious and accessible. (My colleague's experience is precisely an illustration.) This does not mean that there is no way to discriminate between the meanings an utterance will have in different situations, but that the discrimination will already have been made by virtue of our being in a situation (we are never not in one) and that in another situation the discrimination will also have already been made, but differently. In other words, while at any one point it is always possible to order and rank "Is there a text in this class?"$_1$ and "Is there a text in this class?"$_2$ (because they will always have already been ranked), it will never be possible to give them an immutable once-and-for-all ranking, a ranking that is independent of their appearance or nonappearance in situations (because it is only in situations that they do or do not appear).

Nevertheless, there is a distinction to be made between the two that allows us to say that, in a limited sense, one is more normal than the other: for while each is perfectly normal in the context in which their literalness is immediately obvious (the successive contexts occupied by my colleague), as things stand now, one of those contexts is surely more available, and therefore more likely to be the perspective within which the utterance is heard, than the other. Indeed, we seem to have here an instance of what I would call "institutional nesting": if "Is there a text in this class?"$_1$ is hearable only by those who know what is included under the rubric "first day of class," and if "Is there a text in this class?"$_2$ is hearable only by those whose categories of understanding include the concerns of contemporary literary theory, then it is obvious that in a random population presented with the utterance, more people would "hear" "Is there a text in this class?"$_1$ than "Is there a text in this class?"$_2$; and, moreover, that while "Is there a text in this class?"$_1$ could be immediately hearable by someone for whom "Is there a text in this class?"$_2$ would have to be laboriously explained, it is difficult to imagine someone capable of hearing "Is there a text in this class?"$_2$ who was not already capable of hearing "Is there a text in this class."$_1$ (One is hearable by anyone in the profession and by most students and by many workers in the book trade, and the other only by those in the profession who would not think it peculiar to find, as I did recently, a critic referring to a phrase "made popular by Lacan.") To admit as much is not to weaken my argument by reinstating the category of the normal, because the category as it appears in that argument is not transcendental but institutional; and while no institution is so universally in force and so perdurable that the meanings it enables will be normal for ever, some institutions or forms of life are so widely lived in that for a great many people the meanings they enable seem "naturally" available and it takes a special effort to see that they are the products of circumstances.

The point is an important one, because it accounts for the success with which an Abrams or an E. D. Hirsch can appeal to a shared understanding of ordinary language and argue from that understanding to the availability of a core of determinate meanings. When Hirsch offers "The air is crisp" as an example of a "verbal meaning," that is, accessible to all speakers of the language, and distinguishes what is sharable and determinate about it from the associations that may, in certain circumstances, accompany it (for example, "I should have eaten less at supper," "Crisp air reminds me of my childhood in Vermont"),[2] he is counting on his readers to agree so completely with his sense of what that shared and normative verbal meaning is that he does not bother even to specify it; and although I have not taken a survey, I would venture to guess that his optimism, with respect to this particular example, is well founded. That is, most, if not all, of his readers immediately understand the utterance as a rough meteorological description predicting a certain quality of the local atmosphere. But the "happiness" of the example, far from making Hirsch's point (which is always, as he has recently reaffirmed, to maintain "the stable determinacy of meaning")[3] makes mine. The obviousness of the utterance's meaning is not a function of the values its words have in a linguistic system that is independent of context; rather, it is because the words are heard as already embedded in a context that they have a meaning that Hirsch can then cite as obvious. One can see this by embedding the words in another context and observing how quickly another "obvious" meaning emerges.

Suppose, for example, we came upon "The air is crisp" (which you are even now hearing as Hirsch assumes you hear it) in the middle of a discussion of music ("When the piece is played correctly the air is crisp"); it would immediately be heard as a comment on the performance by an instrument or instruments of a musical air. Moreover, it would *only* be heard that way, and to hear it in Hirsch's way would require an effort on the order of a strain. It could be objected that in Hirsch's text "The air is crisp"₁ has no contextual setting at all; it is merely presented, and therefore any agreement as to its meaning must be because of the utterance's acontextual properties. But there *is* a contextual setting and the sign of its presence is precisely the absence of any reference to it. That is, it is impossible even to think of a sentence independently of a context, and when we are asked to consider a sentence for which no context has been specified, we will automatically hear it in the context in which it has been most often encountered. Thus Hirsch invokes a context by not invoking it; by not surrounding the utterance with circumstances, he directs us to imagine it in the circumstances in which it is most likely to have been produced; and to so imagine it is already to have given it a shape that seems at the moment to be the only one possible.

What conclusions can be drawn from these two examples? First of all, neither my colleague nor the reader of Hirsch's sentence is constrained by the meanings words have in a normative linguistic system; and yet neither is free to confer on an utterance any meaning he likes. Indeed, "confer" is exactly the wrong word because it implies a two stage procedure in which a reader or hearer first scrutinizes an utterance and *then* gives it a meaning. The argument of the preceding pages can be reduced to the assertion that there is no such first stage, that one hears an utterance within, and not as preliminary to determining, a knowledge of its purposes and concerns, and that to so hear it is already to have assigned it a shape and given it a meaning. In other words, the problem of how meaning is determined is only a problem if there is a point at which its determination has not yet been made, and I am saying that there is no such point.

I am *not* saying that one is never in the position of having to self-consciously figure out what an utterance means. Indeed, my colleague is in just such a position when he is informed by his student that he has not heard her question as she intended it ("No, No, I mean in this class do we believe in poems and things, or is it just us?") and therefore must now figure it out. But the "it" in this (or any other) case is not a collection of words waiting to be assigned a meaning but an utterance whose already assigned meaning has been found to be inappropriate. While my colleague has to begin all over again, he does not have to begin from square one; and indeed he never was at square one, since from the very first his hearing of the student's question was informed by his assumption of what its concerns could possibly be. (That is why he is not "free" even if he is unconstrained by determinate meanings.) It is that assumption rather than his performance within it that is challenged by the student's correction. She tells him that he has mistaken her meaning, but this is not to say that he has made a mistake in combining her words and syntax into a meaningful unit; it is rather that the meaningful unit he immediately discerns is a function of a mistaken identification (made before she speaks) of her intention. He was prepared as she stood before him to hear the kind of thing students ordinarily say on the first day of class, and therefore that is precisely what he heard. He has not misread the text (his is not an error in calculation) but mis*pre*read the text, and if he is to correct himself he must make another (pre)determination of the structure of interests from which her question issues. This, of course, is exactly what he does and the question of how he does it is a crucial one, which can best be answered by first considering the ways in which he *didn't* do it.

He didn't do it by attending to the literal meaning of her response. That is, this is not a case in which someone who has been misunderstood clarifies her meaning by making more explicit, by varying or adding to her words in such a way as to render their sense inescapable. Within the circumstances of utterance as he has assumed them her words are perfectly clear, and what she is doing is asking him to imagine other circumstances in which the same words will be equally, but differently, clear. Nor is it that the words she does add ("No, No, I mean

. . .") direct him to those other circumstances by picking them out from an inventory of all possible ones. For this to be the case there would have to be an inherent relationship between the words she speaks and a particular set of circumstances (this would be a higher level literalism) such that any competent speaker of the language hearing those words would immediately be referred to that set. But I have told the story to several competent speakers of the language who simply didn't get it, and one friend—a professor of philosophy—reported to me that in the interval between his hearing the story and my explaining it to him (and just how I was able to do that is another crucial question) he found himself asking "What kind of joke is this and have I missed it?" For a time at least he remained able only to hear "Is there a text in this class" as my colleague first heard it; the student's additional words, far from leading him to another hearing, only made him aware of his distance from it. In contrast, there are those who not only get the story but get it before I tell it; that is, they know in advance what is coming as soon as I say that a colleague of mine was recently asked, "Is there a text in this class?" Who are these people and what is it that makes their comprehension of the story so immediate and easy? Well, one could say, without being the least bit facetious, that they are the people who come to hear me speak because they are the people who already know my position on certain matters (or know that I will *have* a position). That is, they hear, "Is there a text in this class?" even as it appears at the beginning of the anecdote (or for that matter as a title of an essay) in the light of their knowledge of what I am likely to do with it. They hear it coming from *me,* in circumstances which have committed me to declaring myself on a range of issues that are sharply delimited.

My colleague was finally able to hear it in just that way, as coming from me, not because I was there in his classroom, nor because the words of the student's question pointed to me in a way that would have been obvious to any hearer, but because he was able to think of me in an office three doors down from his telling students that there are no determinate meanings and that the stability of the text is an illusion. Indeed, as he reports it, the moment of recognition and comprehension consisted of his saying to himself, "Ah, there's one of Fish's victims!" He did not say this because her words identified her as such but because his ability to see her as such informed his perception of her words. The answer to the question "How did he get from her words to the circumstances within which she intended him to hear them?" is that he must already be thinking within those circumstances in order to be able to hear her words as referring to them. The question, then, must be rejected, because it assumes that the construing of sense leads to the identification of the context of utterance rather than the other way around. This does not mean that the context comes first and that once it has been identified the construing of sense can begin. This would be only to reverse the order of precedence, whereas precedence is beside the point because the two actions it would order (the identification of context and the making of sense) occur simultaneously. One does not say "Here I am in a situation; now I can begin to determine what these words mean." To be in a situation is to see the words, these or any other, as already meaningful. For my colleague to realize that he may be confronting one of my victims is *at the same time* to hear what she says as a question about his theoretical beliefs.

But to dispose of one "how" question is only to raise another: if her words do not lead him to the context of her utterance, how does he get there? Why did he think of me telling students that there were no determinate meanings and not think of someone or something else? First of all, he might well have. That is, he might well have guessed that she was coming from another direction (inquiring, let us say, as to whether the focus of this class was to be the poems and essays or our responses to them, a question in the same line of country as hers but quite distinct from it) or he might have simply been stymied, like my philosopher friend, confined, in the absence of an explanation, to his first determination of her concerns and unable to make any sense of her words other than the sense he originally made. How, then, did he do it? In part, he did it because he *could* do it; he was able to get to this context because it was already part of his repertoire for organizing the world and its events. The category "one of Fish's victims" was one he already had and didn't have to work for. Of course, *it* did not always have *him*, in that his world was not always being organized by it, and it certainly did not have him at the beginning of the conversation; but it was available to him, and he to it, and all he had to do was to recall it or be recalled to it for the meanings it subtended to emerge. (Had it not been available to him, the career of his comprehension would have been different and we will come to a consideration of that difference shortly.)

This, however, only pushes our inquiry back further. How or why was he recalled to it? The answer to this question must be probabilistic and it begins with the recognition that when something changes, not everything changes. Although my colleague's understanding of his circumstances is transformed in the course of this conversation, the circumstances are still understood to be academic ones, and within that continuing (if modified) understanding, the directions his thought might take are already severely limited. He still presumes, as he did at first, that the student's question has something to do with university business in general, and with English literature in particular, and it is the organizing rubrics associated with these areas of experience that are likely to occur to him. One of those rubrics is "what-goes-on-in-other-classes" and one of those other classes is mine. And so, by a route that is neither entirely unmarked nor wholly determined, he comes to me and to the notion "one of Fish's victims" and to a new construing of what his student has been saying.

Of course that route would have been much more circuitous if the category "one of Fish's victims" was not already available to him as a device for producing intelligibility. Had that device not been part of his repertoire, had he been incapable of being recalled to it because he never knew it in the first place, how would he have proceeded? The answer is that he could not have proceeded at all, which does not mean that one is trapped forever in the categories of understanding at one's disposal (or the categories at whose disposal one is), but that the introduction of new categories or the expansion of old ones to include new (and therefore newly seen) data must always come from the outside or from what is perceived, for a time, to be the outside. In the event that he was unable to identify the structure of her concerns because it had never been his (or he its), it would have been her obligation to explain it to him. And here we run up against another instance of the problem we have been considering all along. She could not explain it to him by varying or adding to her words, by being more explicit, because her words will only be intelligible if he already has the knowledge they are supposed to convey, the knowledge of the assumptions and interests from which they issue. It is clear, then, that she would have to make a new start, although she would not have to start from scratch (indeed, starting from scratch is never a possibility); but she would have to back up to some point at which there was a shared agreement as to what was reasonable to say so that a new and wider basis for agreement could be fashioned. In this particular case, for example, she might begin with the fact that her interlocutor already knows what a text is; that is, he has a way of thinking about it that is responsible for his hearing of her first question as one about bureaucratic classroom procedures. (You will remember that "he" in these sentences is no longer my colleague but someone who does not have his special knowledge.) It is that way of thinking that she must labor to extend or challenge, first, perhaps, by pointing out that there are those who think about the text in other ways, and then by trying to find a category of his own understanding which might serve as an analogue to the understanding he does not yet share. He might, for example, be familiar with those psychologists who argue for the constitutive power of perception, or with Gombrich's theory of the beholder's share, or with that philosophical tradition in which the stability of objects has always been a matter of dispute. The example must remain hypothetical and skeletal, because it can only be fleshed out after a determination of the particular beliefs and assumptions that would make the explanation necessary in the first place; for whatever they were, they would dictate the strategy by which she would work to supplant or change them. It is when such a strategy has been successful that the import of her words will become clear, not because she has reformulated or refined them but because they will now be read or heard within the same system of intelligibility from which they issue.

In short, this hypothetical interlocutor will in time be brought to the same point of comprehension my colleague enjoys when he is able to say to himself, "Ah, there's one of Fish's victims," although presumably he will say something very different to himself if he says anything at all. The difference, however, should not obscure the basic similarities between the two experiences, one reported, the other imagined. In both cases the words that are uttered are immediately heard within a set of assumptions about the direction from which they could possibly be coming, and in both cases what is required is that the hearing occur within another set of assumptions in relation to which the same words ("Is there a text in this class?") will no longer be the same. It is just that while my colleague is able to meet that requirement by calling to mind a context of utterance that is already a part of his repertoire, the repertoire of his hypothetical stand-in must be expanded to include that context so that should he some day be in an analogous situation, he would be able to call it to mind.

The distinction, then, is between already having an ability and having to acquire it, but it is not finally an essential distinction, because the routes by which that ability could be exercised on the one hand, and learned on the other, are so similar. They are similar first of all because they are similarly *not* determined by words. Just as the student's words will not direct my colleague to a context he already has, so will they fail to direct someone not furnished with that context to its discovery. And yet in neither case does the absence of such a mechanical determination mean that the route one travels is randomly found. The change from one structure of understanding to another is not a rupture but a modification of the interests and concerns that are already in place; and because they are already in place, they constrain the direction of their own modification. That is, in both cases the hearer is already in a situation informed by tacitly known purposes and goals, and in both cases he ends up in another situation whose purposes and goals stand in some elaborated relation (of contrast, opposition, expansion, extension) to those they supplant. (The one relation in which they could not stand is no relation at all.) It is just that in one case the network of elaboration (from the text as an obviously physical object to the question of whether or not the text is a physical object) has already been articulated (although not all of its articulations are in focus at one time; selection is always occurring), while in the other the articulation of the network is the business of the teacher (here the student) who begins, necessarily, with what is already given.

The final similarity between the two cases is that in neither is success assured. It was no more inevitable that my colleague tumble to the context of his student's utterance than it would be inevitable that she could introduce that context to someone previously unaware of it; and, indeed, had my colleague remained puzzled (had he simply not thought of me), it would have been necessary for the student to bring him along in a way that was finally indistinguishable from the way she would bring someone to a new knowledge, that is, by beginning with the shape of his present understanding.

I have lingered so long over the unpacking of this anecdote that its relationship to the problem of authority in the classroom and in literary criticism may seem obscure. Let me recall you to it by recalling the contention of Abrams and others that authority depends upon the existence of a determinate core of meanings because in the absence of such a core there is no normative or public way of construing what anyone says or writes, with the result that interpretation becomes a matter of individual and private construings none of which is subject to challenge or correction. In literary criticism this means that no interpretation can be said to be better or worse than any other, and in the classroom this means that we have no answer to the student who says my interpretation is as valid as yours. It is only if there is a shared basis of agreement at once guiding interpretation and providing a mechanism for deciding between interpretations that a total and debilitating relativism can be avoided.

But the point of my analysis has been to show that while "Is there a text in this class?" does not have a determinate meaning, a meaning that survives the sea change of situations, in any

situation we might imagine the meaning of the utterance is
either perfectly clear or capable, in the course of time, of being
clarified. What is it that makes this possible, if it is not the
"possibilities and norms" already encoded in language? How
does communication ever occur if not by reference to a public
and stable norm? The answer, implicit in everything I have
already said, is that communication occurs within situations and
that to be in a situation is already to be in possession of (or to
be possessed by) a structure of assumptions, of practices understood to be relevant in relation to purposes and goals that are
already in place; and it is within the assumption of these purposes and goals that any utterance is *immediately* heard. I stress
immediately because it seems to me that the problem of communication, as someone like Abrams poses it, is a problem only
because he assumes a distance between one's receiving of an utterance and the determination of its meaning—a kind of dead space
when one has only the words and then faces the task of construing them. If there were such a space, a moment before interpretation began, then it would be necessary to have recourse
to some mechanical and algorithmic procedure by means of
which meanings could be calculated and in relation to which one
could recognize mistakes. What I have been arguing is that
meanings come already calculated, not because of norms embedded in the language but because language is always perceived, from the very first, within a structure of norms. That
structure, however, is not abstract and independent but social;
and therefore it is not a single structure with a privileged relationship to the process of communication as it occurs in any
situation but a structure that changes when one situation, with
its assumed background of practices, purposes, and goals, has
given way to another. In other words, the shared basis of agreement sought by Abrams and others is never not already found,
although it is not always the same one.

Many will find in this last sentence, and in the argument to
which it is a conclusion, nothing more than a sophisticated version of the relativism they fear. It will do no good, they say, to
speak of norms and standards that are context specific, because
this is merely to authorize an infinite plurality of norms and

standards, and we are still left without any way of adjudicating between them and between the competing systems of value of which they are functions. In short, to have many standards is to have no standards at all.

On one level this counterargument is unassailable, but on another level it is finally beside the point. It is unassailable as a general and theoretical conclusion: the positing of context- or institution-specific norms surely rules out the possibility of a norm whose validity would be recognized by everyone, no matter what his situation. But it is beside the point for any particular individual, for since everyone is situated somewhere, there is no one for whom the absence of an asituational norm would be of any practical consequence, in the sense that his performance or his confidence in his ability to perform would be impaired. So that while it is generally true that to have many standards is to have none at all, it is not true for anyone in particular (for there is no one in a position to speak "generally"), and therefore it is a truth of which one can say "it doesn't matter."

In other words, while relativism is a position one can entertain, it is not a position one can occupy. No one can *be* a relativist, because no one can achieve the distance from his own beliefs and assumptions which would result in their being no more authoritative *for him* than the beliefs and assumptions held by others, or, for that matter, the beliefs and assumptions he himself used to hold. The fear that in a world of indifferently authorized norms and values the individual is without a basis for action is groundless because no one is indifferent to the norms and values that enable his consciousness. It is in the name of personally held (in fact they are doing the holding) norms and values that the individual acts and argues, and he does so with the full confidence that attends belief. When his beliefs change, the norms and values to which he once gave unthinking assent will have been demoted to the status of opinions and become the objects of an analytical and critical attention; but that attention will itself be enabled by a new set of norms and values that are, for the time being, as unexamined and undoubted as those they displace. The point is that there is never a moment when one believes nothing, when consciousness is innocent of any and all categories of thought, and whatever categories of thought are operative at a given moment will serve as an undoubted ground.

Here, I suspect, a defender of determinate meaning would cry "solipsist" and argue that a confidence that had its source in the individual's categories of thought would have no public value. That is, unconnected to any shared and stable system of meanings, it would not enable one to transact the verbal business of everyday life; a shared intelligibility would be impossible in a world where everyone was trapped in the circle of his own assumptions and opinions. The reply to this is that an individual's assumptions and opinions are not "his own" in any sense that would give body to the fear of solipsism. That is, *he* is not their origin (in fact it might be more accurate to say that they are his); rather, it is their prior availability which delimits in advance the paths that his consciousness can possibly take. When my colleague is in the act of construing his student's question ("Is there a text in this class?"), none of the interpretive strategies at his disposal are uniquely his, in the sense that he thought them up; they follow from his preunderstanding of the interests and goals that could possibly animate the speech of someone functioning within the institution of academic America, interests and goals that are the particular property of no one in particular but which link everyone for whom their assumption is so habitual as to be unthinking. They certainly link my colleague and his student, who are able to communicate and even to reason about one another's intentions, not, however, because their interpretive efforts are constrained by the shape of an independent language but because their shared understanding of what could possibly be at stake in a classroom situation results in language appearing to them in the same shape (or successions of shapes). That shared understanding is the basis of the confidence with which they speak and reason, but its categories are their own only in the sense that as actors within an institution they automatically fall heir to the institution's way of making sense, its systems of intelligibility. That is why it is so hard for someone whose very being is defined by his position within an institution (and if not this one, then some other) to explain to someone outside it a practice or a meaning that seems to him to require no explanation, because he regards it as natural. Such a person, when pressed, is likely to say, "but that's just the way it's done" or "but isn't it obvious" and so testify that the practice of meaning in question is community property, as, in a sense, he is too.

We see then that (1) communication does occur, despite the absence of an independent and context-free system of meanings, that (2) those who participate in this communication do so confidently rather than provisionally (they are not relativists), and that (3) while their confidence has its source in a set of beliefs, those beliefs are not individual-specific or idiosyncratic but communal and conventional (they are not solipsists).

Of course, solipsism and relativism are what Abrams and Hirsch fear and what lead them to argue for the necessity of determinate meaning. But if, rather than acting on their own, interpreters act as extensions of an institutional community, solipsism and relativism are removed as fears because they are not possible modes of being. That is to say, the condition required for someone to be a solipsist or relativist, the condition of being independent of institutional assumptions and free to originate one's own purposes and goals, could never be realized, and therefore there is no point in trying to guard against it. Abrams, Hirsch, and company spend a great deal of time in a search for the ways to limit and constrain interpretation, but if the example of my colleague and his student can be generalized (and obviously I think it can be), what they are searching for is never not already found. In short, my message to them is finally not challenging, but consoling—not to worry.

14

How To Recognize a Poem
When You See One

L AST TIME I sketched out an argument by which meanings are the property neither of fixed and stable texts nor of free and independent readers but of interpretive communities that are responsible both for the shape of a reader's activities and for the texts those activities produce. In this lecture I propose to extend that argument so as to account not only for the meanings a poem might be said to have but for the fact of its being recognized as a poem in the first place. And once again I would like to begin with an anecdote.

In the summer of 1971 I was teaching two courses under the joint auspices of the Linguistic Institute of America and the English Department of the State University of New York at Buffalo. I taught these courses in the morning and in the same room. At 9:30 I would meet a group of students who were interested in the relationship between linguistics and literary criticism. Our nominal subject was stylistics but our concerns were finally theoretical and extended to the presuppositions and assumptions which underlie both linguistic and literary practice. At 11:00 these students were replaced by another group whose concerns were exclusively literary and were in fact confined to English religious poetry of the seventeenth century. These students had been learning how to identify Christian symbols and how to recognize typological patterns and how to move from the observation of these symbols and patterns to the specification of a poetic intention that was usually didactic or homiletic. On the day I am thinking about, the only connection between the two classes was an assignment given to the first which was still on the blackboard at the beginning of the second. It read:

Jacobs–Rosenbaum
Levin
Thorne
Hayes
Ohman (?)

I am sure that many of you will already have recognized the names on this list, but for the sake of the record, allow me to identify them. Roderick Jacobs and Peter Rosenbaum are two linguists who have coauthored a number of textbooks and co-edited a number of anthologies. Samuel Levin is a linguist who was one of the first to apply the operations of transformational grammar to literary texts. J. P. Thorne is a linguist at Edinburgh who, like Levin, was attempting to extend the rules of transformational grammar to the notorious irregularities of poetic language. Curtis Hayes is a linguist who was then using transformational grammar in order to establish an objective basis for his intuitive impression that the language of Gibbon's *Rise and Fall of the Roman Empire* is more complex than the language of Hemingway's novels. And Richard Ohmann is the literary critic who, more than any other, was responsible for introducing the vocabulary of transformational grammar to the literary community. Ohmann's name was spelled as you see it here because I could not remember whether it contained one or two n's. In other words, the question mark in parenthesis signified nothing more than a faulty memory and a desire on my part to appear scrupulous. The fact that the names appeared in a list that was arranged vertically, and that Levin, Thorne, and Hayes formed a column that was more or less centered in relation to the paired names of Jacobs and Rosenbaum, was similarly accidental and was evidence only of a certain compulsiveness if, indeed, it was evidence of anything at all.

In the time between the two classes I made only one change. I drew a frame around the assignment and wrote on the top of that frame "p. 43." When the members of the second class filed in I told them that what they saw on the blackboard was a religious poem of the kind they had been studying and I asked them to interpret it. Immediately they began to perform in a

manner that, for reasons which will become clear, was more or
less predictable. The first student to speak pointed out that the
poem was probably a hieroglyph, although he was not sure
whether it was in the shape of a cross or an altar. This question
was set aside as the other students, following his lead, began to
concentrate on individual words, interrupting each other with
suggestions that came so quickly that they seemed spontaneous.
The first line of the poem (the very order of events assumed
the already constituted status of the object) received the most
attention: Jacobs was explicated as a reference to Jacob's ladder,
traditionally allegorized as a figure for the Christian ascent to
heaven. In this poem, however, or so my students told me, the
means of ascent is not a ladder but a tree, a rose tree or rosenbaum. This was seen to be an obvious reference to the Virgin
Mary who was often characterized as a rose without thorns, itself an emblem of the immaculate conception. At this point the
poem appeared to the students to be operating in the familiar
manner of an iconographic riddle. It at once posed the question, "How is it that a man can climb to heaven by means
of a rose tree?" and directed the reader to the inevitable answer:
by the fruit of that tree, the fruit of Mary's womb, Jesus. Once
this interpretation was established it received support from, and
conferred significance on, the word "thorne," which could only
be an allusion to the crown of thorns, a symbol of the trial suf-
fered by Jesus and of the price he paid to save us all. It was
only a short step (really no step at all) from this insight to the
recognition of Levin as a double reference, first to the tribe of
Levi, of whose priestly function Christ was the fulfillment, and
second to the unleavened bread carried by the children of Israel
on their exodus from Egypt, the place of sin, and in response to
the call of Moses, perhaps the most familiar of the old testament types of Christ. The final word of the poem was given at
least three complementary readings: it could be "omen," especially since so much of the poem is concerned with foreshadowing and prophecy; it could be Oh Man, since it is man's story
as it intersects with the divine plan that is the poem's subject;
and it could, of course, be simply "amen," the proper conclusion

to a poem celebrating the love and mercy shown by a God who gave his only begotten son so that we may live.

In addition to specifying significances for the words of the poem and relating those significances to one another, the students began to discern larger structural patterns. It was noted that of the six names in the poem three—Jacobs, Rosenbaum, and Levin—are Hebrew, two—Thorne and Hayes—are Christian, and one—Ohman—is ambiguous, the ambiguity being marked in the poem itself (as the phrase goes) by the question mark in parenthesis. This division was seen as a reflection of the basic distinction between the old dispensation and the new, the law of sin and the law of love. That distinction, however, is blurred and finally dissolved by the typological perspective which invests the old testament events and heroes with new testament meanings. The structure of the poem, my students concluded, is therefore a double one, establishing and undermining its basic pattern (Hebrew vs. Christian) at the same time. In this context there is finally no pressure to resolve the ambiguity of Ohman since the two possible readings—the name is Hebrew, the name is Christian—are both authorized by the reconciling presence in the poem of Jesus Christ. Finally, I must report that one student took to counting letters and found, to no one's surprise, that the most prominent letters in the poem were S, O, N.

Some of you will have noticed that I have not yet said anything about Hayes. This is because of all the words in the poem it proved the most recalcitrant to interpretation, a fact not without consequence, but one which I will set aside for the moment since I am less interested in the details of the exercise than in the ability of my students to perform it. What is the source of that ability? How is it that they were able to do what they did? What is it that they did? These questions are important because they bear directly on a question often asked in literary theory, What are the distinguishing features of literary language? Or, to put the matter more colloquially, How do you recognize a poem when you see one? The commonsense answer, to which many literary critics and linguists are committed, is that the act of recognition is triggered by the observable presence of distinguishing features. That is, you know a poem when you see one because its language displays the characteristics that you know to be proper to poems. This, however, is a model that quite obviously does not fit the present example. My students did not proceed from the noting of distinguishing features to the recognition that they were confronted by a poem; rather, it was the act of recognition that came first—they knew in advance that they were dealing with a poem—and the distinguishing features then followed.

In other words, acts of recognition, rather than being triggered by formal characteristics, are their source. It is not that the presence of poetic qualities compels a certain kind of attention but that the paying of a certain kind of attention results in the emergence of poetic qualities. As soon as my students were aware that it was poetry they were seeing, they began to look with poetry-seeing eyes, that is, with eyes that saw everything in relation to the properties they knew poems to possess. They knew, for example (because they were told by their teachers), that poems are (or are supposed to be) more densely and intricately organized than ordinary communications; and that knowledge translated itself into a willingness—one might even says a determination—to see connections between one word and another and between every word and the poem's central insight. Moreover, the assumption that there *is* a central insight is itself poetry-specific, and presided over its own realization. Having assumed that the collection of words before them was unified by an informing purpose (because unifying purposes are what poems have), my students proceeded to find one and to formulate it. It was in the light of that purpose (now assumed) that significances for the individual words began to suggest themselves, significances which then fleshed out the assumption that had generated them in the first place. Thus the meanings of the words and the interpretation in which those words were seen to be embedded emerged together, as a consequence of the operations my students began to perform once they were told that this was a poem.

It was almost as if they were following a recipe—if it's a

poem do this, if it's a poem, see it that way—and indeed definitions of poetry *are* recipes, for by directing readers as to what
to look for in a poem, they instruct them in ways of looking that
will produce what they expect to see. If your definition of poetry
tells you that the language of poetry is complex, you will scrutinize the language of something identified as a poem in such
a way as to bring out the complexity you know to be "there."
You will, for example, be on the look-out for latent ambiguities;
you will attend to the presence of alliterative and consonantal
patterns (there will always be some), and you will try to make
something of them (you will always succeed); you will search
for meanings that subvert, or exist in a tension with the meanings that first present themselves; and if these operations fail
to produce the anticipated complexity, you will even propose
a significance for the words that are *not* there, because, as everyone knows, everything about a poem, including its omissions,
is significant. Nor, as you do these things, will you have any
sense of performing in a willful manner, for you will only be
doing what you learned to do in the course of becoming a skilled
reader of poetry. Skilled reading is usually thought to be a matter of discerning what is there, but if the example of my students can be generalized, it is a matter of knowing how to *produce* what can thereafter be said to be there. Interpretation is
not the art of construing but the art of constructing. Interpreters
do not decode poems; they make them.

To many, this will be a distressing conclusion, and there are
a number of arguments that could be mounted in order to forestall it. One might point out that the circumstances of my students' performance were special. After all, they had been concerned exclusively with religious poetry for some weeks, and
therefore would be uniquely vulnerable to the deception I had
practiced on them and uniquely equipped to impose religious
themes and patterns on words innocent of either. I must report,
however, that I have duplicated this experiment any number
of times at nine or ten universities in three countries, and the
results were always the same, even when the participants know
from the beginning that what they are looking at was originally
an assignment. Of course this very fact could itself be turned into

an objection: doesn't the reproducibility of the exercise prove
that there is something about these words that leads everyone
to perform in the same way? Isn't it just a happy accident that
names like Thorne and Jacobs have counterparts or near counterparts in biblical names and symbols? And wouldn't my students have been unable to do what they did if the assignment
I gave to the first class had been made up of different names?
The answer to all of these questions is no. Given a firm belief
that they were confronted by a religious poem, my students
would have been able to turn any list of names into the kind of
poem we have before us now, because they would have read the
names within the assumption that they were informed with
Christian significances. (This is nothing more than a literary
analogue to Augustine's rule of faith.) You can test this assertion
by replacing Jacobs-Rosenbaum, Levin, Thorne, Hayes, and
Ohman with names drawn from the faculty of Kenyon College—
Temple, Jordan, Seymour, Daniels, Star, Church. I will not
exhaust my time or your patience by performing a full-dress
analysis, which would involve, of course, the relation between
those who saw the River Jordan and those who saw *more* by
seeing the Star of Bethlehem, thus fulfilling the prophecy by
which the temple of Jerusalem was replaced by the inner temple
or church built up in the heart of every Christian. Suffice it to
say that it could easily be done (you can take the poem home and
do it yourself) and that the shape of its doing would be constrained not by the names but by the interpretive assumptions
that gave them a significance even before they were seen. This
would be true even if there were no names on the list, if the
paper or blackboard were blank; the blankness would present
no problem to the interpreter, who would immediately see in
it the void out of which God created the earth, or the abyss
into which unregenerate sinners fall, or, in the best of all possible poems, both.

Even so, one might reply, all you've done is demonstrate
how an interpretation, if it is is prosecuted with sufficient vigor,
can impose itself on material which has its own proper shape.
Basically, at the ground level, in the first place, when all is said
and done, "Jacobs-Rosenbaum Levin Thorne Hayes Ohman(?)"

is an assignment; it is only a trick that allows you to transform it into a poem, and when the effects of the trick have worn off, it will return to its natural form and be seen as an assignment once again. This is a powerful argument because it seems at once to give interpretation its due (as an act of the will) and to maintain the independence of that on which interpretation works. It allows us, in short, to preserve our commonsense intuition that interpretation must be interpretation of *something*. Unfortunately, the argument will not hold because the assignment we all see is no less the product of interpretation than the poem into which it was turned. That is, it requires just as much work, and work of the same kind, to see this as an assignment as it does to see it as a poem. If this seems counterintuitive, it is only because the work required to see it as an assignment is work we have already done, in the course of acquiring the huge amount of background knowledge that enables you and me to function in the academic world. In order to know what an assigment is, that is, in order to know what to do with something identified as an assignment, you must first know what a class is (know that it isn't an economic grouping) and know that classes meet at specified times for so many weeks, and that one's performance in a class is largely a matter of performing between classes.

Think for a moment of how you would explain this last to someone who did not already know it. "Well," you might say, "a class is a group situation in which a number of people are instructed by an informed person in a particular subject." (Of course the notion of "subject" will itself require explication.) "An assignment is something you do when you're not in class." "Oh, I see," your interlocutor might respond, "an assignment is something you do to take your mind off what you've been doing in class." "No, an assignment is a part of a class." "But how can that be if you only do it when the class is not meeting?" Now it would be possible, finally, to answer that question, but only by enlarging the horizons of your explanation to include the very concept of a university, what it is one might be doing there, why one might be doing it instead of doing a thousand other things, and so on. For most of us these matters do not re-

quire explanation, and indeed, it is hard for us to imagine someone for whom they do; but that is because our tacit knowledge
of what it means to move around in academic life was acquired
so gradually and so long ago that it doesn't seem like knowledge
at all (and therefore something someone else might *not* know)
but a part of the world. You might think that when you're on
campus (a phrase that itself requires volumes) that you are
simply walking around on the two legs God gave you; but your
walking is informed by an internalized awareness of institutional goals and practices, of norms of behavior, of lists of do's
and don't's, of invisible lines and the dangers of crossing them;
and, as a result, you see everything as *already* organized in relation to those same goals and practices. It would never occur to
you, for example, to wonder if the people pouring out of that
building are fleeing from a fire; you *know* that they are exiting
from a class (what could be more obvious?) and you know that
because your perception of their action occurs within a knowledge of what people in a university could possibly be doing and
the reasons they could have for doing it (going to the next class,
going back to the dorm, meeting someone in the student union).
It is within that same knowledge that an assignment becomes
intelligible so that it appears to you immediately as an obligation, as a set of directions, as something with parts, some of which
may be more significant than others. That is, it is a proper question to ask of an assignment whether some of its parts might be
omitted or slighted, whereas readers of poetry know that no part
of a poem can be slighted (the rule is "everything counts") and
they do not rest until every part has been given a significance.

In a way this amounts to no more than saying what everyone alreadys knows: poems and assignments are different, but
my point is that the differences are a result of the different interpretive operations we perform and not of something inherent
in one or the other. An assignment no more compels its own
recognition than does a poem; rather, as in the case of a poem,
the shape of an assignment emerges when someone looks at
something identified as one with assignment-seeing eyes, that
is, with eyes which are capable of seeing the words as already
embedded within the institutional structure that makes it pos-

sible for assignments to have a sense. The ability to see, and therefore to make, an assignment is no less a learned ability than the ability to see, and therefore to make, a poem. Both are constructed artifacts, the products and not the producers of interpretation, and while the differences between them are real, they are interpretive and do not have their source in some bedrock level of objectivity.

Of course one might want to argue that there is a bedrock level at which these names constitute neither an assignment or a poem but are merely a list. But that argument too falls because a list is no more a natural object—one that wears its meaning on its face and can be recognized by anyone—than an assignment or a poem. In order to see a list, one must already be equipped with the concepts of seriality, hierarchy, subordination, and so on, and while these are by no mean esoteric concepts and seem available to almost everyone, they are nonetheless learned, and if there were someone who had not learned them, he or she would not be able to see a list. The next recourse is to descend still lower (in the direction of atoms) and to claim objectivity for letters, paper, graphite, black marks on white spaces, and so on; but these entities too have palpability and shape only because of the assumption of some or other system of intelligibility, and they are therefore just as available to a deconstructive dissolution as are poems, assignments, and lists.

The conclusion, therefore, is that all objects are made and not found, and that they are made by the interpretive strategies we set in motion. This does not, however, commit me to subjectivity because the means by which they are made are social and conventional. That is, the "you" who does the interpretative work that puts poems and assignments and lists into the world is a communal you and not an isolated individual. No one of us wakes up in the morning and (in French fashion) reinvents poetry or thinks up a new educational system or decides to reject seriality in favor of some other, wholly original, form of organization. We do not do these things because we could not do them, because the mental operations we can perform are limited by the institutions in which we are *already* embedded. These institutions precede us, and it is only by inhabiting them,

or being inhabited by them, that we have access to the public
and conventional senses they make. Thus while it is true to say
that we create poetry (and assignments and lists), we create it
through interpretive strategies that are finally not our own but
have their source in a publicly available system of intelligibility. Insofar as the system (in this case a literary system) constrains us, it also fashions us, furnishing us with categories of
understanding, with which we in turn fashion the entities to
which we can then point. In short, to the list of made or constructed objects we must add ourselves, for we no less than the
poems and assignments we see are the products of social and
cultural patterns of thought.

   To put the matter in this way is to see that the opposition
between objectivity and subjectivity is a false one because
neither exists in the pure form that would give the opposition
its point. This is precisely illustrated by my anecdote in which
we do *not* have free-standing readers in a relationship of
perceptual adequacy or inadequacy to an equally free-standing
text. Rather, we have readers whose consciousnesses are constituted by a set of conventional notions which when put into
operation constitute in turn a conventional, and conventionally
seen, object. My students could do what they did, and do it in
unison, because as members of a literary community they knew
what a poem was (their knowledge was public), and that knowledge led them to look in such a way as to populate the landscape
with what they knew to be poems.

   Of course poems are not the only objects that are constituted
in unison by shared ways of seeing. Every object or event that
becomes available within an institutional setting can be so characterized. I am thinking, for example, of something that happened in my classroom just the other day. While I was in the
course of vigorously making a point, one of my students, William Newlin by name, was just as vigorously waving his hand.
When I asked the other members of the class what it was that
Mr. Newlin was doing, they all answered that he was seeking
permission to speak. I then asked them how they knew that. The
immediate reply was that it was obvious; what else could he
be thought to be doing? The meaning of his gesture, in other

words, was right there on its surface, available for reading by anyone who had the eyes to see. That meaning, however, would not have been available to someone without any knowledge of what was involved in being a student. Such a person might have thought that Mr. Newlin was pointing to the fluorescent lights hanging from the ceiling, or calling our attention to some object that was about to fall ("the sky is falling," "the sky is falling"). And if the someone in question were a child of elementary or middle-school age, Mr. Newlin might well have been seen as seeking permission not to speak but to go to the bathroom, an interpretation or reading that would never occur to a student at Johns Hopkins or any other institution of "higher learning" (and how would we explain to the uninitiated the meaning of *that* phrase).

The point is the one I have made so many times before: it is neither the case that the significance of Mr. Newlin's gesture is imprinted on its surface where it need only be read off, or that the construction put on the gesture by everyone in the room was individual and idiosyncratic. Rather, the source of our interpretive unanimity was a structure of interests and understood goals, a structure whose categories so filled our individual consciousnesses that they were rendered as one, immediately investing phenomena with the significance they *must* have, given the already-in-place assumptions about what someone could possibly be intending (by word or gesture) in a classroom. By seeing Mr. Newlin's raised hand with a single shaping eye, we were demonstrating what Harvey Sacks has characterized as "the fine power of a culture. It does not, so to speak, merely fill brains in roughly the same way, it fills them so that they are alike in fine detail."[1] The occasion of Sacks's observation was the ability of his hearers to understand a sequence of two sentences—"The baby cried. The mommy picked it up."—exactly as he did (assuming, for example that "the 'mommy' who picks up the 'baby' is the mommy of that baby"), despite the fact that alternative ways of understanding were demonstrably possible. That is, the mommy of the second sentence could well have been the mommy of some other baby, and it need not even have been a baby that this "floating" mommy was picking up. One is tempted to say that in the absence of a specific context we are authorized to take the words literally, which is what Sacks's hearers do; but as Sacks observes, it is within the assumption of a context—one so deeply assumed that we are unaware of it—that the words acquire what seems to be their literal meaning. There is nothing *in the words* that tells Sacks and his hearers how to relate the mommy and the baby of this story, just as there is nothing *in the form* of Mr. Newlin's gesture that tells his fellow students how to determine its significance. In both cases the determination (of relation and significance) is the work of categories of organization—the family, being a student—that are from the very first giving shape and value to what is heard and seen.

Indeed, these categories are the very shape of seeing itself, in that we are not to imagine a perceptual ground more basic than the one they afford. That is, we are not to imagine a moment when my students "simply see" a physical configuration of atoms and *then* assign that configuration a significance, according to the situation they happen to be in. To be in the situation (this or any other) is to "see" with the eyes of its interests, its goals, its understood practices, values, and norms, and so to be conferring significance *by* seeing, not after it. The categories of my students' vision are the categories by which they understand themselves to be functioning as students (what Sacks might term "doing studenting"), and objects will appear to them in forms related to that way of functioning rather than in some objective or preinterpretive form. (This is true even when an object is seen as not related, since nonrelation is not a pure but a differential category—the specification of something by enumerating what it is not; in short, nonrelation is merely one form of relation, and its perception is always situation-specific.)

Of course, if someone who was not functioning as a student was to walk into my classroom, he might very well see Mr. Newlin's raised hand (and "raised hand" is already an interpretation-laden description) in some other way, as evidence of a disease, as the salute of a political follower, as a muscle-improving exercise, as an attempt to kill flies; but he would always see it in *some* way, and never as purely physical data waiting for his in-

interpretation v. judgement(?) Same? other?

terpretation. And, moreover, the way of seeing, whatever it was, would never be individual or idiosyncratic, since its source would always be the institutional structure of which the "see-er" was an extending agent. This is what Sacks means when he says that a culture fills brains "so that they are alike in fine detail"; it fills them so that no one's interpretive acts are exclusively his own but fall to him by virtue of his position in some socially organized environment and are therefore always shared and public. It follows, then, that the fear of solipsism, of the imposition by the unconstrained self of its own prejudices, is unfounded because the self does not exist apart from the communal or conventional categories of thought that enable its operations (of thinking, seeing, reading). Once one realizes that the conceptions that fill consciousness, including any conception of its own status, are culturally derived, the very notion of an unconstrained self, of a consciousness wholly and dangerously free, becomes incomprehensible.

we are only a community of something held in common —

But without the notion of the unconstrained self, the arguments of Hirsch, Abrams, and the other proponents of objective interpretation are deprived of their urgency. They are afraid that in the absence of the controls afforded by a normative system of meanings, the self will simply substitute its own meanings for the meanings (usually identified with the intentions of the author) that texts bring with them, the meanings that texts *"have"*; however, if the self is conceived of not as an independent entity but as a social construct whose operations are delimited by the systems of intelligibility that inform it, then the meanings it confers on texts are not its own but have their source in the interpretive community (or communities) of which it is a function. Moreover, these meanings will be neither subjective nor objective, at least in the terms assumed by those who argue within the traditional framework: they will not be objective because they will always have been the product of a point of view rather than having been simply "read off"; and they will not be subjective because that point of view will always be social or institutional. Or by the same reasoning one could say that they are *both* subjective and objective: they are subjective because they inhere in a particular point of view and are there-

then there then no personal Relationships.

fore not universal; and they are objective because the point of view that delivers them is public and conventional rather than individual or unique.

To put the matter in either way is to see how unhelpful the terms "subjective" and "objective" finally are. Rather than facilitating inquiry, they close it down, by deciding in advance what shape inquiry can possibly take. Specifically, they assume, without being aware that it is an assumption and therefore open to challenge, the very distinction I have been putting into question, the distinction between interpreters and the objects they interpret. That distinction in turn assumes that interpreters and their objects are two different kinds of *a*contextual entities, and within these twin assumptions the issue can only be one of control: will texts be allowed to constrain their own interpretation or will irresponsible interpreters be allowed to obscure and overwhelm texts. In the spectacle that ensues, the spectacle of Anglo-American critical controversy, texts and selves fight it out in the persons of their respective champions, Abrams, Hirsch, Reichert, Graff on the one hand, Holland, Bleich, Slatoff, and (in some characterizations of him) Barthes on the other. But if selves are constituted by the ways of thinking and seeing that inhere in social organizations, and if these constituted selves in turn constitute texts according to these same ways, then there can be no adversary relationship between text and self because they are the necessarily related products of the same cognitive possibilities. A text cannot be overwhelmed by an irresponsible reader and one need not worry about protecting the purity of a text from a reader's idiosyncrasies. It is only the distinction between subject and object that gives rise to these urgencies, and once the distinction is blurred they simply fall away. One can respond with a cheerful yes to the question "Do readers make meanings?" and commit oneself to very little because it would be equally true to say that meanings, in the form of culturally derived interpretive categories, make readers.

Indeed, many things look rather different once the subject–object dichotomy is eliminated as the assumed framework within which critical discussion occurs. Problems disappear, not because they have been solved but because they are shown never to have

been problems in the first place. Abrams, for example, wonders
how, in the absence of a normative system of stable meanings,
two people could ever agree on the interpretation of a work
or even of a sentence; but the difficulty is only a difficulty if the
two (or more) people are thought of as isolated individuals
whose agreement must be compelled by something external to
them. (There is something of the police state in Abrams's vision,
complete with posted rules and boundaries, watchdogs to enforce them, procedures for identifying their violators as crim-
inals.) But if the understandings of the people in question are
informed by the same notions of what counts as a fact, of what
is central, peripheral, and worthy of being noticed—in short,
by the same interpretive principles—then agreement between
them will be assured, and its source will not be a text that enforces its own perception but a way of perceiving that results in
the emergence to those who share it (or those whom it shares) of
the same text. That text might be a poem, as it was in the case of
those who first "saw" "Jacobs-Rosenbaum Levin Hayes Thorne
Ohman(?)," or a hand, as it is every day in a thousand classrooms;
but whatever it is, the shape and meaning it appears immediately
to have will be the "ongoing accomplishment"[2] of those who
agree to produce it.

15

What Makes an Interpretation Acceptable?

L AST TIME I ended by suggesting that the fact
of agreement, rather than being a proof of the
stability of objects, is a testimony to the power
of an interpretive community to constitute the objects upon
which its members (also and simultaneously constituted) can
then agree. This account of agreement has the additional advantage of providing what the objectivist argument cannot supply, a coherent account of *dis*agreement. To someone who believes in determinate meaning, disagreement can only be a theological error. The truth lies plainly in view, available to anyone
who has the eyes to see; but some readers choose not to see it
and perversely substitute their own meanings for the meanings
that texts obviously bear. Nowhere is there an explanation of
this waywardness (original sin would seem to be the only relevant
model), or of the origin of these idiosyncratic meanings (I have
been arguing that there could be none), or of the reason why
some readers seem to be exempt from the general infirmity.
There is simply the conviction that the facts exist in their own
self-evident shape and that disagreements are to be resolved by
referring the respective parties to the facts as they really are. In
the view that I have been urging, however, disagreements cannot
be resolved by reference to the facts, because the facts emerge
only in the context of some point of view. It follows, then, that
disagreements must occur between those who hold (or are held
by) different points of view, and what is at stake in a disagreement is the right to specify what the facts can hereafter be said to
be. Disagreements are not settled by the facts, but are the means
by which the facts are settled. Of course, no such settling is final,
and in the (almost certain) event that the dispute is opened

338

again, the category of the facts "as they really are" will be reconstituted in still another shape.

Nowhere is this process more conveniently on display than in literary criticism, where everyone's claim is that his interpretation more perfectly accords with the facts, but where everyone's purpose is to persuade the rest of us to the version of the facts he espouses by persuading us to the interpretive principles in the light of which those facts will seem indisputable. The recent critical fortunes of William Blake's "The Tyger" provide a nice example. In 1954 Kathleen Raine published an influential essay entitled "Who Made the Tyger" in which she argued that because the tiger is for Blake "the beast that sustains its own life at the expense of its fellow-creatures" it is a "symbol of . . . predacious selfhood," and that therefore the answer to the poem's final question—"Did he who made the Lamb make thee"—"is, beyond all possible doubt, No."[1] In short, the tiger is unambiguously and obviously evil. Raine supports her reading by pointing to two bodies of evidence, certain cabbalistic writings which, she avers, "beyond doubt . . . inspired *The Tyger*," and evidence from the poem itself. She pays particular attention to the word "forests" as it appears in line 2, "In the forests of the night:" "Never . . . is the word 'forest' used by Blake in any context in which it does not refer to the natural, 'fallen' world" (p. 48).

The direction of argument here is from the word "forests" to the support it is said to provide for a particular interpretation. Ten years later, however, that same word is being cited in support of a quite different interpretation. While Raine assumes that the lamb is for Blake a symbol of Christ-like self-sacrifice, E. D. Hirsch believes that Blake's intention was "to satirize the singlemindedness of the Lamb": "There can be no doubt," he declares, "that *The Tyger* is a poem that celebrates the holiness of tigerness."[2] In his reading the "ferocity and destructiveness" of the tiger are transfigured and one of the things they are transfigured by is the word "forests": " 'Forests' . . . suggests tall straight forms, a world that for all its terror has the orderliness of the tiger's stripes or Blake's perfectly balanced verses" (p. 247).

What we have here then are two critics with opposing interpretations, each of whom claims the same word as internal
and confirming evidence. Clearly they cannot both be right,
but just as clearly there is no basis for deciding between them.
One cannot appeal to the text, because the text has become an
extension of the interpretive disagreement that divides them;
and, in fact, the text as it is variously characterized is a *consequence* of the interpretation for which it is supposedly evidence. It is not that the meaning of the word "forests" points in
the direction of one interpretation or the other; rather, in the
light of an already assumed interpretation, the word will be seen
to *obviously* have one meaning or another. Nor can the question be settled by turning to the context—say the cabbalistic
writings cited by Raine—for that too will only be a context
for an already assumed interpretation. If Raine had not already
decided that the answer to the poem's final question is "beyond
all possible doubt, No," the cabbalistic texts, with their distinction between supreme and inferior deities, would never have
suggested themselves to her as Blake's source. The rhetoric of
critical argument, as it is usually conducted in our journals, depends upon a distinction between interpretations on the one
hand and the textual and contextual facts that will either support or disconfirm them on the other; but as the example of
Blake's "Tyger" shows, text, context, and interpretation all
emerge together, as a consequence of a gesture (the declaration
of belief) that is irreducibly interpretive. It follows, then, that
when one interpretation wins out over another, it is not because
the first has been shown to be in accordance with the facts but
because it is from the perspective of its assumptions that the facts
are now being specified. It is these assumptions, and not the facts
they make possible, that are at stake in any critical dispute.

Hirsch and Raine seem to be aware of this, at least sublim-
inally; for whenever their respective assumptions surface they
are asserted with a vehemence that is finally defensive: "The
answer to the question . . . is beyond all possible doubt, No."
"There can be no doubt that *The Tyger* is . . . a poem that celebrates the holiness of tigerness." If there were a doubt, if the
interpretation with which each critic begins were not firmly in

place, the account of the poem that follows from that interpretation could not get under way. One could not cite as an "obvious" fact that "forests" is a fallen word or, alternatively, that it "suggests tall and straight forms." Whenever a critic prefaces an assertion with a phrase like "without doubt" or "there can be no doubt," you can be sure that you are within hailing distance of the interpretive principles which produce the facts that he presents as obvious.

In the years since 1964 other interpretations of the poem have been put forward, and they follow a predictable course. Some echo either Raine or Hirsch by arguing that the tiger is either good or evil; others assert that the tiger is *both* good and evil, or beyond good and evil; still others protest that the questions posed in the poem are rhetorical and are therefore not meant to be answered ("It is quite evident that the critics are not trying to understand the poem at all. If they were, they would not attempt to answer its questions.")[3] It is only a matter of time before the focus turns from the questions to their asker and to the possibility that the speaker of the poem is not Blake but a limited persona ("Surely the point . . . is that Blake sees further or deeper than his *persona*").[4] It then becomes possible to assert that "we don't know who the speaker of 'The Tyger' is," and that therefore the poem "is a maze of questions in which the reader is forced to wander confusedly."[5] In this reading the poem itself becomes rather "tigerish" and one is not at all surprised when the original question—"Who made the Tiger?"—is given its quintessentially new-critical answer: the tiger is the poem itself and Blake, the consummate artist who smiles "his work to see," is its creator.[6] As one obvious and indisputable interpretation supplants another, it brings with it a new set of obvious and indisputable facts. Of course each new reading is elaborated in the name of the poem itself, but the poem itself is always a function of the interpretive perspective from which the critic "discovers" it.

A committed pluralist might find in the previous paragraph a confirmation of his own position. After all, while "The Tyger" is obviously open to more than one interpretation, it is not open to an infinite number of interpretations. There may be disagreements as to whether the tiger is good or evil, or whether the speaker is Blake or a persona, and so on, but no one is suggesting that the poem is an allegory of the digestive processes or that it predicts the Second World War, and its limited plurality is simply a testimony to the capacity of a great work of art to generate multiple readings. The point is one that Wayne Booth makes when he asks, "Are we *right* to rule out at least some readings?"[7] and then answers his own question with a resounding yes. It would be my answer too; but the real question is what gives us the right so to be right. A pluralist is committed to saying that there is something in the text which rules out some readings and allows others (even though no *one* reading can ever capture the text's "inexhaustible richness and complexity"). His best evidence is that in practice "we all in fact" do reject unacceptable readings and that more often than not we agree on the readings that are to be rejected. Booth tells us, for example, that he has never found a reader of *Pride and Prejudice* "who sees no jokes against Mr. Collins" when he gives his reasons for wanting to marry Elizabeth Bennet and only belatedly, in fifth position, cites the "violence" of his affection.[8] From this and other examples Booth concludes that there are justified limits to what we can legitimately do with a text," for "surely we could not go on disputing at all if a core of agreement did not exist." Again, I agree, but if, as I have argued, the text is always a function of interpretation, then the text cannot be the location of the core of agreement by means of which we reject interpretations. We seem to be at an impasse: on the one hand there would seem to be no basis for labeling an interpretation unacceptable, but on the other we do it all the time.

This, however, is an impasse only if one assumes that the activity of interpretation is itself unconstrained; but in fact the shape of that activity is determined by the literary institution which at any one time will authorize only a finite number of interpretative strategies. Thus, while there is no core of agreement *in* the text, there is a core of agreement (although one subject to change) concerning the ways of *producing* the text. Nowhere is this set of acceptable ways written down, but it is a part of everyone's knowledge of what it means to be operating within the literary institution as it is now constituted. A student of mine recently demonstrated this knowledge when, with an air of giving away a trade secret, she confided that she could go into any classroom, no matter what the subject of the course, and win approval for running one of a number of well-defined interpretive routines: she could view the assigned text as an instance of the tension between nature and culture; she could look in the text for evidence of large mythological oppositions; she could argue that the true subject of the text was its own composition, or that in the guise of fashioning a narrative the speaker was fragmenting and displacing his own anxieties and fears. She could not, however, at least at Johns Hopkins University today, argue that the text was a prophetic message inspired by the ghost of her Aunt Tilly.

My student's understanding of what she could and could not get away with, of the unwritten rules of the literary game, is shared by everyone who plays that game, by those who write and judge articles for publication in learned journals, by those who read and listen to papers at professional meetings, by those who seek and award tenure in innumerable departments of English and comparative literature, by the armies of graduate students for whom knowledge of the rules is the real mark of professional initiation. This does not mean that these rules and the practices they authorize are either monolithic or stable. Within the literary community there are subcommunities (what will excite the editors of *Diacritics* is likely to distress the editors of *Studies in Philology*), and within any community the boundaries of the acceptable are continually being redrawn. In a classroom whose authority figures include David Bleich and Norman Holland, a student might very well relate a text to her memories of a favorite aunt, while in other classrooms, dominated by the spirit of Brooks and Warren, any such activity would immediately be dismissed as nonliterary, as something that isn't done.

The point is that while there is always a category of things that are not done (it is simply the reverse or flip side of the category of things that *are* done), the membership in that category is continually changing. It changes laterally as one moves from subcommunity to subcommunity, and it changes through time when once interdicted interpretive strategies are admitted into the ranks of the acceptable. Twenty years ago one of the things that literary critics didn't do was talk about the reader, at least in a way that made his experience the focus of the critical act. The prohibition on such talk was largely the result of Wimsatt's and Beardsley's famous essay "The Affective Fallacy," which argued that the variability of readers renders any investigation of their responses ad-hoc and relativistic: "The poem itself," the authors complained, "as an object of specifically critical judgment, tends to disappear."[9] So influential was this essay that it was possible for a reviewer to dismiss a book merely by finding in it evidence that the affective fallacy had been committed. The use of a juridical terminology is not accidental; this was in a very real sense a *legal* finding of activity in violation of understood and institutionalized decorums. Today, however, the affective fallacy, no longer a fallacy but a methodology, is committed all the time, and its practitioners have behind them the full and authorizing weight of a fully articulated institutional apparatus. The "reader in literature" is regularly the subject of forums and workshops at the convention of the Modern Language Association; there is a reader newsletter which reports on the multitudinous labors of a reader industry; any list of currently active schools of literary criticism includes the school of "reader response," and two major university presses have published collections of essays designed both to display the variety of reader-centered criticism (the emergence of factions within a once interdicted activity is a sure sign of its having achieved the status of an orthodoxy) and to detail its history. None of this of course means that a reader-centered criticism is now invulnerable to challenge or attack, merely that it is now recognized as a competing literary strategy that cannot be dismissed simply by being named. It is acceptable not because everyone accepts it but because those who do not are now obliged to argue against it.

The promotion of reader-response criticism to the category of things that are done (even if it is not being done by everyone) brings with it a whole new set of facts to which its practitioners can now refer. These include patterns of expectation and dis-

appointment, reversals of direction, traps, invitations to premature conclusions, textual gaps, delayed revelations, temptations,
all of which are related to a corresponding set of authors' intentions, of strategies designed to educate the reader or humiliate
him or confound him or, in the more sophisticated versions of
the mode, to make him enact in his responses the very subject
matter of the poem. These facts and intentions emerge when
the text is interrogated by a series of related questions—What is
the reader doing? What is being done to him? For what purpose?
—questions that follow necessarily from the assumption that the
text is not a spatial object but the occasion for a temporal experience. It is in the course of answering such questions that a reader-
response critic elaborates "the structure of the reading experience," a structure which is not so much discovered by the
interrogation but demanded by it. (If you begin by assuming that
readers do something and the something they do has meaning,
you will never fail to discover a pattern of reader activities that
appears obviously to be meaningful.) As that structure emerges
(under the pressure of interrogation) it takes the form of a
"reading," and insofar as the procedures which produced it are
recognized by the literary community as something that some
of its members do, that reading will have the status of a competing interpretation. Of course it is still the case, as Booth insists,
that we are "right to rule out at least some readings," but there
is now one less reading or kind of reading that can be ruled out,
because there is now one more interpretive procedure that has
been accorded a place in the literary institution.

The fact that it remains easy to think of a reading that most
of us would dismiss out of hand does not mean that the text
excludes it but that there is as yet no elaborated interpretive
procedure for producing that text. That is why the examples of
critics like Wayne Booth seem to have so much force; rather
than looking back, as I have, to now familiar strategies that
were once alien and strange sounding, they look forward to
strategies that have not yet emerged. Norman Holland's analysis of Faulkner's "A Rose for Emily" is a case in point. Holland
is arguing for a kind of psychoanalytic pluralism. The text, he
declares, is "at most a matrix of psychological possibilities for its

readers," but, he insists, "only some possibilities . . . truly fit the matrix": "One would not say, for example, that a reader of . . . 'A Rose for Emily' who thought the 'tableau' [of Emily and her father in the doorway] described an Eskimo was really responding to the story at all—only pursuing some mysterious inner exploration."[10]

Holland is making two arguments: first, that anyone who proposes an Eskimo reading of "A Rose for Emily" will not find a hearing in the literary community. And that, I think, is right. ("We are right to rule out at least some readings.") His second argument is that the unacceptability of the Eskimo reading is a function of the text, of what he calls its "sharable promptuary" (p. 287), the public "store of structured language" (p. 287) that sets limits to the interpretations the words can accommodate. And that, I think, is wrong. The Eskimo reading is unacceptable because there is at present no interpretive strategy for producing it, no way of "looking" or reading (and remember, all acts of looking or reading are "ways") that would result in the emergence of obviously Eskimo meanings. This does not mean, however, that no such strategy could ever come into play, and it is not difficult to imagine the circumstances under which it would establish itself. One such circumstance would be the discovery of a letter in which Faulkner confides that he has always believed himself to be an Eskimo changeling. (The example is absurd only if one forgets Yeat's *Vision* or Blake's Swedenborgianism or James Miller's recent elaboration of a homosexual reading of *The Waste Land*). Immediately the workers in the Faulkner industry would begin to reinterpret the canon in the light of this newly revealed "belief" and the work of reinterpretation would involve the elaboration of a symbolic or allusive system (not unlike mythological or typological criticism) whose application would immediately transform the text into one informed everywhere by Eskimo meanings. It might seem that I am admitting that there is a text to be transformed, but the object of transformation would be the text (or texts) given by whatever interpretive strategies the Eskimo strategy was in the process of dislodging or expanding. The result would be that whereas we now have a Freudian "A Rose for Emily," a mytho-

logical "A Rose for Emily," a Christological "A Rose for Emily,"
a regional "A Rose for Emily," a sociological "A Rose for Emily,"
a linguistic "A Rose for Emily," we would in addition have an
Eskimo "A Rose for Emily," existing in some relation of com-
patibility or incompatibility with the others.

Again the point is that while there are always mechanisms
for ruling out readings, their source is not the text but the presently recognized interpretive strategies for producing the text.
It follows, then, that no reading, however outlandish it might
appear, is inherently an impossible one. Consider, for another
example, Booth's report that he has never found a reader who
sees no jokes against Mr. Collins, and his conclusion that the
text of *Pride and Prejudice* enforces or signals an ironic reading.
First of all, the fact that he hasn't yet found such a reader does
not mean that one does not exist, and we can even construct his
profile; he would be someone for whom the reasons in Mr. Collins's list correspond to a deeply held set of values, exactly the
opposite of the set of values that must be assumed if the passage
is to be seen as obviously ironic. Presumably no one who has
sat in Professor Booth's classes holds that set of values or is
allowed to hold them (students always know what they are expected to believe) and it is unlikely that anyone who is now
working in the Austen industry begins with an assumption other
than the assumption that the novelist is a master ironist. It is
precisely for this reason that the time is ripe for the "discovery"
by an enterprising scholar of a nonironic Austen, and one can
even predict the course such a discovery would take. It would
begin with the uncovering of new evidence (a letter, a lost manuscript, a contemporary response) and proceed to the conclusion
that Austen's intentions have been misconstrued by generations
of literary critics. She was not in fact satirizing the narrow and
circumscribed life of a country gentry; rather, she was celebrating that life and its tireless elaboration of a social fabric, complete with values, rituals, and self-perpetuating goals (marriage,
the preservation of great houses, and so on). This view, or something very much like it, is already implicit in much of the criticism, and it would only be a matter of extending it to local
matters of interpretation, and specifically to Mr. Collins's list of

[margin annotation: intentional fallacy — ?]

reasons which might now be seen as reflecting a proper ranking of the values and obligations necessary to the maintenance of a way of life.

Of course any such reading would meet resistance; its opponents could point for example to the narrator's unequivocal condemnation of Mr. Collins; but there are always ways in the literary institution of handling this or any other objection. One need only introduce (if it has not already been introduced) the notion of the fallible narrator in any of its various forms (the dupe, the moral prig, the naif in need of education), and the "unequivocal condemnation" would take its place in a structure designed to glorify Mr. Collins and everything he stands for. Still, no matter how many objections were met and explained away, the basic resistance on the part of many scholars to this revisionist reading would remain, and for a time at least *Pride and Prejudice* would have acquired the status of the fourth book of *Gulliver's Travels,* a work whose very shape changes in the light of two radically opposed interpretive assumptions.

Again, I am aware that this argument is a tour-de-force and will continue to seem so as long as the revolution it projects has not occurred. The reading of *Pride and Prejudice,* however, is not meant to be persuasive. I only wanted to describe the conditions under which it might *become* persuasive and to point out that those conditions are not unimaginable given the procedures within the literary institution by which interpretations are proposed and established. Any interpretation could be elaborated by someone in command of those procedures (someone who knows what "will do" as a literary argument), even my own "absurd" reading of "The Tyger" as an allegory of the digestive processes. Here the task is easy because according to the critical consensus there is no belief so bizarre that Blake could not have been committed to it and it would be no trick at all to find some elaborate system of alimentary significances (Pythagorean? Swedenborgian? Cabbalistic?) which he could be presumed to have known. One might then decide that the poem was the first-person lament of someone who had violated a dietary prohibition against eating tiger meat, and finds that forbidden food burning brightly in his stomach, making its fiery way through the forests of the intestinal tract, beating and hammering like some devil-wielded anvil. In his distress he can do nothing but rail at the tiger and at the mischance that led him to mistake its meat for the meat of some purified animal: "Did he who made the Lamb make thee?" The poem ends as it began, with the speaker still paying the price of his sin and wondering at the inscrutable purposes of a deity who would lead his creatures into digestive temptation. Anyone who thinks that this time I have gone too far might do very well to consult some recent numbers of *Blake Studies*.

In fact, my examples are very serious, and they are serious in part because they are so ridiculous. The fact that they *are* ridiculous, or are at least perceived to be so, is evidence that we are never without canons of acceptability; we are always "right to rule out at least some readings." But the fact that we can imagine conditions under which they would *not* seem ridiculous, and that readings once considered ridiculous are now respectable and even orthodox, is evidence that the canons of acceptability can change. Moreover, that change is not random but orderly and, to some extent, predictable. A new interpretive strategy always makes its way in some relationship of opposition to the old, which has often marked out a negative space (of things that aren't done) from which it can emerge into respectability. Thus, when Wimsatt and Beardsley declare that "the Affective Fallacy is a confusion between the poem and its *results,* what it *is* and what it *does*," the way is open for an affective critic to argue, as I did, that a poem *is* what it does. And when the possibility of a reader-centered criticism seems threatened by the variability of readers, that threat will be countered either by denying the variability (Stephen Booth, Michael Riffaterre) or by controlling it (Wolfgang Iser, Louise Rosenblatt) or by embracing it and making it into a principle of value (David Bleich, Walter Slatoff).

Rhetorically the new position announces itself as a break from the old, but in fact it is radically dependent on the old, because it is only in the context of some differential relationship that it can be perceived as new or, for that matter, perceived at all. No one would bother to assert that Mr. Collins is the hero of *Pride and Prejudice* (even as an example intended to be absurd) were that position not already occupied in the criticism by Elizabeth and Darcy; for then the assertion would have no force; there would be nothing in relation to which it could be surprising. Neither would there be any point in arguing that Blake's tiger is both good and evil if there were not already readings in which he was declared to be one or the other. And if anyone is ever to argue that he is both old and young, someone will first have to argue that he is *either* old or young, for only when his age has become a question will there be any value in a refusal to answer it. Nor is it the case that the moral status of the tiger (as oposed to its age, or nationality, or intelligence) is an issue raised by the poem itself; it becomes an issue because a question is put to the poem (is the tiger good or evil?) and once that question (it could have been another) is answered, the way is open to answering it differently, or declining to answer it, or to declaring that the absence of an answer is the poem's "real point."

The discovery of the "real point" is always what is claimed whenever a new interpretation is advanced, but the claim makes sense only in relation to a point (or points) that had previously been considered the real one. This means that the space in which a critic works has been marked out for him by his predecessors, even though he is obliged by the conventions of the institution to dislodge them. It is only by their prevenience or prepossession that there is something for him to say; that is, it is only because something has already been said that he can now say something different. This dependency, the reverse of the anxiety of influence, is reflected in the unwritten requirement that an interpretation present itself as remedying a deficiency in the interpretations that have come before it. (If it did not do this, what claim would it have on our attention?) Nor can this be just any old deficiency; it will not do, for example, to fault your predecessors for failing to notice that a poem is free of split infinitives or dangling participles. The lack an interpretation supplies must be related to the criteria by which the literary community recognizes and evaluates the objects of its professional attention. As things stand now, text-book grammaticality is not one of those criteria, and therefore the demonstration of its presence in a poem will not reflect credit either on the poem or on the critic who offers it.

Credit *will* accrue to the critic when he bestows the *proper* credit on the poem, when he demonstrates that it possesses one or more of the qualities that are understood to distinguish poems from other verbal productions. In the context of the "new" criticism, under many of whose assumptions we still labor, those qualities include unity, complexity, and universality, and it is the perceived failure of previous commentators to celebrate their presence in a poem that gives a critic the right (or so he will claim) to advance a new interpretation. The unfolding of that interpretation will thus proceed under two constraints: not only must what one says about a work be related to what has already been said (even if the relation is one of reversal) but as a consequence of saying it the work must be shown to possess in a greater degree than had hitherto been recognized the qualities that properly belong to literary productions, whether they be unity and complexity, or unparaphrasability, or metaphoric richness, or indeterminacy and undecidability. In short, the new interpretation must not only claim to tell the truth about the work (in a dependent opposition to the falsehood or partial truths told by its predecessors) but it must claim to make the work better. (The usual phrase is "enhance our appreciation of.") Indeed, these claims are finally inseparable since it is assumed that the truth about a work will be what penetrates to the essence of its literary value.

This assumption, along with several others, is conveniently on display in the opening paragraph of the preface to Stephen Booth's *An Essay on Shakespeare's Sonnets:*[11]

The history of criticism opens so many possibilities for an essay on Shakespeare's sonnets that I must warn a prospective reader about what this work does and doesn't do. To begin with the negative, I have not solved or tried to solve any of the puzzles of Shakespeare's sonnets. I do not attempt to identify Mr. W. H. or the dark lady. I do not speculate on the occasions that may have evoked particular sonnets. I do not attempt to date them. I offer neither a reorganization of the sequence, nor a defense of

the quarto order. What I have tried to do is find out what about
the sonnets has made them so highly valued by the vast majority
of critics and general readers.

This brief paragraph can serve as an illustration of almost everything I have been saying. First of all, Booth self-consciously locates and defines his position in a differential opposition to the
positions he would dislodge. He will not, he tells us, do what
any of his predecessors have done; he will do something else,
and indeed if it were not something else there would be no
reason for him to be doing it. The reason he gives for doing it
is that what his predecessors have done is misleading or beside
the point. The point is the location of the source of the sonnets'
value ("what about the sonnets has made them so highly valued") and his contention (not stated but strongly implied) is
that those who have come before him have been looking in the
wrong places, in the historical identity of the sequence's characters, in the possibility of recovering the biographical conditions of composition, and in the determination of an authoritative ordering and organization. He, however, will look in the
right place and thereby produce an account of the sonnets that
does them the justice they so richly deserve.

   Thus, in only a few sentences Booth manages to claim for his
interpretation everything that certifies it as acceptable within
the conventions of literary criticism: he locates a deficiency in
previous interpretations and proposes to remedy it; the remedy
will take the form of producing a more satisfactory account of
the work; and as a result the literary credentials of the work—
what makes it of enduring value—will be more securely established, as they are when Booth is able to point in the closing
paragraph of his book to Shakespeare's "remarkable achievement." By thus validating Shakespeare's achievement, Booth
also validates his own credentials as a literary critic, as someone who knows what claims and demonstrations mark him as
a competent member of the institution.

   What makes Stephen Booth so interesting (although not at
all atypical) is that one of his claims is to have freed himself and
the sonnets from that very institution and its practices. "I do

not," he declares, "intentionally give any interpretations of the sonnets I discuss. I mean to describe them, not to explain them." The irony is that even as Booth is declaring himself out of the game, he is performing one of its most familiar moves. The move has several versions, and Booth is here availing himself of two: (1) the "external-internal," performed when a critic dismisses his predecessors for being insufficiently literary ("but that has nothing to do with its qualities *as a poem*"); and (2) the "back-to-the-text," performed when the critical history of a work is deplored as so much dross, as an obscuring encrustation ("we are in danger of substituting the criticism for the poem"). The latter is the more powerful version of the move because it trades on the assumption, still basic to the profession's sense of its activities, that the function of literary criticism is to let the text speak for itself. It is thus a move drenched in humility, although it is often performed with righteousness: those other fellows may be interested in displaying their ingenuity, but *I* am simply a servant of the text and wish only to make it more available to its readers (who happen also to be my readers).

The basic gesture, then, is to disavow interpretation in favor of simply presenting the text; but it is actually a gesture in which one set of interpretive principles is replaced by another that happens to claim for itself the virtue of not being an interpretation at all. The claim, however, is an impossible one since in order "simply to present" the text, one must at the very least describe it ("I mean to describe them") and description can occur only within a stipulative understanding of what there is to be described, an understanding that will produce the object of its attention. Thus, when Booth rejects the assumptions of those who have tried to solve the puzzles of the sonnets in favor of "the assumption that the source of our pleasure in them must be the line by line experience of reading them," he is not avoiding interpretation but proposing a change in the terms within which it will occur. Specifically, he proposes that the focus of attention, and therefore of description, shift from the poem conceived as a spatial object which *contains* meanings to the poem conceived as a temporal experience in the course of which meanings become momentarily available, before disappearing under the pressure of other meanings, which are in their turn superseded, contradicted, qualified, or simply forgotten. It is only if a reader agrees to this change, that is, agrees to accept Booth's revisionary stipulation as to where the value and the significance of a poem are to be located, that the facts to which his subsequent analyses point will be seen to be facts at all. The description which Booth offers in place of an interpretation turns out to be as much of an interpretive construct as the interpretations he rejects.

Nor could it be otherwise. Strictly speaking, getting "back-to-the-text" is not a move one can perform, because the text one gets back to will be the text demanded by some other interpretation and that interpretation will be presiding over its production. This is not to say, however, that the "back-to-the-text" move is ineffectual. The fact that it is not something one can do in no way diminishes the effectiveness of claiming to do it. As a rhetorical ploy, the announcement that one is returning to the text will be powerful so long as the assumption that criticism is secondary to the text and must not be allowed to overwhelm it remains unchallenged. Certainly, Booth does not challenge it; indeed, he relies on it and invokes it even as he relies on and invokes many other assumptions that someone else might want to dispute: the assumption that what distinguishes literary from ordinary language is its invulnerability to paraphrase; the assumption that a poem should not mean, but be; the assumption that the more complex a work is, the more propositions it holds in tension and equilibrium, the better it is. It would not be at all unfair to label these assumptions "conservative" and to point out that in holding to them Booth undermines his radical credentials. But it would also be beside the point, which is not that Booth isn't truly radical but that he *couldn't* be. Nor could anyone else. The challenge he mounts to some of the conventions of literary study (the convention of the poem as artifact, the convention of meaningfulness) would not even be *recognized* as a challenge if others of those conventions were not firmly in place and, for the time being at least, unquestioned. A wholesale challenge would be impossible because there would be no terms in which it could be made; that is, in order to be wholesale, it would have to be made in terms wholly outside the institution; but if that were the case, it would be unintelligible because it is only within the institution that the facts of literary study—texts, authors, periods, genres—become available. In short, the price intelligibility exacts (a price Booth pays here) is implication in the very structure of assumptions and goals from which one desires to be free.

So it would seem, finally, that there are no moves that are not moves in the game, and this includes even the move by which one claims no longer to be a player. Indeed, by a logic peculiar to the institution, one of the standard ways of practicing literary criticism is to announce that you are avoiding it. This is so because at the heart of the institution is the wish to deny that its activities have any consequences. The critic is taught to think of himself as a transmitter of the best that had been thought and said by others, and his greatest fear is that he will stand charged of having substituted his own meanings for the meanings of which he is supposedly the guardian; his greatest fear is that he be found guilty of having interpreted. That is why we have the spectacle of commentators who, like Stephen Booth, adopt a stance of aggressive humility and, in the manner of someone who rises to speak at a temperance meeting, declare that they will never interpret again but will instead do something else ("I mean to describe them"). What I have been saying is that whatever they do, it will only be interpretation in another guise because, like it or not, interpretation is the only game in town.

LIBRARY ST. MARY'S COLLEGE

16
Demonstration vs. Persuasion: Two Models of Critical Activity

BY ASSERTING, as I did at the close of my last lecture, that interpretation is the only game in town, I may have seemed only to confirm the fears of those who argue for the necessity of determinate meaning: for, one might say, if interpretation covers the field, there is nothing to constrain its activities and no way to prevent, or even to recognize, its irresponsible exercise. But this is to think of interpretation as something external to the center it supposedly threatens, whereas I have been arguing that interpretation is constitutive of the center—of what will count as a fact, as a text, as a piece of evidence, as a reasonable argument—and thus defines its own limits and boundaries. The mistake is to think of interpretation as an activity in need of constraints, when in fact interpretation is a *structure* of constraints. The field interpretation covers comes complete with its own internal set of rules and regulations, its list of prescribed activities which is also, and at the same time, a list of activities that are proscribed. That is, within a set of interpretive assumptions, to know what you can do is, *ipso facto,* to know what you can't do; indeed, you can't know one without the other; they come together in a diacritical package, indissolubly wed. So that while irresponsible behavior certainly exists (in that one can always recognize it), it exists not as a threat to the system but as a component within it, as much defining responsible behavior as responsible behavior defines it.

That is why the fear of interpretation that is anarchic or totally relativistic will never be realized; for in the event that a fringe or off-the-wall interpretation makes its way into the center, it will merely take its place in a new realignment in which *other* interpretations will occupy the position of being off-the-wall. That is, off-the-wallness is not a property of interpretations that have been judged inaccurate with respect to a free-standing text but a property of an interpretive system within whose confines the text is continually being established and re-established. It is not a pure but a relational category; an off-the-wall interpretation is simply one that exists in a reciprocally defining relationship with interpretations that are on the wall (you know it by what it is not, and you know what it is not by it); and since the stipulation of what is and is not off the wall is a matter of dispute (the system is precisely a mechanism for the endless negotiation of what will be authorized or nonauthorized) there is always the possibility, and indeed the certainty, that the shape of the stipulation will change. What is not a possibility, however, is that there be *only* off-the-wall interpretation (that "anything goes") because the category only has meaning by virtue of its binary opposite, which is, of course, no less dependent on it. The conclusion is paradoxical, but only superficially so: there is no such thing as an off-the-wall interpretation if by that one means an interpretation that has nothing to do with the text; and yet there is always an off-the-wall interpretation if by that one means an interpretation constitutive of the boundaries within which the text can emerge.

The further conclusion is that off-the-wallness is not inimical to the system but essential to it and to its operation. The production and perception of off-the-wall interpretations is no less a learned and conventional activity than the production and perception of interpretations that are judged to be acceptable. They are, in fact, the same activities enabled by the same set of in-force assumptions about what one can say and not say as a certified member of a community. It is, in short, no easier to disrupt the game (by throwing a monkey wrench into it) than it is to get away from it (by performing independently of it), and for the same reasons. One cannot disrupt the game because any interpretation one puts forward, no matter how "absurd," will already be *in* the game (otherwise one could not even conceive of it as an interpretation); and one cannot get away from the game because anything one does (any account of a text one offers) will be possible and recognizable only within the conditions the game has established.

It is because one can neither disrupt the game nor get away from it that there is never a rupture in the practice of literary criticism. Changes are always produced and perceived within the rules of the game, that is, within its stipulations as to what counts as a successful performance, what claims can be made, what procedures will validate or disconfirm them; and even when some of these stipulations are challenged, others must still be in place in order for the challenge to be recognized. Continuity in the practice of literary criticism is assured not despite but because of the absence of a text that is independent of interpretation. Indeed, from the perspective I have been developing, the fear of discontinuity is an incoherent one. The irony is that discontinuity is only a danger within the model erected to guard against it; for only if there is a free-standing text is there the possibility of moving away from it. But in the system I have been describing any movement away from the text is simultaneously a movement toward it, that is, toward its reappearance as an extension of whatever interpretation has come to the fore.

It could be objected that the continuity I have demonstrated is purchased at its own price, the price of an even greater incoherence attaching to the rationale for engaging in the activity at all; for if changes are to be explained with reference to the conventions of criticism rather than to the ideal of more accurately presenting an independent text, then their succession is pointless, and there is no reason, except for the opportunities made available by the conventions, to argue for one interpretation rather than another. Criticism thus becomes a supremely cynical activity in which one urges a point of view only because it is likely to win points or because it is as yet unsponsored by anyone else. In this view, while all developments are related and therefore not random, in the absence of any extrainstitutional goal such as the progressive clarification of the text, they are empty.

Not only is such a view disturbing but it seems counterintuitive given the very real sense we all have, both as critics and teachers, of advancing toward a clearer sight of our object. Jonathan Culler speaks for all of us when he declares that "often one feels that one has indeed been shown the way to a fuller understanding of literature," and, as he points out, "the time and effort devoted to literary education by generations of students and teachers creates a strong presumption that there is something to be learned, and teachers do not hesitate to judge their pupils' progress toward a general literary competence."[1] Of all the objections to the denial of determinate meaning, this is the most powerful because it trades on the fear, as Culler expresses it, "that the whole institution of literary education is but a gigantic confidence trick." That is to say, if we really believe that a text has no determinate meaning, then how can we presume to judge our students' approximations of it, and, for that matter, how can we presume to teach them anything at all? The question is the one posed by E. D. Hirsch in 1967—"On what ground does [the teacher of literature] claim that his 'reading' is more valid than that of any pupil?"—and common sense as well as professional self-respect are on the side of asserting that the ground must be something other than the accidental fact of a teacher's classroom authority.

The issue is not simply the basis of the confidence we ask our students to have in us but the basis of the confidence we might have in ourselves. How can someone who believes that the force and persuasiveness of an interpretation depends on institutional circumstances (rather than any normative standard of correctness), and that those circumstances are continually changing, argue with conviction for the interpretation he happens to hold at the present time? The answer is that the general or metacritical belief (to which I am trying to persuade you in these lectures) does not in any way affect the belief or set of beliefs (about the nature of literature, the proper mode of critical inquiry, the forms of literary evidence, and so on) which yields the interpretation that now seems to you (or me) to be inescapable and obvious. I may, in some sense, *know* that my present reading of *Paradise Lost* follows from assumptions that I did not always hold and may not hold in a year or so, but that "knowledge" does not prevent me from knowing that my present reading of *Paradise Lost* is the correct one. This is because the reservation with which I might offer my reading amounts to no more than saying "of course I may someday change my mind," but the fact that my mind may someday be other than it now is does not alter the fact that it *is* what it now is; no more than the qualifying "as far as I know" with which someone might preface an assertion means that he doesn't know what he knows —he may someday know something different, and when he does, that something will *then* be as far as he knows and he will know it no less firmly than what he knows today. An awareness that one's perspective is limited does not make the facts yielded by that perspective seem any less real; and when that perspective has given way to another, a new set of facts will occupy the position of the real ones.

Now one might think that someone whose mind had been changed many times would at some point begin to doubt the evidence of his sense, for, after all, "this too may pass," and "what I see today I may not see tomorrow." But doubting is not something one does outside the assumptions that enable one's consciousness; rather doubting, like any other mental activity, is something that one does *within* a set of assumptions that cannot at the same time be the object of doubt. That is to say, one does not doubt in a vacuum but from a perspective, and that perspective is itself immune to doubt until it has been replaced by another which will then be similarly immune. The project of radical doubt can never outrun the necessity of being situated; in order to doubt *everything*, including the ground one stands on, one must stand somewhere else, and that somewhere else will then be the ground on which one stands. This infinite regress could be halted only if one could stand free of any ground whatsoever, if the mind could divest itself of all prejudices and presuppositions and start, in the Cartesian manner, from scratch; but then of course you would have nothing to start *with* and anything with which you *did* start (even "I think, therefore I am") would be a prejudice or a presupposition. To put the matter in a slightly different way: radical skepticism is a possibility only if the mind exists independently of its furnishing, of the categories of understanding that inform it; but if, as I have been arguing, the mind is constituted by those categories, there is no possibility of achieving the distance from them that would make them available to a skeptical inquiry. In short, one cannot, properly speaking, *be* a skeptic, and one cannot be a skeptic for the same reason that one cannot be a relativist, because one cannot achieve the distance from his own beliefs and assumptions that would result in their being no more authoritative *for him* than the beliefs and assumptions held by others or the beliefs and assumptions he himself used to hold. The conclusion is tautological but inescapable: one believes what one believes, and one does so without reservation. The reservation inherent in the general position I have been arguing—that one's beliefs and therefore one's assumptions are always subject to change—has no real force, since until a change occurs the interpretation that seems self-evident to me will continue to seem so, no matter how many previous changes I can recall.

This does not mean that one is always a prisoner of his present perspective. It is always possible to entertain beliefs and opinions other than one's own; but that is precisely how they will be seen, as beliefs and opinions *other than one's own*, and therefore as beliefs and opinions that are false, or mistaken, or partial, or immature, or absurd. That is why a revolution in one's beliefs will always feel like a progress, even though, from the outside, it will have the appearance merely of a change. If one believes what one believes, then one believes that what one believes is *true,* and conversely, one believes that what one doesn't believe is not true, even if that is something one believed a moment ago. We can't help thinking that our present views are sounder than those we used to have or those professed by others. Not only does one's current position stand in a privileged relation to positions previously held, but previously held positions will always have the status of false or imperfect steps, of wrongly taken directions, of clouded or deflected perceptions. In other words, the idea of progress is inevitable, not, however, because there *is* a progress in the sense of a clearer and clearer sight of an independent object but because the *feeling* of having

progressed is an inevitable consequence of the firmness with
which we hold our beliefs, or, to be more precise, of the firmness
with which our beliefs hold us.[2]

That firmness does not preclude a certain nostalgia for the
beliefs we used to hold; the sense of progress that attends belief
is not always a comfortable one. Quite often we find it incon-
venient to believe the things we currently believe, but we find
too that it is impossible not to believe them. The recent history
of formal linguistics provides a nice example. Whatever judgment history will finally make on the "Chomsky revolution,"
there can be no doubt of its effects on the practitioners of the
discipline. The promise, held out by the generative model, that
linguistic behavior could be reduced to a set of abstract formal
rules with built-in recursive functions united linguists in a sustained and exhilirating search for those rules. Not only did success seem just around the corner but the generality of the model
(it seemed to offer no less than a picture of the operations of the
human mind) was such that it recommended itself to a succession of neighboring and not so neighboring disciplines—an-
thropology, philosophy, sociology, psychology, educational theory, literary criticism. Suddenly in each of these fields one heard
the increasingly familiar talk of transformations, deep and surface structures, the distinction between competence and performance, and so on. Linguistics, which had occupied a position in the intellectual world not unlike that of Classics—well
thought of but little attended to—suddenly found itself at the
center of discussion and debate. In the late sixties, however, a
group of Chomsky's best students mounted a disquieting and
finally successful challenge to the model within whose assumptions researchers were working by pointing to data that could
not be accommodated within those assumptions. In a classic
instance of a Kuhnian paradigm shift, the now orthodox Chom-
skians (defending what they called, significantly, the "standard
theory") responded by either ignoring the data, or consigning
them to the wastebasket of "performance," or declaring them
to be assimilable within the standard model given a few minor
revisions or refinements (here a key phrase was "notational
variant"). In time, however, the weight of the unassimilable

data proved too much for the model, and it more or less collapsed, taking with it much of the euphoria and optimism that had energized the field for a brief but glorious period. The workers in the field (or at least many of them) were in the position of no longer being able to believe in something they would have liked to believe in.

One sees this clearly, for example, in the opening paragraph of Barbara Partee's survey, in 1971, of linguistic metatheory:

> It was much easier to teach a course in syntax in 1965 or 1966 than it is now. In 1965 we had Chomsky's *Aspects* model, and if one didn't pay too much attention to disquieting things like Lakoff's thesis and Postal's underground *Linguistic anarchy notes,* one could present a pretty clear picture of syntax with a well understood phonological component tacked on one end and a not-yet-worked-out imaginable semantic component tacked on the other end. There were plenty of unsolved problems to work on, but the *paradigm* (in Kuhn's sense) seemed clear. But now we're in a situation where there is no theory which is both worked out in a substantial and presentable form and compatible with all the data considered important.[3]

In the face of this situation, Professor Partee finds herself still teaching the *Aspects* model, but only as an "elegant solution" to some syntactic problems; she spends most of her time, she reports, showing her students the "data which doesn't seem amenable to treatment in the framework at all" (p. 652). This is not what she would like to do, but what she *has* to do. "I'm by now sure," she declares regretfully, "that the Katz-Postal-*Aspects* model can't work, and I consider that a great pity" (p. 675). Pity or not, she can't help herself. No matter how convenient it would be if she still believed in the *Aspects* model— convenient for her teaching, for her research, for her confidence in the very future of the discipline—she can only believe what she believes. That is, she can't *will* a belief in the *Aspects* model any more than she can will a disbelief in the arguments that persuaded her that it was unworkable. (Willing, like doubting, is an action of the mind, and like doubting, it cannot be performed outside the beliefs that are the mind's furniture.)

In literary studies the analogous situation would be one in

which a critic or teacher felt compelled (against his wishes, if
not his will) to give up an interpretation because it no longer
seemed as self-evident as it once did. I myself am now precisely
in that position with respect to Spenser's *Shepheardes Calender*.
For more than fifteen years I have taught the *Calender* as a serious exploration of pastoral attitudes and possibilities, as a sequence more or less preliminary to Milton's "Lycidas"; but recently I have been persuaded to a different idea of pastoral, one
less serious (in the sense of solemn) and more informed by a
spirit of play and playful inquiry. As a result when I now look
at the *Calender,* I no longer see what I used to see and things
that I never saw before now seem obvious and indisputable.
Moreover, my sense of which eclogues are central, and in what
ways, has changed entirely so that I am now (self-) deprived of
some of the set pieces with which I used to adorn my teaching.
Instead, I spend most of my time talking about eclogues to
which I had previously paid no attention at all, and fielding questions that sound disconcertingly like objections from my former
self.

Of course everyone will have had similar experiences, and
they will all point to the same conclusion: not only does one
believe what one believes but one *teaches* what one believes even
if it would be easier and safer and more immediately satisfying
to teach something else. No one ever tells a class that he will
not teach the interpretation he believes in because he thinks
that the interpretation he used to believe in is better. If he
thought that his former interpretation was better, he would
still believe in it, because to believe in an interpretation is to
think that it is better. And since you will always believe in something, there will always be something to teach, and you will
teach that something with all the confidence and enthusiasm
that attends belief, even if you know, as I do, that the belief
which gives you that something, and gives it to you so firmly,
may change. The question sometimes put to me—"If what you
are saying is true, what is the point of teaching or arguing for
anything?"—misses *my* point, which is not that there is no
perspective within which one may proceed confidently but that
one is always and already proceeding within just such a perspec-

tive because one is always and already proceeding within a structure of beliefs. The fact that a standard of truth is never available independently of a set of beliefs does not mean that we can never know for certain what is true but that we *always* know for certain what is true (because we are always in the grip of some belief or other), even though what we certainly know may change if and when our beliefs change. Until they do, however, we will argue *from* their perspective and *for* their perspective, telling our students and readers what it is that we certainly see and trying to alter their perceptions so that, in time, they will come to see it too.

In short, we try to persuade others to our beliefs because if they believe what we believe, they will, as a consequence of those beliefs, see what we see; and the facts to which we point in order to support our interpretations will be as obvious to them as they are to us. Indeed, this is the whole of critical activity, an attempt on the part of one party to alter the beliefs of another so that the evidence cited by the first will be seen *as* evidence by the second. In the more familiar model of critical activity (codified in the dogma and practices of New Criticism) the procedure is exactly the reverse: evidence available apart from any particular belief is brought in to judge between competing beliefs, or, as we call them in literary studies, interpretations. This is a model derived from an analogy to the procedures of logic and scientific inquiry, and basically it is a model of *demonstration* in which interpretations are either confirmed or disconfirmed by facts that are independently specified. The model I have been arguing for, on the other hand, is a model of *persuasion* in which the facts that one cites are available only because an interpretation (at least in its general and broad outlines) has already been assumed. In the first model critical activity is controlled by free-standing objects in relation to which its accounts are either adequate or inadequate; in the other model critical activity is constitutive of its object. In one model the self must be purged of its prejudices and presuppositions so as to see clearly a text that is independent of them; in the other, prejudicial or perspectival perception is all there is, and the question is from which of a number of equally interested per-

spectives will the text be constituted. In one model change is (at least ideally) progressive, a movement toward a more accurate account of a fixed and stable entity; in the other, change occurs when one perspective dislodges another and brings with it entities that had not before been available.

Obviously the stakes are much higher in a persuasion than in a demonstration model, since they include nothing less than the very conditions under which the game, in all of its moves (description, evaluation, validation, and so on), will be played. That is why Jonathan Culler is only half right when he says that "the possibility of bringing someone to see that a particular interpretation is a good one assumes shared points of departure and common notions of how to read" (p. 28). Culler is right to insist that notions of correctness and acceptability are institution-specific and that knowledge of these "shared points of departure" is a prerequisite of what he calls "literary competence." But he is wrong to imply (as he does here and elsewhere) that literary competence is an unchanging set of rules or operations to which critics must submit in order to be recognized as players in the game. Culler's model of critical activity is one that will hold for the majority of critical performances; for it is certainly true that most of the articles we read and write do little more than confirm or extend assumptions that are already in place. But the activity that is most highly valued by the institution (even if it is often resisted) is more radically innovative. The greatest rewards of our profession are reserved for those who challenge the assumptions within which ordinary practices go on, not so much in order to eliminate the category of the ordinary but in order to redefine it and reshape its configurations. This act of challenging and redefining can occur at any number of levels: one can seek to overturn the interpretation of a single work, or recharacterize the entire canon of an important author, or argue for an entirely new realignment of genres, or question the notion of genre itself, or even propose a new definition of literature and a new account of its function in the world. At any of these levels one will necessarily begin, as Culler says, "with shared points of departure and common notions of how to read," but the goal of the performance will be the refashion-

ing of those very notions and the establishments of new points of departure. That is why, as I said, the stakes in a persuasion model are so high. In a demonstration model our task is to be adequate to the description of objects that exist independently of our activities; we may fail or we may succeed, but whatever we do the objects of our attention will retain their ontological separateness and still be what they were before we approached them. In a model of persuasion, however, our activities are directly constitutive of those objects, and of the terms in which they can be described, and of the standards by which they can be evaluated. The responsibilities of the critic under this model are very great indeed, for rather than being merely a player in the game, he is a maker and unmaker of its rules.

That does not, however, mean that he (or you or I) is ever without rules or texts or standards or "shared points of departure and common notions of how to read." It has been my strategy in these lectures to demonstrate how little we lose by acknowledging that it is persuasion and not demonstration that we practice. We have everything that we always had—texts, standards, norms, criteria of judgment, critical histories, and so on. We can convince others that they are wrong, argue that one interpretation is better than another, cite evidence in support of the interpretations we prefer; it is just that we do all those things within a set of institutional assumptions that can themselves become the objects of dispute. This in turn means that while we still have all the things we had before (texts, standards, norms, criteria of judgment), we do not always have them in the same form. Rather than a loss, however, this is a gain, because it provides us with a principled account of change and allows us to explain to ourselves and to others why, if a Shakespeare sonnet is only 14 lines long, we haven't been able to get it right after four hundred years.

It also allows us to make sense of the history of literary criticism, which under the old model can only be the record of the rather dismal performances of men—like Sidney, Dryden, Pope, Coleridge, Arnold—who simply did not understand literature and literary values as well as we do. Now we can regard those performances not as unsuccessful attempts to approximate our own but as extensions of a literary culture whose assumptions were not inferior but merely different. That is, once we give up the essentialist notions that inform a demonstration model—the notion that literature is a monolith and that there is a single set of operations by which its characteristics are discovered and evaluated—we are free to consider the various forms the literary institution has taken and to uncover the interpretative strategies by which its canons have been produced and understood. But perhaps the greatest gain that falls to us under a persuasion model is a greatly enhanced sense of the importance of our activities. (In certain quarters of course, where the critical ideal is one of self-effacement, this will be perceived to be the greatest danger.) No longer is the critic the humble servant of texts whose glories exist independently of anything he might do; it is what he does, within the constraints embedded in the literary institution, that brings texts into being and makes them available for analysis and appreciation. The practice of literary criticism is not something one must apologize for; it is absolutely essential not only to the maintenance of, but to the very production of, the objects of its attention.

Two questions remain and they are both concerned with what the poststructuralists would term "the status of my own discourse." I have been saying that all arguments are made within assumptions and presuppositions that are themselves subject to challenge and change. Well, isn't that also an argument, and one therefore that is no more securely based than the arguments it seeks to dislodge? The answer, of course, is yes; but the answer is also "so what?" According to the position presented here, no one can claim privilege for the point of view he holds and therefore everyone is obliged to practice the art of persuasion. This includes me, and persuasion is the art that I have been trying to practice here. I have not merely presented my position; I have been arguing for it, and I have been arguing for it in a way that can serve as an example (not necessarily a successful one) of how one must proceed if one operates within a model of persuasion. The first thing that one must do is not assume that he is preaching to the converted. That means that whatever the point of view you wish to establish, you will have to establish it in the face of anticipated objections. In general, people resist what you have to say when it seems to them to have undesirable or even disastrous consequences. With respect to what I have been saying, those consequences include the absence of any standards by which one could determine error, the impossibility of preferring one interpretation to another, an inability to explain the mechanisms by which interpretations are accepted and rejected, or the source of the feeling we all have of progressing, and so on. It has been my strategy to speak to these fears, one by one, and to remove them by showing that dire consequences do not follow from the position I espouse and that in fact it is only within that position that one can account for the phenomena my opponents wish to preserve. In short, I have been trying to persuade you to believe what I believe because it is in your own best interests as *you* understand them. (Notice that the determination of what would count as being persuasive is a function of what is understood to be at stake. That is, the mechanisms of persuasion, like everything else, are context-specific; what will be persuasive in any argument depends on what the parties have agreed to in advance; there must be some shared assumption about what is important and necessary and undesirable, for if there were not, neither party could make a point that would be recognized by the other as telling.)

Of course there is always the possibility that it could happen the other way around: you could persuade me that everything I want to preserve depends on a position other than the one I hold, and if you did that, your position would then be mine and I would believe what you believe; but until that happens I will argue for my position with all the confidence that attends belief even though I know that under certain conditions at some time in the future I might believe something else. Another way to put this is to say that the fact that I am subject to the same challenge I have put to my predecessors is not a weakness in my position but a restatement of it. The idea of a position that was invulnerable to challenge makes sense only if you believe in the possibility of a position innocent of assumptions; this of course is exactly what I do not believe and therefore the fact that my assumptions are capable of being dislodged does not refute my argument but confirms it, because it is an extension of it.

The final question concerns the practical consequences of that argument. Since it is primarily a literary argument, one wonders what implications it has for the practice of literary criticism. The answer is, none whatsoever. That is, it does not follow from what I have been saying that you should go out and do literary criticism in a certain way or refrain from doing it in other ways. The reason for this is that the position I have been presenting is not one that you (or anyone else) could live by. Its thesis is that whatever seems to you to be obvious and inescapable is only so within some institutional or conventional structure, and that means that you can never operate outside some such structure, even if you are persuaded by the thesis. As soon as you descend from theoretical reasoning about your assumptions, you will once again inhabit them and you will inhabit them without any reservations whatsoever; so that when you are called on to talk about Milton or Wordsworth or Yeats, you will do so from within whatever beliefs you held about these authors. The fear that one consequence of this position might be that you would be unable to do practical criticism depends on the possibility of your not believing anything at all about them; but it is impossible even to think about them independently of some or other belief, and so long as you can think about them, there is no danger of your being without something to say or without the confidence to say it. That is why this is not a position you can live by, because to live by it you would have to be forever analyzing beliefs, without ever being committed to any, and that is not a position any of us can occupy. It is, however, a position that we are all living *out,* as one set of firmly held beliefs gives way to another, bringing with them an endless succession of practical activities that we are always able to perform.

I can imagine someone saying at this point that if your argument will have no effect on the way I read and teach poetry, why should I be interested in it? What does it matter? There are two answers to this question. The first is to point out that the question itself assumes that in order for something to be interesting, it must directly affect our everyday experience of poetry; and that assumption is in turn attached to a certain antitheoretical bias built into the ideology of New Criticism. In other words, the fact that a thesis has no consequences for practical criticism is damning only from a parochial point of view and it is that point of view I have been challenging. The other answer to the question is institutional, as it must be. The elaboration of this position is something that matters because the issues it takes up are considered central to the institution's concerns. The status of the text, the source of interpretive authority, the relationship between subjectivity and objectivity, the limits of interpretation—these are topics that have been discussed again and again; they are basic topics, and anyone who is able to advance the discussion of them will automatically be accorded a hearing and be a candidate for the profession's highest rewards. One incontestable piece of evidence in support of this assertion is the fact that I have been here speaking to you for an entire week, and that you have been listening; and for that, and for very much more, I thank you.

That last has the ring of a concluding sentence, but before we adjourn I must remember to tell you the end of the story with which this series of lectures began. You will recall that my colleague was finally able to recognize his student as one of my victims and to hear her question ("Is there a text in this class?") as an inquiry into his theoretical beliefs and therefore as an inquiry into the nature of the standards and accepted practices that would be in force in his classroom. I have deliberately withheld his final reply because if I had reported it earlier you might have heard in it a ringing defense of determinate meaning as something available independently of social and institutional circumstances. But if I have been at all persuasive, you will now be able to hear it as a testimony to the power of social and institutional circumstances to establish norms of behavior not despite, but because of, the absence of transcendental norms. He said: "Yes, there *is* a text in this class; what's more, it has meanings; and I am going to tell you what they are."

Notes

1. Literature in the Reader

1. *The Verbal Icon* (Lexington: University of Kentucky Press, 1954), p. 21.

2. Thus the line could read: "They did not not perceive," which is not the same as saying they did perceive. (The question is still open.) One could also argue that "not" is not really a negative.

3. Of course, "That" is no longer read as "the fact that," but this is because the order of the clauses has resulted in the ruling out of that possibility.

4. This is not true of the Oxford school of ordinary language philosophers (Austin, Grice, Searle), who discuss meaning in terms of hearer–speaker relationships and intention–response conventions, that is, "situational meaning."

5. I borrow this phrase from P. W. Bridgman, *The Way Things Are* (Cambridge: Harvard University Press, 1959).

6. Ed. W. C. Helmbold and W. G. Rabinowitz (New York: Liberal Arts Press, 1956), p. 53.

7. See Paul Alpers, *The Poetry of "The Faerie Queen"* (Princeton: Princeton University Press, 1967), where exactly this point is made.

8. Wimsatt and Beardsley, *The Verbal Icon*, p. 34.

9. Ronald Wardhaugh, *Reading: A Linguistic Perspective* (New York: Harcourt, Brace & World, 1969), p. 60.

10. That is to say, there is a large difference between the two competences. One is uniform through human history, the other different at different points in it.

11. *Syntactic Structures* (The Hague: Mouton, 1957), pp. 21–24.

12. See Wardhaugh, *Reading*, p. 55: "Sentences have a 'depth' to them, a depth which grammatical models such as phrase structure models and generative-transformational models attempt to represent. These models suggest that if a left-to-rightness principle is relevant to sentence processing, it must be a left-to-rightness of an extremely sophisticated kind that requires processing to take place concurrently at several levels, many of which are highly abstract; phonological or graphological, structural, and semantic."

13. *Language and Mind* (New York: Harcourt, Brace & World, 1968), p. 32.

14. *The Rhetoric of Fiction* (Chicago: University of Chicago Press, 1961), p. 139.

15. What follows is by no means exhaustive; it is selective in three directions. First, I arbitrarily exclude, and therefore lump together in one undifferentiated mass, all those whose models of production and comprehension are primarily spatial; all those who are more interested in what goes into a work rather than what goes into and out of the reader; all those who offer top to bottom rather than left to right analyses: statisticians of style (Curtis Hayes, Josephine Miles, John Carroll), descriptive linguists (Halliday and Company), formalist-structuralists (Roman Jakobson, Roland Barthes), and many more. (In the longer study to which this essay is preliminary, these men and women will be considered and discriminated.) I am also selective in my discussion of psychologically oriented critics; and within that selection I must make further apologies for considering their work only in relation to my own methodological concerns, which are on the whole narrower and less ambitious than theirs. In short, with the possible exception of Michael Riffaterre, I shall do less than justice to my predecessors.

16. *Principles of Literary Criticism* (New York: Harcourt, Brace & World, 1959 [1924]), pp. 20–22.

17. London: K. Paul, Trench, Trubner, 1926.

18. London: K. Paul, Trench, Trubner, 1929.

19. *The Structure of Complex Words* (London: Chatto & Windus, 1951), pp. 10, 56–57.

20. "Criticism and the Language of Literature: Some Traditions and Trends in Great Britain," *Style,* 3 (1969), 59.

21. *Some Versions of Pastoral* (Norfolk, Conn.: New Directions), p. 121.

22. "Describing Poetic Structures," *Yale French Studies,* 36–37 (1966).

23. "Criteria for Style Analysis," *Word* 15 (1959), 158.

24. *Word,* 16 (1960).

25. "The Stylistic Function," *Proceedings of the Ninth International Congress of Linguistics* (The Hague: Mouton, 1964), pp. 320, 321.

26. "Criteria for Style Analysis," pp. 154–155.

27. "Stylistic Context," p. 207.

28. "Describing Poetic Structures," pp. 215–216.

29. Ibid., p. 223.

30. "Criteria for Style Analysis," pp. 172—173.

31. Since this essay was written I have had the opportunity to read Walter J. Slatoff's *With Respect to Readers: Dimensions of Literary Response* (Ithaca: Cornell University Press, 1970), a new book which addresses itself, at least rhetorically, to many of the issues raised here. The direction Slatoff takes, however, is quite different from mine.

The chief difference (and difficulty) is Slatoff's notion of what constitutes "response." In his analyses, response is something that occurs either before or after the activity of reading. What concerns him is really not response, in the sense of the interaction between the flow of word on the page and an active mediating consciousness, but a response to that response. Recalling Conrad Aiken's description of Faulkner's novels as "a calculated system of screens and obtrusions, of confusions and ambiguous interpolations and delays," Slatoff makes the following distinction on the basis, or so he would claim, of a "divergence in responses": "Some actively enjoy the delays and suspensions of a writer like Faulkner; others can barely abide them; still others are deeply ambivalent. Similarly we must vary greatly in our instinctive responses" (p. 62). Now "response" here clearly means what a reader is, by nature, disposed to like or dislike; and in that context there is surely a divergence. But there is no divergence at the level of response which is preliminary to this disposition. Whether the reader likes or dislikes or both likes and dislikes the experience of Faulkner's delays he will, in common with every other reader, experience them. That is, he will negotiate the confusions, struggle through the screens, endure the suspensions; and of course this uniformity of experience (and of response) is acknowledged by Slatoff himself when he makes it the basis of his observation of difference.

It could be said I suppose that Slatoff and I are simply interested in different stages of response: I am concerned with the response that *is* the act of perception, the moment-to-moment experience of adjusting to the sequential demands of prose and poetry, while Slatoff speculates on the "divergent" attitudes (what he really means by "response") a reader might take toward that experience after he has had it. But the case is more serious than that because Slatoff confuses the two (I wonder if they can really be separated) and makes the variability of one the basis of denying the uniformity of the other, even though it is that uniformity which makes talk about divergence possible.

The two thesis chapters of the book are entitled "Varieties of Involvement" and "The Divergence of Responses," and it becomes increasingly clear that the variations and divergences occur when a finished reader encounters a finished work. That is, in his theory the work is a respository of properties and meanings (corresponding to the intention of the author) which then come into contact with a reader more or less comformable to them. In other words, his is an "adversary" model—work *versus* reader—in which readers, rather than actualizing meanings, react to them on the basis of attitudes they hold prior to the encounter.

In the end, Slatoff's program for putting the reader back into reading amounts to no more than this: acknowledging the fact that a reader has likes and dislikes which are not always compatible with the likes and dislikes informing a particular work. Despite his pronouncements to the contrary, Slatoff finally effects a radical divorce between work and reader and, what is more important, between reader and meaning. They are fixed in their respective positions before they meet, and their interaction does nothing but define the degree of their incompatibility. This is all that Slatoff intends by the phrase "divergence of response," and since the divergence is from a received (that is, handed over) meaning—a response *after* the fact, whereas in my model the response *is* the fact—it can be tolerated without compromising the integrity of the work. Indeed, it can be celebrated, and this is exactly what Slatoff proceeds to do in the name, of course, of relevance.

2. What Is Stylistics?

1. "Unconscious Ordering in the Prose of Swift," in *The Computer and Literary Style,* ed. Jacob Leed (Kent, Ohio: Kent State University Press, 1966), pp. 79–106.

2. Roman Jakobson and Morris Halle, *The Fundamentals of Language* (The Hague: Mouton, 1955), pp. 69–96.

3. "Generative Grammars and the Concept of Literary Style," in *Contemporary Essays on Style,* ed. Glen A. Love and Michael Payne (Glenview, Ill.: Scott, Foresman, 1969), pp. 133–148. This essay originally appeared in *Word,* 20 (December 1964), 423–439.

4. Ibid., p. 148.

5. "Literature as Sentences," in *Contemporary Essays on Style,* p. 154. This essay originally appeared in *College English,* 27 (January 1966), 261–267.

6. Ibid., p. 156.

7. Ibid., p. 154.

8. *Contemporary Essays on Style,* p. 143.

9. J. P. Thorne, "Generative Grammar and Stylistic Analysis," in *New Horizons in Linguistics,* ed. John Lyons (Baltimore: Penguin, 1970), p. 188.

10. For other examples of Thorne's work, see "Stylistic and Generative Grammars," *Journal of Linguistics,* 1 (1965), 49–59; "Poetry, Stylistics and Imaginary Grammars," *Journal of Linguistics,* 5 (1969), 147–150.

11. *Contemporary Essays on Style,* pp. 152–153.

12. Roderick A. Jacobs and Peter S. Rosenbaum, *Transformations, Style and Meaning* (Waltham, Mass.: Xerox College Publishing, 1971), pp. 103–106.

13. My argument here has affinities with Hubert Dreyfus's explanation in *What Computers Can't Do* (New York: Harper & Row, 1972) of the impasse at which programmers of artificial intelligence find themselves. "The programmer must either claim that some features are intrinsically relevant and have a fixed meaning regardless of content . . . or the programmer will be faced with an infinite regress of contexts" (p. 133). Dreyfus's conclusion anticipates the proposal I will offer at the end of this essay for the reform of stylistics. "Human beings seem to embody a third possibility which would offer a way out of this dilemma. Instead of a hierarchy of contexts, the present situation is recognized as a continuation or modification of

the previous one. Thus we carry over from the immediate past a set of anticipations based on what was relevant and important a moment ago. This carry-over gives us certain predispositions as to what is worth noticing" (p. 134).

14. In *Literary Style: A Symposium,* ed. Seymour Chatman (New York: Oxford University Press, 1971), pp. 330–365. See also Halliday, "Categories of the Theory of Grammar," *Word,* 17 (1961), 241–292; "The Linguistic Study of Literary Texts," in *Proceedings of the Ninth International Congress of Linguistics,* ed. H. Hunt (The Hague: Mouton, 1964), pp. 302–307; "Descriptive Linguistics in Literary Studies," in *Linguistics and Literary Style,* ed. Donald C. Freeman (New York: Holt, Rinehart and Winston, 1970), pp. 57–72; "Notes of Transitivity and Theme in English," *Journal of Linguistics,* 3 (1967), 37–81, 199–244, and *Journal of Linguistics,* 4 (1968), 179–215; "Language Structure and Language Function," in *New Horizons in Linguistics,* pp. 140–165. For an exposition of Halliday's grammar and its application to literary analysis, see John Spencer and Michael J. Gregory, "An Approach to the Study of Style," in *Linguistics and Literary Style,* pp. 59–105. For a critique of the tradition in which Halliday works, see D. T. Langendoen, *The London School of Linguistics* (Cambridge: M.I.T. Press, 1968).

15. *Literary Style: A Symposium,* p. 339.

16. Martin Joos, "Linguistic Prospects in the United States," in *Trends in European and American Linguistics,* ed. Christine Mohrmann (Utrecht: Spectrum, 1961), p. 18.

17. John R. Searle, *Speech Acts: An Essay in the Philosophy of Language* (Cambridge: Cambridge University Press, 1969), p. 52.

18. *What Computers Can't Do,* p. 200.

19. "Criteria for Style Analysis," *Word,* 15 (1959), 164.

20. "Describing Poetic Structures," in *Structuralism,* ed. Jacques Ehrmann (New York: Doubleday/Anchor, 1970), p. 197. This volume was originally published in 1966 as numbers 36 and 37 of *Yale French Studies.*

21. Ibid. See also "Criteria for Style Analysis," p. 164.

22. See "Literature as Act," in *Approaches to Poetics,* ed. Seymour Chatman (New York: Columbia University Press, 1973), pp. 81–108; "Speech Acts and the Definition of Literature," *Philosophy and Rhetoric,* 4 (Winter 1971), 1–19; "Speech, Action and Style," in *Literary Style: A Symposium,* pp. 241–259; "Speech, Literature, and the Space Between," *New Literary History,* 4 (Autumn 1972), 47–64; "Instrumental Style: Notes on the Theory of Speech as Actions," in *Current Trends in Stylistics,* ed. Braj. B. Kachru (Edmonton, 1972).

23. "Speech Acts," p. 25.

24. See "Speech, Action, and Style," pp. 249–250.

25. That is to say, stylistics requires that there be two separate systems— one of content or message, the other of everything else—which it is the stylistician's job to match up or correlate. Otherwise, they complain, there

would be nothing for them to do. Ohmann is consistent in his dualism from his earliest writings (when his grammar was structural) to his "middle period" (when the deep-surface distinction of transformational grammar seemed to give new authorization to the form-content split) to the present day (when the illocutionary force–propositional content distinction serves the same need). In "Instrumental Style" (manuscript) he states, [In] the distinction between the unactivated meaning and the fully launched illocutionary act we have the kind of split required for style to exist."

26. "Speech Acts," p. 13. The definition is impossible because discourse without illocutionary force would be discourse unrelated to the conventions of everyday speech and therefore discourse that was unintelligible (just a series of noises). To put in another way, the language of literature would be wholly discontinuous with the language we ordinarily speak, and in order to read it one would have to learn it from scratch. (Of course there *are* special poetic vocabularies, for example, silver-age Latin, but these are always precisely parallel to, that is, paristic on, everyday usage.) Ohmann seems aware of this difficulty in his definition, since he modifies it on the very next page, admitting that a literary work has illocutionary force, but declaring that it is "mimetic." These mimetic speech acts, however, turn out to be just like real ones, and it seems that this strange class has been instituted only to remedy the deficiency of the original definition.

27. That is, like the stylisticians, the structuralists dislodge man from his privileged position as the originator of meanings, and locate meaning instead in the self-sufficient operation of a timeless formalism. The difference in that they do consciously what the stylisticians do inadvertently; they deliberately raise the implied antihumanism of other formalist methodologies to a principle. The parallel holds too in the matter of interpretation. Since the structuralists' goal is the system of signifiers—intelligibility rather than what is made intelligible—they either decline interpretation or perform it in such a way as to make its arbitrary contingent nature inescapable; see for example Roland Barthes, *S/Z* (Paris: Editions du Seuil, 1970). Again the similarity with what the stylisticians do is less important than the self-consciousness with which it is done. One may disagree with the assumptions impelling the structuralists' enterprise, but one cannot accuse them of being unaware of those assumptions.

28. "A Framework for the Statistical Analysis of Style," in *Statistics and Style,* ed. Lubomir Doležel and Richard W. Bailey (New York: American Elsevier, 1969), p. 22.

29. Indeed the stylisticians often make incredibily damaging admissions and then walk away from them as if their entire program were still intact. Two examples from the work of Manfred Bierwisch will have to suffice. In an article entitled "Semantics" written for *New Horizons in Linguistics* Bierwisch points out that a semantic theory will have to be able "to explain how one of the several meanings associated with a particular word or sentence is selected in accordance with a particular universe of dis-

course" (p. 183). He then admits that at the present time there seems no way precisely to formalize (that is, make predictable) the process by which, for example, the various meanings of the word "group" are selected; but he can still conclude (with no warrant whatsoever) that "although little progress has yet been made in the systematic treatment of these problems, they do not seem to pose difficulties of principle" (p. 184). In another of his articles, the problem is not an unsupported conclusion but a conclusion he fails to make. The article is "Poetics and Linguistics" (in *Lingustics and Literary Style*) and at the close of it Bierwisch points out that references in poems to to other poems or to other universes of discourse (for example, art history) "can never be expressed in an exhaustive linguistic semantics and . . . thus mark . . . the boundaries of a complete theory of poetic effect and style" (p. 112). The conclusion that he does not reach (although it seems inescapable) is that a theory with those limitations is of questionable value.

30. See "Literature in the Reader" (chap. 1, above); see also *Self-Consuming Artifacts: The Experience of Seventeenth-Century Literature* (Berkeley: University of California Press, 1972) and *Surprised by Sin: The Reader in Paradise Lost* (New York and London: Macmillan, 1967).

31. Louis Milic, "Connectives in Swift's Prose Style," in *Linguistics and Literary Style*, pp. 243–257.

32. *Contemporary Essays on Style*, p. 156.

33. Let me take the opportunity this example offers to clarify what I mean by *the* reader or, as I have elsewhere termed him, the "informed" reader. There are at least four potential readers of this sentence: (1) the reader for whom the name Iago means nothing; (2) the reader who knows that Iago is a character in a play by Shakespeare; (3) the reader who has read the play; (4) the reader who is aware that the question has its own history, that everyone has had a whack at answering it, and that it has become a paradigm question for the philosophical-moral problem of motivation. Now each of these readers will assume the role of answerer because each of them (presumably) is a native speaker of English who knows what is involved in a felicitous question. (His knowledge is the content of Searle's formalizations.) But the precision with which that role is played will be a function of the reader's particular knowledge of Iago. That is, the reader who is a member of my fourth class will not only recognize that he is being asked to perform the activity of answering but will perform it in a very specific direction (and consequently the speaker's withdrawal from that direction will be felt by him all the more sharply). He will be my informed reader and I would want to say that his experience of the sentence will be not only different from, but better than, his less-informed fellows. Note that this is not a distinction between real and ideal readers; all the readers are real, as are all their experiences. Nor do I assume a uniformity of attitude and opinion among informed readers. Some readers may believe that Iago is motivated by jealousy, others that he is motiveless, still others

that he is not evil but heroic. It is the ability of the reader to have an opinion (or even to know that having an opinion is what is called for), and not the opinion he has, which makes him informed in my sense; for then, no matter what opinion he has, he will have committed himself to considering the issues of motivation and agency. That commitment will be the *content* of his experience and it will not be the content of the experience of readers less informed than he.

34. Again my argument intersects with that of Dreyfus in *What Computers Can't Do:* "There must be some way of avoiding the self-contradictory regress of contexts, or the incomprehensible notion of recognizing an ultimate context, as the only way of giving significance to independent, neutral facts. The only way out seems to be to deny the separation of fact and situation . . . to give up the independence of the facts and understand them as a product of the situation. This would amount to arguing that only in terms of situationally determined relevance are there any facts at all" (p. 136).

35. Roger Fowler, *The Languages of Literature: Some Linguistic Contributions to Criticism* (London: Barnes & Noble, 1971), pp. 38–39.

36. The resulting "single-shot" procedure also spells the end of another distinction, the distinction between style and meaning. This distinction depends on the primacy of propositional content (that which it is the reader's job to extract), but in an analysis which has as its object the structure of the reader's experience, the achieving of propositional clarity is only one among many activities, and there is no warrant for making it the privileged center in relation to which all other activities are either appendages or excrescences. Rather than the traditional dichotomy between process and product (the how and the what), everything becomes process and nothing is granted the stability that would lead to its being designated "content." Thus there is only style, or, if you prefer, there is only meaning, and what the philosophers have traditionally called meaning becomes an abstraction from the total meaning experience. Describing that experience becomes the goal of analysis and the resulting shape is both the form and the content of the description. (This is a "monism" not open to the usual objection that it leaves you with nothing to do.)

37. I am thinking, for example, of the work of T. G. Bever. See "Perceptions, Thought, and Language," in *Language Comprehension and the Acquisition of Knowledge,* ed. Roy O. Freedle and John B. Carroll (New York: Halsted Press, 1972), pp. 99–112.

3. How Ordinary Is Ordinary Language?

This is an expanded version of a paper originally read before the meeting of General Topics I (Poetic Theory) in New York, December 1972.

1. "From Linguistics to Criticism," *Kenyon Review,* 13 (1951), 713.

2. "The Application of Linguistics to the Study of Poetic Language," in *Style in Language,* ed. Thomas A. Sebeok (Cambridge: M.I.T. Press, 1960), p. 83.

3. "Notes on Linguistics and Literature," *College English,* 32 (1970), 184.

4. For a recent confrontation see the essays by Roger Fowler and F. W. Bateson in *The Languages of Literature: Some Linguistic Contributions to Criticism,* ed. Roger Fowler (London: Barnes & Noble, 1971), pp. 43–79. See also William Youngren, *Semantics, Linguistics, and Criticism* (New York: Random House, 1972), and T. K. Pratt, "Linguistics, Criticism, and Smollett's *Roderick Random,*" *University of Toronto Quarterly,* 42 (1972), 26–99. Youngren and Bateson line up on the Schwartz side, arguing that criticism and linguistics are simply different kinds of activities. Fowler and Pratt, on the other hand, regard it as axiomatic that a connection between the two disciplines exists.

5. Gordon Messing, "The Impact of Transformational Grammar upon Stylistics and Literary Analysis," *Linguistics,* 66 (1971), 65.

6. David H. Hirsch, "Linguistic Structure and Literary Meaning," *Journal of Literary Semantics,* 20, no. 1 (1972), 86.

7. *Semantics, Linguistics, and Criticism,* pp. 101–113.

8. On this point see pp. 100–101.

9. In addition to those cited in note 4, see Mark Lester, "The Relation of Linguistics to Literature," *College English,* 30 (1969), 367, 375; Manfred Bierwisch, "Poetics and Linguistics," in *Linguistics and Literary Style,* ed. Donald C. Freeman (New York: Holt, Rinehart and Winston, 1970), pp. 111–112; Bennison Gray, "Stylistics: The End of a Tradition," *FAAC,* 31 (1973), 501–504.

See also in the Autumn 1972 issue of *New Literary History:* Henryk Markiewicz, "The Limits of Literature," pp. 6–9; George Steiner, "Whorf, Chomsky and the Student of Literature," pp. 30–31; Manuel Duran, "Inside the Glass Cage: Poetry and 'Normal' Language," pp. 66–67; Richard Kuhns, "Semantics for Literary Languages," p. 103. The easy confidence with which these writers distinguish between ordinary language and literature is questioned in two commentaries by Francis Berry and Paul de Man. De Man's caveat on page 181 seems to me particularly incisive: "Taking for granted there is such a thing as 'literary language,' one can describe a particular subset of the class, but as soon as one confronts the question of defining the specificity of literary language as such, complications arise."

10. "Unconscious Ordering in the Prose of Swift," in *The Computer and Literary Style,* ed. Jacob Leed (Kent, Ohio: Kent State University Press, 1966), p. 80.

11. Louis Milic, "Connectives in Swift's Prose Style," in *Linguistics and Literary Style,* p. 253. In another article Milic goes so far as to connect Swift's stylistic habits with his "eventual lunacy": "Rhetorical Choice and Stylistic Option," in *Literary Style: A Symposium,* ed. Seymour Chatman (New York: Oxford University Press, 1971), p. 86.

12. W. K. Wimsatt, "Style as Meaning," in *Essays on the Language of Literature,* ed. Seymour Chatman and Samuel R. Levin (Boston: Houghton Mifflin, 1967), pp. 370–371; M. C. Beardsley, "The Language of Literature," ibid., p. 290.

13. Of course message-plus theories give the lie to the suggestion (contained in the *rhetoric* of the ordinary language/literary language distinction) that there are two orders of value. As soon as the distinction has been made and a norm has been declared, the values have been reduced to one, and logically the only definition of literature possible is message-minus. Message-plus theorists, then, are reacting to an intuition that something undersirable has occurred because of the distinction to which they perversely remain committed.

14. "Criteria for Style Analysis," in *Essays on the Language of Literature,* pp. 414–416.

15. "Closing Statement: Linguistics and Poetics," in *Style in Language,* p. 352.

16. Richard Ohmann, "Speech Acts and the Definition of Literature," *Philosophy and Rhetoric,* 4 (1971), 15.

17. "Style and Good Style," in *Contemporary Essays on Style,* ed. Glen A. Love and Michael Payne (Glenview, Ill.: Scott, Foresman, 1969), p. 8.

18. *Essays on the Language of Literature,* p. 373.

19. *Style in Language,* p. 350.

20. *New York Review of Books,* June 29, 1972, p. 23.

21. An exception is Richard Ohmann, who in a series of articles has been exploring the significance of speech act theory for literary criticism. See especially "Speech Acts and the Definition of Literature." It seems to me that Ohmann misunderstands speech-act theory and turns it into a system which drives a wedge between ordinary and literary language. See my "What Is Stylistics and Why Are They Saying Such Terrible Things about It?" (chap. 2, above). For the work of the philosophical (or generative) semanticists, see *Semantics,* ed. D. Steinberg and L. A. Jakobovits (Cambridge: Cambridge University Press, 1971), pp. 157–482.

22. "Verbs of Judging: An Exercise in Semantic Description," in *Studies in Linguistic Semantics,* ed. C. J. Fillmore and D. T. Langendoen (New York: Holt, Rinehart and Winston, 1971), p. 277.

23. Oxford: Oxford University Press, 1962.

24. John R. Searle, *Speech Acts: An Essay in the Philosophy of Language* (Cambridge: Cambridge University Press, 1969), p. 197.

25. Actually, there is no norm, since rather than a "pure" class of statements (constatives) around which the others are ranged as either appendages or excrescences, we have a continuum of speech acts, no one of which can claim primacy. Moreover, these acts are necessarily the "content" of literature just as they are the content of any other form of discourse engaged in by human beings. There is a suggestive point of contact here between speech-act theory and some pronouncements of the struc-

turalist Roland Barthes. Barthes's repeated objection to the "ideology of the referent" is an objection to the claims (of privilege) made by logical denotative language; and when he declares in *Writing Degree Zero* (London: Cape, 1967), that clarity is not a value but just another style (see *Literary Style: A Symposium,* p. xii), he is doing what Searle and Austin do when they make statements just one among many classes of speech acts. There are, of course, large differences between Oxford philosophers and the structuralists, but they are allied at least in their antipositivism. In this connection we might note, too, the practitioners of what has been called "reader-response" criticism, who reject as a goal the extraction from a text of a propositional "nugget" and concentrate instead on the activities of the reader, only *one* of which is the achieving of the propositional clarity. (See chapter 2, above.)

26. This is basically the sequence in the arguments of Ohmann, Schwartz, and Markiewicz, cited above.

27. On this point see Inger Rosengren, "Style as Choice and Deviation," *Sytle,* 6 (1972), 13. Workers in the field frankly acknowledge that the concept of style depends on the concepts of paraphrasability and synonymy: See, for example, Fowler, *Languages of Literature,* pp. 19–20; Milic, "Theories of Style and Their Implications for the Teaching of Composition," in *Contemporary Essays on Style,* pp. 15–21; Seymour Chatman, "The Semantics of Style," in *Structuralism: A Reader,* ed. Michael Lane (London: Jonathan Cape, 1970), pp. 126–128.

4. What It's Like To Read *L'Allegro* and *Il Penseroso*

This is an expanded version of a paper originally read before Section 6 of the Modern Language Association convention, December 1971.

1. V. B. Halpert, "On Coming to the Window in *L'Allegro,*" *Anglia,* 81 (1963), 200.

2. Edith Riggs, "Milton's *L'Allegro,* 41–50," *Explicator,* 23 (February 1965), item 44.

3. Cleanth Brooks and John E. Hardy, *Poems of Mr. John Milton* (New York: Harcourt, Brace, 1951), p. 136.

4. Lines 47–48. The text used throughout is from *John Milton: Complete Poetry and Major Prose,* ed. Merritt Y. Hughes (New York: Odyssey Press, 1957).

5. For a similar point, see Leslie Brisman, " 'All before Them Where to Choose': 'L'Allegro' and 'Il Penseroso,' " *Journal of English and Germanic Philology,* 71 (April 1972), 239.

6. "Structural Figures of *L'Allegro* and *Il Penseroso,*" in *Milton: Modern Essays in Criticism,* ed. Arthur E. Barker (New York: Oxford University Press, 1965), p. 61.

7. *The Well Wrought Urn* (New York: Reynal & Hitchcock, 1947), p. 54.

8. J. B. Leishman, "*L'Allegro* and *Il Penseroso* in Their Relation to Seventeenth-Century Poetry," *Essays and Studies 1951,* n.s., 4 (1951), 5.

9. D. C. Allen, *The Harmonious Vision* (Baltimore: John Hopkins University Press, 1954), p. 6.

10. *Five Pens in Hand* (New York: Doubleday, 1958), p. 39.

11. Herbert F. West, Jr., "Here's a Miltonic Discovery . . . ," *Renaissance Papers, 1958, 1959, 1960, 1961* (Columbia: Southwest Renaissance Conference), p. 73.

12. The discreteness of the details is noted by F. W. Bateson in "The Money-Lender's Son: 'L'Allegro' and 'Il Penseroso,' " in his *English Poetry: A Critical Introduction* (London: Longmans, Green, 1950), p. 159: " 'Russet' is decidedly not the epithet one would have expected for 'Lawns' . . . nor is 'Gray' what one would have expected for 'Fallows.' " But Bateson then goes on to draw exactly the wrong conclusion: "Milton must have had his eye on a real field." I would say, rather, that Milton wanted to keep the reader's eye from going to the trouble of envisioning a real field.

13. See James Hutton, "Some English Poems in Praise of Music," *English Miscellany*, 2 (1951), 46.

14. Robert Graves, "John Milton Muddles Through," *New Republic*, May 27, 1957, p. 17.

15. I do not mean that the word itself could not appear in *L'Allegro*, but that it could appear with its full logical force. It could appear if it operated (like "while" in line 49) in such a way as to gesture toward a sequence that was, in fact, not there. I would not wish to be understood as suggesting that the presence or absence of a word could automatically (that is, mechanically) be correlated with the presence or absence of a particular effect. The specification of effect always requires a taking into account of the full experiential context.

16. *The Harmonious Vision*, p. 10.

17. Ibid.

18. *A Variorum Commentary on the Poems of John Milton*, vol. 2, pt. 1, ed. A. S. P. Woodhouse and Douglas Bush (New York: Columbia University Press, 1972), p. 337. The commentary continues, "The end is to be read in the light of the beginning and particularly in that supplied by the image of the *Cherub Contemplation* when fully understood." The achieving of that full understanding is both the shape and the content of the reading experience.

19. Lines 95–96. See *Variorum Commentary*, pp. 324–326, for a full discussion of the symbols of power clustered in this passage.

20. *Voices of Melancholy* (London: Routledge and Kegan Paul, 1971), pp. 151–156. Professor Lyons goes on to point out that the central figure in *Il Penseroso* has an imagination of himself "as existing in time" (p. 152) and therefore lives in a world "of possibility and choice" (p. 155). The central figure of *L'Allegro*, on the other hand, "lives in a one day's world in which his imagined experiences follow each other as discrete and disconnected events or scenes" (p. 152). Similar points are made by Leslie Brisman, "All before Them Where To Choose."

21. Thomas G. Rosenmeyer, *The Green Cabinet* (Berkeley: University of California Press, 1969), p. 53.

22. "What Is Stylistics and Why Are They Saying Such Terrible Things about It?" (chap. 2, above).

23. See Brisman, "All before Them Where to Choose," p. 229: "The two may be conceived as choices, but choice is actualized when one has moved from the first to the second."

24. *The Harmonious Vision*, p. 23.

5. Facts and Fictions: A Reply to Ralph Rader

1. My argument will engage two of Rader's articles. They are "Fact, Theory, and Literary Explanation," *Critical Inquiry*, 1, no. 2 (December 1974), 245–272, and "The Concept of Genre and Eighteenth-Century Studies," in *New Approaches to Eighteenth-Century Literature: Selected Papers from the English Institute,* ed. Phillip Harth (New York: Columbia University Press, 1974), pp. 79–115. In what follows they will be referred to as *Fact* and *Concept* along with the appropriate page number.

2. Later *(Fact,* pp. 266–269) Rader will emend Milton's declaration of intention to read "pleasingly justify the ways of God to man." Since he has already defined "pleasingly" as without difficulty or loose ends, he can then proceed to label everything that does not contribute to an *easy* comprehension of that justification an unintended and unavoidable negative consequence of Milton's positive intention.

3. I do not believe that these agreements exist. It is just that Rader must have them, and so he invents or declares them.

4. Some linguists might now point to differences in focus and presupposition, but this would merely lend additional support to my analysis by formalizing (or attempting to formalize) the significance of sequential order, which is actually perceptual order.

5. That is why, when Rader points out *(Fact,* pp. 269–270) that a syntax held to be "expressive" of a single work *(Paradise Lost)* cannot at the same time be predicated of a whole group of works, the horns of his logical dilemma do not catch me at all. My argument is not about syntax or any other physical feature (that is, unit made available by any kind of mechanical parsing) but about readers' activities. It could be objected that these activities are empty, merely closings and openings, and that therefore in my analyses all experiences turn out to be the same. The answer is that these pieces of deliberative reasoning are always reasoning about *something.* The reader is not assuming or approving or concluding or revising or expecting in a vacuum: rather, he does these things with reference to the concerns to which the text has directed him, for example, the question of the responsibility for the Fall. In other words, these acts are not preliminary to the determining of content: they *have* content, and the content they have is the ordering or structuring which constitutes their performance. (See "Interpreting the *Variorum*," chap. 6, below.)

6. I do not like the word "preliminary" because it already devalues the phenomena to which I would call attention. That is, to accept the word is also to accept the product-oriented ontology Rader preaches.

7. In his essay Rader also raises the issues of literary vs. nonliterary discourse and evaluation. I have decided not to consider them here because I have written on them elsewhere. See "How Ordinary Is Ordinary Language?" (chap. 3, above). I might just say (predictably) that I do not believe in the distinction between literature and nonliterature (not that it hasn't been made and acted upon but that it is not a real or essential distinction; it is a convention) and that I regard evaluation not as a theoretical issue but as a subject in the history of taste.

6. Interpreting the *Variorum*

1. All references are to *The Poems of John Milton,* ed. John Carey and Alastair Fowler (London: Longmans, Green, 1968).

2. *A Variorum Commentary on the Poems of John Milton,* vol. 2, pt. 2, ed. A. S. P. Woodhouse and Douglas Bush (New York: Columbia University Press, 1972), p. 475.

3. It is first of all a reference to the city of iniquity from which the Hebrews are urged to flee in Isaiah and Jeremiah. In Protestant polemics Babylon is identified with the Roman Church whose destruction is prophesied in the book of Revelation. And in some Puritan tracts Babylon is the name for Augustine's earthly city, from which the faithful are to flee inwardly in order to escape the fate awaiting the unregenerate. See *Variorum Commentary,* pp. 440–441.

4. *Variorum Commentary,* p. 469.

5. Ibid., p. 457.

6. *Poems upon Several Occasions, English, Italian, and Latin, with Translations, by John Milton,* ed. Thomas Warton (London, 1791), p. 352.

7. See my *Surprised by Sin: The Reader in Paradise Lost* (London and New York: Macmillan, 1967); *Self-Consuming Artifacts: The Experience of Seventeenth-Century Literature* (Berkeley: University of California Press, 1972); "What Is Stylistics and Why Are They Saying Such Terrible Things About It?" (chap. 2, above); "How Ordinary Is Ordinary Language?" (chap. 3, above); "Facts and Fictions: A Reply to Ralph Rader" (chap. 5, above).

8. Structuralist Homiletics

1. Paul Ricoeur, "Symbole et temporalite," *Archivo di Filosofia,* nos. 1–2 (1963), 24.

2. Roland Barthes, "Science versus Literature," in *Structuralism: A Reader,* ed. Michael Lane (London: Jonathan Cape, 1970), p. 414.

3. Roland Barthes, "Action Sequences," in *Patterns of Literary Style,* ed. Joseph Strelka (University Park: Pennsylvania State University Press, 1971), p. 14.

4. Roland Barthes, *Writing Degree Zero,* trans. Annette Lavers and Colin Smith (London: Jonathan Cape, 1967), pp. 52–54.

5. Lancelot Andrewes, *XCVI Sermons,* 3rd ed. (London: Richard Badger, 1635), p. 531.

6. The translation is C. S. Baldwin's, taken from his *Ancient Rhetoric and Poetic* (Gloucester, Mass.: Peter Smith, 1959), pp. 148–149.

7. Baldwin, *Ancient Rhetoric and Poetic,* p. 149.

8. "Linguistics and Poetics," in *Style in Language,* ed. Thomas A. Sebeok (Cambridge: M.I.T. Press, 1960), p. 358.

9. For a demonstration and expansion of this thesis, see my *Self-Consuming Artifacts: The Experience of Seventeenth-Century Literature* (Berkeley: University of California Press, 1972).

9. How To Do Things with Austin and Searle

I gratefully acknowledge the advice and criticism of Rob Cummins, Frank Hubbard, Walter Michaels, and David Sachs, who will find here not only some of their ideas but some of their sentences.

1. Throughout I have used the edition edited by Reuben Brower (New York: Signet, 1966).

2. John Searle, *Speech Acts: An Essay in the Philosophy of Language* (Cambridge: Cambridge University Press, 1969), p. 66. Although I deploy the vocabulary of Searle's version of speech-act theory, I am not committed to its precise formulations.

3. *How To Do Things with Words* (Oxford: Oxford University Press, 1962), pp. 9–10.

4. Why they don't see this is a question beyond the scope of the present analysis, although two explanations suggest themselves: either they are stupid, or they don't want to see. These are Sicinius' explanations (II, iii, 180–182).

5. John Searle, "A Classification of Illocutionary Acts," *Language in Society,* 5 (1976), 13–14.

6. IV, iv, 6–11.

7. "The Reality of Fiction," *New Literary History,* 7, no. 1 (Autumn 1975), 7–38.

8. "Literature as Act," in *Approaches to Poetics,* ed. Seymour Chatman (New York: Columbia University Press, 1973), p. 90.

9. *How To Do Things with Words,* p. 42.

10. "Instrumental Style," in *Current Trends in Stylistics,* ed. Braj B. Kachru (Edmonton, 1972), p. 129.

11. "Speech, Action, and Style," in *Literary Style: A Symposium,* ed. Seymour Chatman (New York: Oxford University Press, 1971), p. 251.

12. *Current Trends in Stylistics,* p. 118.

13. *Speech Acts,* p. 25.

14. It is curious that Ohmann himself does what he repeatedly accuses

traditional stylistics of doing: sliding off from illocutionary to either locutionary or perlocutionary acts.

15. Richard Gale, "The Fictive Use of Language," *Philosophy*, 46 (1971), 339.

16. Richard Ohmann, "Speech, Literature and the Space Between," *New Literary History*, 4 (1972), 53.

17. John Searle, "The Logical Status of Fictional Discourse," *New Literary History*, 6 (1975), 326.

18. "How Ordinary Is Ordinary Language" (chap. 3 above).

19. *How To Do Things with Words*, p. 22. Jakobson's famous "poetic function" or "set toward the message" is another version, as is Richard's distinction between "scientific" and "emotive" language. See also John M. Ellis, *The Theory of Literary Criticism: A Logical Analysis* (Berkeley: University of California Press, 1974), pp. 42–44, and Barbara Smith, "On the Margins of Discourse," *Critical Inquiry*, 1 (June 1975) 769–798.

20. *New Literary History*, pp. 332–333.

21. Of course one could argue that this is coherence of a kind, but that would merely show that, like unity, coherence is an empty term, an attribute we always manage to "discover" in any work we hapen to like.

22. Searle has another answer to this question: "It is the performance of the utterance act with the intention of invoking the horizontal conventions that constitutes the pretended performance of the illocutionary act" (p. 327). In short, it is fiction when an author intends it to be so taken; but by Searle's own account, that intention would be identifying of fictional discourse and not of work of fiction.

23. *Individuals* (New York: Doubleday/Anchor, 1963), p. 5.

24. An earlier and shorter version of this paper was given at the 1974 meeting of the Midwest Modern Language Association in Chicago. The occasion was a panel devoted to the subject "Speech Act Theory and Literary Criticism," headed by Michael Hancher. The proceedings, including a discussion between the panelists and the audience, were published in *Centrum*, 3, no. 2 (Fall 1975), 107–146.

10. What Is Stylistics? Part II

1. "Surfacing from the Deep," in *On the Margin of Discourse: The Relation of Literature to Language* (Chicago: University of Chicago Press, 1978), pp. 157–201.

2. See chapter 2, above.

3. Donald Freeman, "The Strategy of Fusion: Dylan Thomas' Syntax," in *Style and Structure in Literature*, ed. Roger Fowler (Ithaca: Cornell University Press, 1975), p. 19.

4. Samuel Jay Keyser, "Wallace Stevens: Form and Meaning in Four Poems," *College English*, 37, no. 6 (1976), 578 (hereafter cited as *WS*).

5. E. L. Epstein, "The Self-Reflexive Artifact," in *Style and Structure in Literature*, p. 40 (hereafter cited as *SRA*).

6. "The New Stylistics," in *Style and Structure in Literature: Essays in the New Stylistics,* p. 8.

7. "Keats's 'To Autumn': Poetry as Process and Pattern," *Language and Style,* 11, no. 1 (1978), 3–17 (hereafter cited as *TA*).

8. "Generative Grammar and Stylistic Analysis," in *New Horizons in Linguistics,* ed. John Lyons (Baltimore: Penguin, 1970), pp. 194–195.

9. "Is Transformation Stylistics Useful?" *College English,* 35, no. 7 (1974), 823.

11. Normal Circumstances and Other Special Cases

1. Augustine, *On Christian Doctrine,* trans. D. W. Robertson, Jr. (New York: Bobbs-Merrill, 1958), p. 13.

2. William Madsen, *From Shadowy Types to Truth* (New Haven: Yale University Press, 1968), p. 198.

3. *Riggs v. Palmer,* 115 N.Y. 506, 22 N.E. 188 (1889). All further references to this text will be at 189.

4. Kenneth Abraham, "Intention and Authority in Statutory Interpretation" (paper delivered at the 1977 Modern Language Association session on Law and Literature).

5. John T. Grinder and Suzette Haden Elgin, *Guide to Transformational Grammar* (New York: Holt, Rinehart and Winston, 1973), p. 117.

6. M. F. Garrett, "Does Ambiguity Complicate the Perception of Sentences?" in *Advances in Psycholinguistics,* ed. G. B. Flores d'Arcias and W. J. M. Levelt (Amsterdam: North-Holland, 1970), p. 54.

7. John R. Searle, "Indirect Speech Acts," in *Syntax and Semantics, Volume 3: Speech Acts,* ed. Peter Cole and Jerry Morgan (New York: Academic Press, 1975), pp. 60–61.

8. Ibid., pp. 61–62.

9. Herbert H. Clark and Eve V. Clark, *Psychology and Language* (New York: Harcourt, Brace, 1977), pp. 121–122.

13. Is There a Text in This Class?

1. M. H. Abrams, "The Deconstructive Angel," *Critical Inquiry,* 3, no. 3 (Spring 1977), 431, 434.

2. *Validity in Interpretation* (New Haven: Yale University Press, 1967), pp. 218–219.

3. *The Aims of Interpretation* (Chicago: University of Chicago Press, 1976), p. 1.

14. How To Recognize a Poem When You See One

1. "On the Analysability of Stories by Children," in *Ethnomethodology,* ed. Roy Turner (Baltimore: Penguin, 1974), p. 218.

2. A phrase used by the ethnomethodologists to characterize the interpretive activities that create and maintain the features of everyday life.

See, for example, Don H. Zimmerman, "Fact as a Practical Accomplishment," in *Ethnomethodology*, pp. 128–143.

15. What Makes an Interpretation Acceptable?

1. *Encounter,* June 1954, p. 50.
2. *Innocence and Experience* (New Haven: Yale University Press, 1964), pp. 245, 248.
3. Philip Hosbaum, "A Rhetorical Question Answered: Blake's *Tyger* and Its Critics," *Neophilologus,* 48, no. 2 (1964), 154.
4. Warren Stevenson, " 'The Tyger' as Artefact," *Blake Studies,* 2, no. 1 (1969–70), 9.
5. L. J. Swingle, "Answers to Blake's 'Tyger': A Matter of Reason or of Choice," *Concerning Poetry,* 2 (1970), 67.
6. Stevenson, " 'The Tyger' as Artefact," p. 15.
7. "Preserving the Exemplar," *Critical Inquiry,* 3, no. 3 (Spring 1977), 413.
8. Ibid., 412.
9. *The Verbal Icon* (Lexington: University of Kentucky Press, 1954), p. 21.
10. *5 Readers Reading* (New Haven: Yale University Press, 1975), p. 12.
11. New Haven: Yale University Press, 1969.

16. Demonstration vs. Persuasion

1. *Structuralist Poetics* (Ithaca: Cornell University Press, 1975), p. 121.
2. To the objection that this condemns everyone to a state of mass delusion I would answer, "mass delusion in relation to what?" Presumably, in relation to a truth independent of anyone's particular set of beliefs; but if there is no one (with the exception of God) who occupies a position independent of belief, no one, that is, who is not a particular, situated, one, then the objection loses its force because the notion "mass delusion" has no operational validity.
3. "Linguistic Metatheory," in *A Survey of Linguistic Science,* ed. W. Dingwall (College Park: University of Maryland Press, 1971), p. 651.

Index